Modula-2
for
Microcomputer Systems

Go raibh maith agut
Eamon agus Máirín
Tá grá mór lei

Modula-2 for Microcomputer Systems

J.E. Cooling

Department of Electronic and Electrical Engineering
Loughborough University of Technology

CHAPMAN & HALL
London · Glasgow · New York · Tokyo · Melbourne · Madras

Published by Chapman & Hall, 2-6 Boundary Row, London SE1 8HN

Chapman & Hall, 2-6 Boundary Row, London SE1 8HN, UK

Blackie Academic & Professional, Wester Cleddens Road, Bishopbriggs, Glasgow G64 2NZ, UK

Chapman & Hall, 29 West 35th Street, New York NY10001, USA

Chapman & Hall Japan, Thomson Publishing Japan, Hirakawacho Nemoto Building, 6F, 1-7-11 Hirakawa-cho, Chiyoda-ku, Tokyo 102, Japan

Chapman & Hall Australia, Thomas Nelson Australia, 102 Dodds Street, South Melbourne, Victoria 3205, Australia

Chapman & Hall India, R. Seshadri, 32 Second Main Road, CIT East, Madras 600 035, India

First edition 1988
Reprinted 1991, 1992

© 1988 J.E. Cooling

Typeset in 10/12pt Sabon by Best-set Typesetter, Hong Kong
Printed and bound in Great Britain by T.J. Press (Padstow) Ltd, Padstow, Cornwall

ISBN 0 412 43730 9

Apart from any fair dealing for the purposes of research or private study, or criticism or review, as permitted under the UK Copyright Designs and Patents Act, 1988, this publication may not be reproduced, stored, or transmitted, in any form or by any means, without the prior permission in writing of the publishers, or in the case of reprographic reproduction only in accordance with the terms of the licences issued by the Copyright Licensing Agency in the UK, or in accordance with the terms of licences issued by the appropriate Reproduction Rights Organization outside the UK. Enquiries concerning reproduction outside the terms stated here should be sent to the publishers at the London address printed on this page.

   The publisher makes no representation, express or implied, with regard to the accuracy of the information contained in this book and cannot accept any legal responsibility or liability for any errors or omissions that may be made.

A catalogue record for this book is available from the British Library

Contents

Preface		ix
1	**An introduction to Modula-2**	1
	1.1 *A very broad view of Modula's structure*	1
	1.2 *Identifiers*	8
	1.3 *Comments*	9
	1.4 *Console communications*	10
	1.5 *Constants*	12
	1.6 *Basic data types*	14
	Review	18
2	**Arithmetic and logic**	19
	2.1 *Statements and expressions*	19
	2.2 *Arithmetic expressions*	20
	2.3 *Boolean expressions*	29
	Review	31
3	**Program flow control**	32
	3.1 *Program flow control*	32
	3.2 *Selection*	33
	3.3 *Repetition or 'loop control'*	43
	Review	52
4	**Subprograms in Modula-2 – procedures and function procedures**	53
	4.1 *How to handle large jobs*	53
	4.2 *Introduction to the procedure*	58
	4.3 *Using variables in procedures – scope and locality*	59
	4.4 *Procedures with parameters*	65
	4.5 *Function procedures*	73

vi Contents

    4.6 *Nesting and recursion*   77
    4.7 *A final point*   78

5 Types revisited   79

    5.1 *Setting the scene*   79
    5.2 *Data types – basic concepts reviewed*   80
    5.3 *Text operations – type CHAR*   83
    5.4 *BOOLEAN operation*   89
    5.5 *Inventing your own data types*   91
    5.6 *Conversion and transfer of data types*   98
    5.7 *Procedure types*   103
    Review   106

6 Modular construction   107

    6.1 *Fundamental ideas*   107
    6.2 *Modules*   114
    6.3 *Communication between modules*   115
    6.4 *Library modules – independent compilation*   117
    6.5 *Library modules – definition and implementation*   117
    6.6 *Local modules*   122
    6.7 *Initialising modules*   130
    Review   131

7 Structured data types – arrays and sets   132

    7.1 *Introduction to structured variables*   132
    7.2 *Arrays*   134
    7.3 *Sets*   156
    Review   164

8 Structured data types – records and dynamic structures   165

    8.1 *Records*   166
    8.2 *Dynamic data structures*   183
    8.3 *Opaque types*   194
    Review   195

9 Accessing processor hardware   196

    9.1 *Introduction – the need for device access*   196
    9.2 *Facilities needed to access devices*   198
    9.3 *Low-level facilities in Modula-2*   202
    9.4 *Using Modula-2 in a target system*   207
    Review   225

10	**Concurrent processing**	**226**
	10.1 *Concurrency – an introduction*	227
	10.2 *Interacting and non-interacting tasks – their coordination*	229
	10.3 *Subroutines, co-routines and processes*	231
	10.4 *Using co-routines (processes) in Modula-2*	233
	10.5 *Multiple task synchronisation*	243
	10.6 *Interrupt handling*	253
	Review	255

Appendix A	**EBNF and syntax diagrams**	**256**
	A.1 *EBNF as a metalanguage*	256
	A.2 *Syntax diagrams*	258

Appendix B	**Modula-2 language definition**	**260**
	B.1 *The syntax of Modula-2*	260
	B.2 *Modula-2 syntax diagrams*	262

Appendix C	**Modula-2 Language features**	**279**
	C.1 *Reserved words*	279
	C.2 *Operators and delimiters*	279
	C.3 *Operator precedence*	280
	C.4 *Standard predefined identifiers*	280
	C.5 *Control statements*	281

Appendix D	**Program development for micros**	**284**
	D.1 *Introduction*	284
	D.2 *Hexadecimal and assembly language programming*	286
	D.3 *High-level language programming*	289

References	291
Answers to selected questions	292
Index	295

Preface

What is this book about?

The purpose of this book is to give an introduction to the programming language Modula-2. It aims to cover all basic aspects of the language, placing particular emphasis on microcomputer systems (i.e. smaller systems). It also sets out to cover the topic from the point of view of real-time embedded systems design.

What is a real-time embedded microcomputer system?

When a microcomputer is used as an element within a system which must meet fast response times it falls into this category. Examples include aircraft flight control systems, anti-skid braking in vehicles and robotic control.

How does this affect the contents and coverage of the text?

Particular emphasis is placed on the so-called 'low-level' facilities which are needed to interact with processor hardware, and on concurrent (multitasking) processing. Dynamic data structures are treated as an introductory topic, and advanced data structures (more suited to the larger machine) are omitted.

Who should read it?

It is written for those who would like to learn about Modula-2, especially for microcomputer applications. In general, it assumes that the reader has relatively little experience of modern block-structured languages.

What will it do for me, the reader?

It will introduce Modula-2 in (hopefully) a painless way as a learning process. It carefully and clearly explains the structure and rules of the language and shows why it is an ideal candidate for microprocessor applications.

Why should I be interested in Modula?

Good designers have long realised that software reliability, quality, portability, maintainability and cost control are closely bound up with the level of the language used. High-level programming enhances these features. Now, with improvements in both microprocessors and memory devices, it is economical and practicable to use such languages in microcomputer applications. Modula-2 is the latest in the line of such languages and has been designed specifically with those features in mind; moreover, it sets out to eliminate the need for assembly language code in programs.

Will it teach me anything about software design?

Yes, but this is not its main objective. Its aim is to get you actually writing programs in Modula-2 as soon as possible; hence design aspects are subordinated to the task of learning how to use the language.

Isn't this a bit of a limitation?

From the point of view of a computer scientist or an experienced programmer this may be so. However, in my opinion, the 'naive' reader finds that many books on languages are virtually unreadable owing to their complexity. Frustration, boredom and glazed eyes are the product of such texts.

Are design aspects ignored then?

No. The relationship between design requirements and language support for such factors is always shown. Otherwise it's impossible to understand why modern structured languages (the grandchildren of ALGOL) have become so important nowadays.

What level is this book pitched at?

Only one assumption is made: you aren't an experienced high-level language programmer. Although there is an engineering bias, the book should be useful to anybody who *wants* to learn Modula-2.

Are there any other special features about this book?

Yes, it is designed as a learning guide. It also assumes that nobody in their right mind reads a text like this for bedtime relaxation. Only prospective Modula-2 programmers will use it. It therefore seems reasonable to assume that you have access to a computer, probably a PC. So, the text is built on the development of small but illustrative programs which you should work on.

Has anything else been done to smooth the path of progress?

Yes. Special arrangements have been made with a leading UK Modula-2 software house, Real Time Associates, for the provision and support of Modula-2 compilers and software tools.

Will working through this turn me into a proficient Modula programmer?

No. Only design experience can do that. What it will do is to get you over the first (difficult) set of hurdles in learning to understand and use the language.

Modula-2 is still in a state of change. How can I keep up to date on progress?

Three sources can be consulted. There is a British Standard Institute Standardisation Committee hard at work on Modula-2. Real Time Associates, in conjunction with the BSI, operate a mailing list for papers connected with this committee. This is done on a non-profit, at cost, basis.

Another important source of information is MODUS, the Modula-2 Users Association. Its object is to act as a forum for all parties interested in Modula-2 to meet and exchange ideas; it publishes an irregular quarterly newsletter/journal. Contact PO Box 51778, Palo Alto, California 94303, USA or Postfach 289, CH-8045 Zurich, Switzerland.

Finally, consult the *Journal of Pascal, ADA and Modula-2*, published by John Wiley and Sons, New York.

Acknowledgements

This is part that most readers skip, but, to me, it's a very important part. It enables me to thank all those who've made this a much better book than the Mark 1 version.

First, thanks to Vincent Southcott and Steve Williams for acting as guinea pigs on the very early draft during their final year projects. Their enthusiasm for the language convinced me that here Nicholas Wirth really has another winner. Mark Shackman and Nick King of Real Time Associates deserve a special mention for efforts beyond the call of duty in reading through the (almost) final draft. Mark's assessment, as a software specialist, was especially valuable to us. Another important set of comments came from Alan Cuff who, as a friend, was pressured to give the draft a good going-over. His wide experience in hardware and software for real-time telemetry systems enabled him to review this from a professional engineering position. Thanks also to my son Niall for his enthusiasm, support and occasional proof reading. He carries some of the blame for this book ever appearing at all. His experience in using Modula-2 for a Digital Signal Processing system triggered the whole project off. And finally, thanks to Janet Redman for doing such a good job on the diagrams.

Chapter 1

An introduction to Modula-2

The purpose of this chapter is to introduce the reader to the broader aspects of Modula-2 together with specific points needed for future reading. After studying this in conjunction with Appendices A, B and C you should be able to:

- Define the general layout of a Modula-2 program.
- Identify the use of program declarations and statements.
- Describe the use of identifiers, variables, reserved words and comments.
- Understand the concepts of block structuring and data typing.
- Compile a Modula-2 program on a personal computer (PC) and interact with this from the computer console.

1.1 A very broad view of Modula's structure

1.1.1 Structure – why?

It may seem strange to start off talking about structure when the main concern of this book is the Modula-2 language. But the fundamental design of Modula-2 forces us to use structure and organisation in our software. So why should this be so important? Just look around and see the ordered form of the everyday things in our life; books, churches and motorway systems all have these properties. We tend to take these for granted; yet without proper organisation and design they'd be almost useless. All right then, let's look more closely at a book example to see why structuring is so important. It is also quite meaningful because, in many ways, software design can be related to it.

The objective of a book is to communicate information. It doesn't matter whether the subject is 'Gardening for Beginners', a James Bond novel, or 'Electromagnetic Compatibility'; it is pointless printing it unless the reader can understand it. Those of you who've been unfortunate enough to read grindingly boring reports will appreciate this fact. So let's introduce some organisation into our book design as shown in Fig. 1.1.

2 An introduction to Modula-2

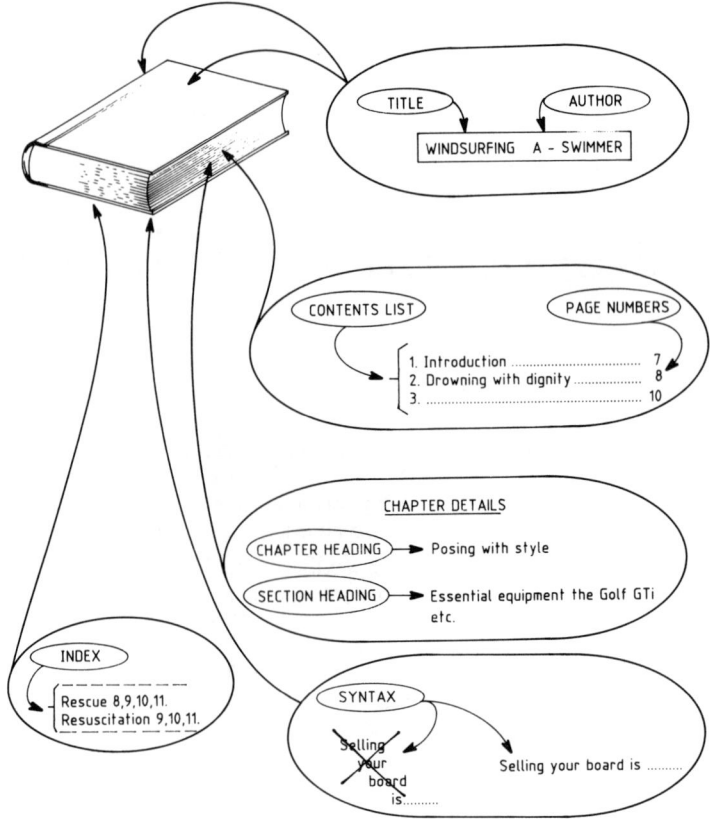

Fig. 1.1 Structure – an essential ingredient

Once the text has been produced we bind the book and put covers on it. On the cover we include the most important items of information: the title and author's name. Now it is easy to catalogue, store and reference the book. And everybody uses the same system. On opening the covers we find that the contents are arranged into chapters. For non-fiction work, logically related items are normally collected together in specific chapters. It then becomes a simple job to use the book as a reference source. But we still need to find our way around the book; that's where the contents list comes in. A quick glance at this will tell us immediately where the relevant information is held. It is also useful when we first come to decide whether or not to buy a book. When we really get down to detailed referencing and cross-checking, the index comes into its own. Try using a technical working text which hasn't got an index; painful is the best description that can be applied to such a case. Finally, the text itself has to obey the rules of grammar and layout, that is, the syntax of the language.

We end up with an item which has a clearly understood function. If we go to the library we know how to track it down. Once in our hands we can very quickly decide whether it is of interest to us from the contents list. Assuming that it is what we want, actually using it should be a straightforward task. Finally, we hope that it is written in a good, clear and correct style. If it does all of these then it will truly convey information.

Software should be designed with the same aims in mind. Unfortunately, past experience shows the reverse case. Three interesting quotations, spanning roughly a 15-year period, illustrate this. The first castigates software developers for having an unprofessional and slap-happy approach. The second neatly highlights the absence of design as part of the software production process, while the last one indicates just how little attention is given to the needs of the end user.

> You software guys are too much like the weavers in the story about the Emperor and his new clothes. When I go out to check on a software development the answers I get sound like, 'We're fantastically busy weaving this magic cloth. Just wait a while and it'll look terrific.' But there's nothing I can see or touch, no numbers I can relate to, no way to pick up signals that things aren't really all that great. And there are too many people I know who have come out at the end wearing a bunch of expensive rags or nothing at all.
>
> A USAF decision maker

> If builders built buildings the same way that programmers wrote programs, the first woodpecker would destroy civilisation.
>
> Gerry Weinberg

> Most so called user friendly systems are about as friendly as a cornered rat.
>
> Eddie Shah

We've realised our mistakes of the past; now we're trying to get it right in the first place. At last software engineering has become a recognised discipline in its own right. But any profession needs the right tools if the jobs are going to be done properly. And one of the major tools is the programming language; enter Modula-2.

1.1.2 General program layout

Modula-2 programs have a defined structure (Fig. 1.2). The layout, in general, takes the following form:

```
MODULE ModuleName;
    .
    .
    . Explanatory statements are inserted here.
    .
    .
    .
```

4 An introduction to Modula-2

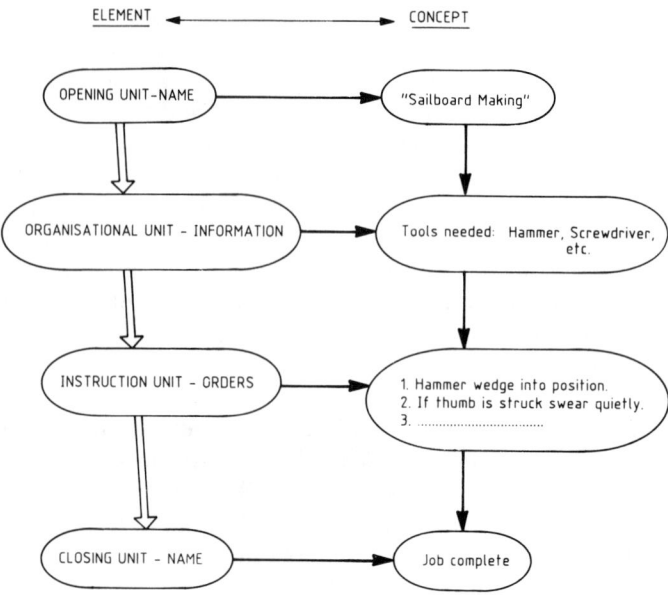

Fig. 1.2 Modula-2 program – general structure

> BEGIN
> .
> .
> . Statements for execution by the program are inserted here.
> .
> .
> END ModuleName.

All high-level languages (HLLs) use certain words to carry out specific actions; Modula-2 is no exception. These are called 'reserved words', and may only be used for their defined purpose. They will be introduced as and when they are needed in these notes. The reserved words here are MODULE, BEGIN, END; these must be written in upper case (Fig. 1.3). A full listing of reserved words is given in Appendix C. Note that Modula-2 is case sensitive, that is, 'END', 'End' and 'end' are treated as different words.

ModuleName is the name given by the author to the program.

Explanatory statements: What is their purpose? Modula-2 is a 'typed' language. That is, all items used within the program must belong to a defined type. The general concepts of types and their attributes are illustrated by Fig. 1.4. More specifically for Modula-2, consider INTEGERs. These are defined in these notes to be whole numbers lying in the range $-32\,768$ to $+32\,767$. If the compiler is to work correctly it must be given information concerning the data types used in the program. This is written in the section shown and is called the 'declarations'. Declarations are needed only for the

Modula's structure   5

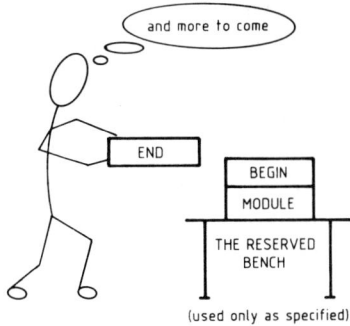

Fig. 1.3 Reserved words

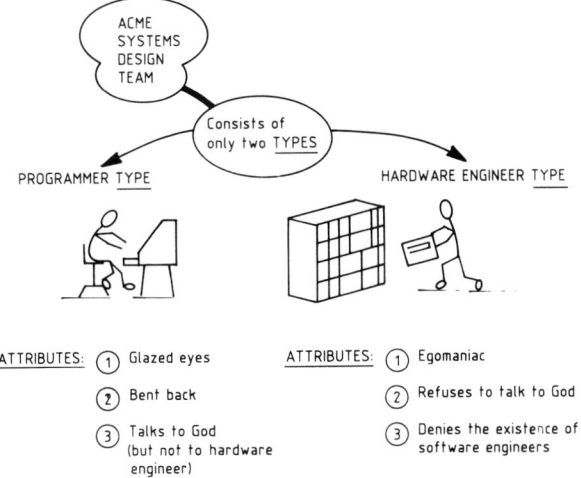

Fig. 1.4 Types – concept and attributes

compilation phase of program development; they take no part in the actual execution of the finished product.

Executable statements: These are the set of instructions which are carried out (executed) by the program when it is run, defined as the program 'statements'.

1.1.3 Declarations and statements

Let's consider a very simple program to carry out the following task:

Y = X1+X2

Before the program can be compiled we must let the compiler know of the existence and the type of the three items Y, X1, X2. We 'declare' them, the relevant facts being written in the declarations section. We then write the program statement in the instructions section. In this case the program structure is:

Line 1	MODULE Example;
Line 2	VAR
Line 3	X1,X2,Y :INTEGER;
Line 4	BEGIN
Line 5	Y:=X1+X2;
Line 6	END Example.

Line numbers have been put in for ease of reference only.

Line 1: This starts with the reserved word 'MODULE', the name of the program ('Example') being inserted next, and the line finished with a semi-colon.

Line 2: Another reserved word has been introduced here, 'VAR'. VAR stands for 'variables'; in this case the variables are X1, X2, Y. The collection of variables is called the 'variable list'.

Line 3: The variable list is written here, terminated by a colon, then followed by the word 'INTEGER', the whole lot being finished off with a semi-colon. Both ':' and ';' belong to a set of Modula-2 units called 'delimiters' (Fig. 1.5). INTEGER defines X1,X2,Y to be of the type INTEGER and has a specific meaning (as already shown) in Modula-2. Hence it can be seen that in the declarations section we must list all variables, state which grouping they belong to (in this instance VAR) and define their type within the group (here being INTEGER).

Line 4: the use of 'BEGIN' indicates the start of the executable statements.

Line 5: Here we meet the assignment symbol ':='. This can be read as 'is given the value of': For this example, Y is given the value of the result of the

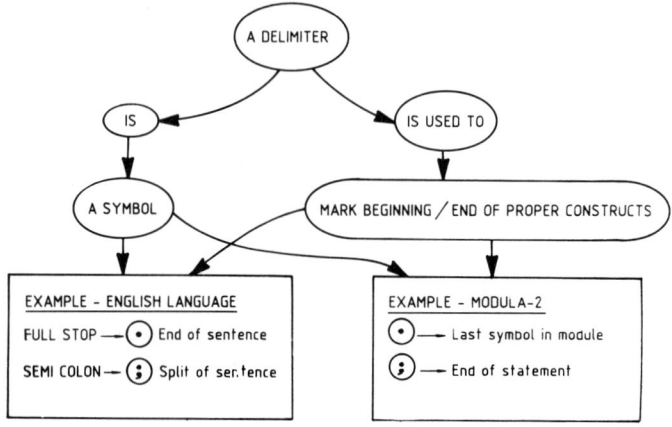

Fig. 1.5 Delimiters

addition of X1+X2. Strictly speaking, we evaluate the expression on the right-hand side of the symbol and assign it to the variable on the left-hand side. In this statement X1 and X2 are defined to be operands and '+' is an operator (Fig. 1.6). Once more note the use of the delimiter ';'.

Line 6: The reserved word 'END' followed by the name of the program and finished off with a full stop defines the end of the executable statements.

In general (and more formal) terms the example consists of:

```
MODULE ProgramName;
VAR
   identifier list:type;
BEGIN
   statements;
END ProgramName.
```

1.1.4 Block structure

The block structure within Modula-2 is provided by the matching BEGIN and END words and also by the use of local modules (see later). Structuring of this nature supports program modularity and visibility, and also simplifies the use of variable names in large programs (see Chapter 4, local and global variables).

1.1.5 Formally describing Modula-2 features

In this text both Extended Backus-Naur Form (EBNF) notation and syntax diagrams are used to describe the functioning of Modula-2. Pertinent information is introduced gradually; therefore a full description of the language

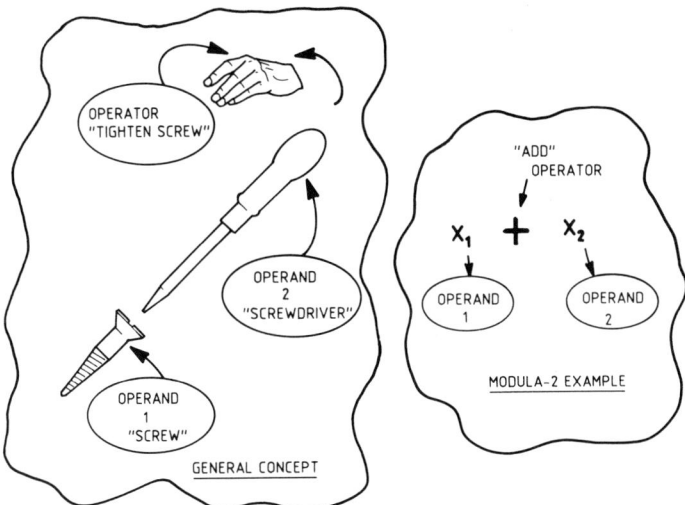

Fig. 1.6 Operators and operands

8 An introduction to Modula-2

is given in Appendix B. This is more suitable for the experienced programmer. EBNF and syntax diagrams are described in Appendix A; read this before going any further.

It is now possible to show the overall structure of Modula-2 using these techniques. Generally, the descriptions given within the text are restricted to show the essential points; formal descriptors are given in Appendix B.

Firstly consider a Modula-2 program expressed using EBNF:

Modula-2program = MODULEIdent";"BlockIdent"."
   block = {declaration}[BEGIN StatementSequence]END

The syntax diagram representation of this case is given in Fig. 1.7.

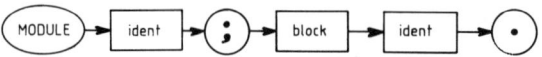

Fig. 1.7 Modula-2 program structure – syntax diagram

1.2 Identifiers

Identifiers are symbolic names used to represent items within the program (Fig. 1.8). So far we have used the identifiers X1, X2 and Y to represent the variables used in the first example program. The format for identifiers is precisely defined, its EBNF description being:

identifier = letter{letter|digit}

The equivalent syntax diagram is that of Fig. 1.9. From this information

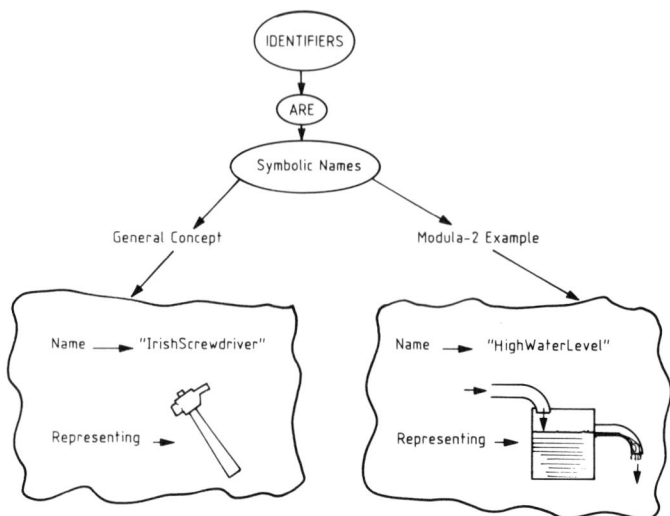

Fig. 1.8 Identifiers

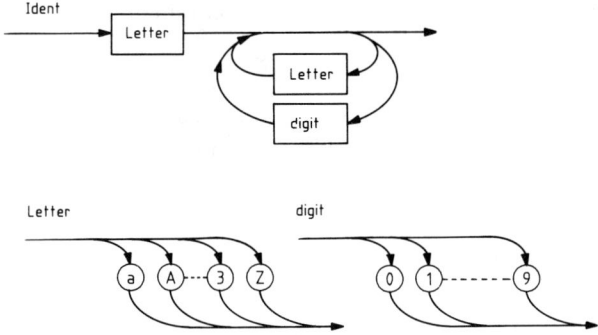

Fig. 1.9 Syntax diagram – identifier

it can be seen that an identifier *must* start with a letter; moreover characters such as the slash, underscore, etc. are not allowed (not legal). Reserved words must not be used as identifiers.

Remember that Modula-2 identifiers are case sensitive. Thus ALARMGROUP, Alarm-group and AlarmGroup are all different identifiers. As a result it would be perfectly legal to use 'Begin' as an identifier; such practices earn one the title 'wally of the year'. Further, only use uppercase text for reserved words and standard identifiers.

An identifier written in the form 'Unit1.AlarmGroup' is defined to be a qualified identifier. That is, the identifier 'AlarmGroup' is qualified (or confined) by the prefix 'Unit1'. As such, identifiers 'Unit1.AlarmGroup' and 'Unit2.AlarmGroup' are regarded as two quite different items. Wait until you reach Chapter 8 before bothering yourself with this information.

Q1.1 What are the standard identifiers of Modula-2?

Q1.2 In many computer languages identifiers are uniquely distinguished only by their first few letters-digits. For instance, where six is the limit, 'Checkpoint' and 'Checkport' would mean the same thing to the compiler. Find out what your Modula-2 compiler does.

Q1.3 How are octal values expressed in Modula-2?

1.3 Comments

Comments have one function only: to make the program easier for the reader to understand. They are ignored by the compiler. A well-designed program will always use comments liberally but selectively, i.e. use them for positive reasons. In Modula-2 comments are inserted into the program by enclosing the text within the character pairs (* and *). For example:

    (*this is a comment*)

Note that comments can be nested within comments, as in

(* (*this is a comment*) *)

Q1.4 Where could this feature be put to good use?

1.4 Console communications

1.4.1 Introduction

In general, programs are developed for two different applications. Either they are required to run under some operating system or else they are to be included in a target (usually microprocessor) machine. In the first case program input data are usually obtained from a console operator, output information normally being sent to the console, printer, plotter or similar output device. For the moment we'll limit ourselves to interactive console operations, dealing with targetted systems later.

1.4.2 Outputs

Why start with output operations? Well, usually the computer must provide some information to the console operator before any interactive processes go into action. Generally, outputs consist of either messages for the operator or else numerical values, say the results of calculations.

In the first case the output is a text string, that is, a sequence or 'string' of printing characters. To send a text string to the console we use the software function 'WriteString'. For instance, to write 'Hello' on the console screen we use the statement:

WriteString('Hello');

This will lead to the word 'Hello' being displayed on the screen. Note that the character string is enclosed between (' and ').

For the second case a number of alternative formats are available to us in Modula; however, let's consider a requirement to print out the integer number 55. For this we write

WriteInt(55,x);

where x sets the minimum numbers of characters which are output to the screen, the so-called fieldwidth (Fig. 1.10).

One last write operation will be introduced here, that of 'WriteLn'. Its function is to send out an end-of-line sequence to the terminal device, i.e. a carriage-return/line-feed action. This is not built into the other write operations.

It should occur to us to ask where these magical quantities WriteString,

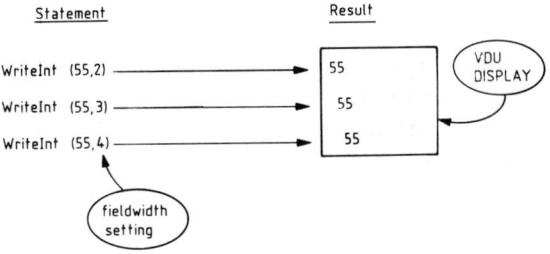

Fig. 1.10 Use of the fieldwidth setting

WriteInt etc. come from and how the program recognises them for what they are. They are, in fact, small software packages provided as part of a Modula-2 library of standard functions. Library features are very common in high-level languages which run under standard operating systems; they are also found in Microprocessor Development Systems (MDSs) for assembly language programming. What makes Modula-2 more like assembly language programming is that library functions must be explicitly brought into the program via import statements. At the present time there is no need to know how they work in detail, only how to use them. Consult your Modula-2 compiler handbook to see what library features are available to you.

A trivial example of the write operations is given in Listing 1.1. Read through this, decide what should be written on the screen of your PC, and then actually compile, link and run the program. You really should do this with all the examples given in the text as there is no substitute for practical experience.

```
MODULE Firstone;
(*****************************************************)
(* Here is a trivial program - but it does work     *)
(*                Listing 1.1                        *)
(*****************************************************)
FROM InOut IMPORT WriteInt, WriteLn, WriteString;

BEGIN
  WriteString('hello');
  WriteLn;
  WriteInt(55,2);
  WriteLn;
  WriteInt(55,3);
  WriteLn;
END Firstone.
```

Listing 1.1

Q1.5 What do you think would happen if the string of characters in a WriteString expression extended into two lines?

1.4.3 Inputs

So how do we get information into the program in the first place? Again we use standard library functions, here the 'ReadInt' one being used. From now on, these will be used without a full explanation being given in the text. The meaning of any such function should be obvious from its use; but you *should* consult your compiler manual for full information.

In Listing 1.2 our very simple program is extended to take in the values of the variables X1 and X2 from the keyboard. Note that comments are also included.

```
MODULE SecondOne;
(*****************************************************)
(* Here is a simple example of inputting data       *)
(*                  Listing 1.2                      *)
(*****************************************************)
FROM InOut IMPORT ReadInt;
VAR
   x1,x2,y :INTEGER;

BEGIN
   ReadInt(x1); (* ReadInt is a function which reads
                   a value from the keyboard (x1) and
                   verifies that it is an integer.  *)
   ReadInt(x2); (*x2 is read from the keyboard*);
   y:=x1+x2;
END SecondOne.
```

Listing 1.2

Now let's further extend the program to provide interactive working with the console as shown in Listing 1.3. Note that the text between BEGIN and END is indented; this makes the program structure clear.

Where text and numerical values are to be mixed we can, for instance, write

WriteString('The value of y is');
WriteInt(y,2);
WriteLn;

When the program is run this would cause the following to appear on the screen (assume that the result of the addition is 36):

The value of y is 36

1.5 Constants

1.5.1 Literal constants

Often it is required to carry out a calculation using a fixed or constant value. One line of a digital filter computation might read

Ynew:=8.5+Yold;

```
MODULE ConsoleComms;
(*************************************************************)
(*     This program illustrates the use of comments and      *)
(*     various read and write functions.                     *)
(*                    Listing 1.3                            *)
(*************************************************************)

FROM InOut IMPORT WriteInt, WriteLn, WriteString, ReadInt;
VAR
    x1,x2,y :INTEGER;

BEGIN
    WriteString('Key in input data')(*this is sent to the Screen*);
    WriteLn;
    ReadInt(x1);
    ReadInt(x2);
    y:=x1+x2;
    WriteInt(y,5)          (*the value of y is written out*);
                           (*it has a fieldwidth of 5 characters*);
    WriteLn;
    WriteString('ok?');
    WriteLn;
END ConsoleComms.
```

Listing 1.3

The number 8.5 is said to be expressed as a literal constant.

1.5.2 Named constants

While the literal form is perfectly all right, a much more flexible technique is to use names for literal constants. The names are defined (declared) in the declarations section; they are also assigned their actual or 'literal' values at this point. In the program itself the identifier name (and not the value) is used, this being called a named constant. The advantages gained are that if the value of the constant has to be changed then:

- only one alteration has to be done;
- the workload is reduced; and
- the likelihood of forgetting to carry the change through the program is eliminated.

Thus, instead of using the literal constant 8.5 in the computation we could use the named constant 'Demand', giving:

   Ynew := Demand + Yold;

where Demand is to be given the value 8.5. This is done in the source program in the following way:

   MODULE M1;

   CONST
     Demand = 8.5; (* note that we use an equals sign *)

BEGIN

   Ynew:=Demand+Yold; (* don't confuse the assignment operator
                          with the equals sign *)

END M1.

The word 'CONST' stands for constant; it is another reserved word. Constants can be expressed in a number of different forms; we are going to meet some of these now. The main point to remember is that constants are fixed; that is, they *never* change during the execution of a program. Contrast this with variables. The value to the right-hand side of the equals sign is called a 'constant expression.'

1.6 Basic data types

1.6.1 Introduction

We organise variables and constants in Modula-2 into various categories or 'types', though so far we have only met type INTEGER. One reason for forming types is to let the compiler know how much memory space is needed for such data values. But once having done this we can then get the compiler to look for program errors caused by using types incorrectly. The use of data typing is a major aid for the elimination of syntax errors in Modula-2 software.

There are two general classes of data types: scalar (or simple) and structured. At this stage only some of the scalar ones will be considered, a full discussion on types being kept until later (Chapter 5).

1.6.2 Type BYTE

This is not available in all Modula-2 implementations. However, where it is, 8 bits are allocated to it. This gives it a number range of 0–255. What the bits actually represent is up to us (Fig. 1.11). Have a good think about this as it is an extremely important aspect of high-level language program-

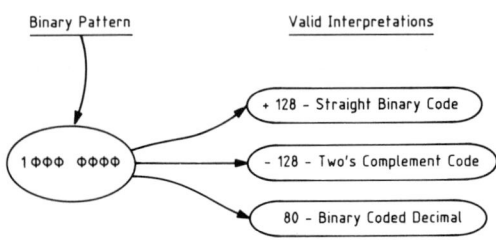

Fig. 1.11 Reality vs. conceptuality

ming. What we're really saying is that the same physical (electrical) object can have totally different meanings to us. When types are covered in Chapter 5 this will become much clearer.

1.6.3 Type INTEGER

Integers are defined as numbers without a decimal point, such as 25 276, −49, etc. The maximum number size which a computer can handle depends on the particular language implementation. In Modula 2/86 from Logitech, for instance, two bytes are set aside for integers, representing numbers between −32 768 and +32 767. You must make sure that your programs do not try to generate numbers greater than these values, otherwise overflow errors will occur, with unpredictable results.

```
MODULE Test;
(*****************************************************************)
(*      This illustrates the use of data type INTEGER          *)
(*                      Listing 1.4                            *)
(*****************************************************************)
FROM InOut IMPORT WriteInt, WriteLn, WriteString, ReadInt;
VAR
    x1,x2,y: INTEGER;
CONST
    demand=50;
BEGIN
    WriteString('Enter Data'); WriteLn;
    ReadInt(x1); WriteLn;
    WriteString('Next digit'); WriteLn;
    ReadInt(x2); WriteLn;
    y:=x1+x2+demand;
    WriteString('The value of y is');
    WriteInt(y,7); WriteLn;
    WriteString('ok?'); WriteLn;
END Test.
```

Listing 1.4

1.6.4 Type CARDINAL

This is allocated two bytes (like INTEGER) but has a range of 0 to +65 535, representing whole numbers only.

1.6.5 Type REAL

Numbers which include decimal points are defined as REAL types and can be expressed in two ways:

- Fixed-point form such as 5.1, 793.29, −6.508, etc.
- Floating-point form such as 2.0E+1 (i.e. 2.0 * 10), 5.2E−2, etc.

The format for REAL numbers is given in Fig. 1.12. The actual degree of precision achieved using floating-point numbers depends entirely on the

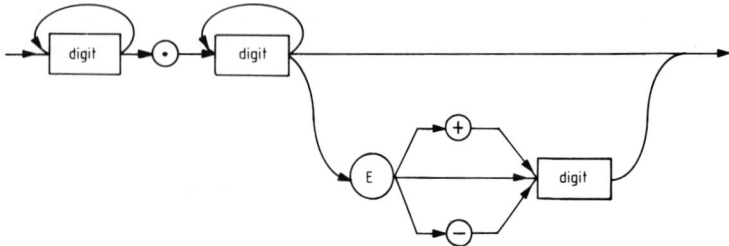

Fig. 1.12 Syntax diagram for type real

compiler implementation. Check yours out; it will be important when handling both large and small numbers in the same expression.

The Logitech compiler (User Manual, 1985), in common with various other implementations of Modula, uses procedures ReadReal and WriteReal for the reading and writing of REAL values. Unfortunately, the normal output printing syntax is restricted, the exponential form of notation normally being used. This can be changed to the more normal form by the use of a 'real to string' conversion (see later).

Accordingly, the following are valid ways to express the number '1000':

   1000   1000E0   10E2   1E3   +1E3   +1E+3

The procedures mentioned above are contained in the library module RealInOut. Thus a trivial example of the use of REAL input/output operations is as shown in Listing 1.5.

```
MODULE RealMath;
(*****************************************************)
(* Here is a simple example which uses REAls       *)
(*                  Listing 1.5                    *)
(*****************************************************)
FROM RealInOut IMPORT ReadReal, WriteReal;
VAR
    x1,x2,y :REAL;

BEGIN
    ReadReal(x1) (*x1 is read from the keyboard*);
    ReadReal(x2) (*x2 is read from the keyboard*);
    y:=x1+x2;
    WriteReal(y,10); (* note the larger fieldwith *)
END RealMath.
```

Listing 1.5

Q1.6 Consult your compiler manual to find the largest and smallest REAL numbers implemented in this system. Find out the internal data representation of the exponent and mantissa parts of the number. Compare this with INTEGER form. Comment on the likely effects on computing times using both representations.

1.6.6 Logical operations – type BOOLEAN

The BOOLEAN type has only two values: true or false. The use of these will be discussed later; for the moment only the method of declaration is shown. It follows the usual form so that for a BOOLEAN variable called 'Test' the declaration is

  Test:BOOLEAN;

1.6.7 Character operations – constants

We have already met the use of text characters for printing out messages to a console. These are set at the time of writing the program; only by rewriting can they be changed. Thus they are known as character constants, the sequence of characters enclosed in single quotes being defined as a 'string'. As an example consider the declaration

  CONST
    Can29 = 'SAE 20 oil';

The presence of the quote marks defines that the enclosed data items are to be interpreted as printable characters. So when we write

  WriteString(Can29);

the text actually printed out on the screen is that between the quote marks.

1.6.8 Character operations – type CHAR

There are many cases where we want to interact with the program, as for instance to manipulate text and variables, or to give a simple yes/no answer. Likewise we may want to output information which depends on the results of a program run. It can be seen that using character constants presents the same difficulties as those found in the use of literal constants.

Modula-2 has a way of easing this burden and giving much greater flexibility by supplying another data type called CHAR. Any variable defined as being of type CHAR can hold one (and only one) printable character. Strictly, there are also non-printing characters of type CHAR. For the moment we'll ignore them. However, it is now possible to define and change the particular printing character under program control, something which can't be done with character constants.

Declarations of character variables are done in the normal way, e.g.

  VAR
    AlphaNumericCharacter :CHAR;

Then, within the program, we can assign any character value to the variable, as follows:

  AlphaNumericCharacter:='7';
  AlphaNumericCharacter:='W';

As an example (Listing 1.6) let us consider the problem of reading in two characters from a keyboard and printing them back in reverse order. You will also see that the operations 'Read' and 'Write' are used with type CHAR.

The more extensive use of CHAR is discussed later in Chapter 5.

```
MODULE CharacterInOut;
(*****************************************************************)
(*     Here is an example of the use of data type CHAR.         *)
(*                    Listing 1.6                                *)
(*****************************************************************)
FROM InOut IMPORT Write, WriteInt, WriteLn, WriteString, Read;
VAR
    digit1,digit2:CHAR (*this is a standard declaration form*);

BEGIN
    WriteString('input digits='); WriteLn;
    Read(digit1); Write(digit1);
    Read(digit2); Write(digit2); WriteLn;
    WriteString('the reverse order is ');
    Write(digit2); Write(digit1);
    WriteLn;
END CharacterInOut.
```

Listing 1.6

Review

Can you now:

- Define the general layout of a Modula-2 program?
- Identify the use of program declarations and statements?
- Describe the use of identifiers, variables, reserved words and comments?
- Understand the concepts of block structuring and data typing?
- Compile a Modula-2 program on a personal computer (PC) and interact with this from the computer console?

Chapter 2
Arithmetic and logic

If you have fully understood Chapter 1 you are now in a position to learn how to manipulate data, both arithmetically and logically. On completing this chapter you will be able to:
- Define and use expressions.
- Perform addition, subtraction, multiplication and division.
- Carry out type changing between REALs and INTEGERs.
- Understand and control the precedence of operations.
- Understand the structure and use of Boolean expressions.

2.1 Statements and expressions

We have already met statements and expressions in quite a number of examples so far. These have been handled in a fairly informal way; now let's define them more precisely. A statement is 'the unit from which a high-level language program is constructed; a program is a sequence of statements'. Another way of viewing statements is that they result in something happening when the program runs. One form of statement is typified by 'WriteLn', another by the assignment operation, as in 'x:=25'.

In the program statement (Fig. 2.1)

$k:=x_1+x_2;$

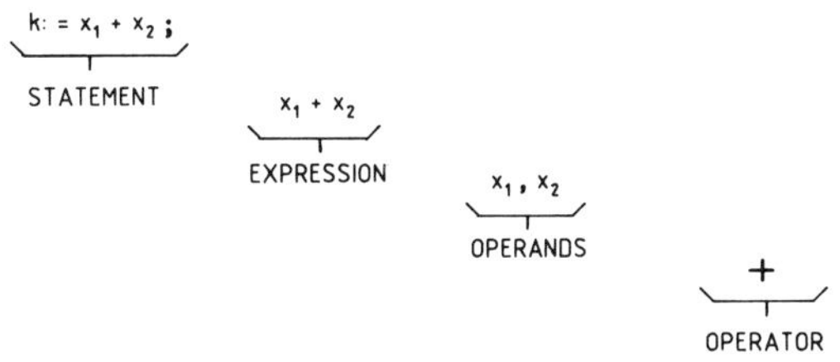

```
k: = x₁ + x₂ ;
└─────┬─────┘
   STATEMENT      x₁ + x₂
                └───┬───┘
                EXPRESSION    x₁ , x₂
                            └──┬──┘
                            OPERANDS       +
                                         └─┬─┘
                                         OPERATOR
```

Fig. 2.1 Statements and expressions

the total right-hand side of the statement is an example of an expression, where x_1 and x_2 are defined to be operands and + is an operator. More formally, an expression can be defined as 'a sequence of operators and operands which can be evaluated to produce a result'. This result may be either numeric or Boolean; the first case arises from arithmetic operations, the second from logical ones.

In this section we are going to look at the ways in which valid expressions may be formed (the syntax rules); then we'll consider the way these are evaluated by the processor (the semantics of the language).

Note in passing that, as a constant expression is defined to be the same as an expression, it is perfectly valid to use constructs such as:

```
CONST
    Six = 6;
    Three = 3;
    TG = Six + Three;
```

Q2.1 The following declaration order will cause the compilation to fail.

```
CONST
    Six = 6;
    TG = Six + Three;
    Three = 3;
```
Why?

2.2 Arithmetic expressions

2.2.1 Introduction

The simplest form of expression only has one operand, as in

```
K:= 55;      or
W:= -36.2;
```

Clearly the value of the expression always stays the same. In most situations it is best to use a symbolic name (as described earlier), giving, for example

```
CONST
    Hightemp = 55;
```

More complex expressions are formed by using a number of operands linked together by arithmetic operators. In Modula-2 we can carry out (Fig. 2.2):

(a) Addition   '+'
(b) Subtraction   '−'
(c) Multiplication   '*'
(d) Division   '/', 'DIV', and 'MOD'.

MATHS NOTATION		MODULA NOTATION
Addition	x + y	x + y
Subtraction	x - y	x - y
Multiplication	x × y	x * y
Division	x / y	x / y or $\begin{cases} x \text{ DIV } y \\ x \text{ MOD } y \end{cases}$

Fig. 2.2 Arithmetic operations

Use of these is straightforward as long as the rules concerning type mixing are followed. For instance, the number '2' is treated as type INTEGER; '2.0' is of type REAL. The statement

y:= 2 + 2.0;

is illegal in Modula. Type mixing is not allowed. Type conversion must be carried out until only one type is present in the statement, and, in an effort to keep errors to a minimum, this must be done explicitly. Modula-2 does *not* do any type changing automatically.

Much greater coverage is given to this aspect of program development in Chapter 5.

2.2.2 Working with REALs and INTEGERs – type conversion

Although it is best to work only with quantities of the same type, in practice it is often necessary to convert from REAL to INTEGER and vice versa. Consider, for instance, carrying out digital filtering of analogue signals. The input is obtained from an analogue-to-digital converter (ADC) whilst the output is provided by a digital-to-analogue converter (DAC); in each case the digital version of the analogue value is in INTEGER (or CARDINAL) form. Normally it is much simpler from the computation point of view to work in floating-point mode. Therefore, before mathematical operations are carried out on the input signal, an INTEGER to REAL type conversion must be performed. Likewise, a conversion back to INTEGER form is needed before the result is sent to the DAC.

Two standard functions are supplied to carry out type conversions between REALs and INTEGERs. These, named FLOAT and TRUNC, are limited in use; hence it is recommended that the library procedures 'real' and 'entier' (French for integer) should normally be used. The use of these is shown in Listing 2.1. Note that variable y1 uses two bytes (16 bits) of data storage. When it is converted to y1R it changes its format and now occupies eight data bytes. On reconversion to INTEGER ('y1:=entier(y1R)') it reverts to two bytes. Furthermore, note that the number of bytes used for data representation may vary from compiler to compiler.

22 Arithmetic and logic

```
MODULE TypeChange;
(*******************************************************************)
(*      Here is an example of type changing of INTEGER          *)
(*      and REAL types.                                         *)
(*              Listing 2.1                                     *)
(*******************************************************************)
FROM InOut IMPORT WriteInt, WriteLn, WriteString, ReadInt;
FROM MathLib0 IMPORT real, entier;
VAR
    x1,x2,y1: INTEGER;
    x1R,x2R,y1R:REAL;

BEGIN
    WriteString('Enter first number'); WriteLn;
    ReadInt(x1); WriteLn;
    WriteString('Next number'); WriteLn;
    ReadInt(x2); WriteLn;
    y1:= x1 + x2;

(*------------------------------------------------------------------*)
    y1R:= real(y1);    (* y1 is converted from INTEGER to REAL *)
    y1:= entier(y1R);  (* y1R is converted from REAL to INTEGER *)
(*------------------------------------------------------------------*)

    WriteString('The integer value of y is');
    WriteInt(y1,5); WriteLn;
    WriteString('ok?'); WriteLn;
END TypeChange.
```

Listing 2.1

Q2.2 The result from 'TRUNC(57.7)' is '57'. What would you expect if 'TRUNC(−57.7)' was used?

2.2.3 Addition

The addition operator '+' has been used on a number of occasions in the specimen programs and has the same meaning as the algebraic symbol.

2.2.4 Subtraction

The operator is '−'; again it has the same meaning as its algebraic counterpart.

2.2.5 Mutliplication

The symbol for multiplication is '*'; operations are similar to the algebraic '×'.

An example with simple addition and multiplication operations is given in Listing 2.2.

2.2.6 Division

Division is slightly more complicated (not the process, just the way we handle it in Modula). For INTEGER division we use the operator DIV:

Arithmetic expressions 23

```
MODULE AddAndMultiply;
(*******************************************************************)
(*    Addition and multiplication of INTEGER and REAL         *)
(*    types are performed by this example.                    *)
(*                    Listing 2.2                             *)
(*******************************************************************)
FROM InOut IMPORT WriteInt, WriteLn, WriteString, ReadInt;
FROM MathLib0 IMPORT real, entier;
FROM RealInOut IMPORT WriteReal, ReadReal;
VAR
   x1,x2,y1: INTEGER;
   x1R,x2R,y1R:REAL;
CONST
   TG=6.3;

BEGIN
   WriteString('Enter first number'); WriteLn;
   ReadInt(x1); WriteLn;
   WriteString('Next number'); WriteLn;
   ReadInt(x2); WriteLn;

(*-------------------------------------------------------------*)
   y1:= x1 + x2;         (* addition of integers *)
   y1R:= real(y1);
   y1R:= TG*y1R;         (* multiplication of REALs *)
(*-------------------------------------------------------------*)

   WriteString('The real value of y is  ');
   WriteReal(y1R,9); WriteLn;
   y1:= entier(y1R);
   WriteString('The integer value of y is  ');
   WriteInt(y1,5); WriteLn;
   WriteString('ok?'); WriteLn;
END AddAndMultiply.
```

Listing 2.2

  9 DIV 3 = 3, an INTEGER result
 10 DIV 3 = 3, a truncated INTEGER result

Thus, if the result of INTEGER division is not a whole number the INTEGER quotient part is returned to us in truncated (and not rounded) form (Fig. 2.3):

 23 DIV 5 = 4 (the truncated part of 4.6)

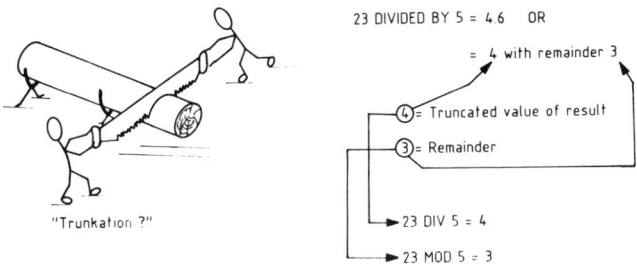

Fig. 2.3 DIV and MOD operators

In this calculation, if we had wanted to find the remainder, then we would have written 23 MOD 5:

23 MOD 5 = 3, the remainder part of the number

DIV can be used with both positive and negative values; for MOD only positive values give a valid result. Both DIV and MOD are reserved words.

For division involving REALs only one operator is used, the '/' symbol. Functionally this is the same as the divider in algebra:

5/2 = 2.5, a REAL value
9/3 = 3, also a REAL value (but written 3.0 in Modula-2)

To avoid confusion between INTEGERs and REALs in Modula, we *must* include a decimal point when writing a REAL number.

These points are demonstrated in Listing 2.3.

```
MODULE DivAndMod;
(*******************************************************************)
(*     This example shows the use of DIV and MOD operators       *)
(*                     Listing 2.3                                *)
(*******************************************************************)
FROM InOut IMPORT WriteInt, WriteLn, WriteString, ReadInt;
VAR
    x1,x2,y1,y2 : INTEGER;

BEGIN
    WriteString('Enter first number'); WriteLn;
    ReadInt(x1); WriteLn;
    WriteString('Next number'); WriteLn;
    ReadInt(x2); WriteLn;
    y1:= x1 DIV x2;
    y2:= x1 MOD x2;

    WriteString('The DIV result, y1, is ');
    WriteInt(y1,5); WriteLn;
    WriteString('The MOD result, y2, is ');
    WriteInt(y2,5); WriteLn;
    WriteString('ok?'); WriteLn;
END DivAndMod.
```

Listing 2.3

Q2.3 ABS is a standard predefined procedure in Modula-2 (see Appendix C.4). ABS(35) gives the result '35'. What would ABS(−35) give?

2.2.7 Operator precedence

Establishing precedence, or 'who gets served first', is something found all the time in ordinary day-to-day life (Fig. 2.4). We meet a similar problem in doing arithmetic, both in the mathematical and in the Modula-2 sense. Consider the following expressions:

Fig. 2.4 Establishing precedence

```
3+4+9
a−b−c
x*y*z
```

In each expression only one class of operator is used. How does Modula-2 set about evaluating the result? Quite simply, it works from left to right in the expression. This may seem to be so self-evident and trivial that it doesn't deem a mention. True, in many situations the order will not matter; in others it is vital to get it right. Consider the statements

$Y1 = 4000 \times 9 \div 2$ and $Y2 = 4000 \div 2 \times 9$

Intermediate results:
$Y1 = 36\,000 \div 2$ $Y2 = 2000 \times 9$

Final results:
$Y1 = 18\,000$ $Y2 = 18\,000$

The intermediate result for Y1 is too large for type INTEGER. Hence, if we were to implement this in Modula-2 using INTEGER arithmetic, Y2 would compute perfectly well but Y1 would give us an overflow problem.

Using REALs will eliminate this particular problem. However, when very large and very small numbers have to be handled in the same expression great care must be taken. A floating-point system may have a very large dynamic range (i.e. smallest to largest number); but that doesn't mean that the smallest and the largest values can be handled simultaneously. Check out your particular implementation of floating-point numbers.

When mixed operators are used we definitely do have to use a set of rules for the precedence of operators. These should state precisely what is supposed to happen, similar to algebraic operations, otherwise results are unpredictable.

We do this by splitting the operators into four precedence classes; as far as arithmetic is concerned the order is:

High * / DIV MOD (equal precedence for these)
Low + − (again, these have equal precedence)

Listing 2.4 demonstrates this point.

```
MODULE Precedence;
(*******************************************************************)
(*      This demonstrates the precedence aspects of            *)
(*      arithmetic operators.                                  *)
(*                      Listing 2.4                            *)
(*******************************************************************)
FROM InOut IMPORT WriteInt, WriteLn, WriteString, ReadInt;
FROM MathLib0 IMPORT real, entier;
FROM RealInOut IMPORT WriteReal, ReadReal;
VAR
   x1,x2,y,k:INTEGER;
CONST
   TG=6;

BEGIN
   WriteString('Enter first number'); WriteLn;
   ReadInt(x1); WriteLn;
   WriteString('Next number'); WriteLn;
   ReadInt(x2); WriteLn;

   k:= TG + x1 DIV x2;
   y:= x1 MOD x2 + TG;

   WriteString('The value of k is ');
   WriteInt(y,5); WriteLn;
   WriteString('The value of y is ');
   WriteInt(y,5); WriteLn;
   WriteString('They should be the same. ok?'); WriteLn;
END Precedence.
```

Listing 2.4

Q2.4 The following algebraic operations give the same answer:

y = (23/4)×6 and (23×6)/4

Why do we get different answers from these Modula-2 arithmetic operations?

y:=23 DIV 4 * 6;
y:=23 * 6 DIV 4;

One final point which has nothing to do with precedence (but it had to go somewhere) needs to be mentioned. Arithmetic operators cannot be placed next to each other; for instance,

y := x *−10; is illegal. Rewrite as y := x * (−10);

2.2.8 The use of parentheses

How do we implement the following: 'add A to B, then multiply the result by C'. If we write 'A+B*C' then the computation will result in B being multiplied by C and then having A added to that value. We could take the following line of attack:

    Y:=A+B;
    K:=Y*C;
or Y:=A+B;
    Y:=Y*C;

Generally it is better to use parentheses to avoid confusion. So for the above example we have

Y:=(A+B)*C;

Parentheses take precedence over the other operators; within the brackets normal rules apply (Listing 2.5).

```
MODULE Arithmetic;
(*****************************************************************)
(*    Just a bit more manipulation of arithmetic expressions    *)
(*    but now involving parentheses.                            *)
(*                      Listing 2.5                             *)
(*****************************************************************)
FROM InOut IMPORT WriteInt, WriteLn, WriteString, ReadInt;
FROM MathLib0 IMPORT real, entier;
FROM RealInOut IMPORT WriteReal, ReadReal;
VAR
    x1,x2,y,k:REAL;
CONST
    TG = 6.3;
    demand = 63.4;

BEGIN
    WriteString('Enter first number'); WriteLn;
    ReadReal(x1); WriteLn;
    WriteString('Next number'); WriteLn;
    ReadReal(x2); WriteLn;

    k:=(TG+x2)/x1;
    y:=demand*k+demand;

    WriteString('The value of y is');
    WriteReal(y,15); WriteLn;
    WriteString('ok?'); WriteLn;
END Arithmetic.
```

Listing 2.5

Summary – evaluating arithmetic expressions

- If an expression contains nested parentheses (brackets within brackets) then work on the innermost pair first.
- Within these brackets carry out all multiplications and divisions, remembering that these operators have equal precedence. In such cases execute the operations working from left to right.
- Now perform all additions and subtractions.
- Repeat this sequence within each matching set of parentheses until the complete expression is finally evaluated.

Normally a range of maths functions are provided in the library module 'MathLib0'. Find out exactly what mathematical support is given by your Modula-2 package.

2.2.9 Some terminology

Expressions are defined as being made up of a number of component parts according to the following rules (Fig. 2.5):

	Example	
	A:= B+C*W−(D*E/F)	The whole right-hand side is defined as the expression
	B	These are defined as the terms of the expression
	C*W	
	D*E/F	
	B,C,D,E,F	These are defined as the factors of the terms
	*,/	These are MulOperators
	+,−	These are AddOperators

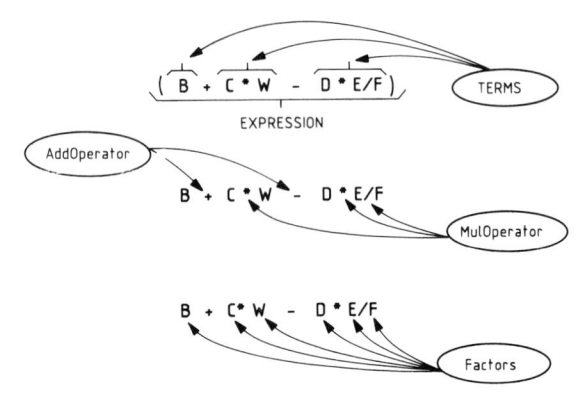

Fig. 2.5 Make-up of a simple expression

2.3 Boolean expressions

2.3.1 Introduction

Boolean expressions are defined as those which have only one of two values, true or false (Fig. 2.6). A variable can be defined as type BOOLEAN and used in the program as required. It is important to realise that such variables are normally used in conjunction with other program statements to make logical decisions. For instance, a control system may have to shut down if a particular alarm occurs; the control processor would make a logical decision based on the state of the alarm signal to define a subsequent course of action.

As the use of Boolean functions is highly dependent on program requirements, only the basic features will be discussed here. It is looked at in much greater depth in Chapter 5.

Fig. 2.6 Values of boolean variables

2.3.2 Logical operations

Two sets of operators are used in logical operations. The first ones describe the logical operations which may be carried out in Modula-2; these consist of the AND, OR and NOT operators.

Having put the expression together it has to be evaluated against a test condition to decide on subsequent actions. The evaluation is carried out using the second set, the 'relational' operators:

Symbol	Operation
=	equal to
<	less than
>	greater than
<>	not equal to
>=	equal to or greater than
<=	equal to or less than
IN	contained in (set membership)

The following simple problems illustrate the basic types of logical operations which are carried out regularly.

30 Arithmetic and logic

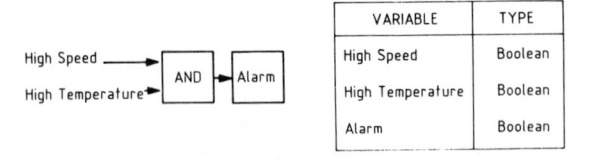

VARIABLE	TYPE
High Speed	Boolean
High Temperature	Boolean
Alarm	Boolean

Alarm = High Speed AND High Temperature

Fig. 2.7 Logical operations using boolean variables

(a) Evaluate the logical value of a AND b AND c OR d.
(b) If X is less than Y then carry out sequence Z.

Consider the first case.

Q2.5 What is the order of precedence for the Boolean evaluation?
Q2.6 What type of operand is involved?

This is further illustrated in Fig. 2.7.

Now look at the second case. Here no Boolean evaluation is involved as we are only comparing the values of two variables. But note that the *result* of the evaluation is a Boolean quantity. Hence, the relational operators can be used with other variable types as well as with Boolean operands; in each case the result is always a Boolean one.

As an example consider the case of monitoring a carrier signal in a data communications system where it is essential to flag up low signal conditions (Fig. 2.8). We could compare the actual signal level with a predefined condition and produce a Boolean result from the comparison; this defines the future course of action.

A variable used as a Boolean must be declared in the normal way, the format being

   Highlevel : BOOLEAN;

Demonstration programs which use BOOLEANs are left until Chapter 5.

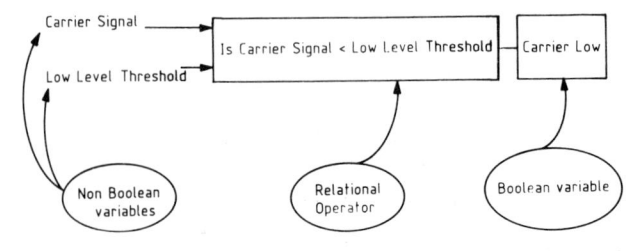

Fig. 2.8 Decisions using the relational operator

Review

Do you feel you can now

- Define and use expressions?
- Perform addition, subtraction, multiplication and division?
- Carry out type changing between REALs and INTEGERs?
- Understand and control the precedence of operations?
- Understand the structure and use of Boolean expressions?

Chapter 3
Program flow control

Up to this point all program examples have followed the same pattern, with statements executed one after the other. This is called the sequence control structure, and in the examples here has been implemented using mainly the straightforward assignment statement. Unfortunately, this won't get us very far in practical situations, especially where calculations and decision making are concerned. Very broadly we can say that the sequential operations are disturbed as soon as we have to answer one or more of the following questions:

- Should this action be performed?
- Should action A or action B be carried out?
- How often should a task be carried out – 1? (WHILE a condition is true do something)
- How often should a task be carried out – 2? (REPEAT something until a terminating condition is reached)
- How often should a task be carried out – 3? (FOR a fixed set of conditions carry out a task)
- How often should a task be carried out – 4? (EXIT from the task when a special terminating point is reached)

On completing this chapter you should be able to:

- Define the basic control structures of sequence, selection and repetition used in Modula-2.
- Understand how and why they are used.
- Write simple programs using these structures.

3.1 Program flow control

It may sound like a gross simplification to say that all programs can be written using only the assignment and conditional statements outlined above. Yet this really is the case in well-designed software, the only exception being the need on rare occasions to take unusual steps to get out of difficulties. And even that should be precisely controlled.

These three structures form the basic syntax for 'structured programming' techniques; all programs can be constructed using just these. Most languages allow the programmer to unconditionally transfer program control, usually by using the GOTO function. This is *not* available in Modula-2.

3.2 Selection

3.2.1 The IF-THEN statement

This is the simplest version of the selection statement, having the following informal form:

IF <condition A> THEN <action W>;

The program evaluates the condition A; if the Boolean result from this is true then the action (statement) W is carried out and program flow continues to the next statement. If the result is false the action is *not* carried out; instead the next sequential statement in the program is executed. Formally, this construct is defined using EBNF as:

IfStatement = IF expression THEN StatementSequence

Figure 3.1 shows the flow of operations for a simple IF-THEN statement, Listing 3.1 being an example of this action. Figure 3.2 gives the statement syntax.

3.2.2 The IF-THEN-ELSE statement

In the example above, if the test condition is evaluated as false, no action is taken. However, we often want to carry out alternative actions as a result of

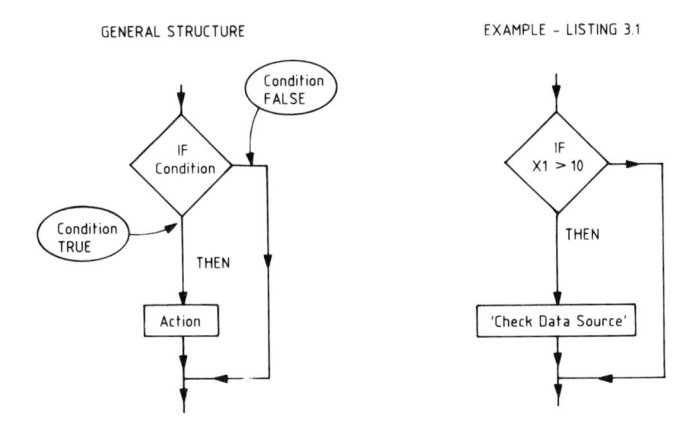

Fig. 3.1 Flow chart of the IF-THEN operation

```
MODULE IfThen;
(*******************************************************************)
(*      This shows the use of 'IF-THEN' statements.                *)
(*                      Listing 3.1                                *)
(*******************************************************************)
FROM InOut IMPORT WriteLn, WriteString;
FROM RealInOut IMPORT WriteReal, ReadReal;
VAR
   x1,x2,y,k:REAL;
CONST
   TG=6.3;
   demand = 63.4;

BEGIN
   WriteString('Enter first number'); WriteLn;
   ReadReal(x1); WriteLn;
   WriteString('Next number'); WriteLn;
   ReadReal(x2); WriteLn;

   IF x1>10.0 THEN
       WriteString('Check data Source');WriteLn;
   END;

   k:=(TG+x2)/x1;
   y:=demand*k+demand;
   WriteString('The value of y is');
   WriteReal(y,15); WriteLn;
   WriteString('ok?'); WriteLn;
END IfThen.
```

If the value of x1 (which is input from the keyboard) is greater than 10 then the message shown will be printed out. If less than 10 no message is generated. In each case the subsequent statements are executed.

Listing 3.1

IF → expression → THEN → StatementSequence → END → ;

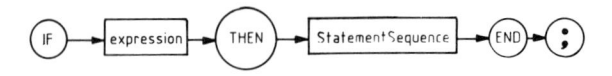

Fig. 3.2 Syntax of the IF-THEN statement

the evaluation, one set for true, the other for false. For instance, IF 'autopilot shows heading error greater than 5 degrees' THEN 'move rudder left for starboard error' ELSE 'move rudder right'. To cater for this we have the IF-THEN-ELSE control structure.

   IF <condition A> THEN <action W> ELSE <action X>;

If the condition is found to be true the action W will be done, if false X will be carried out. The flow chart explanation of the selection process is given in Fig. 3.3, whilst the syntax is described in Fig. 3.4. Listing 3.2 shows how this is used.

The evaluation 'IF x1 > 10,0' gives a Boolean result; it is either true or false. If true, the statements following THEN are executed; otherwise those following ELSE are carried out.

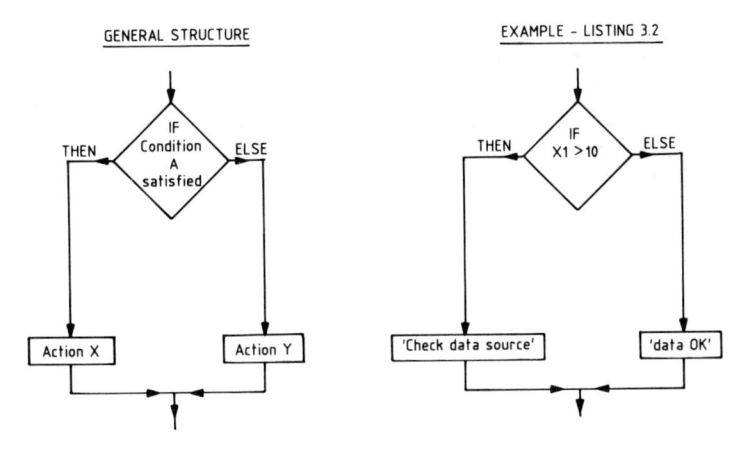

Fig. 3.3 Flow chart of IF-THEN-ELSE sequence

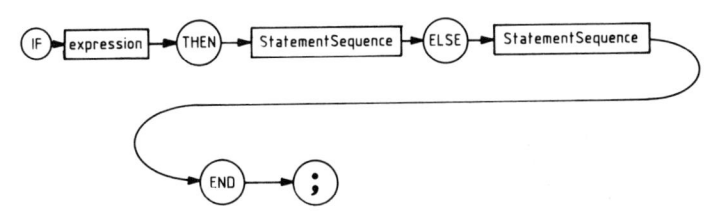

Fig. 3.4 IF-THEN-ELSE syntax diagram

3.2.3 Nested-IF statements

There are situations where we have to carry out a number of checks on, say, incoming data. Using the IF statement we can do it as follows:

```
IF <condition A> THEN
    IF <condition X> THEN <action 1> ELSE <action 2>
ELSE
    IF <condition Y> THEN <action 3> ELSE <action 4>
END
```

This is described as a nested-IF sequence (Fig. 3.5). Listing 3.3 is an example of the **nested-IF statement**.

IF, THEN and ELSE are reserved words.

When nesting is used it can become quite difficult to decide which are the matching pairs of IF and END. It is therefore good practice to use comments to help pick these out, as shown in Listing 3.3.

3.2.4 Multiple choices – ELSIF and CASE statements

Typically this occurs in console interactions where the response from the operator determines the resulting course of events; for instance a message out to the screen might read

36 Program flow control

```
MODULE IfThenElse;
(*****************************************************************)
(*    Here is a simple example of IF THEN ELSE decisions.      *)
(*                  Listing 3.2                                *)
(*****************************************************************)
FROM InOut IMPORT WriteLn, WriteString;
FROM RealInOut IMPORT WriteReal, ReadReal;
VAR
   x1,x2,y,k:REAL;
CONST
   TG=6.3;
   demand = 63.4;
   HighValue = 10.0;

BEGIN
   WriteString('Enter first number'); WriteLn;
   ReadReal(x1); WriteLn;
   WriteString('Next number'); WriteLn;
   ReadReal(x2); WriteLn;

   IF x1> HighValue   THEN
       WriteString('Check data Source');WriteLn;
   ELSE
       WriteString('data OK');WriteLn;
   END; (* end of if *)

   k:=(TG+x2)/x1;
   y:=demand*k+demand;
   WriteString('The value of y is');
   WriteReal(y,15); WriteLn;
   WriteString('ok?'); WriteLn;
END IfThenElse.
```

Listing 3.2

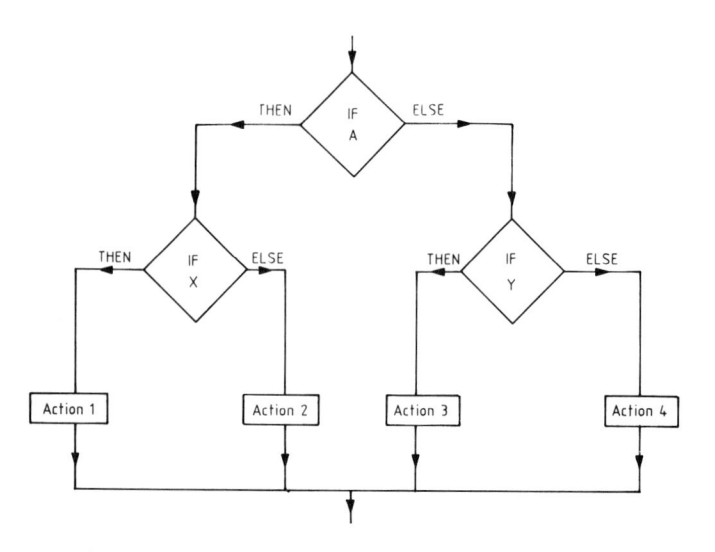

Fig. 3.5 Flow chart of the NESTED-IF sequence

```
MODULE NestedIf;
(***********************************************************)
(*   This illustrates the use of the NESTED IF action.    *)
(*                    Listing 3.3                          *)
(***********************************************************)
FROM InOut IMPORT WriteLn, WriteString;
FROM RealInOut IMPORT WriteReal, ReadReal;
VAR
   x1,x2,y,k:REAL;
CONST
   TG=6.3;
   demand = 63.4;

BEGIN
   WriteString('Enter first number'); WriteLn;
   ReadReal(x1); WriteLn;
   WriteString('Next number'); WriteLn;
   ReadReal(x2); WriteLn;

   IF x1>10.0 THEN
      IF x2<20.0 THEN
         WriteString('Check data Source');WriteLn;
      ELSE
         WriteString('data OK');WriteLn;
      END; (* end x2<20.0 *)
   ELSE
      IF x2>=30.0 THEN
         WriteString('bad data'); WriteLn;
      ELSE
         WriteString('x2 OK'); WriteLn;
      END; (* end x2>30.0 *)
   END; (* end x1>10.0 *)

   k:=(TG+x2)/x1;
   y:=demand*k+demand;
   WriteString('The value of y is');
   WriteReal(y,15); WriteLn;
   WriteString('ok?'); WriteLn;
END NestedIf.
```

Listing 3.3

System Alarms – Set-up procedure
Select alarm group by number
1. Main propulsion
2. Generators
3. Steering
4. Fire and damage control
5. Auxiliaries

The next programmed action would be to read in the response from the operator and begin the set-up sequence for the selected group. Such decision making could be handled either by a sequence of statements as follows:

   IF <1> THEN <action W>;
   IF <2> THEN <action X>;
   etc.

or by a series of IF-THEN-ELSE actions. However, the first case, although it will work, does not by itself ensure that the operations are mutually exclusive. A little bit of creative programming will soon put an end to such good intentions. In the second case use of multiple IF-THEN-ELSEs soon gives rise to a complicated program structure which is difficult to read and understand. Two methods of dealing with situations such as these are provided in Modula-2, the 'ELSIF' and 'CASE' functions.

ELSIF

The basic functioning of the ELSIF statement is shown in Fig. 3.6. When applied to the message handling problem outlined above it would be used as follows:

```
IF    1 THEN <Main propulsion>
ELSIF 2 THEN <Generators>
ELSIF 3 THEN <Steering>
ELSIF 4 THEN <Fire and damage control>
ELSIF 5 THEN <Auxiliaries>
END
```

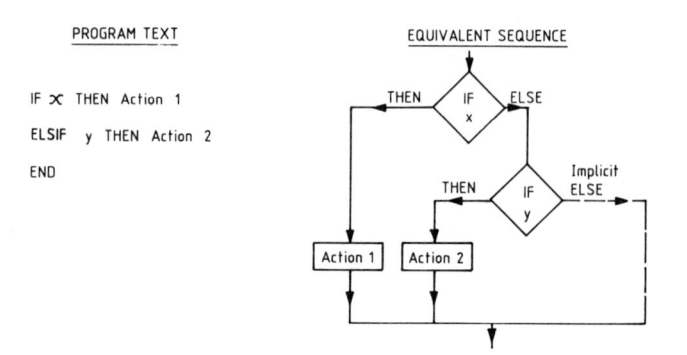

Fig. 3.6 The basic ELSE-IF sequence

The flow of operations is shown in Fig. 3.7.

That's fine as far as it goes. However, in the situation above only numbers 1–5 are valid inputs; what if a 6 is entered by mistake? What will happen is that the program will pass control onto the statement following the ELSIF construct. This could, if the software is carefully designed, indicate that an *invalid* number has been received. You may believe that programmers always incorporate such defensive programming methods as a matter of course. In that case you probably still believe in Santa Claus.

A much safer technique is to combine the ELSIF with an ELSE; this ensures that some action is *always* carried out when the sequence is encountered, for instance

```
IF    1 THEN <Main propulsion>
ELSIF 2 THEN <Generators>
```

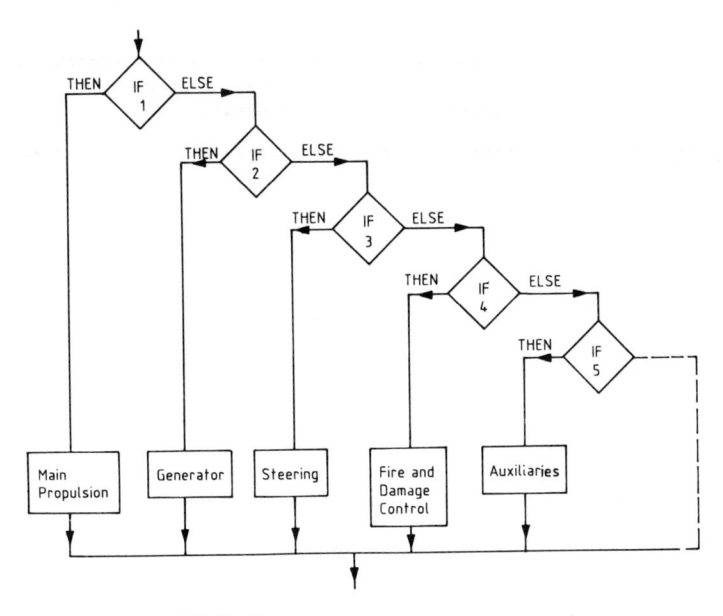

Fig. 3.7 A more general ELSE-IF sequence

```
ELSIF 3 THEN <Steering>
ELSIF 4 THEN <Fire and damage control>
ELSIF 5 THEN <Auxiliaries>
ELSE   <Warning message to operator>
END
```

The complete syntax for the IF statements is therefore as shown in Fig. 3.8.

An example showing how to deal with multiple branches in a program is given in Listing 3.4. In the example here only one statement follows each ELSIF; it is quite permissible to have multiple statements in such places.

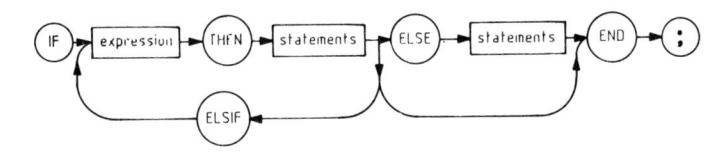

Fig. 3.8 Syntax for the IF construct

CASE

Modula-2 gives us an easier way of handling these multiple-choice problems, called the CASE statement. It acts as a selector switch (Fig. 3.9), selecting one course of action from a number of choices. For instance, to select an action depending on a colour we would write:

40 Program flow control

```
MODULE Chooseone;
(******************************************************************)
(*    In this module the use of ELSIF is demonstrated.            *)
(*    It handles multiple branches in a program.                  *)
(*                    Listing 3.4                                 *)
(******************************************************************)
FROM InOut IMPORT WriteLn, WriteString, ReadInt;
VAR
   Answer:INTEGER;

BEGIN
   WriteString('System Alarms - Set-up procedure'); WriteLn;
   WriteString('Select Alarm group by number'); WriteLn;
   WriteString('1. Main Propulsion'); WriteLn;
   WriteString('2. Generators'); WriteLn;
   WriteString('3. Steering'); WriteLn;
   WriteString('4. Fire and damage control'); WriteLn;
   WriteString('5. Auxiliaries'); WriteLn;
   ReadInt(Answer); WriteLn;
   IF Answer = 1 THEN
      WriteString('Main Propulsion Selected')
   ELSIF Answer = 2 THEN
      WriteString('Generators Selected')
   ELSIF Answer = 3 THEN
      WriteString('Steering Selected')
   ELSIF Answer = 4 THEN
      WriteString('Fire control Selected')
   ELSIF Answer = 5 THEN
      WriteString('Auxiliaries Selected')
   ELSE
      WriteString('Invalid entry');

   END; (*this is the end of the IF statement*)
WriteLn;
WriteString('Program finished - goodbye');
END Chooseone.
```

Listing 3.4

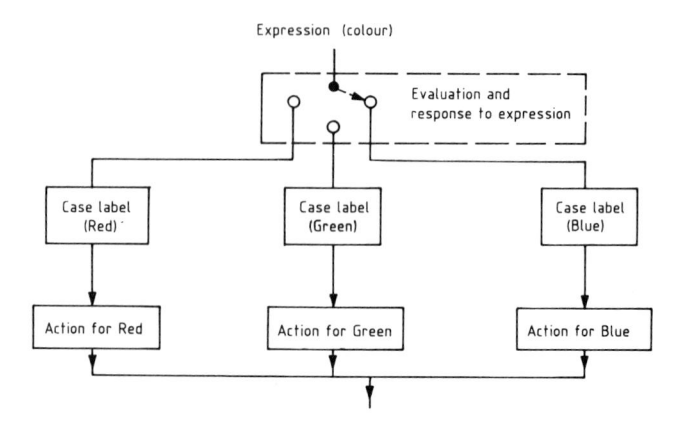

Fig. 3.9 CASE logical control structure

```
CASE Colour OF
   Red: Statements for Red |
   Green: Statements for Green |
   Blue: Statements for Blue
END;
```

The route selected for use is determined by the value of the expression 'colour'. This is demonstrated in Listing 3.5. In this example the expression between CASE and OF (i.e. colour) is first evaluated; then the case list is scanned to find a match. Where this occurs the corresponding statements are carried out. On completion of these statements, program control passes to the one following the CASE operation.

The general CASE syntax is shown in Fig. 3.10. Note that it is optional to include an ELSE statement. However, its use in situations like this is a must to prevent program foul-ups if the answer doesn't correspond to one of the case conditions.

Note also that the vertical bar '|' is used to end each alternative statement sequence except before the ELSE statement.

Now let's re-do the earlier ELSIF example using the CASE feature (Listing 3.6). Even in this simple example the clarity and ease of the CASE statement, compared with mutliple IFs, is obvious.

As defined in Appendix B a case label list has the form:

CaseLabelList = CaseLabels "," CaseLabels
CaseLabels = ConstantExpression[".." ConstantExpression]

Therefore, it is correct and legal to write

```
MODULE CaseExample;
(*********************************************************)
(*    This is an introduction to the CASE feature for     *)
(*    handling multiple branches in a program.            *)
(*                  Listing 3.5                           *)
(*********************************************************)
FROM InOut IMPORT WriteLn, WriteString, Read;
VAR
    Colour:CHAR;

BEGIN
   WriteString('Select colour'); WriteLn;
   WriteString('Red = R, Green = G, Blue =B'); WriteLn;
   Read(Colour); WriteLn;

   CASE Colour OF
       'R': WriteString('Red scores one point')|
       'G': WriteString('Green scores two points')|
       'B': WriteString('Blue scores five points')
   END; (*this is the end of the CASE statement*)
   WriteLn; WriteLn;
   WriteString('Program finished - goodbye');
END CaseExample.
```

Listing 3.5

42 Program flow control

```
MODULE ChooseAnother;
(*********************************************************)
(* This is another example of the CASE construct.  Compare it *)
(* with the ELSIF solution of Listing 3.4.                    *)
(*                    Listing 3.6                             *)
(*********************************************************)
FROM InOut IMPORT WriteInt, WriteLn, WriteString, ReadInt;
VAR
   Answer:INTEGER;

BEGIN
   WriteString('System Alarms - Set-up procedure'); WriteLn;
   WriteString('Select Alarm group by number'); WriteLn;
   WriteString('1. Main Propulsion'); WriteLn;
   WriteString('2. Generators'); WriteLn;
   WriteString('3. Steering'); WriteLn;
   WriteString('4. Fire and damage control'); WriteLn;
   WriteString('5. Auxiliaries'); WriteLn;
   ReadInt(Answer); WriteLn;

   CASE Answer OF
      1: WriteString('Main Propulsion Selected')|
      2: WriteString('Generators Selected')|
      3: WriteString('Steering Selected')|
      4: WriteString('Fire control Selected')|
      5: WriteString('Auxiliaries Selected')
      ELSE WriteString('Invalid entry');
   END; (*this is the end of the CASE statement*)
   WriteLn; WriteLn;
   WriteString('Program finished - goodbye');
END ChooseAnother.
```

Listing 3.6

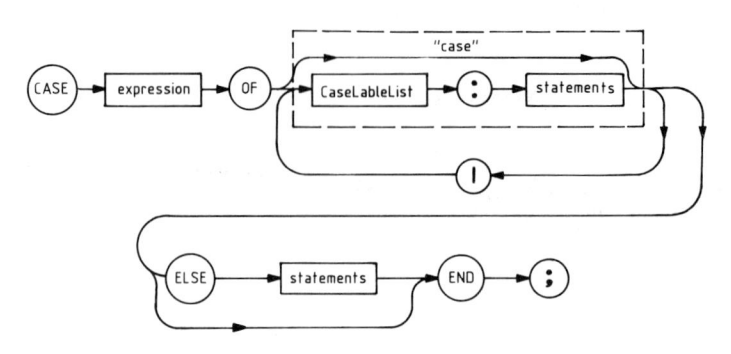

Fig. 3.10 The CASE syntax diagram

CASE Colour OF
  'R', 'r': statements
CASE Answer OF
  1..3: statements

('1..3' means all values from, and including, 1–3).

It is important to recognise that case labels *must* be single-valued constants; variables are not allowed.

3.3 Repetition or 'loop control'

3.3.1 Introduction

Repetition occurs frequently in life (Fig. 3.11). It is no surprise then that we meet similar requirements within programs. For instance, we may want to input characters from a keyboard until the carriage-return key is pressed, or to drive a pump motor while a pressure transducer shows low pressure.

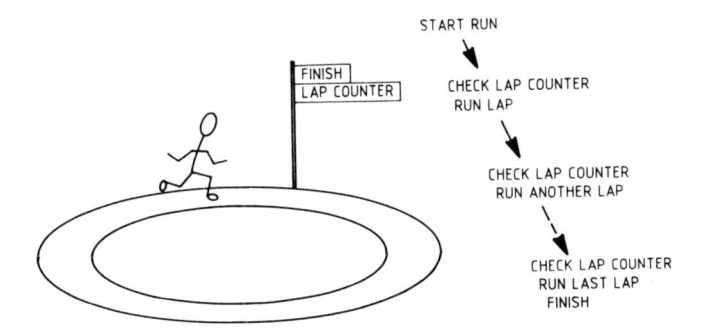

Fig. 3.11 Repetition or 'here we go round again'

Very broadly these repetitive program sequences can be split into two groups (Fig. 3.12). Within the first set repetition depends upon program conditions. The number of loops depends upon the state of some control variable (as in the examples given above). It is also likely that the program may never loop. In contrast, repetitive actions may be defined quite precisely by the program code itself; termination takes place only after the correct number of iterations have been carried out.

Thus, the four basic iterative control structures are (Fig. 3.12):

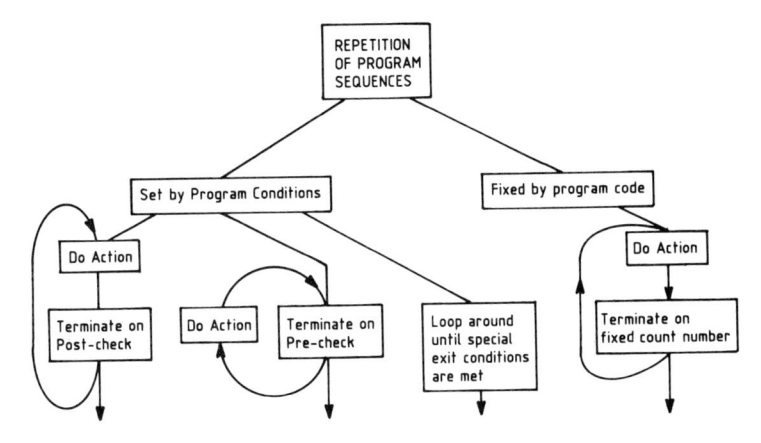

Fig. 3.12 Repetition control structures of Modula-2

- Post-check loop (the REPEAT-UNTIL construct)
- Pre-check loop (WHILE-DO construct)
- Check within loop (the LOOP construct)
- Fixed looping conditions (the FOR-TO construct).

3.3.2 The REPEAT-UNTIL statement

When using this form we first do the required action and then check the test condition. If this condition isn't satisfied then the action is repeated and a further test carried out. Finally, when the test conditions are fulfilled control passes to the next sequential statement in the program.

The flow chart description of the REPEAT-UNTIL operation is given in Fig. 3.13, the syntax diagram being that of Fig. 3.14.

REPEAT and UNTIL are reserved words.

An example of the use of the REPEAT statement is given in Listing 3.7.

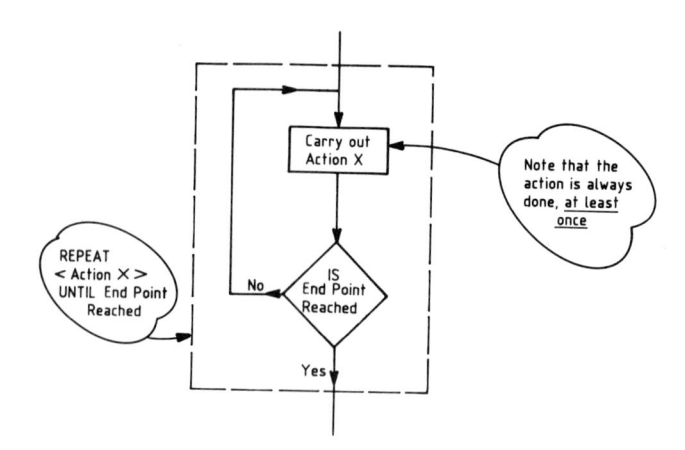

Fig. 3.13 Post-check loop – REPEAT-UNTIL structure

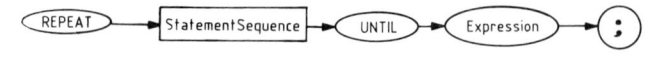

Fig. 3.14 REPEAT-UNTIL statement syntax

3.3.3 The WHILE-DO statement

For this operation the test condition is evaluated before the action is carried out (Fig. 3.15). If it is satisfied then no action is performed and control passes on as usual to the next program statement. Otherwise, the defined action is implemented and the test condition is once more evaluated.

Syntactically it is defined as in Fig. 3.16.

WHILE and DO are reserved words.

Listing 3.8 gives a program which uses the WHILE-DO statement.

Repetition or 'loop control' **45**

```
MODULE RepUntil;
(*****************************************************************)
(*     Here is an example of use of the REPEAT statement.       *)
(*                    Listing 3.7                                 *)
(*****************************************************************)
FROM InOut IMPORT WriteLn, WriteString;
FROM RealInOut IMPORT WriteReal, ReadReal;
VAR
   x1,x2:REAL;

BEGIN
   x2:=0.0;
   REPEAT (* start of the repeat iteration *)
      WriteString('input data')(*a request to the keyboard*);
      ReadReal(x1); WriteLn;
      x2:=x2+x1;
      WriteString('The value of x2 is');
      WriteReal(x2,15); WriteLn; WriteLn;
   UNTIL x1>100.0;  (*this is the test condition, repeat ends*)
   WriteString('Test finished - goodbye'); WriteLn;
END RepUntil.
```

Listing 3.7

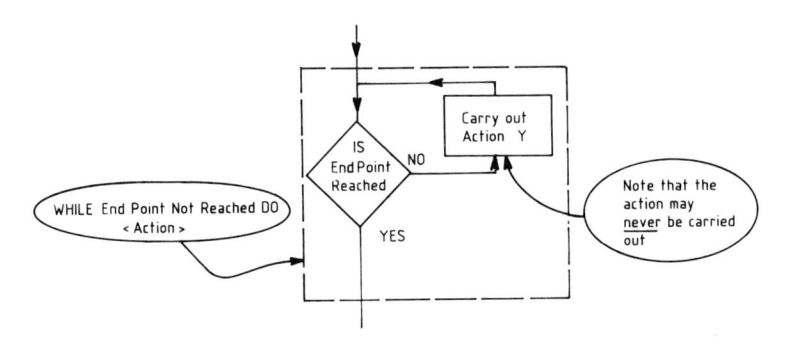

Fig. 3.15 Pre-check loop – WHILE-DO structure

Fig. 3.16 WHILE-DO statement syntax

Q3.1 Show that any WHILE construct can be implemented using a REPEAT operation; show that the reverse is also true.

3.3.4 The FOR statement

Often we want to carry out an action a fixed number of times irrespective of the state of the program being actioned. This can be done in Modula using the FOR-TO loop, this being expressed in very general terms by the diagram

46 Program flow control

```
MODULE WhileDo;
(*****************************************************************)
(*      This is the WHILE statement in action.                    *)
(*                      Listing 3.8                               *)
(*****************************************************************)
FROM InOut IMPORT WriteLn, WriteString;
FROM RealInOut IMPORT WriteReal, ReadReal;
VAR
   x1,x2:REAL;

BEGIN
   x2:=0.0;
   WHILE x1<10.0 DO    (*this is the pre-check condition*)
      WriteString('input data')(*a request to the keyboard*);
      ReadReal(x1); WriteLn;
      x2:=x2+x1;
      WriteString('The value of x2 is');
      WriteReal(x2,15); WriteLn;
   END; (* WHILE x1<10.0 *)
   WriteString('Test finished - goodbye'); WriteLn;
END WhileDo.
```

Listing 3.8

of Fig. 3.17. Suppose, for instance, we wish to read in 6 analogue values to a digital controller. We could write:

FOR Analog:= 1 TO 6 DO
   <statements>;
END;

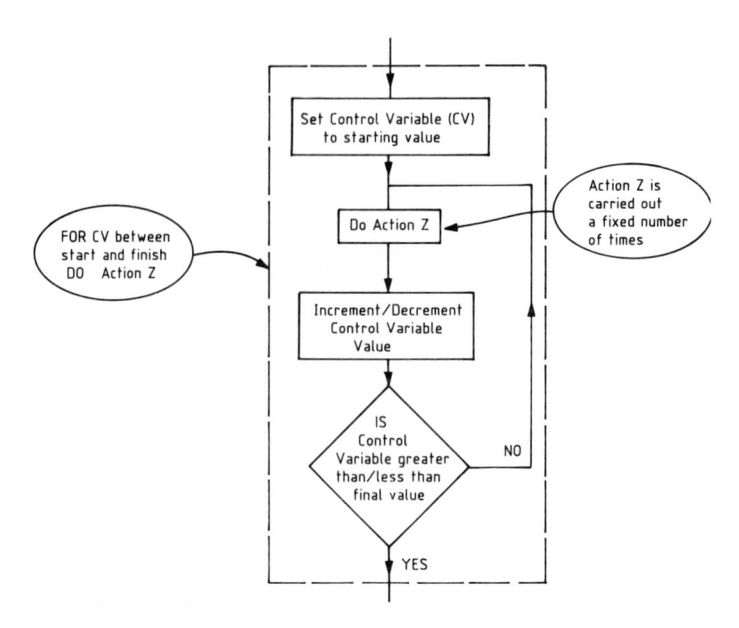

Fig. 3.17 Fixed number of LOOP operations – FOR-TO structure

Repetition or 'loop control' 47

The FOR-TO statement starts off with the control variable (Analog) set to 1 and tests to see if the control variable exceeds the final value. If it doesn't then the statement body is executed and the control variable in incremented by 1. The sequence is repeated until the terminating condition is reached, at which point the statement is concluded.

Figure 3.18 gives the syntax of this statement while Listing 3.9 shows it in use. From the syntax diagram it is clear that both expressions must be the same type. Further, they must be assignment compatible with the identifier (control variable). The control variable cannot be a REAL.

What makes this function quite different is that the starting, terminating and incremental conditions are all clearly stated. As shown so far, the incremental value is one (1) by default. Now in some instances it may be desirable to step in increments other than 1. This can be done by including the step size in the FOR-TO statement using a BY command:

FOR X:=10 TO 100 BY 10 DO < statements > END

In this situation X is first set to 10, the statements are then executed, X is now incremented by 10, its value checked, statements executed, and the whole process repeated until X exceeds 100.

We may also count down from a larger to a smaller value using the FOR-

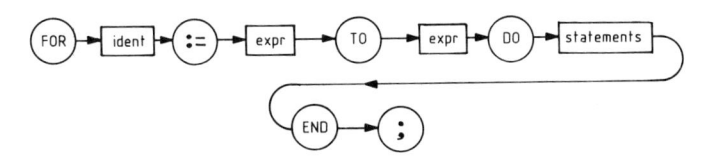

Fig. 3.18 Basic syntax of the FOR-TO statement

```
MODULE ForTo;
(***************************************************************)
(*   This shows a trivial use of the FOR statement.           *)
(*                  Listing 3.9                                *)
(***************************************************************)
FROM InOut IMPORT WriteLn, WriteString;
VAR
   Num :INTEGER;

BEGIN
   FOR Num:= 1 TO 70 DO
      WriteString('*')
   END; (* end of forloop *)
   WriteLn;
END ForTo.
```

This will result is a row of 70 * signs being printed across the screen

Listing 3.9

TO function. However, the BY statement must be used in this case, as for instance in

FOR Num := 70 TO 1 BY −1 DO StatementSequence END.

This control structure is used mainly when the number of operations to be performed is known in advance, when particular items in a complete group are to be accessed, and similar situations. Very often this is met when handling arrays (see later), though the following is a simple application of the FOR-TO action.

Suppose a microprocessor controller has ten output switch channels which, during system initialisation, must be set to a safe condition. A statement of the form

FOR Switches:= 1 TO 10 DO SetSafe END;

is a compact way of carrying this out. An operation similar to this is given in Listing 3.10.

```
MODULE ForToAgain;
(***************************************************************)
(*      This is another example using the FOR statement.      *)
(*                      Listing 3.10                           *)
(***************************************************************)
FROM InOut IMPORT Write, WriteLn, WriteString;
VAR
   Channel:CHAR;

BEGIN
   FOR Channel:= 'A' TO 'E' DO
      WriteString('Now setting channel ');
      Write(Channel); WriteLn;
      WriteString('Channel '); Write(Channel);
      WriteString(' switches set safe'); WriteLn; WriteLn;
   END; (* end of forloop *)
END ForToAgain.
```

Listing 3.10

Q3.2 Carry out a FOR statement on character data types.

Q3.3 On termination of the FOR loop what is the value of the control variable?

Q3.4 In the FOR-TO structure what is the fundamental difference between the step (BY) value and the beginning and ending values? (Have a good look at the syntax diagrams, Appendix B.)

3.3.5 LOOP and EXIT statements

The LOOP statement means exactly what it says, i.e. loop round this set of statements indefinitely (Fig. 3.19). Syntactically it is expressed as shown in Fig. 3.20.

Fig. 3.19 Infinite loop

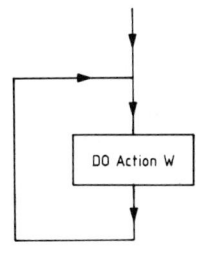

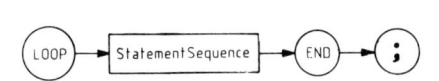

Fig. 3.20 LOOP statement syntax

Where would this be useful? Well, consider the case of a closed loop digital controller which must execute a control function at well-defined time intervals. Normally the control program is interrupt driven using a hardware timer to ensure that timing specifications are met. Often the foreground control program runs as an infinite loop, waiting for the next interrupt. In most high-level languages this is implemented using a GOTO loop which, as has been already pointed out, is not allowable in Modula. In such a situation the LOOP statement can be used.

In our case it is very useful to repeatedly run programs at the console without having to restart them each time. This can be done very simply using the LOOP operation as shown in Listing 3.11.

LOOP operations are much more useful if somehow we can break out from the loop when it's convenient or desirable (if you ran the last example you'll know exactly why). This feature is implemented in Modula by using an EXIT statement. During loop execution, when conditions are met which satisfy the exit requirements, the loop is immediately terminated. Pro-

```
MODULE Looping;
(***************************************************************)
(*            This is the LOOP operation                       *)
(*                  Listing 3.11                               *)
(***************************************************************)
FROM InOut IMPORT WriteLn, WriteString;
FROM RealInOut IMPORT WriteReal, ReadReal;
VAR
   x1,y :REAL;

BEGIN
   LOOP
      WriteString('Enter data'); WriteLn;
      ReadReal(x1); WriteLn;
      y:=0.707*x1;
      WriteString('The rms value is ');
      WriteReal(y,15); WriteLn; WriteLn;
   END;    (* end of LOOP *)

END Looping.
```

Listing 3.11

gram control then passes to the statement which directly follows the loop sequence.

This can be demonstrated by returning to the earlier man–machine interface (MMI) interactions involving the CASE structure (program module 'ChooseAnother', Listing 3.6). From a practical point of view the operator must always be allowed to correct any data entry mistakes but as the program stands this isn't the case. However, by using the LOOP structure with an exit included (Listing 3.12), we can now meet this need.

A major feature of the LOOP operation is to have multiple exit points in a loop (Fig. 3.21), this being extremely useful in MMI interactions (Listing 3.13). Note that EXIT does not in itself require an END; in these last examples this has come about because of the IF clause.

Q3.5 Show how WHILE, REPEAT and FOR-TO statements can be implemented using the LOOP statement. Compare and contrast the results.

```
MODULE LoopExit;
(***************************************************************)
(*      This demonstrates the LOOP statement having an exit    *)
(*      condition.     Listing 3.12                            *)
(***************************************************************)
FROM InOut IMPORT WriteInt, WriteLn, WriteString, Read, ReadInt;
VAR
    Answer:INTEGER;
    Reply:CHAR;

BEGIN
   LOOP
      WriteString('System Alarms - Set-up procedure'); WriteLn;
      WriteString('Select Alarm group by number'); WriteLn;
      WriteString('1. Main Propulsion'); WriteLn;
      WriteString('2. Generators'); WriteLn;
      WriteString('3. Steering'); WriteLn;
      WriteString('4. Fire and damage control'); WriteLn;
      WriteString('5. Auxiliaries'); WriteLn;
      ReadInt(Answer); WriteLn;
      CASE Answer OF
         1: WriteString('Main Propulsion Selected')|
         2: WriteString('Generators Selected')|
         3: WriteString('Steering Selected')|
         4: WriteString('Fire control Selected')|
         5: WriteString('Auxiliaries Selected');
            ELSE WriteString('Invalid entry');
      END; (*this is the end of the CASE statement*)

      WriteLn;WriteString('OK to proceed?'); WriteLn;
      Read(Reply); WriteLn;
      IF Reply = 'y' THEN EXIT
      END;                    (* if the operator answers 'y' then the
                                 program jumps out of the loop      *)
   END;    (* end of loop *)
   WriteString('Program finished - goodbye');
END LoopExit.
```

Listing 3.12

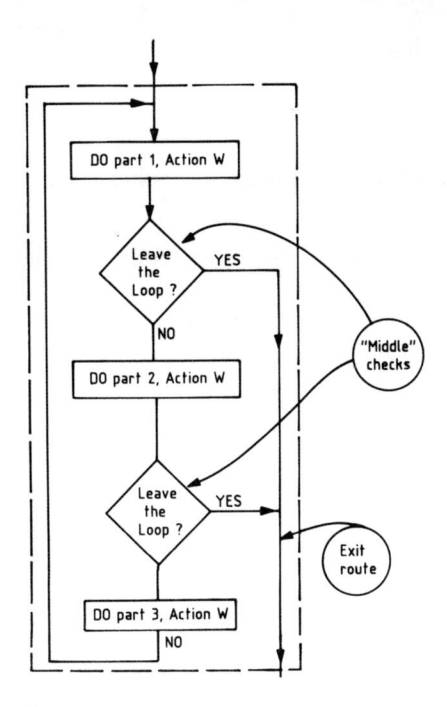

Fig. 3.21 Loop with exits

```
MODULE TwoLoops;
(************************************************************)
(*      This shows a LOOP construct which has two exits.    *)
(*                  Listing 3.13                            *)
(************************************************************)
FROM InOut IMPORT WriteLn, WriteString, Read;
FROM RealInOut IMPORT WriteReal, ReadReal;
VAR
   x1,y :REAL;
   Reply :CHAR;

BEGIN
   LOOP
      WriteString('Enter data'); WriteLn;
      ReadReal(x1); WriteLn;
      y:=0.707*x1;
      WriteString('The rms value is ');
      WriteReal(y,15); WriteLn; WriteLn;
      WriteString('OK to calculate average value?'); WriteLn;
      Read(Reply); WriteLn;
      IF Reply <>'y' THEN EXIT
      END;
      y:=0.637*x1;
      WriteString('The average value is ');
      WriteReal(y,15); WriteLn; WriteLn;
      WriteLn;WriteString('OK to proceed?'); WriteLn;
      Read(Reply); WriteLn;
      IF Reply <>'y' THEN EXIT
      END;
   END;      (* end of LOOP *)
   WriteString('Program finished - goodbye'); 
END TwoLoops.
```

Listing 3.13

Review

Having got to this point you should have achieved the aims of the chapter, that is, to

- Define the basic control structures of sequence, selection and repetition used in Modula-2.
- Understand how and why they are used.
- Write simple programs using these structures.

Chapter 4

Subprograms in Modula-2 procedures and function procedures

We are now ready to tackle one of the most important and useful aspects of high-level languages, the use of subprograms. These are fundamental in the design of good, clear and reliable software. Moreover, if structured programming techniques are to be put into practice these constructs must be used.

After studying this chapter you will

- Understand the reason for and the use of subprograms in high-level languages.
- Understand the structure and use of procedures and function procedures.
- Know the reason for and use of formal and actual parameters in procedures and function procedures.
- Appreciate the difference between local and global variables and grasp the concept of the scope and visibility of variables.

4.1 How to handle large jobs

4.1.1 The background

Small programs are easy to understand. We can see and appreciate both the detail and the overall idea simultaneously (well, almost). New programs can be turned out fast and efficiently. Any mistakes quickly show; equally quickly they can be rectified. So, control and management of software is a simple task? Unfortunately, no. In reality most programs are much, much larger than those shown so far. Moreover, they are usually much more complex and difficult to understand. Such programs often display the idiosyncrasies (a polite way of saying 'quirky peculiarities') of the authors.

How then do we go about handling program development for the larger job? Is it just an extension of our ways of dealing with small ones? Or do we need to completely change our working methods? These are the questions we are going to try to answer here.

4.1.2 An organisational problem

The problems we are faced with are nothing new. Thor the Viking probably got just as frustrated in trying to organise his rape and pillage detail as did the software managers of the Nimrod project. So let's look at the problems, and their solutions, in the context of something we can all understand.

Imagine we've taken over the running of a small garage workshop. Through neglect the servicing manual has degenerated into a huge mass of oil-stained paper (like computer print-outs, though these are usually treated with coffee). As the first step towards changing this chaos into some semblance of order we reorganise the paperwork (Figs. 4.1, 4.2). Now it's properly bound, with related items being grouped together; we've probably also put in contents and index lists. No great effort to imagination is needed to see that this is quite an improvement.

Having just one manual now creates an obvious bottleneck. We could buy one for each mechanic. This, however, might well be an expensive and unnecessary step. The situation is complicated by the need to deal with

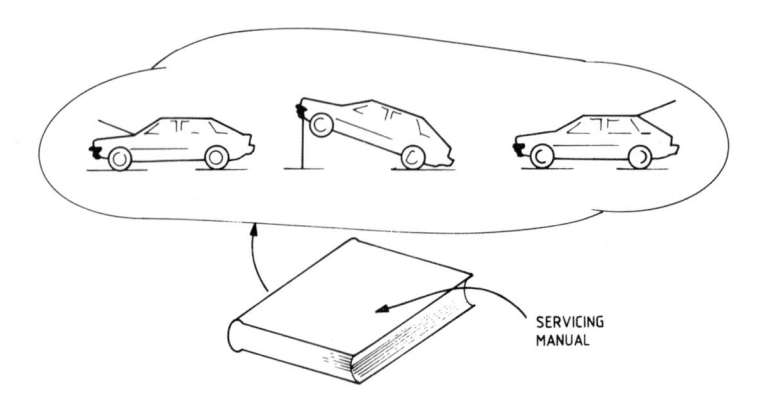

Fig. 4.1

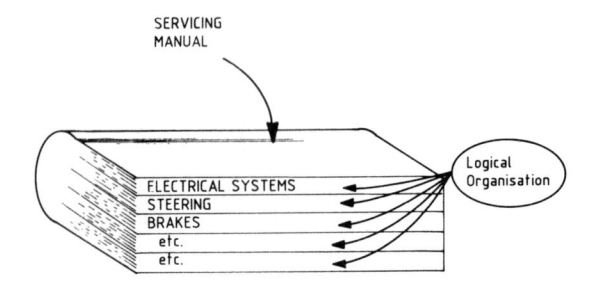

Fig. 4.2

minor variations on a theme (Fig. 4.3). Does this mean that each worker has to be given a manual for each individual model? On top of this, does it really make sense for the electrician to carry information on engine maintenance and repair? Clearly a better solution is needed.

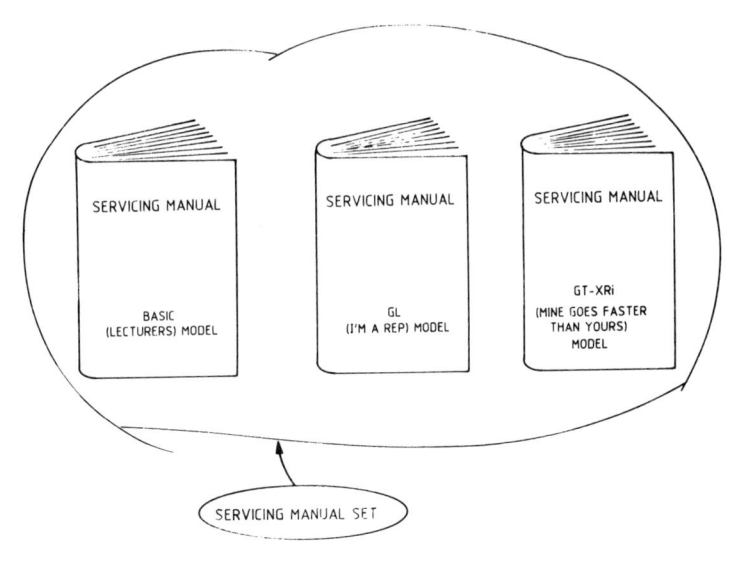

Fig. 4.3

What if we were to make up a set of procedure manuals, each one based on specific topics within the servicing manual? This would simplify the use of the manuals. For instance, the electrician would normally only use the electrical procedure manual; this would hardly upset the engine mechanic. Further, servicing job cards could be simplified by calling up the appropriate procedures (Fig. 4.4). The contents of a procedure manual describes in

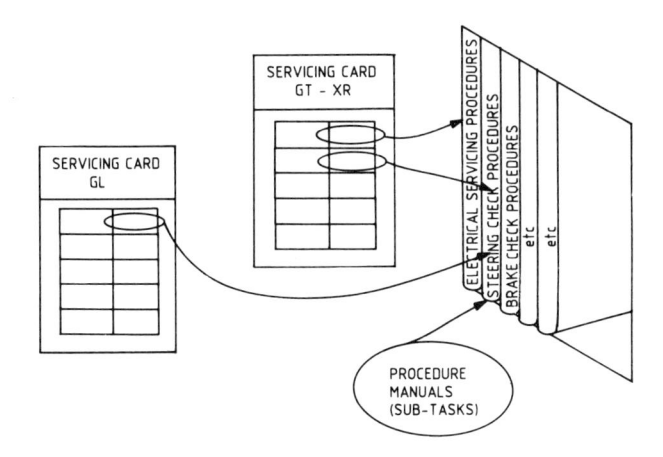

Fig. 4.4

detail what has to be done; this is then given a particular task name (Fig. 4.5). By writing this name on the job card we define the action which is to be carried out; note that no task details are included.

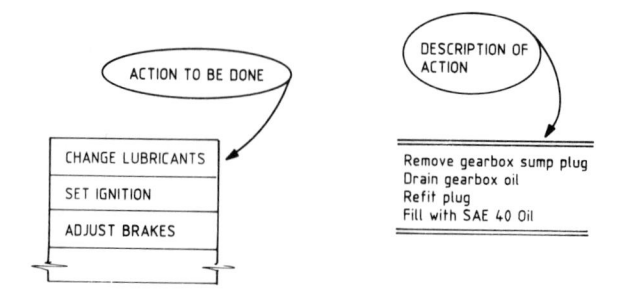

```
                    ACTION TO BE DONE           DESCRIPTION OF
                                                ACTION

         ═══════════════════════
         CHANGE LUBRICANTS                Remove gearbox sump plug
         ─────────────────                Drain gearbox oil
         SET IGNITION                     Refit plug
         ─────────────────                Fill with SAE 40 Oil
         ADJUST BRAKES                    ═══════════════════════
         ═══════════════════════
```

Fig. 4.5

OK, we started out to simplify the documentation system and keep costs down. But, without really appreciating it, we've given ourselves a whole host of benefits. Let's look at exactly what these are.

In the first case, documents may be simply and easily customised (Fig. 4.6). Each individual service can have its own specific job card. These can be put together without too much effort by the front office; after all they aren't exactly going to be tomes of information. By limiting the information on the document we can see what the job is all about (the 'is this really what I'm supposed to be doing?' question).

Fig. 4.6 Customising documents (using building blocks)

The second issue is job sharing (Fig. 4.7). Splitting up the document

Fig. 4.7 Job sharing

makes it is easier for a team to work simultaneously on a task. Moreover, we've effectively 'hidden' details within the procedure manuals. If you don't need to know about a topic you don't have to read about it (this may seem a revolutionary idea to some people).

Finally, it is much easier to maintain the documentation (Fig. 4.8). After the lubrication change manual has attained the texture of greaseproof paper it can be consigned to the boiler, being replaced by a new version. But note that the rest of the manual set is unaffected; there is no 'ripple through' effect. Our documentation set has 'stability'. In the same way, individual manuals can be amended with the minimum of fuss and disruption. If the change merely affects *how* a task is performed nobody else needs to know about it; we can view it as a 'private' item. Only when the actual task affects other items does the change have to made public.

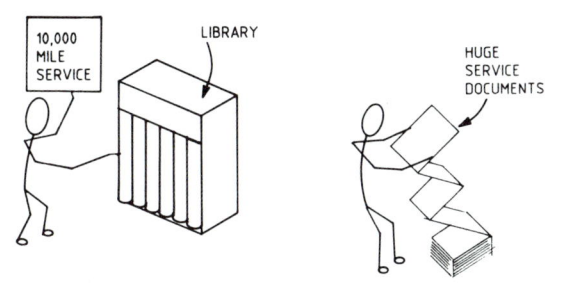

Fig. 4.8 Simplifying documentation maintenance

Finally, we're unlikely to make many mistakes when dealing with a small amount of information. That is, we're building reliability into our working processes.

So, in conclusion, we are, in one sense, putting the qualities of small jobs into a much larger one. It is based on a very simple approach, 'divide and conquer' (now that's an original phrase).

4.1.3 Program design – the Modula-2 approach

The problems discussed above are directly applicable to software development. So too are the solutions. In essence we are looking for techniques which will:

- enable us to split up a complete program into sensible-sized parts;
- associate these with logically related activities;
- develop program building blocks;
- allow a number of programmers to work simultaneously on the project;
- hide information; and
- provide program stability.

The structures provided in Modula to enable us to attain these ends are defined to be 'subprograms'. Three forms are available: procedures, function procedures and modules. In this chapter we'll restrict ourselves to the first two; modules are an important topic in their own right. Note that generally the word 'procedure' will be used to represent both types of procedure.

We've been using procedures all along without having had them described in a formal way. ReadInt, WriteLn and entier are examples of these, being held in library modules. Yet we haven't had to know any details of their construction or implementation to be able to use them. Just re-read the list given above defining desirable qualities for software construction. Surely our experience from earlier chapters shows that procedures go a long way to meet these needs.

4.2 Introduction to the procedure

A standard Modula procedure, sometimes called a 'proper' procedure, may be defined as a textually complete (and usually compact) program construct. It is stored away for use until it is called into action (invoked). The calling may be done by the main program *or* by another procedure. Therefore, it has to be uniquely identified; so we give it a name. The compiler must be made aware of its existence; hence at some point it must be declared in the program.

A procedure code is written within the module construct (Fig. 4.9). We'll see later in Chapter 6 that it is quite permissible for a module to hold nothing but procedures; for the moment consider them to be part of the program module. In such cases the procedure is written before the BEGIN statement which opens the program code. By writing the procedure we also declare its existence to the compiler. That is, no separate declaration is needed.

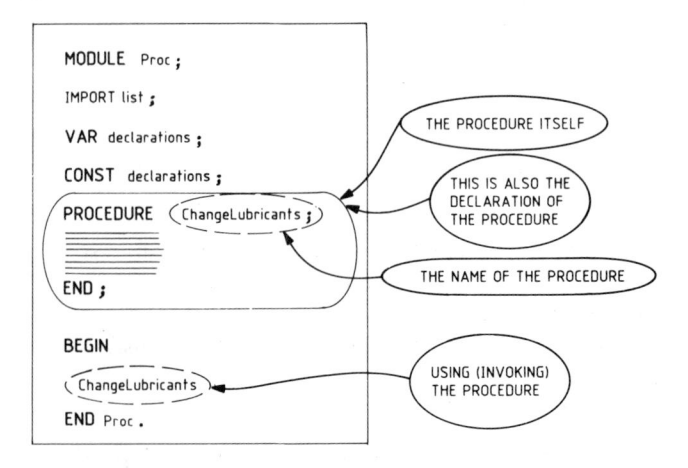

Fig. 4.9 Module format incorporating a procedure

Listing 4.1 is a very simple example of using procedures, the major points being identified in Fig. 4.9. It can be seen that the procedure structure is similar to that of the module. It begins, however, with the word 'PROCEDURE', and ends with the semi-colon delimiter instead of a full stop.

In Listing 4.1 the procedure 'ChangeLubricants' is called twice; yet the procedure code is written once only. The net result is a saving in object code of the executable program. Originally, saving on memory space was a prime reason for using procedures; now it is primarily a basic structuring tool for program development (when using very simple procedures the object code may actually increase).

```
MODULE Proc;
(*****************************************************************)
(*      This illustrates the use of a simple procedure         *)
(*      in a program - Listing 4.1                             *)
(*****************************************************************)
FROM InOut IMPORT WriteLn, WriteString;

(* The actual procedure itself is written here                 *)

PROCEDURE ChangeLubricants;
BEGIN
    WriteString('Lubricants have been changed'); WriteLn;
END ChangeLubricants; (*end of procedure code*)
(* This is also the declaration of the procedure              *)


BEGIN
    WriteString('This is a first demo using procedures'); WriteLn;
    ChangeLubricants;   (*the procedure is called here*)
    WriteString('This is a repeat printout'); WriteLn;
    ChangeLubricants;   (*and again here*)
END Proc. (* end of module *)

    (*                    LISTING 4.1                          *)
```

Listing 4.1

4.3 Using variables in procedures – scope and locality

The procedure above was kept deliberately simple; even variables were omitted from the module. As you can guess, this is the exception rather than the norm. Variables haven't exactly caused us problems up to now. So why pay them special attention just because of procedures? The reason is that the rules governing their use within procedures often causes confusion to the first-time user. So let's look at some simple analogies, using our garage workshop to illustrate these rules.

We've now reorganised our workshop into a general garage space and

60 Subprograms in Modula-2

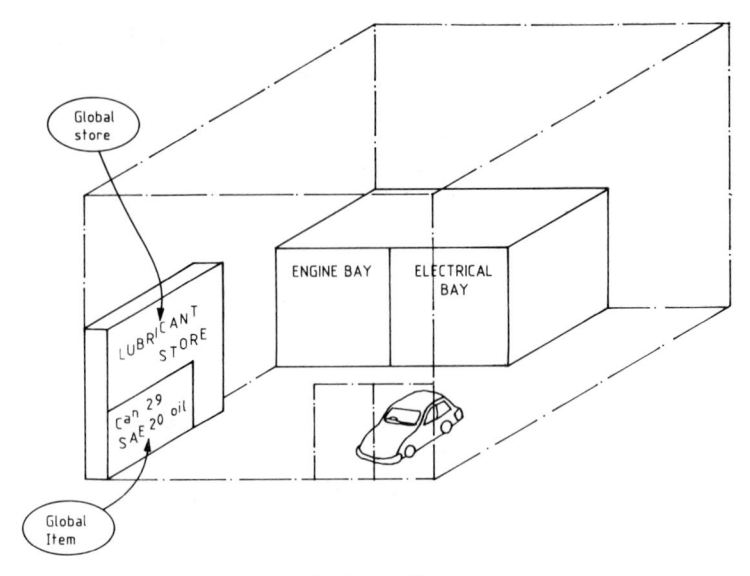

Fig. 4.10 Concept – global storage (Listing 4.2)

two special work bays, the engine and electrical service areas (Fig. 4.10). Inside the general area is located a lubricant store; this may be used by all workers in the garage. One particular item, Can29, holds SAE20 oil. Any worker, in any part of the garage, who receives an instruction to use Can29 goes to the lubricant store; the resulting lubricant is SAE20. We can view this store item as being a 'global' one. That is, its name is known throughout all parts of the garage; further, it means the same thing to all users. Now let's place this in the context of a Modula program. Listing 4.2 is an

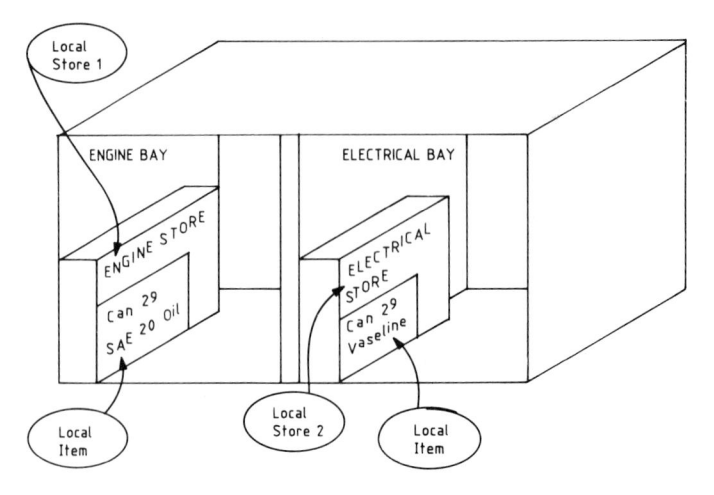

Fig. 4.11 Concept – local storage (Listing 4.3)

Using variables in procedures 61

```
MODULE Proc1;
(*******************************************************************)
(*      This illustrates the use of a global item in a       *)
(*      program which contains procedures - Listing 4.2      *)
(*******************************************************************)
FROM InOut IMPORT WriteLn, WriteString;
CONST
    Can29 = 'SAE 20 oil'; (* The global item *)

PROCEDURE ChangeLubricants;
BEGIN
    WriteString('Lubricants have been changed'); WriteLn;
    WriteString(Can29); WriteLn;
END ChangeLubricants; (*end of procedure code*)

PROCEDURE ServiceElectricals;
BEGIN
    WriteString('Electrics have been serviced'); WriteLn;
    WriteString(Can29); WriteLn;
END ServiceElectricals; (*end of procedure code*)

BEGIN
    WriteString('This is the first procedure'); WriteLn;
    ChangeLubricants;
    WriteString('This is the second procedure'); WriteLn;
    ServiceElectricals;
    WriteString('The global item is '); WriteString(Can29);
END Proc1. (* end of module *)


(*                       LISTING 4.2                         *)

(* When the program is run the following print-out results;

This is the first procedure
Lubricants have been changed
SAE 20 oil
This is the second procedure
Electrics have been serviced
SAE 20 oil
The global item is SAE 20 oil
*)
```

Listing 4.2

extended version of 4.1, now using two procedures. In addition, a string constant 'Can29' has been introduced; this is declared in the usual place. It is used both within the procedures *and* the main program to generate screen printing text. We can therefore infer that the data item is visible throughout the whole module, i.e. it is global.

All is now running smoothly in our garage. However, we realise that it would be both efficient and effective if our servicing bays had their own local stores (Fig. 4.11). We'll identify individual items by can numbers, but then it is essential to make sure that no confusion arises over the numbering system. One solution would be to give every store location a unique identifier. Certainly this would work; but then somebody would have to be given the job of controlling the number system. An alternative, and much simpler, method is to allow each bay manager to control his own numbering system. Thus local items belong to a local store. Even if another store uses exactly the same number it doesn't matter; only those defined to belong to the local store can be used.

These ideas, applied to Modula, are shown in Listing 4.3. Having declarations within a procedure is analogous to building your own local store; local variables and constants correspond to local items. In this listing both procedures have a declarations section; in fact each one has declared a string constant 'Can29'. Although they have the same name they are *not* the same. Now we have to be able to distinguish between the two. The rules for use

```
MODULE Proc2;
(****************************************************************)
(*       This illustrates the use of local items in a           *)
(*       program which contains procedures - Listing 4.3        *)
(****************************************************************)
FROM InOut IMPORT WriteLn, WriteString;

PROCEDURE ChangeLubricants;
CONST
   Can29 = 'SAE 20 oil'; (* First local item *)
BEGIN
   WriteString('Lubricants have been changed'); WriteLn;
   WriteString(Can29); WriteString(' used'); WriteLn;
END ChangeLubricants; (*end of procedure code*)

PROCEDURE ServiceElectricals;
CONST
   Can29 = 'Vaseline'; (* Second local item *)
BEGIN
   WriteString('Electrics have been serviced'); WriteLn;
   WriteString(Can29); WriteString(' used'); WriteLn;
END ServiceElectricals; (*end of procedure code*)

BEGIN (* main program *)
   WriteString('This is the first procedure'); WriteLn;
   ChangeLubricants;
   WriteString('This is the second procedure'); WriteLn;
   ServiceElectricals;
END Proc2. (* end of module *)


(*                      LISTING 4.3                              *)

(* When the program is run the following print-out results;

This is the first procedure
Lubricants have been changed
SAE 20 oil used
This is the second procedure
Electrics have been serviced
Vaseline used
*)
```

Listing 4.3

are very simple; only the one defined in the procedure, the local one, is that which is actually used when the procedure is called. The area of a program in which an identifier is recognised is called its 'scope'. Thus the scope of "Can29 = 'SAE20 oil'" is that of the procedure 'ChangeLubricants'.

What are the advantages of using local variables? The major one is that it helps us to produce reliable (error-free) programs which are maintainable. An identifier is bound to its procedure; therefore it cannot be accessed from other parts of the program. The programmer doesn't have to check through a huge name list to avoid clashes; by limiting scope, identifiers become easily visible and hence controllable. Accidental access to, and modification of, such items is eliminated.

The second advantage is that we can save on computer storage space by using local variables. Such variables are brought into being only while the procedure is active; their storage space is disposed of once the procedure has finished. Obviously this would be an advantage only when dealing with very large quantities of data; for small embedded systems it is unlikely to be important. But what is important is that you realise that variables disappear between procedure calls; they are said to be dynamic. So the value of a local variable in a procedure is undefined each time it is called.

It is very unlikely that we'll write a program which doesn't have some global variables (for variables also read constants in this context). So what are the rules for handling the combination of local *and* global items? These are illustrated by the program in Listing 4.4. 'Can29' and 'GlobalMessage' are globals; observe that we also have local items identified as 'Can29'. The rules for handling clashing names have already been covered (Listing 4.3); the use of non-clashing globals was demonstrated in Listing 4.2. Listing 4.4 merely reinforces these points.

Finally let's consider the highest level of complexity: procedures nested within procedures (Listing 4.5). The structure of the module 'NestedProc' is shown in Fig 4.12; nesting of procedures is clearly visible. The various global and local items are shown, together with their visibility or scope. After studying this figure the following rules should be appreciated and understood:

- Module global identifiers are visible everywhere within the module unless new (inner) redeclarations are made.
- If a module global identifier X is redeclared in a procedure within the module then the local identifier replaces the module identifier. That is, the scope of X does not include such procedures.
- If a procedure (say 'Beta') encloses other procedures then any variables declared in Beta are visible (in scope) throughout all parts of the procedure. Naturally enough this includes the procedures enclosed within Beta unless inner redeclarations are made.
- Assume an identifier Y is declared in a procedure Beta; call this Ybeta. The same identifier is later redeclared in a procedure Delta which is inner

64 Subprograms in Modula-2

```
MODULE Proc3;
(*******************************************************************)
(*       This illustrates the use of both local and global      *)
(*       items in a program - Listing 4.4                       *)
(*******************************************************************)
FROM InOut IMPORT WriteLn, WriteString;
CONST
   Can29 = 'Diesel oil';
   GlobalMessage = 'Service information';

PROCEDURE ChangeLubricants;
CONST
   Can29 = 'SAE 20 oil';
BEGIN
   WriteString(GlobalMessage); WriteLn;
   WriteString('Lubricants have been changed'); WriteLn;
   WriteString(Can29); WriteString(' used'); WriteLn;
END ChangeLubricants; (*end of procedure code*)

PROCEDURE ServiceElectricals;
CONST
   Can29 = 'Vaseline';
BEGIN
   WriteString(GlobalMessage); WriteLn;
   WriteString('Electrics have been serviced'); WriteLn;
   WriteString(Can29); WriteString(' used'); WriteLn;
END ServiceElectricals; (*end of procedure code*)

BEGIN (* main program *)
   WriteString(GlobalMessage); WriteLn;
   WriteString('The boiler fuel supply is ');
   WriteString(Can29); WriteLn;
   WriteString('This is the first procedure'); WriteLn;
   ChangeLubricants;
   WriteString('This is the second procedure'); WriteLn;
   ServiceElectricals;
END Proc3. (* end of module *)

(*                     LISTING 4.4                              *)

   When the program is run the following print-out results;

Service information
The boiler fuel supply is Diesel oil
This is the first procedure
Service information
Lubricants have been changed
SAE 20 oil used
This is the second procedure
Service information
Electrics have been serviced
Vaseline used
```

Listing 4.4

to Beta; call this Ydelta. In these circumstances Ybeta's scope does not extend into Delta. When Delta is invoked the most local identifier (that is, Ydelta) is visible.

```
MODULE NestedProc;
(*********************************************************)
(*      This illustrates the use of both local and global  *)
(*      items with nested procedures - Listing 4.5         *)
(*********************************************************)
FROM InOut IMPORT WriteLn, WriteString;
CONST
   Can29 = 'Diesel oil';
   BannerMessage = 'This is the start of a procedure';

PROCEDURE DoFirstStageService; (* Start of outermost procedure *)
CONST
   LocalMessage = 'This is a nested procedure';

   PROCEDURE ChangeLubricants;
   CONST
      Can29 = 'SAE 20 oil';
   BEGIN
      WriteString(BannerMessage); WriteLn;
      WriteString(LocalMessage); WriteLn;
      WriteString('Lubricants have been changed'); WriteLn;
      WriteString(Can29); WriteString(' used'); WriteLn;
   END ChangeLubricants; (*end of procedure code*)

   PROCEDURE ServiceElectricals;
   CONST
      Can29 = 'Vaseline';
   BEGIN
      WriteString(BannerMessage); WriteLn;
      WriteString(LocalMessage); WriteLn;
      WriteString('Electrics have been serviced'); WriteLn;
      WriteString(Can29); WriteString(' used'); WriteLn;
   END ServiceElectricals; (*end of procedure code*)
BEGIN (* program of outermost procedure *)
   WriteString(BannerMessage); WriteLn;
   ChangeLubricants;
   ServiceElectricals;
END DoFirstStageService; (*end of outermost procedure *)

BEGIN (* main program *)
   WriteString('The boiler fuel supply is ');
   WriteString(Can29); WriteLn;
   DoFirstStageService;
END NestedProc. (* end of module *)


(*                        LISTING 4.5                            *)
```

Listing 4.5

4.4 Procedures with parameters

4.4.1 An introduction

Looking back at our procedure examples, you should be able to see that they have one thing in common; each one carries out a specific task. True,

66 Subprograms in Modula-2

```
MODULE  Nested Proc.
Global items :  Can 29 (Diesel oil)
                BannerMessage

    PROCEDURE  FirstStageService
    Local item :  LocalMessage

        PROCEDURE  ChangeLubricants
        Local item :  Can 29 ('SAE 20 oil')

        PROCEDURE  ServiceElectricals
        Local item :  Can 29 ('Vaseline')
```

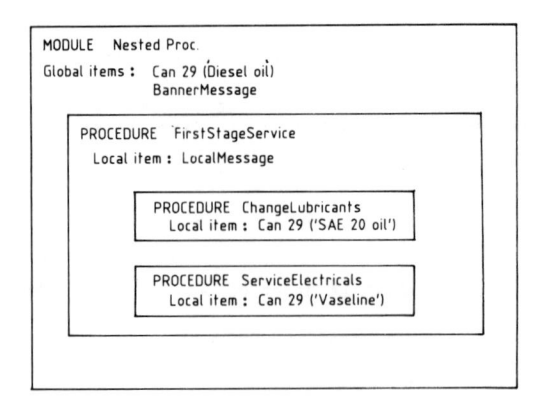

Item	Defined in	Where Visible
Can 29 ('Diesel oil')	Module 'Nested Proc'	Everywhere
Banner Message	Module 'Nested Proc'	Everywhere
Local Message	Procedure 'FirstStageService'	Within all three procedures
Can 29 ('SAE 20 oil')	Procedure 'ChangeLubricants'	Procedure 'ChangeLubricants' only
Can 29 ('Vaseline')	Procedure 'ServiceElectricals'	Procedure 'ServiceElectricals' only

Fig. 4.12 Scope (visibility) within nested procedures

they can be called within a program as many times as needed. But how often in life do we need to carry out, on a repetitive basis, jobs which are identical? Not very often. Much more likely is the need to do jobs which are almost, but not quite, alike. The present procedure construct is thus quite limiting; so we've got to find a way to improve it.

Let's once more use an example from our mythical garage to see what can be done. Each month a check is made on the fuel consumption of the hire cars (business has boomed as a result of reorganisations described earlier). There's no reason why special forms shouldn't be produced for each vehicle, describing exactly what has to be done. Then, every month, the responsible scribe from the front office issues the appropriate paperwork. This gives instructions to the shop floor to fill in the monthly fuel figures, on the special forms, for the vehicles concerned.

As described, this is analogous to the use of a procedure operation. It works, yes, but is very clumsy. Imagine the need to store, order and control all these different forms. At the best it just generates paperwork; at its worst chaos ensues. Now let's consider the method shown in Fig. 4.13. Here a standard 'consumption calculation form' is supplied to the shop floor. This can be used with any car as the details are expressed in general terms. These generalised items of information may be defined as 'formal' details. When the instruction sheet is produced by the front office it asks for fuel consump-

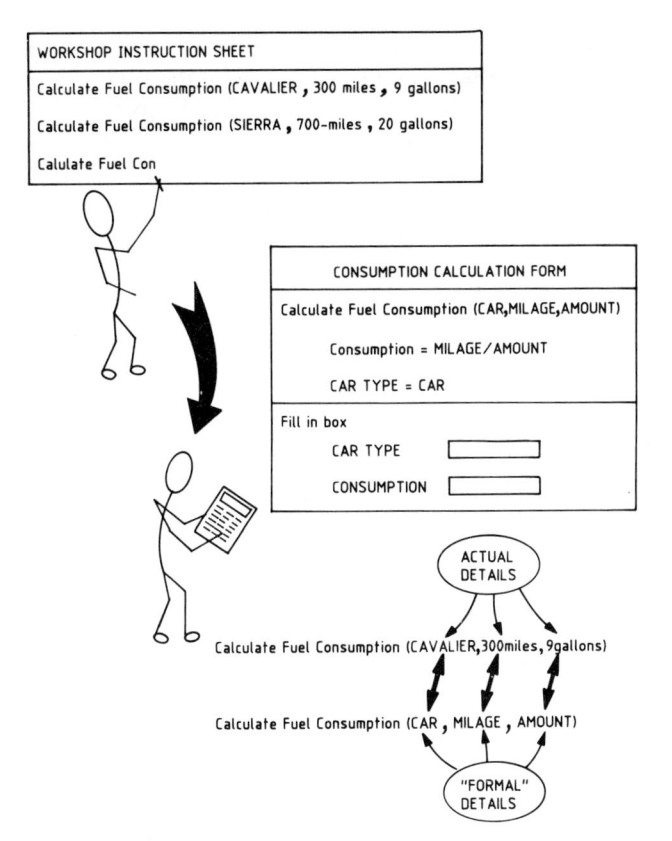

Fig. 4.13 Using generalised sets of instructions

tion figures to be calculated. On this sheet it specifies the actual details of milage and fuel used. By replacing the formal details with the actual details, consumption figures can be produced for specific vehicles. Now we don't need a variety of consumption calculation forms; one is sufficient.

The formal details on our garage form denote items to be supplied when the form is used. In exactly the same way we can devise procedures, using formal data items in our procedure program. These are defined as the 'formal parameters' of the procedure. It (the procedure) is written as if these formal parameters are the actual items used. So, as far as procedure writing is concerned, nothing has really changed. However, when the procedure is invoked, the actual information must be supplied at the time of call. Such items of data are called the 'actual parameters'.

Take, for instance, the procedure WriteInt; this has two formal parameters. When we write 'WriteInt(y,4)' the actual parameters are 'y' and '4'; these replace the formal parameters at execution time.

One important point concerns the order and type of formal and actual parameters. Fundamentally there is no reason to write these in any particular order or to restrict the types which can be used, *but* the actual parameter list must coincide with the formal one, otherwise the procedure results will be nonsense. Fortunately, most errors are likely to be picked up by the compiler. This checks that the formal–actual pairing is correct at compile time.

The parameters can be regarded as the interface between the calling program and the procedure itself (Fig. 4.14). By having parameters we can pass information between the two without using global variables. The safety, security and visibility aspects of this cannot be overstated.

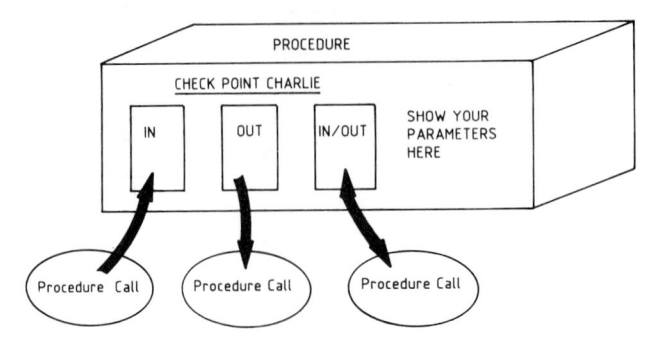

Fig. 4.14 Information-passing using parameters

4.4.2 Value parameters – 'input only'

In our example above we used parameters to pass information into the fuel consumption calculation. This was a one-way process; no reply was asked for. When we do the same thing with Modula procedures the parameters are defined as 'value' parameters. The concept is illustrated in Fig. 4.15, a simple program example being that of Listing 4.6. It can be seen that the procedure ChangeLubricants has one formal parameter only. Its name is 'Oiltype', and is of type CHAR. When the procedure is called the actual parameter used is 'Oil'; this also is a CHAR type.

You will see that, within the procedure, there is no declaration for the variable 'Oiltype'. This comes about because the formal parameter listing is also automatically used as a variable declaration listing (Fig. 4.16).

Now for one very important point. Actual parameters are copied into procedures. Thus when such procedures are invoked the copied items are manipulated, not the originals. This may be demonstrated by running the program of Listing 4.7.

Suppose we have a number of formal parameters to be listed; further, assume there is a mix of types. How is this done? As an example consider parameters as follows:

REAL – K1 K2 K3
INTEGER – X1 X2
CHAR – Error

Procedures with parameters 69

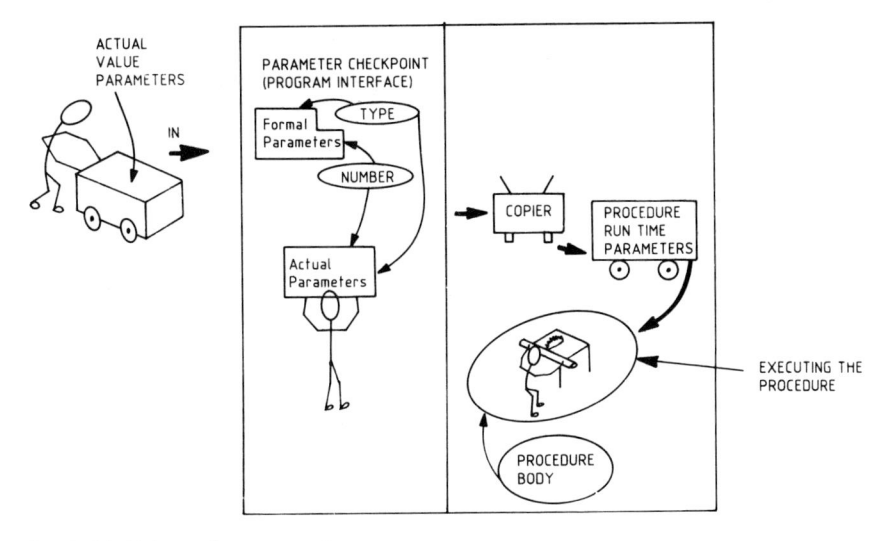

Fig. 4.15 Using value parameters

```
MODULE ValueParam;
(*******************************************************)
(*      This illustrates the use of a value parameter to    *)
(*      pass information to a procedure - Listing 4.6       *)
(*******************************************************)
FROM InOut IMPORT WriteLn, WriteString, Read;
VAR
    Oil:CHAR;

PROCEDURE ChangeLubricants(Oiltype:CHAR);
BEGIN
    IF Oiltype = 'A' THEN
        WriteString('Oil is SAE 20'); WriteLn;
    ELSIF Oiltype = 'B' THEN
        WriteString('Oil is SAE 30-50'); WriteLn;
    ELSE WriteString('Bad entry'); WriteLn;
    END; (*end if-elsif*)
END ChangeLubricants; (*end of procedure code*)

BEGIN
    WriteString('What is the lubricant type?'); WriteLn;
    WriteString('Enter A for SAE20, B for SAE 30-50 oil'); WriteLn;
    Read(Oil); WriteLn;
    ChangeLubricants(Oil);
END ValueParam. (* end of module *)

(*                      LISTING 4.6                          *)
```

Listing 4.6

Then the procedure heading could read

   PROCEDURE Compute (X1,X2:INTEGER; K1,K2,K3:REAL;
                      Error:CHAR);

70 Subprograms in Modula-2

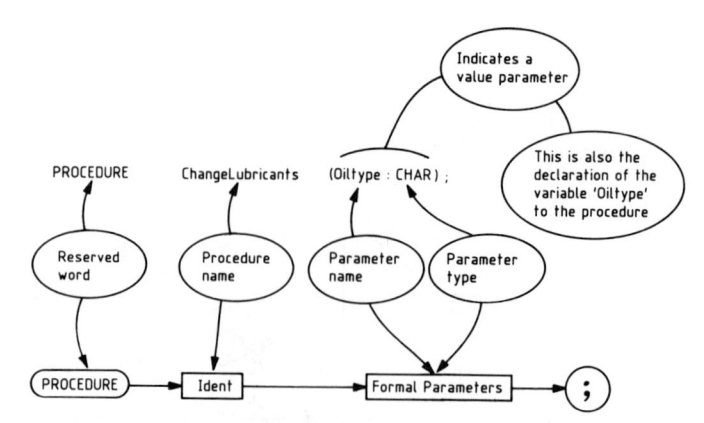

Fig. 4.16 Procedure heading incorporating a value parameter

```
MODULE ValueParam;
(***************************************************************)
(*      This illustrates that value parameters are             *)
(*      passed into a procedure by copying - Listing 4.7       *)
(***************************************************************)
FROM InOut IMPORT WriteLn, WriteString, Read, Write;
VAR
   Oil:CHAR;

PROCEDURE ChangeLubricants(Oiltype:CHAR);
BEGIN
   WriteString('Lubricants have been changed'); WriteLn;
   IF Oiltype = 'A' THEN
      WriteString('Oil is SAE 20'); WriteLn;
   ELSIF Oiltype = 'B' THEN
      WriteString('Oil is SAE 30-50'); WriteLn;
   ELSE WriteString('Bad entry'); WriteLn;
   END; (*end if-elsif*)
   Oiltype:='Z';
   Write(Oiltype); WriteLn;
END ChangeLubricants; (*end of procedure code*)

BEGIN
   WriteString('What is the lubricant type?'); WriteLn;
   WriteString('Enter A for SAE20, B for SAE 30-50 oil'); WriteLn;
   Read(Oil); WriteLn; WriteLn;
   ChangeLubricants(Oil);
   WriteString('Finished with procedure - Oiltype character is ');
   Write(Oil); WriteLn;
END ValueParam. (* end of module *)


      (*              LISTING 4.7                      *)
```

Listing 4.7

The order of writing the formal parameters is unimportant. But make it as readable and understandable as possible.

4.4.3 Variable parameters – 'in-out'

A more illuminating name for these is 'location' parameters. These, in effect, define the location of variables. As a result, two-way transfer of data is possible. Figure 4.17 defines the ideas behind the use of variable parameters, these being quite simple and sound. The essentials are shown in Listing 4.8, but observe the change in the declaration format (Fig. 4.18). The reserved word VAR is used to denote that what follows are variable parameters. What about a formal listing of variable and value parameters then? There is nothing surprising here; we maintain consistency of our rules. In each case the formal parameters must be listed as follows:

- Parameters of different types must be shown separately.
- Variable and value parameters must be separated.

As an example, consider the need to declare:

Value parameters:
  REAL – K1 K2 K3
  INTEGER – X1 X2
Variable parameters:
  REAL – Y1 Y2
  CHAR – Output

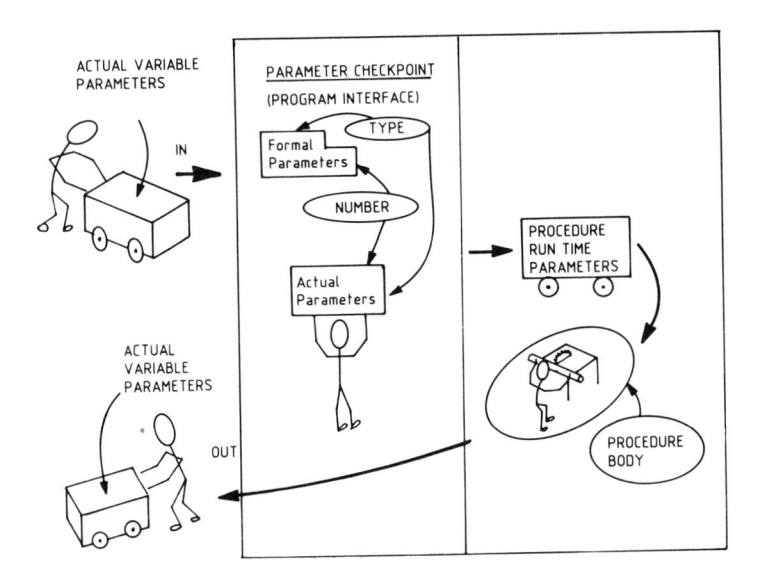

Fig. 4.17 Using variable (location) parameters

72 Subprograms in Modula-2

```
MODULE VariableParam;
(*******************************************************************)
(*        This illustrates the use of a variable parameter to     *)
(*        pass information to/from a procedure - Listing 4.8      *)
(*******************************************************************)
FROM InOut IMPORT WriteLn, WriteString, Read, Write;
VAR
   Oil:CHAR;

PROCEDURE ChangeLubricants(VAR Oiltype:CHAR);
BEGIN
   WriteString('Lubricants have been changed'); WriteLn;
   IF Oiltype = 'A' THEN
      WriteString('Oil is SAE 20'); WriteLn;
   ELSIF Oiltype = 'B' THEN
      WriteString('Oil is SAE 30-50'); WriteLn;
   ELSE WriteString('Bad entry'); WriteLn;
   END; (*end if-elsif*)
   Oiltype:='Z';
END ChangeLubricants; (*end of procedure code*)

BEGIN
   WriteString('What is the lubricant type?'); WriteLn;
   WriteString('Enter A for SAE20, B for SAE 30-50 oil'); WriteLn;
   Read(Oil); WriteLn; WriteLn;
   ChangeLubricants(Oil);
   WriteString('Finished with procedure - Oiltype character is ');
   Write(Oil); WriteLn;
END VariableParam. (* end of module *)

            (*              LISTING 4.8                  *)
```

Listing 4.8

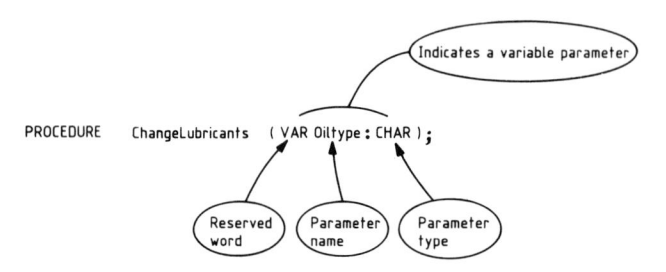

Fig. 4.18 Procedure heading incorporating a variable parameter

The procedure heading has the following form:

PROCEDURE ComputeAgain (VAR Y1,Y2:REAL;
       VAR Output:CHAR; K1,K2,K3:REAL; X1,X2:INTEGER);

Again, the ordering of the formal parameters is not important.

You may well ask why we bother to use value parameters at all. After all, we could do exactly the same job using variable ones. That's true, so there must be more to it than just a matter of moving information about. In fact it is the way the parameters are handled that is important. Running the program of Listing 4.8 proves that the information held by variable 'Oil' is changed by the procedure itself. But when we use value parameters (Listing 4.7) the original value is unaffected by the procedure. Thus, value parameters are intrinsically safer than variable ones; we are prevented from accidently changing what we started with. *Ergo*, use value parameters unless there is a good reason not to.

Q4.1 A mathematically based procedure has an input parameter which contains 10 000 individual elements. A single result is produced by this calculation. Normally a value parameter would be used with an input-only situation. However, in this case there could be a good reason for using location parameters to pass in the information. Why?

4.5 Function procedures

4.5.1 Introduction

In many cases the only item of interest in a procedure run is some result produced by the procedure software. Typically this is the case where mathematical calculations are involved. For instance, we might have a general purpose digital filter equation of the form:

$$Yi = k1*X1 + k2*X2 + k3*X4 - w1*Y1$$

where the k's and the w's are fixed coefficient values and the X's and Y's are measured values within the system.

Exercise: Write a procedure 'NewOutput' to perform this calculation using your knowledge gained so far. Assume that all values, which are reals, may have to be set on the call of the procedure.

If you've done this exercise correctly only Yi will have been declared as a variable parameter, the others being value types. To use the result of this calculation the actual variable corresponding to Yi has to be handled explicitly. That is, it must be declared and then manipulated as an actual parameter. However, it is best to avoid the use of variable parameters unless there is no choice.

Modula gives us a neat way to side-step the need for a variable parameter in such situations. It does this by providing another type of procedure, the 'function' procedure. This should not be seen as a replacement for the proper procedure. Normally it would be used only when the procedure process is designed to give a result. In rather simple terms we can say that a procedure causes something to happen while a function procedure causes a computation to be carried out.

We'll also see that this particular construct makes it relatively simple to form complex expressions using procedure results, as in

$$\text{Tan } X = \frac{\text{Sin } X}{\text{Cos } X}$$

where both 'Sin' and 'Cos' are function procedures.

4.5.2 Using function procedures

The underlying ideas of the function procedure are shown in Fig. 4.19. In most cases input information is needed by the procedure; as before, this is handled using value parameters. Once the procedure has been invoked it churns away, processing the data. Finally a result is generated; its value is then returned to a designated variable in the calling program. To avoid mistakes the item to be returned is clearly specified within the procedure; for this a 'RETURN' statement is provided.

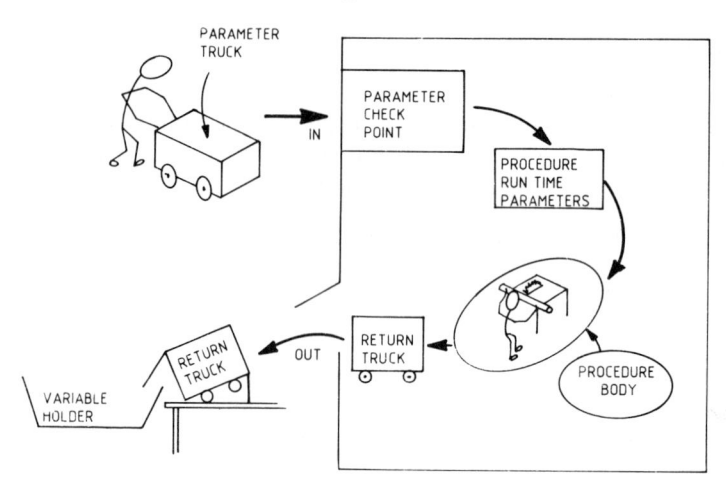

Fig. 4.19 The function procedure concept

As with proper procedures, there are two major points concerning function procedures. The first is the way in which they are written, the second being the method of call. The essentials are illustrated in Figs. 4.20 and 4.21. Here we have a procedure 'AverageFuelConsumption' which has two value parameters. It performs a calculation, returning the computed value of the locally declared variable 'AvConsumption'. This is an INTEGER value, the type being defined in the procedure heading. When the procedure is called we actually assign the result to some variable, in this case 'FuelConsumption' (Fig. 4.21). Read through Listing 4.9 to see how to write and use the function procedure.

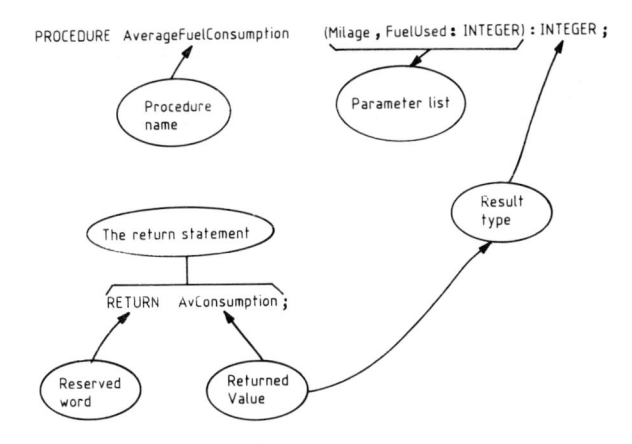

Fig. 4.20 Function procedure details

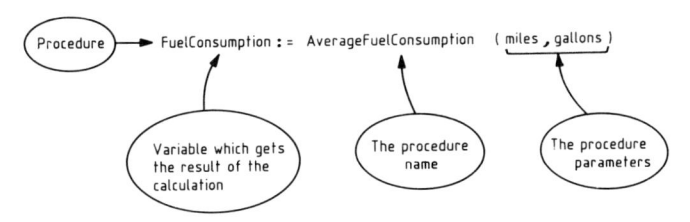

Fig. 4.21 Function procedure call

If additional values have to be saved from the procedure run then variable parameters should be used. Even so, avoid this where possible; it may be better in such cases to use regular procedures. *Never* use global variables to transfer information between procedures and their surrounding environment (Fig. 4.22). It is a form of uncontrolled access method which by-passes all the checks introduced by parameter passing. Almost certainly it will lead to major run-time problems in anything but the smallest of programs. In summary:

- Only one result is returned (here being AvConsumption).
- Its type is defined in the procedure heading (INTEGER).
- The result is given to any desired variable using the assignment statement (FuelConsumption). The returned value and the program variable must be of the same type.
- The returned value must not be a structured variable (the meaning of this will become clear after studying Chapters 7 and 8).
- A parameter list must always be supplied for a function procedure. If no parameters are actually used the list is empty, i.e.

    PROCEDURE IntValueOf():INTEGER;

the corresponding call having the form

76 Subprograms in Modula-2

```
MODULE FunctionProc;
(*******************************************************************)
(*      This illustrates the use of a function procedure to       *)
(*      obtain results from a calculation - Listing 4.9           *)
(*******************************************************************)
FROM InOut IMPORT WriteLn, WriteString, ReadInt, WriteInt;
VAR
   miles, gallons, FuelConsumption:INTEGER;

PROCEDURE AverageFuelConsumption(Milage, FuelUsed :INTEGER):INTEGER;
VAR
   AvConsumption   :INTEGER;
BEGIN
   WriteString('Calculation running'); WriteLn;
   AvConsumption:=Milage DIV FuelUsed;
   RETURN AvConsumption;
END AverageFuelConsumption; (*end of procedure code*)

BEGIN
   WriteString('What is the milage?'); WriteLn;
   ReadInt(miles); WriteLn;
   WriteString('How many gallons have been used?'); WriteLn;
   WriteString('Enter whole numbers only.'); WriteLn;
   ReadInt(gallons); WriteLn;
   FuelConsumption:=AverageFuelConsumption(miles, gallons);
   WriteString('The average fuel consumption is ');
   WriteInt(FuelConsumption, 2);
   WriteString(' miles per gallon.'); WriteLn;
END FunctionProc. (* end of module *)


     (*                     LISTING 4.9                           *)
```
Listing 4.9

Fig. 4.22

IntTime:=IntValueOf();

- The procedure may be called and used within an expression, as, for instance,

    Consumption:=(Consumption + AverageFuelConsumption(miles,gallons))/2;

Such calls are defined as 'function designators'.

Q4.2 There seems little point in having the empty list construct. Can you see any use for it?

4.6 Nesting and recursion

In this chapter many example procedures have themselves invoked other procedures. Such a construct is called 'nesting' of procedures. It is also permissible for a procedure to actually invoke itself. This is defined as 'recursion'. Many mathematical operations involve recursion; in such situations recursive procedures may provide a more elegant solution than alternative methods.

As an example, consider the problem of estimating the number of direct point-to-point signal links in a data communication network. For a system consisting of N nodes, the corresponding number of links, Ln, is calculated as follows:

Ln = (N−1) + (N−2) + (N−3) + ... + (N−N);

i.e. for four nodes,

L4 = (4−1) + (4−2) + (4−3) + (4−4) = 3+2+1 = 6

But this is the same as

L4 = (4−1) + L3

Hence the expression for the number of links involves the calculation for the number of links. This is an example of a recursive action. Generalising:

Ln = (N−1) + L(n−1)

The program to run this is given in Listing 4.10. Here the recursive procedure is 'LinkNumbers'. Note that this is called up in the body of the procedure itself, thus invoking recursive action. It is absolutely essential that the procedure has a definite terminating condition; otherwise it would be impossible to break out from it.

Some readers may find the idea of recursion difficult to grasp at first. If you simply consider that each time the procedure is invoked it behaves like a new procedure the process is easy to follow. Naturally, on each invocation, new parameters are passed and new local variables are created.

Generally, problems solved using recursion can also be handled using iteration. Which method is used depends on individual circumstances.

Q4.3 Why would recursion be avoided in the following situations?
(a) Fast real-time microcomputer controllers.
(b) Small embedded computer systems.

```
MODULE Recursion;
(******************************************************************)
(*       This illustrates the use of recursion in procedures    *)
(*                        Listing 4.10                           *)
(******************************************************************)
FROM InOut IMPORT WriteLn, WriteString, ReadCard, WriteCard;
VAR
    NodePoints :CARDINAL;

PROCEDURE LinkNumbers(Nodes:CARDINAL):CARDINAL;
VAR
    DirectLinks :CARDINAL;
BEGIN
    IF Nodes = 1 THEN
        RETURN 0
    ELSE
    (* here is the recursive call *)
        DirectLinks:= (Nodes-1) + LinkNumbers(Nodes-1);
    END;
    RETURN DirectLinks;
END LinkNumbers; (*end of procedure code*)

BEGIN
    WriteString('Enter number of communication nodes'); WriteLn;
    ReadCard(NodePoints); WriteLn;
    WriteString('The number of direct data links is ');
    WriteCard(LinkNumbers(NodePoints),3); WriteLn;
END Recursion. (* end of module *)
```

Listing 4.10

4.7 A final point

Now is the time to settle down with your system manual and have a good look at the range of procedures provided with the compiler package. In particular, those contained in the module 'InOut' and 'MathLib0' should be recognisable.

Modula doesn't define the structure and use of such utility modules. They depend on the particular system; check on details in your own compiler manual.

To finish this chapter off ensure that you:

- Understand the reason for and the use of subprograms in high-level languages.
- Understand the structure and use of procedures and function procedures.
- Know the reason for and use of formal and actual parameters in procedures and function procedures.
- Appreciate the difference between local and global variables and grasp the concept of the scope and visibility of variables.

Chapter 5
Types revisited

Up to the present we've worked with data objects of various types, such as INTEGER, REAL, and so on. In general it has been a fairly painless experience, made easier by our knowledge of conventional mathematics. What we intend to do here is to extend our understanding and use of data typing. This will show us why strong typing is such an important part of modern high-level computer languages. After having studied this chapter you should be able to:

- See why good typing is an essential part of program security.
- Understand what strong typing is and how it helps the compiler to pick up mistakes in the software.
- Appreciate how typing allows us to take a conceptual view of our problems.
- Understand the ideas of cardinality, ordinality and enumeration.
- Create your own data types.
- Use programmer-defined enumerated types and subrange types.
- Carry out type mixing using both type conversion and type transfer methods.

You will also extend your work on both CHAR and BOOLEAN types.

5.1 Setting the scene

If your objective is to produce software which is complex, obscure and bug-ridden (in short, a kludge) then miss out this chapter. Data typing is a powerful tool for the development of good, understandable and reliable programs; in which case it won't interest you. On the other hand, just in case you don't belong to the hackers brigade, read on.

The use of types is an abstraction process, being a fundamental instrument of high-level language working. It is virtually unknown in assembly languages. Now, it is a well-known fact that many kludges have been produced by such low-level programs. Yet often these have been produced by conscientious professionals for use in critical applications. So it is interesting to start off the discussion on types by looking at the difficulties of working in assembly language.

In developing assembler software, what are the main considerations for the programmer? They are, basically, how does he represent the data in the computer store system (memory), where does he store it and what operations must he carry out on such data?

- Is it possible to examine the contents of a data store and define its meaning? Well, only as a binary number.
- What happens if you try to store a data word in the wrong location? The system will do exactly what you tell it to do.
- By examining the detailed operations carried out on the data can you deduce what is supposed to be happening? Only if the text is littered with comments and you have a good understanding of the processor instruction set.

It is no surprise that programming in assembly language takes a lot of time. It is also a fact that it is very easy to make mistakes, the most serious ones being the so-called algorithmic and logical ones. In other words, from the machine's point of view the code runs; unfortunately it just doesn't do what was intended by the designer.

This situation arises because we spend most time concentrating on machine details and data-handling features, much less on the problem itself. Data typing, however, helps us to focus on what we're trying to do (that is, to solve a particular problem) instead of getting trapped in the bog of machine detail.

5.2 Data types – basic concepts reviewed

5.2.1 Background

Show the circuit symbol in Fig. 5.1 to an electrical engineering student and ask him what it is. He'll probably reply 'Oh, that's a capacitor'. Well, of course, it is nothing of the sort, it is merely marks on a piece of paper. What

Fig. 5.1 The basic idea of abstraction

the student really means is that it 'represents' a capacitor in his mind. Not that it has a particular shape and size, etc., but that it has the electrical circuit properties that we define as being capacitance. 'Very clever', I hear you say in a sarcastic tone, 'how totally irrelevant'. Not so. This is, in fact, an extremely important point; it demonstrates our ability to separate concepts from implementations.

Dealing with abstract ideas affects the way in which we interact with the real world. How, for instance, do we view the jet engine of an aircraft? To the aircraft designer it is a power unit, the driving force of the vehicle (Fig. 5.2). To the company accountant it is a profit centre (we hope), existing only on the balance books. Yet we're talking about the same physical device.

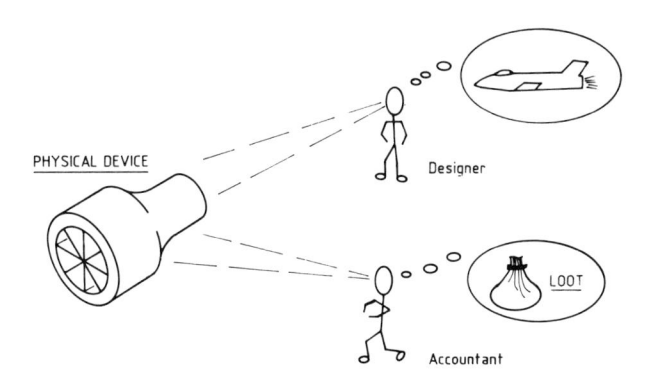

Fig. 5.2 Reality and concepts

Let's put this in the context of Modula-2, specifically for the type REAL. The value 100 000 is too large to be expressed as an INTEGER number, therefore it must become a REAL type. We can write it as 100000.0 or as 1.0E5, two ways of viewing the same quantity. The difference exists in our mind.

One very important point to consider is whether our computer can actually hold this value. Practical implementations for REAL (floating-point) numbers usually use 32, 64 or 80 bits. Thus the actual number range available and its degree of precision depend entirely on the machine being used. At the conceptual level this doesn't affect us. That is why it is so easy to fool ourselves when running mathematical calculations. The resulting print-out may look very impressive, having a large number range and a high degree of precision; yet the actual hardware may be incapable of producing such results accurately.

5.2.2 Abstract ideas – typing and type conversion

A data type is essentially a conceptual idea. Each type defined within a programming language has two attributes:

(a) a set of values; and
(b) a set of operations which can be carried out on these values.

Consider, for instance, type INTEGER. This has a set of values consisting of whole numbers lying in the range $-32\,768$ to $+32\,767$, the step size being 1 (one). We are allowed to carry out the following set of operations on these values:

addition (+)
subtraction (−)
multiplication (*)
division (DIV)
modulus (MOD)
negation (~)

Note that we haven't said anything about how INTEGER values are held within the machine itself. Thus at the programming level we work with the abstract concept of a type; the particular implementation only becomes important when we load and run a program into a target machine.

For the moment we'll deal only with scalar types. Some of these we've met before in Chapters 1 and 2, the so-called predefined types:

INTEGER
CARDINAL
REAL
BOOLEAN
CHAR

It is fundamental to high-level language design that data objects should be named and not accessed using memory addresses. This, of course, can't hold in all situations, a point covered in low-level programming.

Having done this we then find that Modula-2 subjects us to a further set of rules and constraints, i.e. it is said to be a 'strongly typed' language.

- Every data object must belong to one (unique) type.
- Associated with each type is a set of values and operations.
- Every operator used with a data type must belong to the set defined for that type.
- Where assignments are carried out, data objects must be of the same type.

This last point shows why explicit type assignments have to be made from INTEGERs to REALs and vice versa. For instance, given

VAR
  X1:INTEGER;
  Y1:REAL;

then the statement

Y1:=X1;

would be thrown out by the compiler as the types are incompatible. However, writing

Y1:=real(X1);

is perfectly valid as this is a 'type conversion' action.

5.2.3 A few more qualities we've taken for granted!

Let's consider our old friend type INTEGER again, and look more closely at its qualities.

First, it has a finite range: $-32\,768$ to $32\,767$. The measure of the size of the set is its 'cardinality', in this case being $65\,535$ elements.

Second, there is a defined order for the elements, e.g. 10 precedes 11 but follows 9. Thus the type is said to have 'ordinality'.

Third, following from these first two qualities, not only can we list all elements of type INTEGER, we can also place them in order in the list. Listing items in order is defined as 'enumeration'.

Therefore, by definition, an enumerated type must have both cardinality and ordinality.

Q5.1 As an exercise look out the cardinality and ordinality of type BOOLEAN.

5.3 Text operations – type CHAR

So far type CHAR has been used extensively to support programmer interaction with running programs via a display/keyboard unit (Fig. 5.3). Very roughly then, we can say that character types are needed to support communications between the computer and the outside world. The external

Fig. 5.3 Use of type CHAR

84 Types revisited

devices include not only visual display units (VDUs), but printers, plotters, Prom programmers and other computer systems.

How many elements do we need within our data type CHAR, and what should they contain? If we include all the symbols found on a typewriter keyboard then we're a long way towards a solution. Added to this is the need to emulate typewriter functions (carriage return, line feed, etc.) and to control the actual communications activities (end-of-text message, acknowledge message, etc.). Thus we have a set of printable characters plus the control (non-printing) ones.

One major obstacle still lies ahead. How can we be sure that the recipient of our message (say) is using the same character set? Without having an agreed set of ground-rules we can't. Therefore, it is necessary to enforce standardisation on our communications system. The most widely used methods are those of ASCII (American Standard Code for Information Interchange) and EBCDIC (Extended Binary Coded Decimal Interchange Code).

Objects of type CHAR are normally held by a single data byte, thus allowing 256 different data items to be represented. ASCII actually defines 128 characters, as shown in Table 5.1.

Hence it should be realised that type CHAR is an enumerated type. It has a cardinality of 128, the order defined in Table 5.1. Type CHAR constants, if they were defined explicitly, would be written as

Type CHAR = (nul, soh, ... 'a', 'b', 'c', ... del);

No arithmetic operations are defined on CHAR, but we *can* work with the ordinal numbers of the type.

Two standard Modula-2 function procedures which may be used with characters are ORD and CHR (Fig. 5.4). ORD enables us to obtain the ordinal value of a character; for instance

ORD('B') gives the result 66, i.e. the ordinal value of B
ORD('C') gives 67

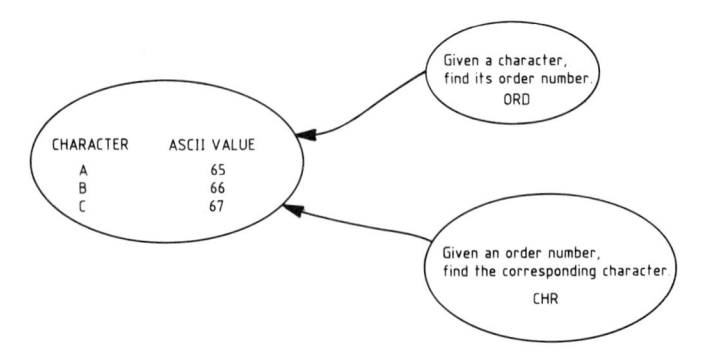

Fig. 5.4 ORD and CHR

ORD('0') gives 48
ORD('1') gives 49

Thus we can write (assuming Y to be a CARDINAL variable)

Y:=ORD('C') i.e. Y is assigned the value 67 or
Y:=ORD('C')−ORD('B') Y is assigned (67−66), i.e. 1

CHR allows us to obtain a character from its ordinal number, as follows:

CHR(66) gives the result 'B'

Hence Alpha:=CHR(66) results in the letter B being assigned to the variable Alpha (assumed to be a CHAR type).

Exercise: Write a program which takes in a character from the keyboard, extracts its ordinal value, and outputs the result to the screen (Listing 5.1).

Exercise: Write a program which takes in a numeric character from the keyboard, computes its actual numeric value, and outputs the result to the screen (Listing 5.2).

Why should we ever need to use the ORD and CHR functions for handling characters? We've managed quite well up to now without them. True, but only because the necessary conversion work has been done by the standard functions such as ReadInt, WriteCard, etc. And, our programs have been very simple with the keyboard types, e.g. INTEGER or REAL, etc., being clearly defined. Further, these only work correctly if the coding scheme is ASCII.

```
MODULE Ordinal;
(*****************************************************************)
(*    This demonstrates use of the ORD function.           *)
(*               Listing 5.1                               *)
(*                                                         *)
(*****************************************************************)
FROM InOut IMPORT Write, WriteInt, WriteLn, WriteString, Read;
VAR
    digit1:CHAR;
    Y:INTEGER;

BEGIN
    LOOP
        WriteString('input digit='); WriteLn;
        Read(digit1); Write(digit1); WriteLn;
        IF ORD(digit1) = 30 THEN EXIT END; (*exit on CR*)
        Y:=ORD(digit1);
        WriteInt(Y,3); WriteLn;
    END; (*end of loop*)
END Ordinal.
```

Listing 5.1

86 Types revisited

Table 5.1 ASCII character set

Decimal No.	Hex. No.	Character	Decimal No.	Hex. No.	Character	Decimal No.	Hex. No.	Character	Decimal No.	Hex. No.	Character
0	00	nul	32	20	sp	64	40	‰	96	60	
1	01	soh	33	21	!	65	41	A	97	61	a
2	02	stx	34	22	"	66	42	B	98	62	b
3	03	etx	35	23	£	67	43	C	99	63	c
4	04	eot	36	24	$	68	44	D	100	64	d
5	05	enq	37	25	%	69	45	E	101	65	e
6	06	ack	38	26	&	70	46	F	102	66	f
7	07	bel	39	27	'	71	47	G	103	67	g
8	08	bs	40	28	(	72	48	H	104	68	h
9	09	tab	41	29	)	73	49	I	105	69	i
10	0A	lf	42	2A	*	74	4A	J	106	6A	j
11	0B	vt	43	2B	+	75	4B	K	107	6B	k
12	0C	ff	44	2C	,	76	4C	L	108	6C	l
13	0D	cr	45	2D	-	77	4D	M	109	6D	m
14	0E	so	46	2E	.	78	4E	N	110	6E	n
15	0F	si	47	2F	/	79	4F	O	111	6F	o

Table 5.1 continued

Decimal No.	Hex. No.	Character	Decimal No.	Hex. No.	Character	Decimal No.	Hex. No.	Character	Decimal No.	Hex. No.	Character
16	10	dle	48	30	0	80	50	P	112	70	p
17	11	dc1	49	31	1	81	51	Q	113	71	q
18	12	dc2	50	32	2	82	52	R	114	72	r
19	13	dc3	51	33	3	83	53	S	115	73	s
20	14	dc4	52	34	4	84	54	T	116	74	t
21	15	nak	53	35	5	85	55	U	117	75	u
22	16	syn	54	36	6	86	56	V	118	76	v
23	17	etb	55	37	7	87	57	W	119	77	w
24	18	can	56	38	8	88	58	X	120	78	x
25	19	em	57	39	9	89	59	Y	121	79	y
26	1A	sub	58	3A	:	90	5A	Z	122	7A	z
27	1B	esc	59	3B	;	91	5B	[	123	7B	{
28	1C	fs	60	3C	<	92	5C	≠	124	7C	!
29	1D	gs	61	3D	=	93	5D	]	125	7D	}
30	1E	rs	62	3E	>	94	5E	ˆ	126	7E	˜
31	1F	us	63	3F	?	95	5F	—	127	7F	del

88 Types revisited

```
MODULE Ord2;
(************************************************************)
(*    Here the ORD function is used to convert numeric       *)
(*    CHARACTERS to their actual numerical value             *)
(*                    Listing 5.2                            *)
(************************************************************)
FROM InOut IMPORT Write, WriteInt, WriteLn, WriteString, Read;
VAR
    digit1:CHAR;
    Y:INTEGER;

BEGIN
   LOOP
      WriteString('input digit='); WriteLn;
      Read(digit1); Write(digit1); WriteLn;
      IF ORD(digit1) = 30 THEN EXIT END; (*exit on CR*)
      Y:=ORD(digit1)-ORD('0');
      WriteInt(Y,1); WriteLn; WriteLn;
   END; (*end of loop*)
END Ord2.
```

Listing 5.2

Exercise: Write a program to take in characters from the keyboard until the CR key is pressed. It is then to compute the value of the input number and output the result to the screen. During the data entry process it must reject non-numeric characters. For simplicity, work within the INTEGER number range (Listing 5.3).

Exercise: Use the CHR function to print out the uppercase letters of the alphabet on the VDU screen (Listing 5.4).

```
MODULE Ord3;
(************************************************************)
(*    In this example the ORD function is used to convert    *)
(*    a numeric character string to its decimal value.       *)
(*                    Listing 5.3                            *)
(************************************************************)
FROM InOut IMPORT Write, WriteInt, WriteLn, WriteString, Read;
VAR
    digit1:CHAR;
    X,Y:INTEGER;

BEGIN
   Y:=0;
   WriteString('input digits ');
   LOOP
      Read(digit1);
      IF ('0'<=digit1)&(digit1<='9') THEN
         Write(digit1);
         X:=ORD(digit1)-ORD('0');
         Y:=10*Y + X;
      END; (*IF*)
      IF ORD(digit1) = 30 THEN
         WriteLn; WriteString('input value is  ');
         WriteInt(Y,5); WriteLn; WriteLn;
         EXIT (*exit on CR*)
      END; (*IF ORD*)
   END; (*end of loop*)
END Ord3.
```

Listing 5.3

```
MODULE Character;
(*****************************************************************)
(*      This illustrates the use of the CHR function.          *)
(*                     Listing 5.4                              *)
(*****************************************************************)
FROM InOut IMPORT Write, WriteInt, WriteLn, WriteString, Read;
VAR
   Num:INTEGER;

BEGIN
   FOR Num:=65 TO 90 DO
   Write(CHR(Num));
   END; (*end of FOR*)

   (* now you can work out what the following does.  Hint: have
       a look at the standard procedure list, appendix C.    *)
   WriteLn; WriteLn;
   FOR Num:=97 TO 122 DO
   Write(CAP(CHR(Num)));
   END; (*of second FOR*)
END Character.
```

Listing 5.4

5.4 BOOLEAN operation

The basis and use of BOOLEAN types has already been covered in Chapter 2; now let's re-evaluate these in more formal terms.

(a) It is an enumerated type.
(b) The set consists of two elements, false and true.
(c) The order is false, true. Thus false = 0, true = 1.
(d) The set of operations which can be carried out on these are:
   Logical NOT (Negation) – highest precedence
   Logical AND (Conjunction)
   Logical OR (Disjunction) – lowest precedence

The truth tables for these are given in Table 5.2

Now for an important point, applicable specifically to Boolean operations in Modula-2. The truth tables imply that the input variables X and Y exist. In an electronic circuit this would have to be the case. After all, in the absence of faults, the inputs to a logic gate must either be in the logic 0 or logic 1 state. However, in software it is possible to make a decision based on one variable only (it may not be the right way to do it but it can still be done). In this case we describe the others as being 'undefined'. The resulting output of the Boolean operation may be either defined or undefined when one of the inputs is undefined. This comes about because, in Modula-2, if the first operand defines the result of an operation the second one is not evaluated. For instance, in the AND operation, if the first operand (X) is false (logic 0) then the result *must* also be false. Such evaluations are said to be 'short-circuit' ones.

Table 5.2 Truth tables for Boolean functions

AND (basic logic) X Y (Z=X AND Y)	AND (positive logic form) X Y Z	OR X Y (Z=X OR Y)	OR X Y Z
F F F	0 0 0	F F F	0 0 0
F T F	0 1 0	F T T	0 1 1
T F F	1 0 0	T F T	1 0 1
T T T	1 1 1	T T T	1 1 1

NOT T = F   NOT 0 = 1
NOT F = T   NOT 1 = 0

Q5.2 Draw up a new table for the AND and OR functions, similar to Table 5.2, but now including a set of undefined states for both X and Y.

The order of precedence of the Boolean and associated conditional operators must be taken into account when writing logical expressions. For instance

x>w AND c<d is interpreted logically as x> (w AND c) <d

Because of this, such a construct is not allowed. The compiler should flag it up as an error. Just the same, to be safe, use parentheses to enforce correct logic operations. For the case above we write

(x>w) AND (c<d)

Now let's clarify a few more points using the example given in Listing 5.5. When this is run it first assigns the condition (or value) TRUE to the variable x. The statement 'IF x' really means 'if x is true'; hence, as x has been set to be true the teststring 'x is true' is printed out on the screen.

Expanding on this, Listing 5.6 illustrates a few more aspects of Boolean operations. In line 3 of the program we evaluate the statement (relation-

```
MODULE Bool1;
(*****************************************************************)
(*      This is an elementary use of a BOOLEAN type.       *)
(*                  Listing 5.5                            *)
(*****************************************************************)
FROM InOut IMPORT Write, WriteInt, WriteLn, WriteString, Read;
VAR
   x:BOOLEAN;

BEGIN
   x:=TRUE;
   IF x THEN WriteString('x is true'); END;
END Bool1.
```

Listing 5.5

```
MODULE Bool2;
(***************************************************************)
(*       Some more examples of boolean operations.             *)
(*                      Listing 5.6                            *)
(***************************************************************)
FROM InOut IMPORT Write, WriteInt, WriteLn, WriteString, Read;
VAR
    x,y:BOOLEAN;
    a,b:INTEGER;

BEGIN
    a:=10;
    b:=20;
    x:=(b>a);
    IF x THEN
        WriteString('x is true'); WriteLn;
    END;
    y:=(a>b);
    IF NOT y THEN
        WriteString('y is false'); WriteLn;
    END;
END Bool2.
```

Listing 5.6

ship) 'b is greater than a'; in this case the answer is clearly true. The result of this evaluation (TRUE) is assigned to the Boolean variable x; consequently the textstring is printed out. Line 7, however, evaluates the relationship 'a greater than b', which is obviously false. Hence 'NOT y' is true, and so the final textstring is also printed out on the screen.

As a final example read and run Listing 5.7. In this example, more statements have been used than are necessary, although this tends to make it easier to follow the program. Therefore, as an exercise compress

Running:=(Status = 'R');
LowOilPressure:=(OilPressure<LowPressurePoint);
Alarm:=LowOilPressure AND Running;

into a single-line statement.

5.5 Inventing your own data types

5.5.1 Why new data types?

Let's open with a very reasonable question. Why should we bother to devise new data types in the first place? This feature isn't available on the older languages, including Coral66, one of the most widely used real-time languages in the UK. Well, the issue is one of program design and maintenance. Remember that the whole object of typing is to help us to produce reliable programs. By using type information the compiler can pick up many errors which otherwise would go through to the run-time code (as I'm sure you've discovered by now). However, the number of types supplied in Modula-2

92   Types revisited

```
MODULE Bool3;
(*****************************************************************)
(*           A more detailed boolean operation.                  *)
(*                       Listing 5.7                             *)
(*****************************************************************)
FROM InOut IMPORT Write, WriteInt, WriteLn, WriteString, Read,
                  ReadInt;
VAR
    Running, LowOilPressure, Alarm:BOOLEAN;
    OilPressure:INTEGER;
    Status,c:CHAR;
CONST
    LowPressurePoint= 20;

BEGIN
   LOOP
      WriteLn; WriteLn;
      WriteString('Low oil pressure alarm point is ');
      WriteInt(LowPressurePoint,2); WriteLn;
      WriteString('Enter actual oil pressure - psi'); WriteLn;
      ReadInt(OilPressure);WriteLn;
      WriteString('What is the engine status - ');
      WriteString('R = running    S = stopped'); WriteLn;
      Read(Status);
      Running:=(Status = 'R');
      LowOilPressure:=(OilPressure < LowPressurePoint);
      Alarm:= LowOilPressure AND Running;
      WriteLn;
      IF Alarm THEN
         WriteString('Engine fault'); WriteLn;
      ELSE
         WriteString('System OK'); WriteLn;
      END; (*end of if statement*)
      WriteString('Test finished? Y or N'); WriteLn;
      Read(c);
      IF ORD(c) = 89 THEN
         EXIT
      END;
   END; (*end of loop*)
END Bool3.
```

Listing 5.7

(the predefined ones) is relatively small. As a result any individual type (e.g. INTEGER) will probably represent a wide range of variables. Many of these will be logically quite different (from the programmer's point of view). Thus the compiler isn't able to find logical errors where types are compatible. Consider the simple example in Listing 5.8 for computing the average of four analogue measurements. If for any reason the programmer had written

   TotalValue:=TotalValue + Num;

the compiler would accept it as a perfectly valid statement; yet logically it is completely wrong. What can be done to help the compiler stop us implementing such code? There is no way that it can possibly spot the flaws in program logic; after all each program is unique. What is needed is another mechanism which, while not being totally foolproof, significantly improves

```
    VAR
        NewValue,TotalValue,AverageValue,Num:INTEGER;

    ......................................
    TotalValue:=0;
    FOR Num:= 1 TO 4 DO
        ReadInt(NewValue); WriteLn;
        TotalValue:=TotalValue + NewValue;
    END; (*end of for*)

    AverageValue:=TotalValue DIV 4;
    WriteString('The average value is');
    WriteInt(AverageValue,5); WriteLn;
    ......................................
```

Listing 5.8

the situation. It is rather like putting up 'stop' signs at a dangerous junction. They don't prevent motorists driving dangerously, yet they certainly reduce the accident rate. By analogy, our contribution to software safety is first to invent new data types; then we can use this information to distinguish between logically different items. In effect, we force the compiler to check for name equivalence; until now it has been looking for structural compatibility.

The ideas behind defining and using your own types are given in Fig. 5.5; these will become clearer as we go along.

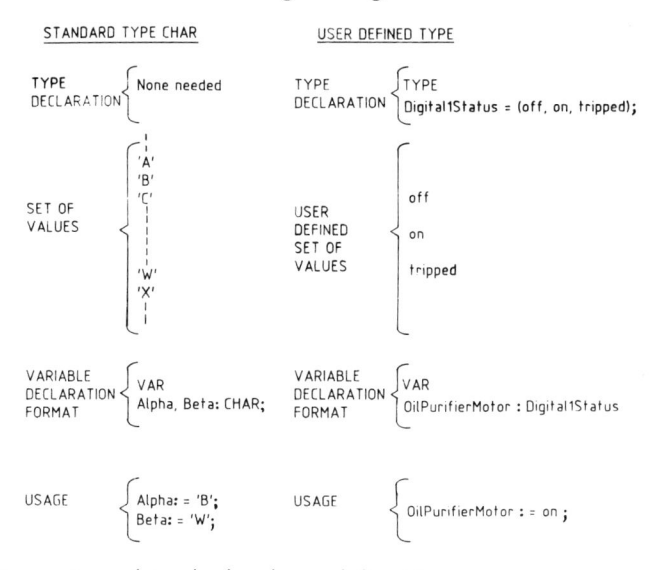

Fig. 5.5 Comparison of standard and user-defined types

5.5.2 Defining new types – enumerated types

Let's modify the averaging program by introducing a new type which is enumerated, i.e. we have to list the values of the type, the ordinality of the

94 Types revisited

values being given by the listing order. For the example above a new type, 'Counter', will be introduced. It consists of four elements (its cardinality), the ordinality being

one=0   two=1   three=2   four=3
TYPE Counter = (one,two,three,four);

Now let's use this in the averaging program (Listing 5.9). Here Num has been declared as being of type 'Counter'; hence it cannot be mixed with INTEGER values in an expression. Just to prove this, alter the code to read 'TotalValue:=TotalValue + Num;' and verify that the compiler generates a 'type incompatibility' message.

```
MODULE UserType1;
(***************************************************************)
(*       This incorporates user defined types.                *)
(*                    Listing 5.9                             *)
(***************************************************************)
FROM InOut IMPORT WriteLn, WriteString, ReadInt, WriteInt;
TYPE
   Counter = (one,two,three,four);
VAR
   x1, NewValue, TotalValue, AverageValue:INTEGER;
   Num:Counter;

BEGIN
   TotalValue:=0;
   FOR Num:= one TO four DO
      WriteString('Enter data'); WriteLn;
      ReadInt(x1); WriteLn;
      TotalValue:=TotalValue + x1;
   END; (*end of for*)
   AverageValue:=TotalValue DIV 4;
   WriteString('The average value is');
   WriteInt(AverageValue,5); WriteLn;

END UserType1.
```

Listing 5.9

The syntax diagram for enumerated type declaration is shown in Fig. 5.6. Only assignment and relational operations apply to such types.

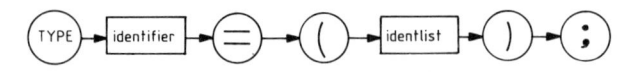

Fig. 5.6 Syntax diagram – enumerated type declaration

In general then, how do we benefit from using programmer-defined types? Well, consider the program abstract of Listing 5.10. First, for the two user-defined types (Digital1Status, Digital2Status) we've clearly and unambiguously spelt out all possible conditions. The reader doesn't have to interpret the meaning of the source code. Second, we've used names which are logically associated with the type attributes. This makes the program easier to

```
TYPE Digital1Status = (off, on, tripped);
     Digital2Status = (low, high);

VAR
    OilPurifierMotor, CPPpumpmotor:Digital1Status;
    BearingTemp, SealTemp:Digital2Status;

BEGIN
    CPPpumpmotor:=on;
    OilPurifierMotor:=tripped;
    BearingTemp:=high;
```

Listing 5.10

read, understand and maintain. Third, we've built in extra safety factors. Consider that, by accident, we write

BearingTemp:=off;

When the program is compiled a 'type incompatibility' error message will be flagged up.

For the small number of variables shown in this example such a mistake is unlikely. Consider, though, the job of developing software for the machinery control systems on a modern warship. The number of items to be monitored and controlled runs into thousands. Do you still think that mistakes like this are unimaginable?

Q5.3 Suppose we had included the following declaration in Listing 5.9:

TYPE Counter = (one,two,three,four);
TYPE Limits = (four,five,six);

What would you expect to happen at compile time?

5.5.3 Subrange types

There are some situations where we want to limit ('constrain') the range of values that a variable may take, usually on the grounds of safety. Let's look at a specific example. If 4095 INTEGER is fed to a 12-bit digital-to-analogue converter it will produce full range output. This corresponds to all 12 bits being in a logic '1' condition. If now 4096 is output to the converter these 12 bits will go to the logic '0' state, resulting in the DAC output going to its minimum value. Now visualise this device being used within a digital control system to set the blade pitch angle of a ship's propeller. For a 4095 output, maximum ahead blade pitch is set. We're trundling across the ocean at full power (probably about 35 knots for a Frigate) when the DAC signal goes from full ahead pitch (4095) to full astern (4096). Not a pretty sight!

In many languages the only way to prevent such an event is to positively check for out-of-range conditions. Thus, the responsibility for avoiding invalid or dangerous conditions rests with the programmer. As a result, one

96 Types revisited

single program mistake made on an off-day could produce catastrophy.

In Modula-2 the problem *could* be handled by defining a new type having the required cardinality and ordinality. This, however, may not be necessary or even desirable. Note that in many cases our program variables, although being a standard type, don't use the full range of values available to us. An example is the instance of the use of the DAC; here the number range needed for full range operation is 0–4095. As such it could be considered to be part of the INTEGER or CARDINAL set. This leads us to the idea of a 'subrange' data type. A subrange is defined as a contiguous subset of a given data type (Fig. 5.7). Note that this doesn't say that the range values need to be INTEGER, merely CONSTANT values which must contiguous.

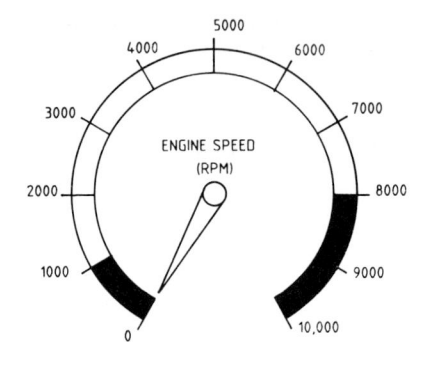

Fig. 5.7 Subrange concept

The declaration form, using the above example, is:

TYPE DacRange = [0..4095];

In a system having four DACs the declaration section could be written as:

TYPE
   DacRange = [0..4095];
VAR
   DAC1,DAC2,DAC3,DAC4:DacRange;

Thus, the subrange syntax is

Subrange type = '['ConstExpression '..' ConstExpression']'

the corresponding syntax diagram being that of Fig. 5.8.

How does the compiler recognise the parent or 'base' type? Simply by checking the type of the two bounds. However, in the DAC example here,

Inventing your own data types   97

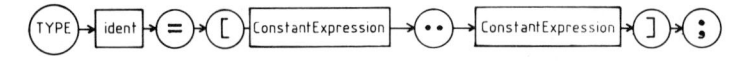

Fig. 5.8 Syntax of a subrange type

```
TYPE
    Digital 1 Status = ( primed, off, on, standby, tripped);
TYPE
    Digital 2 Status = [ off .. Standby ];
```

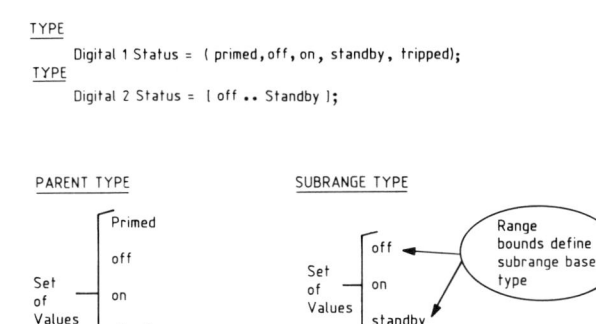

Fig. 5.9 Subrange of an enumerated type

the base type isn't clear, it may be either INTEGER or CARDINAL. The rules in Modula-2 are that if the lower bound is a negative integer value then type INTEGER is assumed, otherwise it is CARDINAL.

The subrange bounds are fairly self-explanatory for INTEGERs and CARDINALs. What, though, of other base types (Fig. 5.9)? Consider the example in Listing 5.11, part of a program module. Here we've first defined (declared) an enumerated type 'Digital1Status' and then declared a subrange of this type 'Digital2Status'. Digital2Status has a lower bound of 'off', an upper bound of 'standby', its cardinality is 3 and the ordinality is 'off', 'on', 'standby'.

As a result the oil purifier motor can be defined to be in one of five conditions, but the CPP motor in only three.

```
TYPE Digital1Status = (primed, off, on, standby, tripped);
     Digital2Status = [off..standby];
VAR
   OilPurifierMotor:Digital1Status;
   CPPpumpmotor:Digital2Status;

BEGIN
   CPPpumpmotor:=on;
   OilPurifierMotor:=standby;
END Subrange.
```

Listing 5.11

Q5.4 What would result from writing

   CPPpumpmotor:=tripped;

in the source code of Listing 5.11?

A few more aspects of subranges are illustrated in Listing 5.12.

Important note 1: There are *no* subranges of type REAL. Note also that bounds can be any constant expression; therefore these allow for the use of constant (CONST) declarations.

Important note 2: It is important to realise that subranges may not give protection against out-of-range values at run time. Consider the example quoted above using the DAC. When the program executes it could possibly compute a value lying outside the defined subrange and send this to the DAC; it would probably be accepted as a valid input by the program. Consult your compiler for run-time support facilities.

Subranges can make it easier to read and understand programs, examples being given later when arrays are discussed.

```
MODULE Subrange;
(*****************************************************************)
(*          More usage of the subrange construct.               *)
(*                    Listing 5.12                              *)
(*****************************************************************)
FROM InOut IMPORT WriteLn, WriteString;
TYPE
   Digital1Status = (primed, off, on, standby, tripped);
   Digital2Status = [off..standby];
VAR
   OilPurifierMotor:Digital1Status;
   CPPpumpmotor:Digital2Status;

BEGIN
   CPPpumpmotor:=on;
   OilPurifierMotor:=tripped;
   IF (CPPpumpmotor = on) AND (OilPurifierMotor = tripped) THEN
      WriteString('Shut down CPP'); WriteLn;
   END; (*end of if*)
END Subrange.
```

Listing 5.12

5.6 Conversion and transfer of data types

5.6.1 The problem of strong typing

It might look as if we're painting ourselves into a bit of a corner with such strong typing characteristics. Situations do arise where variables have to be handled as different types. Yet Modula-2 appears to resolutely forbid the mixing of such types. A case, perhaps, of the immovable object and the irresistible force. Well, not quite. After all, if this were true the language would become unusable. Modula-2, in fact, gives us two ways to deal with type mixing operations.

Before studying these, let's distinguish between the computer representation (bit pattern) of a value and its conceptual value:

Entity	Conceptual representation	Data representation
Five units	5 (INTEGER)	00000000 00000101 −>(0005 Hex)
	Five (character)	00110101 −> (35 Hex)

When dealing with the binary data values we *have* to know what types we are dealing with to make sense of these values. For instance, the value 1000H is either decimal 32 768 (interpreted as CARDINAL) or −32 768 (INTEGER). Yet if we had to mentally add '10 to 10.0 to ten' it would be no surprise to come up with the answer 'thirty' (or even 30). This is an example of a conceptual change during the addition process.

Modula-2 supports both the changing of the *actual* binary representation, called type conversion, and the changing of conceptual representation, called type transfer. Figure 5.10 shows how conversion and transfer works in real life.

5.6.2 Type conversion

When a type is converted, its binary representation is changed from the old to the new type. We've actually been doing this in the use of ORD and CHR, and earlier with 'real' and 'entier'. ORD is not restricted to use with type CHAR, it can generally be applied to enumerated types.

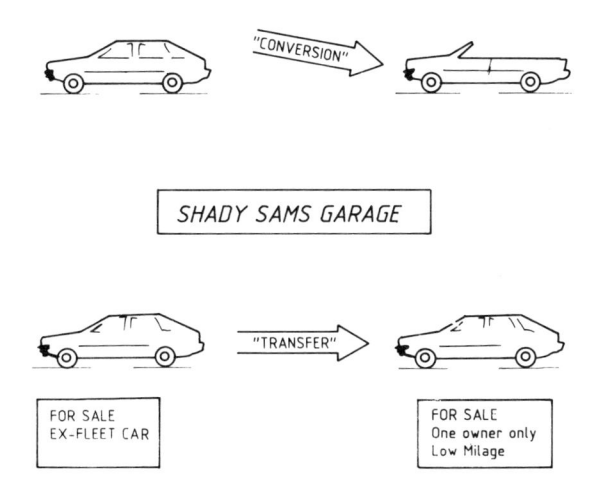

Fig. 5.10 Conversion vs. Transfer operations

The standard type conversion functions supplied in Modula-2 are:

ORD
CHR
VAL
FLOAT
TRUNC

whilst ones supplied with the Logitech library are

real
entier

We've used real and entier extensively in earlier specimen programs; little more needs to be said about them. For the others, though, we can now more formally define their properties. Note in passing that these are actually properly formed function procedures.

ORD
When ORD is applied to an element of an enumerated type it returns the ordinal value of that element. We've previously met this with the ASCII character code set. For instance, the letter A has the position 65 in this set, hence writing

   y:=ORD('A');

results in y being assigned the value 65 (as demonstrated earlier). ORD isn't restricted for use with just the character set. Declaring

   TYPE Pressure = (Low, Normal, High);

then the program statement

   y:=ORD(Normal);

causes y to get the value 1.

CHR
As shown earlier, this converts the CARDINAL set 0–127 to the corresponding character representation (usually ASCII). Essentially it is the inverse of the ordinal function but can only be used with characters.

Q5.5 If we declare
   VAR
   y:BOOLEAN;

and then write the following amongst the program statements

   y:=TRUE;
   WriteInt(ORD(Y),2);

what will be printed out on the screen?

VAL

VAL performs the same function as CHR but is used with all other types, both predefined and programmer-defined. Its format is shown in the following example:

y:=VAL(BOOLEAN,0);

Note that two parameters must be given to the procedure VAL. The first one specifies the type (in this case BOOLEAN), the second the ordinal value in that type. As a result, y becomes FALSE.

For instance, if in a control program we make the following declaration:

TYPE
   Robot1Parameters = (Xlength, Ylength, Zlength);
   Robot2Parameters = (Radius, Theta, Phi);
VAR
   Move1:Robot1Parameters;
   Move2:Robot2Parameters;

and then, as a program statement, write

Move1:=VAL(Robot1Parameters, 2);

the result is that 'Move1' gets 'Zlength'.

Q5.6 What would be the effect if, by mistake, we had written
Move2:=VAL (Robot1Parameters, Ylength);

FLOAT

FLOAT is used to convert CARDINALs to REALs. It is therefore less versatile than the library function 'real'. However, it is standard in Modula-2 and so can be used with any valid compiler. This gives us portability of our source code.

Declaring

VAR
   ADCinput, DACoutput :CARDINAL;
   A0, B1, Ynew, Yold :REAL;

the following statements are valid;

Ynew:= FLOAT(ADCinput);

or

Ynew:= (A0 * FLOAT(ADCinput)) + (B1 * Yold);

TRUNC

This is the reverse function of FLOAT, giving a truncated value of a REAL quantity. It is of type CARDINAL, hence negative numbers are not supported. Using TRUNC we could add to the statements above, as follows:

Ynew:= (A0 * FLOAT(ADCinput)) + (B1 * Yold);
DACoutput:= TRUNC(Ynew);

5.6.3 Type transfer

Here the data is not converted into a new format but is merely interpreted in a different way. As an example, suppose we have the following situation:

VAR
 x, y :INTEGER;
 z :CARDINAL

then writing

y:= z;

is illegal on type incompatibility grounds. However, we can write

y:= INTEGER(z);

and have it accepted by the compiler. When this program statement is compiled, object code is generated for the assignment only. No other code is produced as the variable z is *not* converted into a new number form. Clear your mind on this point by compiling and running the simple test program of Listing 5.13. Run this program and, as a demo, enter the following values:

CARDINALs: 0, 32764, 32765
INTEGERs: 0, 32764, −1

Explain the results.

```
MODULE Transfer;
(*****************************************************************)
(*       This illustrates type transfer in action.              *)
(*                   Listing 5.13                                *)
(*****************************************************************)
FROM InOut IMPORT Write, WriteLn, WriteInt, WriteString, ReadCard,
                  WriteCard, ReadInt;
VAR
   X :INTEGER;
   Y :CARDINAL;

BEGIN
   WriteString('enter cardinal number   ');
   ReadCard(Y); WriteLn;
   X:=INTEGER(Y);
   WriteInt(X,6); WriteLn; WriteLn;
   WriteString('enter integer number   ');
   ReadInt(X); WriteLn;
   Y:=CARDINAL(X);
   WriteCard(Y,6);WriteLn; WriteLn;
END Transfer.
```

Listing 5.13

Type transfer (sometimes called type coercion) must be used with care. Different systems may use different representations for data (e.g. 16 or 32 bits for integers). So the meaning of a bit pattern may change from machine to machine. Hence programs using type transfer functions may not be portable between machines or compilers.

A further limitation is that transfer is allowed only between types which occupy the same amount of processor storage space.

Therefore, type transfers should be used only when necessary, and even then with the greatest caution.

5.7 Procedure types

5.7.1 Introduction

This topic logically belongs in Chapter 4, so it may seem odd to introduce it here. However, it has been held back until types have been covered in detail. This should make it easier to grasp the concepts and uses of procedures as types.

A procedure body consists of a sequence of statements; we identify this particular sequence by giving the procedure a name. Every time that name is used (i.e. the procedure is invoked) that same sequence is called into action. From this point of view the procedure declaration acts like a constant declaration. Consider the procedure 'ReadInt'. We could visualise this as having the following declaration:

```
TYPE
   ProperProcedure1 = PROCEDURE(INTEGER);
VAR
   ReadInt :ProperProcedure1;
```

and similarly, for 'WriteInt':

```
TYPE
   ProperProcedure2 = PROCEDURE(INTEGER, CARDINAL);
VAR
   WriteInt :ProperProcedure2;
```

and so on. If we regard the procedure as a variable then it should be possible to perform operations on it. And that is what we're going to see now.

Note: A procedure type declaration must define the number of parameters required and their types.

5.7.2 Assignment operations

Let's consider one use of the procedure type which involves assignment statements. What this does is allow us to allocate functions to procedures without actually changing their names. We can make a program much more readable and understandable using this approach (after all, that's exactly why we use names for identifiers).

A simple example is given in Listing 5.14 which gives an idea of its use. Before considering it let's recap on what was said above, relating it to function procedures.

The procedure 'sin' is considered to have an implicit declaration:

TYPE FunctionProcedure1 = PROCEDURE(REAL):REAL;
VAR sin : FunctionProcedure1;

Therefore, *any* procedure declared in the same way is assignment compatible. Now, if the following explicit declaration is made:

TYPE CartesianCalculation = PROCEDURE(REAL):REAL;
VAR RealPart :CartesianCalculation;

then 'RealPart:=sin;' is a valid operation.

The object of the following program is to take in a complex number in polar form (i.e. R ∠ Θ) and calculate its cartesian values A + jB. The basic mathematical relationships are that:

```
MODULE TestProc;
(*************************************************************)
(*    This demonstrates the use of a procedure type to       *)
(*    enable one procedure to refer to another.              *)
(*                    Listing 5.14                           *)
(*************************************************************)
FROM RealInOut IMPORT WriteReal, ReadReal;
FROM InOut IMPORT WriteString, WriteLn;
FROM MathLib0 IMPORT sin, cos;

(* Here is the type declaration for the procedure *)
TYPE
    CartesianCalculation = PROCEDURE(REAL): REAL;

VAR
    Radius, Theta, A, jB :REAL;
    RealPart, ImaginaryPart :CartesianCalculation;

BEGIN
    RealPart:=cos; (* first assignment of procedures *)
    ImaginaryPart:=sin; (* second assignment *)
    WriteString('enter Theta, degrees'); WriteLn;
    ReadReal(Theta); WriteLn;
    WriteString('enter Radius '); WriteLn;
    ReadReal(Radius); WriteLn;
    Theta:=(Theta*3.142)/180.0;
    A:=Radius*(RealPart(Theta)); (* use of the user defined procedure *)
    WriteString('The Real part A is ');
    WriteReal(A,15); WriteLn;
    jB:=Radius*(ImaginaryPart(Theta)); (* and another one *)
    WriteString('The Imaginary part jB is ');
    WriteReal(jB,15); WriteLn;
END TestProc.
```

Listing 5.14

A = R(cos θ) – the real part
B = R(sin θ) – the imaginary part

5.7.3 Procedures as parameters

What we've just demonstrated is that procedures can be treated as variables. It seems logical, therefore, to be able to use them as parameters of other procedures. And that is exactly what is done in the example of Listing 5.15.

Here we've written a procedure 'AxisValue'; one of its parameters is 'TrigFunction'. From the declaration format it can be seen that this parameter is of type 'CartesianCalculation', which is a procedure type. Thus the actual parameter which is inserted in place of TrigFunction must be a procedure; it must also conform to the structure of the procedure declaration.

In this example, when AxisValue is first called, the procedure passed in via the parameter mechanism is 'cos'. On the second call 'sin' is used.

```
MODULE TestProc1;
(*************************************************************)
(*    This demonstrates the use of a procedure as a          *)
(*    parameter of another procedure.                        *)
(*              Listing 5.15                                 *)
(*************************************************************)
FROM RealInOut IMPORT WriteReal, ReadReal;
FROM InOut IMPORT WriteString, WriteLn;
FROM MathLib0 IMPORT sin, cos;
TYPE
    CartesianCalculation = PROCEDURE(REAL): REAL;

VAR
    Radius, Theta, A, jB :REAL;

PROCEDURE AxisValue (TrigFunction :CartesianCalculation;
                     R, Angle :REAL):REAL;
VAR
   Length :REAL;
BEGIN
   Length:=R*(TrigFunction(Angle));
   RETURN Length;
END AxisValue;

BEGIN
    WriteString('enter Theta, degrees'); WriteLn;
    ReadReal(Theta); WriteLn;
    WriteString('enter Radius '); WriteLn;
    ReadReal(Radius); WriteLn;
    Theta:=(Theta*3.142)/180.0;
    A:=AxisValue(cos, Radius, Theta); (* first call of the procedure *)
    WriteString('The Real part A is ');
    WriteReal(A,15); WriteLn;
    jB:=AxisValue(sin, Radius, Theta); (* second call *)
    WriteString('The Imaginary part jB is ');
    WriteReal(jB,15), WriteLn;
END TestProc1.
```

Listing 5.15

Important note: (a) Procedures used as described here in Section 5.7 must not be declared local to any other procedure. (b) Standard procedures (see Appendix C) cannot be assigned to a procedure variable. The second limitation can be overcome by enclosing standard procedures within user-designed procedures.

On a closing note, Modula-2 provides a standard procedure type named PROC. This is implicitly defined as

```
TYPE
  PROC = PROCEDURE;
```

If now, for instance, we include a program declaration such as

```
VAR
  ProcessAction :PROC;
```

then 'ProcessAction' coresponds to a procedure without parameters. It is then assignment compatible with any procedure having the same structure.

Review

Do you now:

- See why good typing is an essential part of program security?
- Understand what strong typing is and how it helps the compiler to pick up mistakes in the software?
- Appreciate how typing allows us to take a conceptual view of our problems?
- Understand the ideas of cardinality, ordinality and enumeration?
- Appreciate how to create your own data types?
- Understand the use of programmer-defined enumerated and subrange types?
- Grasp the ideas behind, and the use of, type mixing using both type conversion and type transfer?

Chapter 6
Modular construction

We now come to what probably makes Modula-2 different to virtually all earlier programming languages, the 'module'. Through the use of the module we can divide a total program into a number of smaller segments, the objective being to enhance reliability and productivity. Earlier we saw how procedures help us to attain such goals; the module takes us many more steps along this road.

After studying this chapter you will:

- Understand the need for modularity to achieve reliable programming.
- Appreciate the difference between monolithic, modular and independent compilation techniques.
- Know which module types are provided in Modula-2, what their functions are, how they communicate with each other and how they are structured.
- Understand the difference between static and dynamic variables.
- Be able to write and compile program, definition, implementation and local modules.
- Perceive the design formality and control introduced by Modula-2 through the use of modules and related import and export statements.

6.1 Fundamental ideas

6.1.1 Introduction

The work we've carried out so far shows that a Modula-2 program consists of a series of major building blocks called modules. Every specimen program has been put together to conform with the modular structure of the language, in two ways. First, each program has used the reserved word MODULE as the opening word of the source text. Second, various library modules (e.g. InOut) have been called into use within the programs. Fine. So why do we need to study the topic of modularity? Why bother to complicate life with yet another set of rules for program production? After all, people have (apparently) managed quite all right with Basic for years now.

This question goes right to the heart of good software design and is much broader than the simple 'Basic vs. Modula' type of duel. In essence it questions the whole design approach of the block-structured languages (the grand-daddy of them all being Algol 58). Modula-2 has taken these ideas much further than earlier languages such as Pascal, Coral66, Fortran 77 and RTL2, the purpose being to implicitly support reliable software design. Hence the key question is 'what are we trying to do?', the 'how?' actually being much less important. In this chapter we're going to answer both, at the same time showing how Modula-2's structure forces us into good design techniques.

6.1.2 Fundamental design methods

Software design techniques can be split into three major groups, each having pro's and con's. Actually I suspect that most programmers use combinations of these when writing source code; this probably says more about the rigour and discipline of software design as practised rather than preached.

The concepts behind these methods can be grasped fairly easily by looking at a simple DIY task: design and build of a kit-car.

Method 1, here called 'monolithic', is illustrated in Fig. 6.1. Work begins by producing an all-embracing design plan, i.e. the problem is considered as being a single design task. Once the design is complete the car can be built to the plan's specifications and instructions.

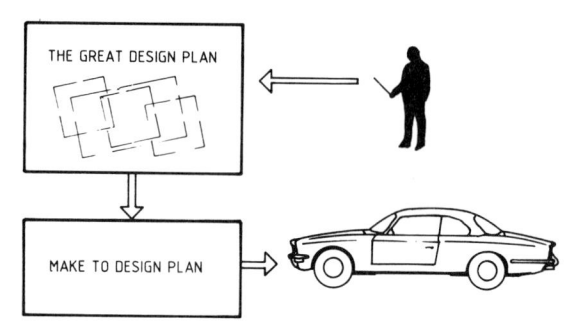

Fig. 6.1 Monolithic design and make

Method 2 (Fig. 6.2) tackles the problem in a different way at the design stage. An overall design plan is produced together with individual designs for major subsystems such as chassis, wheels, etc. The design can be carried out either by one individual, as in method 1, or else a number of designers can work on the job simultaneously. When design work is finished, the various subsystem designs are integrated to produce a manufacturing workplan. Manufacture takes place as in method 1.

Note a significant difference between these two methods. In the first one, as the design is monolithic, all information relating to the system is im-

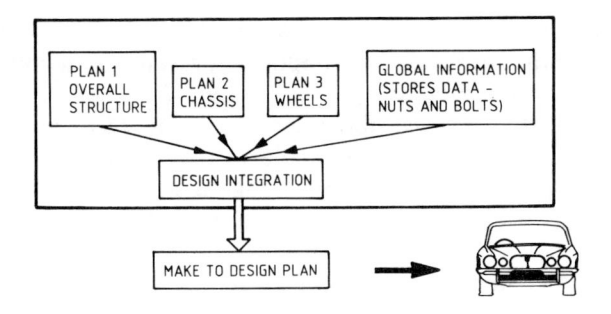

Fig. 6.2 Modular design

plicitly available at all times. However, in the second ('modular') design method this may not necessarily be the case. Some information just doesn't need sharing; it's private or 'local' to that particular design activity. Other information does have to be made generally available. For instance, both the wheel and the suspension system designers need to know the wheel/drive shaft coupling arrangement; otherwise there's no guarantee that the items will fit together correctly. Question: How are these details made known throughout the design team? Simply by explicitly defining design data which is to be made available to all parties, so-called 'global' information.

In the third design method the concept of splitting the total task into a number of ('independent') subtasks is taken one stage further. Not only is the design compartmentalised; the same ideas are applied to manufacturing as well (Fig. 6.3). Not until the final stage of production do all the parts

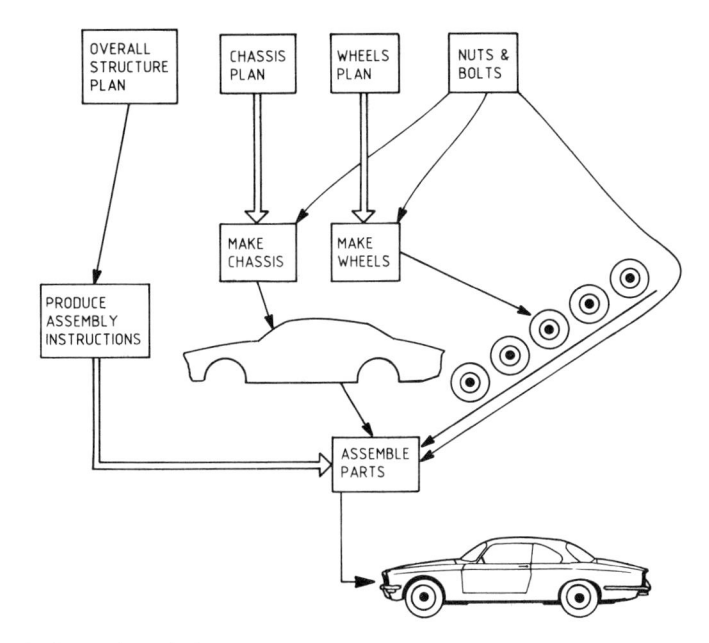

Fig. 6.3 Independent design

come together in what is basically an assembly operation. Only the interfacing details of the subsystems are important, assuming, of course, that the design itself is satisfactory.

Note also that the final assembly is essentially divorced from the detailed design process. This means that we can develop optional designs and choose the most appropriate one at assembly stage (compare this with selecting either a 1.3 or 1.6 litre engine in a standard production car).

6.1.3 Monolithic, modular and independent operations – an evaluation

Monolithic operation

The monolithic method will clearly work best where one person only is concerned with the design and build programme. For simple tasks it works quite well. As the project becomes more complex, though, the design document itself becomes equally complex. In the end only one person may be capable of understanding it: the original designer (Fig. 6.4). Further, the technique inherently makes it very difficult to split the job amongst a number of designers (Fig. 6.5).

Now consider what happens when a revision to the operation of a unit is requested. The complete design plan has to be assessed in the light of any changes, a time-consuming and costly effort. Once changes are made, a full rebuild is necessary before we can even begin to evaluate the change effects.

Fig. 6.4 The only person who understands the design

Fig. 6.5 Work-sharing in a monolithic design

And this is where many problems really start. In a complex system the introduction of just a single revision may very well produce a 'knock-on' effect, leading to totally undesirable (and unpredicted) side-effects (Fig. 6.6). As a result it can be extremely difficult to maintain such designs once they are in service (usually handled by whoever draws the short straw).

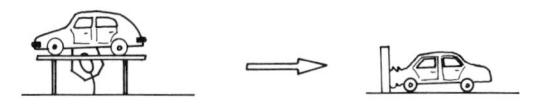

Fig. 6.6 Undesirable side-effects

Modular operation
By breaking the complete problem into a series of smaller ones, even quite complex designs can be managed comfortably. Moreover, individual subtasks may be handled simultaneously by different designers. This assumes, of course, that the job is properly coordinated. As a result, designs become more understandable and can be completed more quickly.

What about introducing modifications to an existing program? Here significant advantages have been gained over the monolithic approach. Individual changes are likely to be quite localised, possibly affecting only one subtask. Hence the effects of such changes can be quickly evaluated. Further, they are far less likely to lead to unwanted side-effects. However, as shown, a complete rebuild is needed to carry out the change in a production unit.

Apart from this last point, does the modular approach have any other major drawback? Unfortunately, yes. Global information, by definition, is available to all design sections; consequently it may also be modified by any designer as work progresses. Where only one designer is involved this probably won't be a problem. Where the design is a team effort global information falls into the category of 'accidents waiting to happen' (Fig. 6.7). Without rigorous project control, changes to the global values (especially undocumented ones) can produce design chaos.

Fig. 6.7 Uncontrolled access has its problems

Independent operation
This sets out to minimise the shortcomings of the modular method of working. All of the advantages gained at the design stage are retained but are now extended into manufacture as well. This has a tremendous impact on product development and maintenance. For instance, suppose a fault shows up in a gearbox which necessitates redesign action. Now we can limit the

design and build operations to the gearbox and its interfacing components (Fig. 6.8). This minimises the time taken to implement and test the change; it also reduces the likelihood of side-effects.

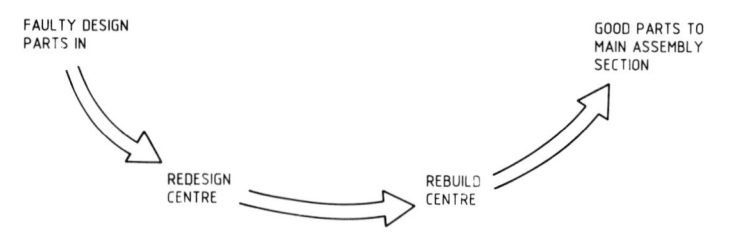

Fig. 6.8 Design modification procedure – independent operation

What about global information? Clearly, when designs are carried out as described here, information has to be passed between individual subtasks. Which brings us back to the use of a 'global bin' of information. The only way to prevent (in reality, minimise) errors caused by the abuse of global values is *not* to use globals. This means that information interchange must be handled in a more controlled (and probably more complex) way (Fig. 6.9). Later we'll see how this topic is treated in the Modula-2 language, for the moment accept it as a necessity.

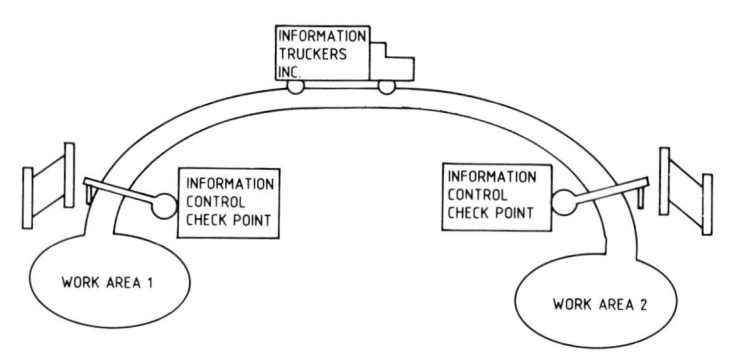

Fig. 6.9 Controlling information flow

6.1.4 Software compilation methods

From the previous section you should have grasped the basic concepts of the three different constructional methods. Now let's put them in the context of software design and compilation.

Monolithic program development is directly analogous to the first method outlined above. Standard Basic forces us to use this approach, the language essentially being simple and straightforward. Here the source program is written out in its entirety as a series of successive statements, i.e. it forms one large block. Compilation to object code may then be carried out.

Standard Pascal allows us to use a 'building-block' approach in the design of the software. The blocks are realised as a series of subtasks (or subprograms) based on the use of procedures and functions. But compilation of the source code is, like Basic, still carried out on the complete program.

Modula-2 and various extended Pascals use the independent design method. In Modula-2 the fundamental program building block is the module, individual modules being written and compiled as complete items. These come together only at the final stage of 'linkage', equivalent to the assembly operation of vehicle component parts.

Table 6.1 compares the advantages and weaknessess of the three methods discussed above.

Table 6.1 Comparison of compilation methods

Compilation method	For	Against
Monolithic	Simple to use. Suitable for small programs.	Large programs are difficult to handle. Program document soon becomes complex. Difficult for more than one designer to work on the job. Revisions can be costly and time consuming. Unwanted effects may easily be inserted when doing changes.
Modular	Overall structure can be made highly 'visible' using modularity of design. Design can be split amongst a number of programmers, giving faster program development. Changes are easier to implement. Side-effects are reduced. Standard program building blocks can be developed (e.g. I/O to console).	Any change means a complete program re-compilation. Global variables are a source of potential danger.
Independent	As for the modular compilation method.	More complex cross-referencing needed

6.1.5 A last comment

What we have been discussing here is a highly emotive issue, so don't expect these conclusions to be accepted without question. Program writing reflects very much the attitudes and intellectual attributes of the programmer. Criticise the method and, by implication, you are attacking the man. Just try getting sensible discussions in such a situation. What is generally agreed though is that programming, in the past, has lacked the formality and rigour of engineering design. This has resulted in some pretty awful software (if you don't believe this I recommend that you read *The Mythical Man-Month* by F.P. Brooks). Nowadays the emphasis is on getting it right at the design stage, so consigning 'hacking' to a place in history. Modula-2 is a language intended to support these laudable aims.

6.2 Modules

Having said that one of the most important items in Modula-2 is the Module we need to show:

- what module types are available;
- what functions they perform and where they are used;
- how they communicate with each other; and
- what their structure is.

Let's consider the first two points here. Figure 6.10 defines the various modules, these being program, library and local (sometimes called internal) types. A library module actually consists of two related modules: definition and implementation. More of these later.

Program modules are regarded as existing at the highest level in the system, using library and local modules as required. The kit-car analogy to the use of a program module is mechanical assembly of a complete vehicle or any of its major components. Library modules are the building blocks of the language (Fig. 6.11), equivalent to the nuts and bolts of the car. Already we've met many library features provided by Modula-2, mainly for text handling and maths operations. The primary purpose is to let us build up a 'library' of useful software routines which can be called into use as needed. These are developed, compiled and tested individually; once proven they can be used immediately at the program module level. No further detailed

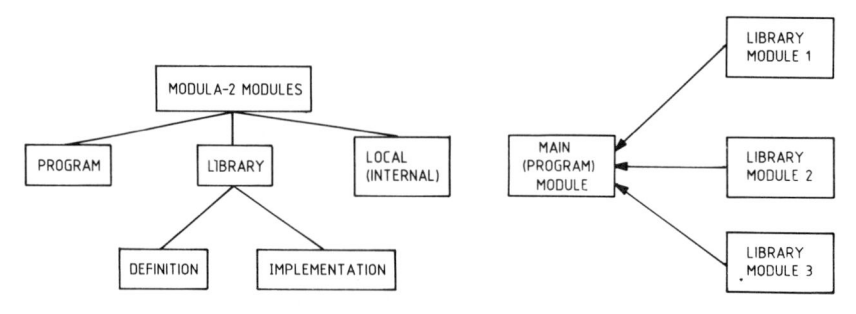

Fig. 6.10 Modula-2 module types

Fig. 6.11 Basic program structure

development or compilation needs to be carried out; this streamlines the development phase and increases software reliability.

So far, all examples of Modula-2 programs have been program modules. However, a large program is likely to consist of a number of program modules which may be called in sequence in the main body of the module (Fig. 6.12). This represents one form of modularisation: 'hierarchical decomposition'. The other form of modularisation, 'functional decomposition', is that produced by generating a set of 'building bricks' using standard procedures. In Modula-2 both are implemented using the library module method.

The final variant, local modules, does not have an independent existence; in fact they can only be used within program or library modules (Fig. 6.13). They have one purpose only, that of 'hiding' information concerning locally defined objects. This is a subtle aspect, best illustrated by example (see Section 6.6).

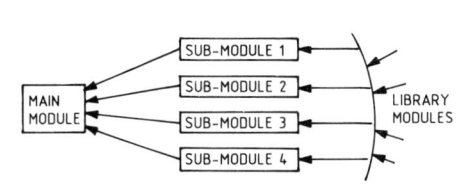

Fig. 6.12 Decomposition of a main module

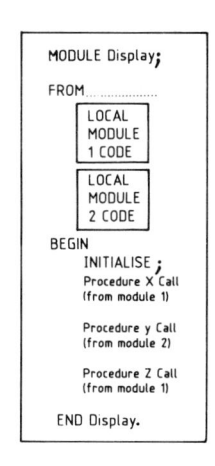

```
MODULE Display;
FROM..................
    LOCAL
    MODULE
    1 CODE
    LOCAL
    MODULE
    2 CODE
BEGIN
    INITIALISE ;
    Procedure X Call
    (from module 1)

    Procedure y Call
    (from module 2)

    Procedure Z Call
    (from module 1)
END Display.
```

Fig. 6.13 Local modules – location and use (typical)

6.3 Communication between modules

Any practical program will contain several modules which normally have to exchange information. This could be done using global variables; but, as pointed out earlier, this is a potentially dangerous method. How then can we provide a communications method which is well defined and controlled, yet avoids global information?

Let's go back to our kit-car again. Consider first the build of a chassis unit and then the overall assembly operation. Nuts and bolts are just two of the items needed for the construction of the chassis; these can be considered to be 'imported' into the chassis operation. On completion of

116 Modular construction

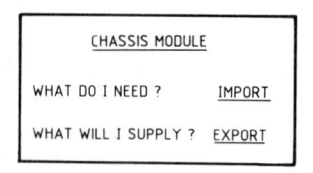

```
         CHASSIS MODULE

WHAT DO I NEED ?         IMPORT

WHAT WILL I SUPPLY ?     EXPORT
```

Fig. 6.14 Import–export concept

chassis build the finished unit is sent off to the final assembly stage, i.e. it is 'exported' to the overall build module (Fig. 6.14). As far as the build module is concerned it is importing the chassis into its operation; further it also imports nuts and bolts to fix units together. Nuts and bolts come from the stores module, thus forming export items. So in this simple example we've defined the concept of import only, export only, and both import and export (Fig. 6.15).

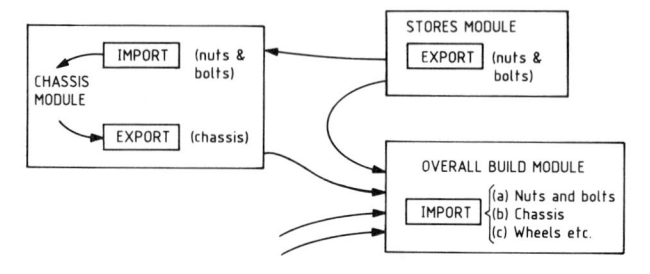

Fig. 6.15 Use of imports and exports

So far, so good. But how do we control the exchange of the parts (information) flow to minimise unwanted changes to this information? Simply by *defining* the list of items to be imported/exported, in some cases explicitly stating the source/destination. The rules are:

- Any item to be imported must somewhere appear on an export list (but see Section 6.5.2).
- A module can only get at items in another module through importing these items in the first place.
- Program modules normally import only.
- Library and local modules can import and export.
- Importing modules are known as 'clients' (of the exporting modules).
- *Modules* cannot be imported.

Hence items can only be made available by using export statements (but see the section on 'Definition modules', 6.5.2). Even then they aren't available for use throughout the program (as with globals) but are limited to modules which import them. This combination makes it quite difficult to accidentally misuse program information (although don't underestimate the ability of hackers).

At long last the fundamental ideas behind the import listings used in our specimen programs should be clear. Export operations are now further discussed in the context of library and local modules.

6.4 Library modules – independent compilation

We've already discussed the reason for using library modules; now let's consider their structure and implementation in a Modula-2 program.

A library module typically consists of a set of procedures and data items made available for use by other modules. For instance, in the example program 'RealMath' (Listing 1.5), the imported procedures are ReadReal and WriteReal. Now, when we write the main module we probably don't know exactly how these procedures are implemented; in most cases we really don't care as long as they work correctly. What *is* important is that the procedures are used correctly, and that any parameters used are also of the correct type. On compilation of the program module the library procedures are called into action, *but* the actual procedure code is not inserted with the main module code; this is done at the linkage stage. In well-designed software the program module is relatively short, generally consisting of a sequence of procedure calls. The ratio of library to program modules may well be 10 : 1 (or even more). What is the significance of these facts? First, if a change has to be made to a library procedure which is purely an internal one (i.e. operation is unchanged as far as the program module is concerned), then only the library module itself is modified and recompiled. Second, if the program module is changed, that and that only is recompiled. In both cases the time taken is much less than that needed for a total recompilation. As program sizes grow this becomes even more marked.

Note: If changes to a library module have effects in client modules then the clients *must* be recompiled.

6.5 Library modules – definition and implementation

6.5.1 Overview

Coral66 or Fortran77 programmers will be familiar with the idea of decoupling the definition of procedures from their implementation. This is done through the use of the so-called 'common communicators' section. In assembly language the same results can be achieved using either external or library subroutine declarations. The underlying idea is to separate *what* a procedure does from *how* it does it. Modula-2 does this by using two paired modules for each library application (Fig. 6.16): a definition module ('what') and an implementation module ('how').

The definition module is the interface between library modules and their clients (Fig. 6.17). Its primary purpose is to supply information on items

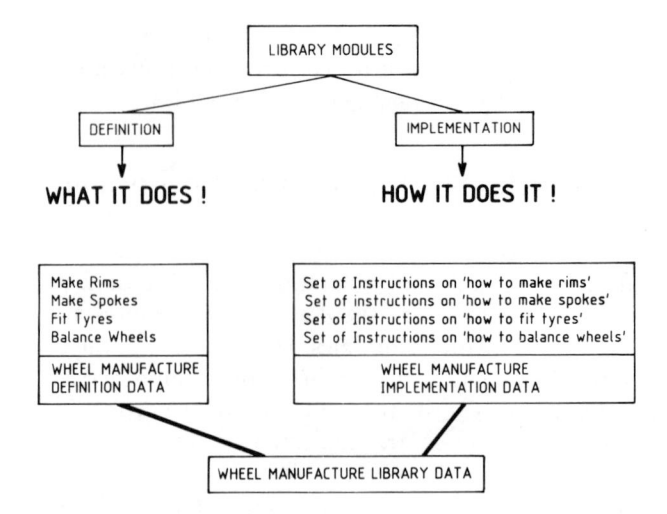

Fig. 6.16 Library module structure

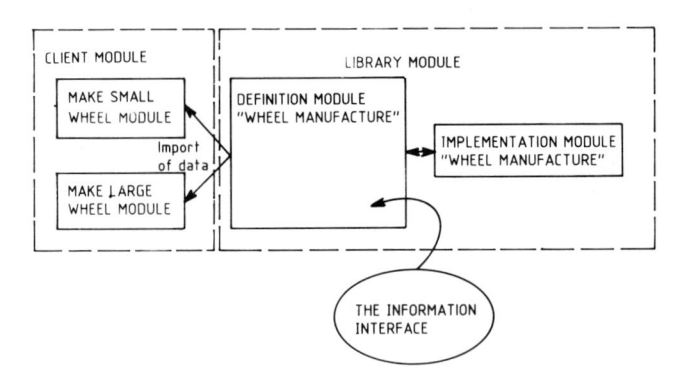

Fig. 6.17 Modules and their clients

exported to the clients; it does *not* have a code statement section. On the other hand, the implementation module holds the actual source code which is used by the client module.

As an example, let's redo the coordinate conversion program of Listing 5.14. Instead of writing all the source code in one module it is now broken down into a series of procedures. These are hidden away in a library module, being called as required by the main module.

For this demonstration we have the following modules:

Definition module 'CoordinateConversion'
Implementation module 'CoordinateConversion'
Client module 'PolarToCartesian'

6.5.2 Definition modules

The basic structure of the definition module is:

> DEFINITION MODULE ModuleName;
>
> IMPORT...
> EXPORT QUALIFIED...
>
> CONST declarations
> TYPE declarations
> VAR declarations
>
> Procedure declarations (heading only)
>
> END ModuleName.

Note:

- 'DEFINITION' is the opening word.
- Items can be imported into the module.
- Items to be exported are defined in the export list (but this may depend on the actual compiler, see note below).
- There is a declarations but no statement section.
- The module is finished off in the usual way.

For our example, the definition module is done first (Listing 6.1). In general,

```
DEFINITION MODULE CoordinateConversion;
(*************************************************)
(*       This is a definition module.          *)
(*       The disk file name is 'coordina.def'. *)
(*                Listing 6.1                  *)
(*************************************************)

EXPORT QUALIFIED GetPolarValues, CalculateRealPart,
                 CalculateImaginaryPart;

PROCEDURE GetPolarValues(VAR Radius, Theta: REAL);
PROCEDURE CalculateRealPart(Radius, Theta: REAL);
PROCEDURE CalculateImaginaryPart(Radius, Theta: REAL);

END CoordinateConversion. (* end of the definition module *)
```

Listing 6.1

for every item defined in the export list, there must be a corresponding declaration. Failure to do this will cause the compiler to generate an error when the definition module is compiled.

The definition module must be compiled before either the implementation

120 Modular construction

or main modules can be compiled. A main module can be compiled without an implementation module even being present in the system.

The use of an export list is the subject of some controversy. Originally it was implemented as part of the Modula-2 language, mainly to provide tight control of objects. No item could be exported from a library module unless it was shown in the export list. Moreover, these exports could be qualified or unqualified. This feature has been deleted from the latest definition of the language. Now all identifiers declared in the definition module are automatically exported. Many feel that this change is a retrograde one. Pressure is being applied to have this feature re-introduced; only time will tell.

It is recommended that the export listing should always be used. In the first case it is good documentation practice. Second, you may have a compiler which was written to meet an earlier specification of the language. Third, most recent good compilers accept the export list but ignore it. Hence there is no problem in actually including it.

6.5.3 Implementation modules

The basic structure of an implementation module is:

```
IMPLEMENTATION MODULE ModuleName;
IMPORT...

PROCEDURE Name1Proc(Parameters);
   Declarations
BEGIN
      StatementSequence
END NameProc;

PROCEDURE Name2Proc(Parameters);
   Declarations
BEGIN
      StatementSequence
END Name2Proc;

END ModuleName.
```

Note:
- The opening word is 'IMPLEMENTATION'.
- Procedure1 declaration (the actual writing of the procedure).
- Procedure2 declaration.
- The module is finished off in the usual way.

Module declarations may be located within the definition or the implementation module. The effect of this depends on the compiler being used. Procedures may, as usual, contain their own declaration listing.

Both function and normal procedures can be used; in each case the parameter listing conforms to the standard rules of Modula-2.

The definition module 'CoordinateConversion.def' has a corresponding implementation module 'CoordinateConversion.mod' (Listing 6.2).

```
IMPLEMENTATION MODULE CoordinateConversion;
(*************************************************************)
(* This is the implementation module for listing 6.1.    *)
(*         The disk file name is 'coordina.mod'.         *)
(*                 Listing 6.2                           *)
(*************************************************************)
FROM RealInOut IMPORT WriteReal, ReadReal;
FROM InOut IMPORT WriteString, WriteLn;
FROM MathLib0 IMPORT sin, cos;

PROCEDURE GetPolarValues(VAR Radius, Theta: REAL);
BEGIN
    WriteString('enter Theta, degrees'); WriteLn;
    ReadReal(Theta); WriteLn;
    WriteString('enter Radius '); WriteLn;
    ReadReal(Radius); WriteLn;
    Theta:=(Theta*3.142)/180.0;
END GetPolarValues;

PROCEDURE CalculateRealPart(Radius, Theta:REAL);
VAR
    A :REAL;
BEGIN
    A:=Radius*(cos(Theta));
    WriteString('The Real part A is ');
    WriteReal(A,15); WriteLn;
END CalculateRealPart;

PROCEDURE CalculateImaginaryPart(Radius, Theta:REAL);
VAR
    jB :REAL;
BEGIN
    jB:=Radius*(sin(Theta));
    WriteString('The Imaginary part jB is ');
    WriteReal(jB,15); WriteLn;
END CalculateImaginaryPart;

END CoordinateConversion.
```

Listing 6.2

6.5.4 Using the implementation module

The program (client) module which uses the procedures located in the library module 'CoordinateConversion' is named 'PolarToCartesian' (Listing 6.3). As you can see, procedures used by the module now feature in its import list, defined as being in module 'CoordinateConversion'. This has two consequences. The first is fairly easy to understand, the other being appreciated only after writing a reasonable-sized program.

First, by putting procedures in a library module we create a set of building blocks. More important, these can be made available and called into use by *any* client module. In the previous case procedures could only be accessed

122 Modular construction

```
MODULE PolarToCartesian;
(*************************************************************)
(*      This module uses the procedures contained in       *)
(*      library module 'CoordinateConversion'.             *)
(*                  Listing 6.3                            *)
(*************************************************************)
FROM InOut IMPORT WriteString, WriteLn;
FROM CoordinateConversion IMPORT GetPolarValues,
                       CalculateRealPart, CalculateImaginaryPart;
VAR
   Amplitude, Angle :REAL;

BEGIN
   WriteString('This is a demonstration of the use of. library modules');
   WriteLn; WriteLn;
   GetPolarValues(Amplitude, Angle);
   CalculateRealPart(Amplitude, Angle);
   CalculateImaginaryPart(Amplitude, Angle);
   WriteString('Run finished'); WriteLn;
END PolarToCartesian.
```

Listing 6.3

by the module in which they were written. Programming is full of wheel re-invention techniques; the use of libraries helps to keep this problem under control. It also has a major impact on debugging time by providing a set of proven, verified programs. The software designer can call on these as needed, knowing that he is using proven programs. The only alternative is to develop new programs for each new application. Naturally enough, these come complete with a new lot of errors.

The second point is that programs become more readable and understandable. We've reduced the amount of text which has to be assimilated at any one time and also suppressed the detail of the software. With the example given this isn't particularly obvious; but once you start using Modula-2 for real this will become very apparent.

6.6 Local modules

6.6.1 The lifetime of variables

An interesting question is 'for how long do variables exist in a running program?'. This might seem to be an academic diversion. In fact it is a very important point, applying at the program, procedure and local module level. The true value of local modules can only be seen when we understand what happens to variables when programs are executed.

This point is best illustrated by an example. Suppose that we wish to produce a software simulation of an analogue (continuous) integrator (Fig. 6.18). A discrete equivalent to this, using trapezoidal approximation rules, is:

$$y(T) = K1^*[x(T)+x(T-1)] + y(T-1)$$

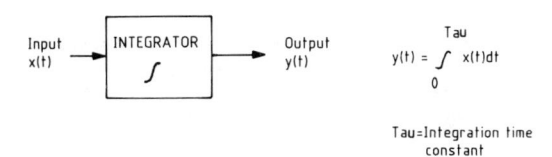

Fig. 6.18 System to be simulated

where T is the current sample, (T−1) is the previous one and K1 is the algorithm coefficient computed from:

K1 = Ts/(2*Tau)

where Ts is the sample time and Tau is the integrator time constant.

Let's generate this in software using a function procedure. Return the computed value y(T) (i.e. Ynew) from the procedure and pass in x(T) (i.e. Xnew) and K1 as value parameters. Then it would appear that x(T−1) (i.e. Xold) and y(T−1) (i.e. Yold) can be local to the procedure, as shown in Listing 6.4.

```
(* This procedure calculates the integral of an input value *)
(* Xnew, outputting the result as Ynew.                     *)

PROCEDURE Integral(Xnew, K1:REAL):REAL;
VAR
   Xold,Yold,Ynew:REAL;

BEGIN
   Ynew:=K1*(Xnew+Xold) + Yold;
   Yold:=Ynew;
   Xold:=Xnew;
   RETURN Ynew;
END Integral; (* end of procedure *)
```

Listing 6.4

This looks fine but just try running it; the results will be most unexpected (and wrong). In Listing 6.5 part of a simple but complete integrator simulation program is given. This *does* run correctly. The reason why the first one failed is that the local variables in 'Integral' were not kept alive after running the procedure. Yet we rely on having these past values for correct operation of the algorithm. In this situation the variables are said to be 'dynamic' as shown in Fig. 6.19.

Fig. 6.19 Dynamic and static variables

```
MODULE SimulateIntegrator;
(***************************************************************)
(* This is part of a program to digitally simulate a            *)
(* continuous integrator. It uses a procedure 'Integral'        *)
(* to perform the actual mathematical integration.              *)
(*                    Listing 6.5                               *)
(***************************************************************)
VAR
   Xold,Yold :REAL;

PROCEDURE Integral(Xnew, K1:REAL):REAL;
VAR
   Xnew :REAL;

BEGIN
   Ynew:=K1*(Xnew+Xold) + Yold;
   Yold:=Ynew;
   Xold:=Xnew;
   RETURN Ynew;
END Integral; (* end of procedure *)

BEGIN (* start of program *)
   STATEMENT SEQUENCE
END SimulateIntegrator. (* end of program *)
```

Listing 6.5

For the second case (Listing 6.5), Xold and Yold, being declared at the module level, are kept active for the program duration. These are defined as 'static' variables. As a result, past values are available to the algorithm on each run, so allowing it to work correctly.

Hence the rule is: variables defined at the module level are static whilst those in procedures are dynamic.

Now what about the case of variables in library modules? Again the rule is simple. If the variable has been declared at the implementation or definition module level, and a client module uses this variable, it remains active for the duration of the program.

6.6.2 Why local modules?

We've stated earlier that local modules don't exist by themselves. Instead they reside inside program and library (strictly implementation) modules. So why do we use them? Basically the reason is to control the visibility and scope of identifiers. But we've seen that the scope of identifiers can be quite closely controlled using procedures; hence the local module must have something more (and significant) to offer.

The example given above has raised a serious problem (or didn't you spot it?). In order to keep variables alive they have, in effect, had to be declared globally. Yet the one thing we strive for is the elimination of global items. Have we run ourselves into an impossible position? Fortunately, no; this is where local modules come to the rescue. In these, all local variables declared at the module level are static. Further, we can confine these within the module and prevent them being known globally.

Let's return to the previous example and replace procedure 'Integral' with a local module 'LocalIntegration'. Inside this module we'll actually incorporate a procedure 'CalcIntegral'. The body of the module is given in Listing 6.6. Putting this inside a local module is analogous to surrounding it with a

```
(*      BODY OF THE LOCAL MODULE            *)
(*      /////////////////////////           *)
        VAR
            Xold, Ynew, Yold :REAL;
        PROCEDURE CalcIntegral;
        BEGIN
            Ynew:=K1*(Xnew+Xold) + Yold;
            Yold:=Ynew;
            Xold:=Xnew;
        END CalcIntegral;
```

Listing 6.6

software 'skin'. There can be no information flow between the surrounding program and the enclosed area unless a positive action is carried out. 'Puncturing' this skin is done through the use of import and export statements (Fig. 6.20). Moreover, all information used inside the local module must be imported unless it is declared locally; this applies to library functions as well as variables, etc.

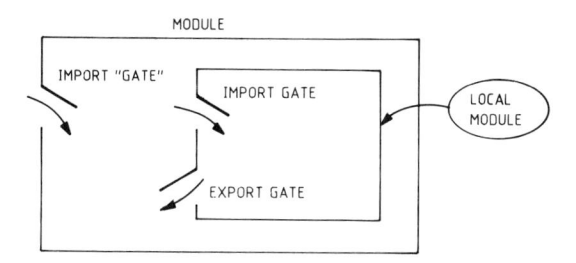

Fig. 6.20 Information flow to and from a local module

Also, to reiterate a point, all information transfer is to and from the enclosing module. Hence library procedures are imported from this and *not* directly from the library module itself.

For the case above the local module becomes that shown in Listing 6.7. Compare this with that of procedure 'Integral' (Listing 6.4). They're virtually identical. This version, however, does work by virtue of the module variables being static. And these are invisible outside the module.

What we've done so far is to write the code of the module; it is still to be executed. Just for the moment it has been kept simple, containing only a single procedure 'CalcIntegral'. This has been declared to be an exported item. To use the procedure we merely call it in the normal way (see the next section).

126 Modular construction

```
MODULE LocalIntegration; (* start of local module declaration *)
IMPORT Xnew ,K1;
EXPORT CalcIntegral, Ynew;
VAR
   Xold, Yold, Ynew :REAL;
PROCEDURE CalcIntegral;
BEGIN
   Ynew:=K1*(Xnew+Xold) + Yold;
   Yold:=Ynew;
   Xold:=Xnew;
END CalcIntegral;
END LocalIntegration. (*end of local module *)
```

Listing 6.7

6.6.3 Using a local module

Listing 6.8 is a full program to test out integrator simulation using keyboard interaction. It uses a local module named 'LocalIntegration2'. Note its position. Like procedures it is declared by writing it. Also like procedures it precedes the statement sequence. Inside the module is the procedure 'Calc-

```
MODULE SimulateIntegrator;
(*****************************************************************)
(*  This provides interactive simulation to carry out a step    *)
(*  test response of a continuous integrator.                   *)
(*                    Listing 6.8                               *)
(*****************************************************************)
FROM InOut IMPORT Read, WriteInt, WriteLn, WriteString, ReadInt;
FROM RealInOut IMPORT WriteReal, ReadReal;
FROM RealConversions IMPORT RealToString;
VAR
   S:ARRAY [1..10] OF CHAR;
   Reply:CHAR;
   OK, FirstRun: BOOLEAN;
   Samples, Stepnumber:INTEGER;
   K1, Xnew, Output, TimeConstant, SampleTime:REAL;

PROCEDURE GetSystemVariables (VAR Tau, T, Input, K2: REAL;
                              VAR Steps : INTEGER);
BEGIN
   WriteString('Enter Integrator time constant'); WriteLn;
   ReadReal(Tau); WriteLn;
   WriteString('Enter Sample time'); WriteLn;
   ReadReal(T); WriteLn;
   WriteString('Enter number of samples'); WriteLn;
   ReadInt(Steps); WriteLn;
   WriteString('Enter test input'); WriteLn;
   ReadReal(Input); WriteLn;
   K2:=T/(2.0*Tau);
END GetSystemVariables;

(*****************************************************************)
(*              start of local module declaration              *)
(*****************************************************************)
MODULE LocalIntegration2;
IMPORT FirstRun, Xnew, K1, WriteString, WriteLn;
EXPORT CalcIntegral, Ynew;
VAR
   Xold,Ynew,Yold:REAL;
```

Local modules

```
      PROCEDURE CalcIntegral;
      BEGIN
         IF FirstRun THEN
            Xold:=0.0;
            Yold:=0.0;
         END; (* end if *)
         Ynew:=K1*(Xnew+Xold) + Yold;
         Yold:=Ynew;
         Xold:=Xnew;
      END CalcIntegral; (* end of procedure *)

   BEGIN
      WriteString('Now setting initial conditions'); WriteLn;
      WriteLn;
      Xold:=0.0;
      Yold:=0.0;
   END LocalIntegration2; (* end of local module *)

(*****************************************************************)

   BEGIN (* start of main module statement sequence *)
      LOOP
         GetSystemVariables(TimeConstant, SampleTime, Xnew,
                            K1, Samples);
         FirstRun:=TRUE;
         FOR Stepnumber:=1 TO Samples DO
            CalcIntegral;  (* using the procedure from the local module *)
            Output:=Ynew;
            RealToString(Output,4,10,S,OK); (* look out module          *)
            WriteString('output = ');       (* 'RealConversions' for this *)
            WriteString(S); WriteLn;
            FirstRun:=FALSE;
         END; (* end of forloop*)

         WriteString('Another test?');WriteLn;
         Read(Reply); WriteLn;
         IF CAP(Reply) = 'N' THEN EXIT (* see appendix C for CAP *)
         END;
      END; (*end of LOOP *)
      WriteString('Finished, goodbye');
   END SimulateIntegrator. (* end of program *)
```

Listing 6.8

Integral'; this is called into use by the main program during the simulation run. One new aspect has also been sneakily introduced; that is, the insertion of program code within the local module. If you compile and run this simulation program the first line of print-out will be 'Now setting initial conditions'. This demonstrates that code within the local module is executed as soon as the program is activated. Here it has been put to good use to set initial conditions for variables used within the program. Such a facility is extremely useful, but only experience will show you why.

In summary, there are two major differences between procedures and local modules concerning the scope of identifiers:

(a) As far as a procedure is concerned, any identifier declared at the module level is visible within the procedure (e.g. K1 of the simulation program).

...refore, it is legal to access and manipulate such variables. This ...ns that such items may be changed by accident or plain bad pro-...nming. But, identifiers can only be brought into a local module (i.e. ...e visible) by an explicit import statement (note the import of K1). ...ariable which is declared locally to a procedure cannot be 'seen' ...ide the procedure (e.g. K2 of procedure 'GetSystemVariables'). ... is, its scope is confined to the procedure itself. In contrast, identi-...declared within local modules (Ynew, for instance) can be made ...le by using the export statement.

Module compilation – independence and order

...nodules truly independent in Modula-2? Does it matter in which order ...y are compiled? One can get into a fruitless discussion concerning the ...irst point, but the second one *is* highly relevant.

To define modules as being totally independent means that, from the design point of view, they can be regarded as watertight compartments. Somehow we manage to plan these in total isolation; then, when the time comes, integrate them into a greater whole which will actually work. Just imagine trying to design and build a vehicle in such a way. So, in the real world, total independence is an imaginary, unattainable goal. But, as shown earlier, we do have an extremely high degree of independence in Modula-2.

How then do we arrive at the order of compilation? A client module imports library functions. Then clearly a library module must exist before the client can use it. However, to insist that the implementation code must be written and compiled will create a real bottleneck in the design process. Further, it isn't necessary, as the client only needs to know *what* the library module does, not *how* it does it. In Modula-2 the definition module acts as the interface between the client and the implementation module. This allows independent compilation of both modules; also it means that these can be modified separately and independently.

Thus the basic rules are (Fig. 6.21):

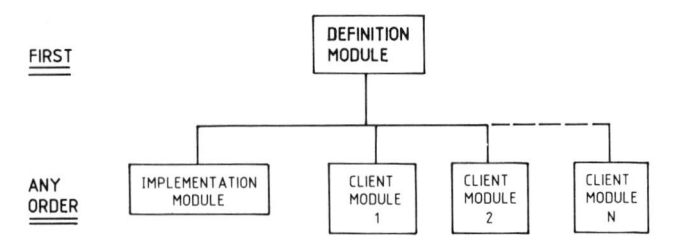

Fig. 6.21 Order of module compilation

- Definition modules must be compiled first.
- Implementation and client modules can then be compiled separately.

Note that an implementation module can be a client, i.e. it uses smaller building blocks from the library. In this case, using the rules above, it can be compiled only after both its own definition module and relevant library definition modules have been compiled.

If an implementation module is revised and recompiled does this affect clients? The answer is No; after all, the client essentially calls on the library module to perform its defined task, passing parameters as necessary. And these haven't been changed in any way. We do, however, have a problem if the implementation is no longer correct (but that is an entirely different problem of software design).

What is the situation concerning definition modules? Suppose, for instance, we change the number of parameters used in an implementation procedure. This means that the corresponding definition module must be altered in line with the change. So we recompile the definition module. Fine. But what about client modules which use this library procedure? Even more complex, what about library modules which use library modules which use further library modules which have just been changed? Grim!

So we have to maintain a strict code of conduct when dealing with changes like this. Remember that the definition module forms the interface between the client and the implementation. Therefore the only safe rule is to always recompile client modules whenever definition modules are changed. In turn this means that documentation control must be both clear and rigorous. Most Modula-2 compilers should have an automatic change record mechanism to keep track of the situation. It should also flag up a warning if incorrect versions are being handled simultaneously. Check your system.

Is there a unique order of compilation? Consider the situation in Listing 6.9 where a program calls up three separate library procedures. But observe that all modules are themselves interrelated by just one procedure:

```
/*****************************************************************/

DEFINITION MODULE Compute;
EXPORT QUALIFIED CheckLimits;
PROCEDURE Checklimits(Input:REAL);
END Compute.


DEFINITION MODULE ControlAlgorithm;
FROM Compute IMPORT Checklimits;
EXPORT QUALIFIED Integral;
PROCEDURE Integral(Signal:REAL):REAL;
END ControlAlgorithm.


DEFINITION MODULE Filter;
FROM Compute IMPORT Checklimits;
EXPORT QUALIFIED MovingAverage;
PROCEDURE MovingAverage(Value:REAL):REAL;
END Filter.
```

130 Modular construction

```
MODULE ProcessSignal;
FROM Compute IMPORT Checklimits;
FROM ControlAlgorithm IMPORT Integral;
FROM Filter IMPORT MovingAverage;

VAR
   MeasuredValue, SmoothedValue, IntegratedValue:REAL;

BEGIN
   SmoothedValue:=MovingAverage(MeasuredValue);
   IntegratedValue:=Integral(SmoothedValue);
   CheckLimits(IntegratedValue);
END ProcessSignal.
/***********************************************************/
```

Listing 6.9

'CheckLimits'. This is used by the library modules 'ControlAlgorithm' and 'Filter' as well as the main program module. To comply with the rules given earlier, module 'Compute' must be compiled first and the program module 'Process-Signal' last. The others are done in-between. The order is not important; that is, it doesn't matter whether 'Integral' is compiled before 'Moving-Average' or vice versa.

6.7 Initialising modules

Up to the present time implementation modules have generally contained procedures only. In fact it is perfectly legal to write program code within the body of the module (see Listing 6.8). This raises two questions: why should we want to do it and, having done so, when is the code executed?

Consider a very common situation of interacting with a VDU from an embedded processor system. When we write code to handle message transfer we assume that the communications hardware has been correctly set up. But has it? One way of dealing with this is to insert set-up code within the communications library module. This ensures that whenever a communications routine is used the hardware is set into the right state.

In this situation, when is the set-up code actually executed? This can be demonstrated using the example in Listing 6.10. Here a program module 'SignalProcessing' imports a procedure 'CalculateAverage2' from a library module 'Filter2'. This module contains initialisation code (only a text message for demo purposes). Note that 'CalculateAverage2' is called twice in the program module.

When the program is run it will be found that the initialisation code is

```
(***********************************************************)
DEFINITION MODULE Filter2;
EXPORT QUALIFIED CalculateAverage2;
PROCEDURE CalculateAverage2(Value:INTEGER);
END Filter2.
(***********************************************************)
```

```
(************************************************************)
IMPLEMENTATION MODULE Filter2;
FROM InOut IMPORT WriteInt, WriteLn, WriteString;

PROCEDURE CalculateAverage2(Value:INTEGER);
BEGIN
    WriteString(' The moving average value is   ');
    WriteInt(Value,4); WriteLn;
END CalculateAverage2; (* end of procedure *)

BEGIN
    WriteString(' This is a dummy set-up routine'); WriteLn; WriteLn;
END Filter2. (* end of implementation module *)
(************************************************************)


(************************************************************)
MODULE SignalProcessing;
(* The client module *)
FROM InOut IMPORT WriteInt, WriteLn, WriteString;
FROM Filter2 IMPORT CalculateAverage2;
CONST
    InputSignal = 100;
    OutputSignal = 1024;

BEGIN
    WriteString(' Demo of initialisation code'); WriteLn;
    CalculateAverage2(InputSignal);
    WriteString(' First calculation done'); WriteLn;
    CalculateAverage2(OutputSignal);
    WriteString(' Second calculation done'); WriteLn;
    WriteString(' End of program, Au Revoir'); WriteLn;
END SignalProcessing. (* end of the client module *)
(************************************************************)
```

Listing 6.10

executed once only, on the first access to the library module. Subsequent calls do not re-activate the code. This is a defined feature of Modula-2.

Review

Do you now consider that you:

- Understand the need for modularity to achieve reliable programming.
- Appreciate the difference between monolithic, modular and independent compilation techniques.
- Know which module types are provided in Modula-2, what their functions are, how they communicate with each other and how they are structured.
- Understand the difference between static and dynamic variables.
- Are able to write and compile program, definition, implementation and local modules.
- Perceive the design formality and control introduced by Modula-2 through the use of modules and related import and export statements.

Chapter 7

Structured data types – arrays and sets

Up to this point we have dealt with only a single data item at a time. In previous examples, for instance, we had NUM, D1, D2 etc., each name representing a single variable of a particular type. These are called 'simple' variables. There are many cases where we work with variables which are related to each other; it may be the set of computation coefficients for a digital filter, the collection of all monitored parameters on a diesel engine, or the set of exam marks for a course. All of these can be organised as a grouping of simple variables of course, but in many cases significant benefits are gained by arranging these in a defined structure. This organisation is called a 'data structure', variables used within the structure being 'structured data' types.

On completing this chapter you will

- Understand the use of structured data types.
- Appreciate the need for a variety of structures.
- Understand and use array and set types.

7.1 Introduction to structured variables

Why should we want to structure, i.e. arrange or order, our information in the first place? Or, if we don't use structured types, are certain jobs beyond our capabilities as programmers? In answering the second question we also give the reply to the first one. No, we don't *need* to use structured types in programming; it is just that they make life much easier for many tasks. After all, you don't need to use a mechanical digger to dig a hole for a swimming pool, it *could* be done by hand.

There are a number of reasons for structuring. In each and every case we will be dealing with a collection of data items; more importantly these items are somehow related to each other. The nature of the relationships varies; as a result a number of different data structures have been produced, each having particular features and uses.

Let's consider what we want from the data structure:

(a) It must first allow us to group data objects together (Fig. 7.1).

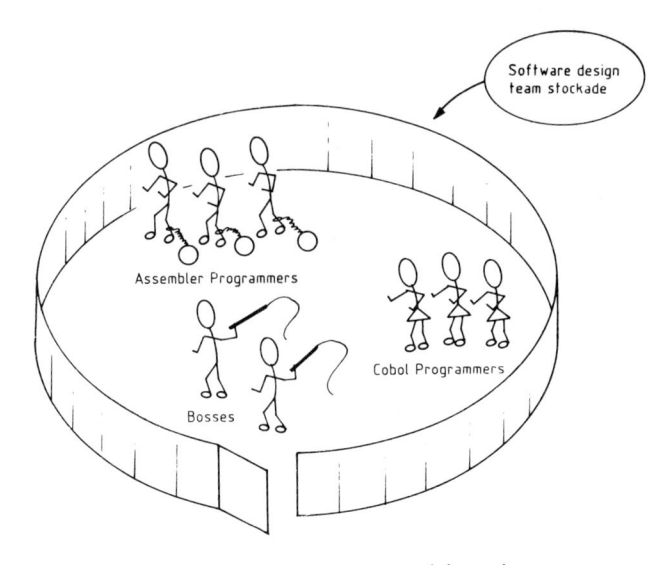

Fig. 7.1 Data structure requirement 1 – grouping of data objects

(b) It must support the grouping of objects of the same type ('homogeneous') and those of different types ('hetrogeneous') (Figs 7.2 and 7.3).

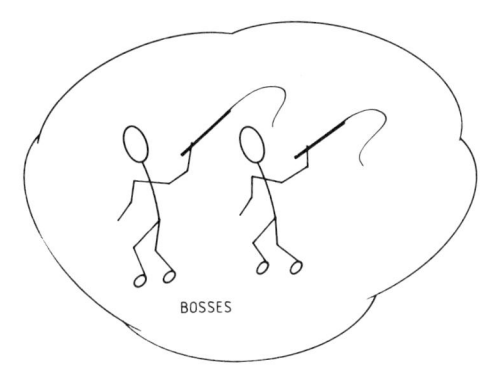

Fig. 7.2 Grouping of homogeneous objects

(c) It must let us handle individual objects within the group as well as manipulating the group (or parts of the group) as a single entity (Figs 7.4 and 7.5).
(d) It some cases it must enable single items to be accessed at random. In others it should allow us to work with large quantities of data using sequential accessing methods. (Figs 7.6 and 7.7).
(e) Accessing the information should be both simple and efficient.

134 Structured data types – arrays and sets

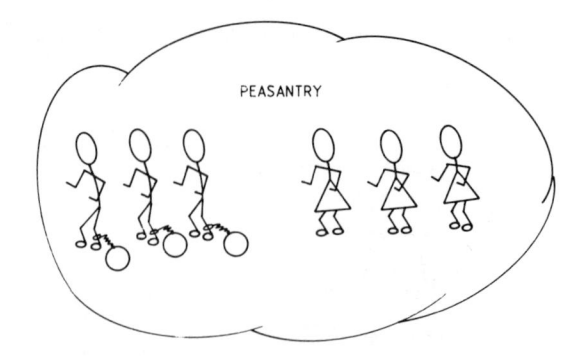

Fig. 7.3 Grouping of heterogeneous objects

Fig. 7.4 Handling individual objects

Fig. 7.5 Group manipulation

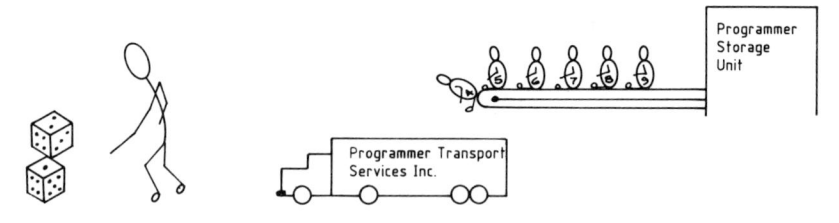

Fig. 7.6 Random selection

Fig. 7.7 Sequential selection

In the following sections we'll see what the various data structures of Modula-2 do for us.

7.2 Arrays

7.2.1 Overview

The array structure is provided in virtually all high-level programming languages, being used with homogeneous data objects (Fig. 7.8). As an example of its use consider the following digital control algorithm:

$$Ynew = A_0*Xnew + A_1*Xold - B_1*Yold$$

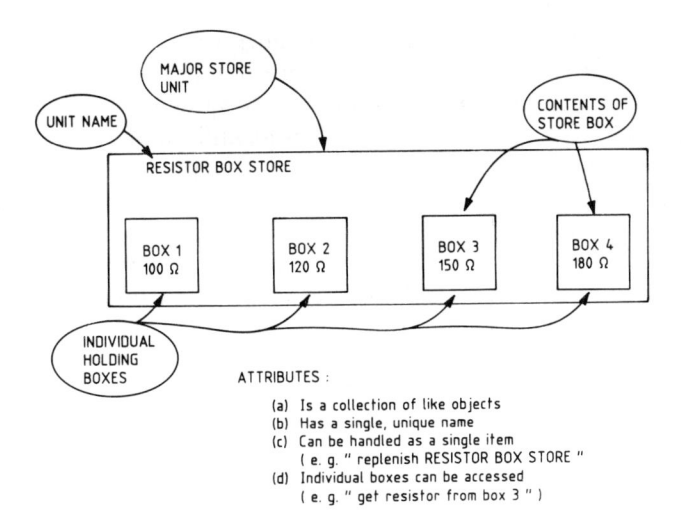

Fig. 7.8 Array structure – concept

where the A's and B's are algorithm coefficients of the *same* data type. Our objective is to form a data type which

- holds the values of the algorithm coefficients;
- is uniquely identified by a single name;
- enables us to handle the whole set of coefficients as if it is a single variable;
- enables us to manipulate each coefficient separately; and
- is easy to manage.

First, group the coefficients into a single compound type (the 'array'), identifying the unit so formed as a named variable (Fig. 7.9). In this case we'll identify the coefficient grouping as 'Accel', having three individual components ('elements').

Now we need to implement an efficient and simple way of identifying the

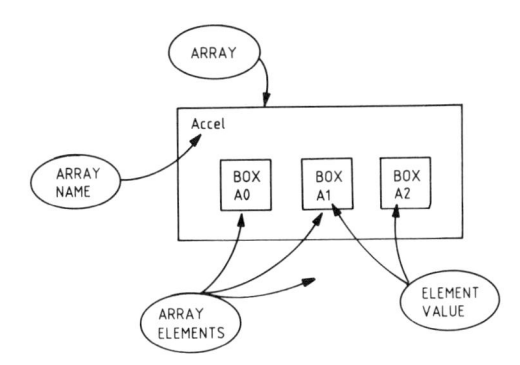

Fig. 7.9 Array structure of algorithm coefficients

elements. Each element in the array is unique; hence it needs a unique reference or identifier. Obviously this identifier must also carry the array name. The fact that all elements belong to the variable 'Accel' means that names don't have to be used as individual identifiers, only numbers (as in house numbering in a street). We'll see later how it pays to use simple ordering of the elements rather than a random grouping. In fact, elements are always arranged in a contiguous sequence. Each one is then identified by a number suffix attached to the array identifier. Note that we use a similar method for numbering houses; this makes it easy to find houses and organise postal deliveries.

7.2.2 Declaring and using arrays – a first introduction

For the above example let us suppose that we are calculating the acceleration (Ynew) of an engine from the speed measurements (X). The array could be identified as Accel, having three elements named as Accel[1], Accel[2] and Accel[3]. Four factors have to be declared to the compiler:

The presence of the array variable ('Accel').
The fact that it is an array.
The number of elements in the array.
The type of its elements.

As all elements are organised in a contiguous sequence we can specify the array size using only two values. These are the numbers of the first and last elements positions. Thus the standard array declaration format is:

   VAR
      Accel: ARRAY [1..3] OF INTEGER;

Here the variable Accel is declared to be an array, having three elements (Fig. 7.10). The first element is identified as number 1, the last being 3; all elements are of type INTEGER.

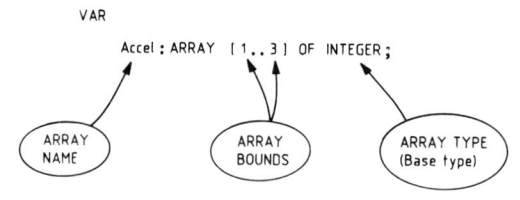

Fig. 7.10 Array declaration format

A simple example of the use of arrays is given in Listing 7.1 where it can be seen that:

- Arrays are declared in the variable block as with simple variables.
- The declaration starts with the identifier name.
- It is followed by the word 'ARRAY'.

```
MODULE CalcAcceleration;
(************************************************************)
(*      This is the simple use of an array.                 *)
(*                Listing 7.1                               *)
(************************************************************)
FROM InOut IMPORT WriteInt, WriteLn, WriteString, ReadInt;
VAR
    Accel : ARRAY [1..3] OF INTEGER;
    Xnew, Xold, Ynew, Yold:INTEGER;

BEGIN

    Accel[1]:=2;
    Accel[2]:=1;
    Accel[3]:=1;
    WriteString('input Xnew'); WriteLn;
    ReadInt(Xnew); WriteLn;
    WriteString('input Xold'); WriteLn;
    ReadInt(Xold); WriteLn;
    WriteString('input Yold'); WriteLn;
    ReadInt(Yold); WriteLn;
    Ynew:= Accel[1]*Xnew + Accel[2]*Xold +Accel[3]*Yold;
    WriteString('the value of Ynew is   ');
    WriteInt(Ynew,5); WriteLn;
END CalcAcceleration.
```

Listing 7.1

- The array bounds are placed in square brackets, lower and upper limits being separated by '..'.
- The word 'OF' comes next.
- The declaration is finished off with the type of the array elements.
- Within the program, array elements are accessed using a 'subscript' or 'array index' enclosed in square brackets (Fig. 7.11).

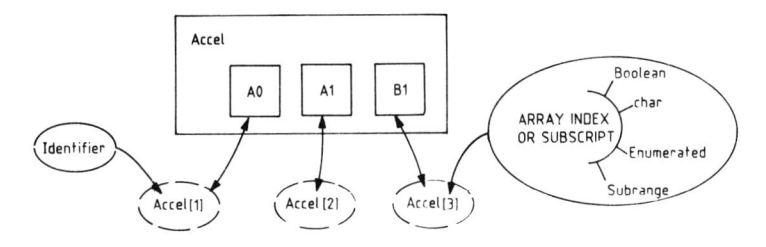

Fig. 7.11 Array elements

7.2.3 Why arrays are powerful constructs

Up to this time we don't seem to have gained very much. In fact in the above example, by using the array construct, we've probably created more work for ourselves. So, in some situations, such as

(a) where only a few variables are involved, or
(b) where the number of variables remains unchanged,

array operations are of limited use. However, if the converse is true, then arrays come into their own. This is best shown by using simple examples, including

(a) presetting values;
(b) transferring data between variables;
(c) handling information of varying size; and
(d) transferring data between array elements.

Presetting a series of program variables (often needed during program initialisation)
Consider the simplicity of the following statement:

FOR J:=1 TO 3 DO
Accel[J]:=0;

When this statement is executed all elements of the array Accel are set to zero (Fig. 7.12). When the number of elements becomes large (say a few hundred) this construct really pays off.

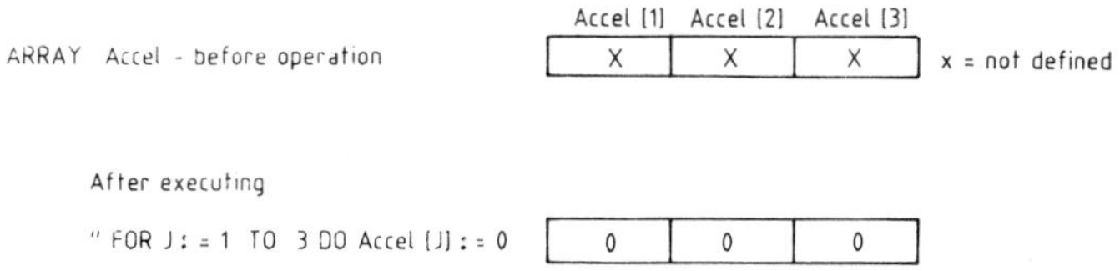

Fig. 7.12

Note that the array index identifier 'J' must also be declared to the compiler.

Transferring values within a group of related variables
Suppose that we have to carry out the following computation:

$$Y_i := X_i + X_{i-1} + X_{i-2} + X_{i-3}$$

where X is the sampled value of the input parameter (say speed), X_i is the most recent sample, X_{i-1} the last value, etc. Each time the calculation is carried out a new value of X is obtained whilst the past values all 'slip' back one sample time (i.e. the value in location X_{i-1} is replaced by the value that was in location X_i, etc.). By forming an 'X' or speed array, this can be done in a neat, simple, way. First of all form a four-element array 'Speed' so that:

Speed[0] holds the value of X_i
Speed[1] holds the value of X_{i-1}
Speed[2] holds the value of X_{i-2}
Speed[3] holds the value of X_{i-3}

Then the values can be slipped back as follows:

FOR J:= 2 TO 0 BY −1 DO
Speed[J+1]:=Speed[J];

Finally, the new measured input is placed into Speed[0], i.e. writing (Fig. 7.13)

Speed[0]:=Xi;

Source Code	STAGE ITEM	BEFORE LOOP OPERATION	END LOOP 1	2	3	4	5
LOOP							
FOR J:= 2 TO 0 BY -1 DO	Speed [0]	0	5	4	2	3	7
Speed [J +1]:= Speed [J];	Speed [1]	0	0	5	4	2	3
END;	Speed [2]	0	0	0	5	4	2
Speed [0]:= Xi;	Speed [3]	0	0	0	0	5	4
END;							
	Xi	5	4	2	3	7	

Fig. 7.13

Q7.1 What would be the effect of writing

FOR J:= 0 TO 2 DO
Speed[J+1]:=Speed[J];

in the example just described?

Handling arrays whose size can vary
Consider the task of modelling a real plant or system using its input and output signal values, signal processing being carried out using a digital computer. Such modelling is used extensively in simulation and self-tuning control systems. Our measured values can be formed into an array within the processor system; subsequently these are manipulated mathematically to extract model information. One parameter which will almost certainly change is the number of data samples taken during the measurement process. But if the array size is fixed how do we deal with this requirement?

The answer is to use named values as bounds, adjusting these as needed. In the following example two uses of named bounds are given. The first one ('MaxNumber') is used to set the maximum size of the array. Note that this is declared as a constant value. The second, 'ActualNumber', is used to select the number of elements accessed when the program is run. However, it is important to realise that the array size is set by the program declaration. It cannot change during a program run (Listing 7.2).

Structured data types – arrays and sets

```
MODULE ArrayBounds;
(******************************************************************)
(*   Here is an example of the basic use of named array bounds.  *)
(*                    Listing 7.2                                 *)
(******************************************************************)
FROM InOut IMPORT WriteInt, WriteLn, WriteString, ReadInt;
CONST
   MaxNumber = 100;
VAR
   J, ActualNumber:INTEGER;
   Speed :ARRAY [1..MaxNumber] OF INTEGER;

BEGIN
   WriteString('input number of data points'); WriteLn;
   ReadInt(ActualNumber); WriteLn;
   FOR J:= 1 TO ActualNumber DO
      Speed[J]:=0;
      WriteInt(Speed[J],2); WriteLn;
   END; (* end of forloop *)
END ArrayBounds.
```

Listing 7.2

Q7.2 If the value entered for 'ActualNumber' was greater than 100 what effect would this have? What then are the implications of this for embedded systems programming?

Transferring data between array variables

Suppose that we have data contained in an array ('Input') which we wish to copy but still retain the original data. Then by forming a second array ('InputCopy') we can transfer data between the two arrays. For instance the statement

   InputCopy[15]:=Input[15];

will simply assign the value of element 15 of Input to element 15 of InputCopy.

Q7.3 Is there any reason for the index numbers to be the same?

The following statement (Fig. 7.14) will cause the entire array to be copied:

FOR i:= 1 TO MaxNumber DO
InputCopy[i]:=Input [i];
END;

Exercise: Copy the contents of an array into a second array, but with the order reversed (i.e. InputCopy[1] gets Input[MaxNumber]).

Source Code	ELEMENT No.	BEFORE		AFTER	
		InputCopy	Input	InputCopy	input
FOR i: = 1 TO MaxNumber DO	1	X	6	6	6
InputCopy [i] : = Input [i] ;	2	X	3	3	3
END ;	3	X	2	2	2
X = not defined here	MaxNumber	X	1	1	1

Fig. 7.14

7.2.4 Arrays – more on bounds, indexing, declarations and types

Bounds and indexing
Look back to the section on subranges; it can be seen that subrange bound definitions ('[x..y]') are identical to those of array bounds. Therefore we can view the array bound type as being a subrange of some existing type, either predefined or user-defined. In the declaration

 Vector: ARRAY[1..100] OF INTEGER;

the bounds are of type CARDINAL. This also illustrates the point (implicit in examples up to now) that the index type does *not* have to be the same as the array type.

Q7.4 Describe the form of the data structure produced by the declaration
 VAR
  Vector: ARRAY[1..100] OF REAL;

 Now the bounds define the number of stored elements. In the case above clearly there are 100 elements. Thus index bounds must be enumerated types; further, in Modula-2 they must also be scalars.

Q7.5 If the following declaration is made in a module:
 CONST
  MaxNumber = 100.0;
 VAR
  Vector: ARRAY[1..MaxNumber] OF REAL;
then, at compile time an error will be flagged up, the message being 'incorrect range for array'. Why?

 In the earlier example we've used a named constant as one of the bounds ([1..MaxNumber]). Such values must be declared prior to the array declara-

142 Structured data types – arrays and sets

tion. Furthermore, bounds must be fixed values, variable quantities being disallowed.

Q7.6 Both of the following sets of declarations will fail at compile time. Why?

(i) VAR
    Vector: ARRAY[1..MaxNumber] OF REAL;
  CONST
    MaxNumber = 50;

(ii) VAR
    MaxNumber: INTEGER;
    Vector: ARRAY[1..MaxNumber] OF REAL;

As an aid to program clarity we can also declare the bounds to be a subrange, associating a name with this type, as follows:

TYPE Measurements = [1..100];
TYPE Vector = ARRAY Measurements OF REAL;

Note that the array type designator ('Measurements') is not enclosed in square brackets (see Listing 7.3).

```
MODULE ArrayBounds;
(**********************************************************)
(* Here a subrange is defined and used to set the array bounds *)
(*                    Listing 7.3                           *)
(**********************************************************)
TYPE
    Measurements = [1..100];
VAR
    J :INTEGER;
    Speed, Delta :ARRAY Measurements OF REAL;

BEGIN
    FOR J:= 1 TO 10 DO
        Speed[J]:= Delta[J];
    END; (*end of forloop*)
    Speed:=Delta;
END ArrayBounds.
```

Listing 7.3

User-defined enumerated types can also be used as an index type, as shown in Listing 7.4. This example has also slipped in an operation which produces a Boolean result ('IF Speed[SpeedData]>...'). As shown it seems a perfectly natural operation; therefore it should be no surprise to learn that all the relational operators can be used with array elements.

Declarations
And now for something really confusing. What's the difference between the declaration

```
MODULE EnumeratedBounds;
(*************************************************************)
(*       This uses an enumerated type as array bounds         *)
(*                    Listing 7.4                             *)
(*************************************************************)
FROM InOut IMPORT WriteInt, WriteLn, WriteString, ReadInt;
TYPE
    DataPoints = (i0, i1, i2, i3, i4);
VAR
    SpeedData :DataPoints;
    Speed :ARRAY DataPoints OF INTEGER;

BEGIN
    FOR SpeedData:= i0 TO i4 DO
        WriteString('enter speed value '); WriteInt(ORD(SpeedData),2);
        WriteLn;
        ReadInt(Speed[SpeedData]); WriteLn;
    END; (*end of forloop*)
    WriteString('The Speed values are'); WriteLn; WriteLn;
    FOR SpeedData:= i0 TO i4 DO
        WriteString('Entry No.'); WriteInt(ORD(SpeedData),2);
        WriteString( ' = '); WriteInt(Speed[SpeedData],5); WriteLn;
        IF Speed[SpeedData]> 100 THEN
            WriteString('Recheck this value'); WriteLn;
        END; (* end if *)
    END; (*end of forloop*)
    WriteString('Program finished');
END EnumeratedBounds.
```

Listing 7.4

Delta, Speed :ARRAY [1..MaxNumber] OF INTEGER;

and that written as

Speed :ARRAY [1..MaxNumber] OF INTEGER;
Delta :ARRAY [1..MaxNumber] OF INTEGER;

For the first case the following two sets of statements are valid:

(i) FOR J:= 1 TO MaxNumber DO
        Speed[J]:=Delta[J];
     END; (* end of forloop *)
(ii) Speed:=Delta;

Actually these are directly equivalent. Statement (ii) is merely a compact way of writing the array assignment operation.

However, when the second declaration format is used, statement (ii) will be rejected by the compiler (different, eh!). This comes about because, in the first declaration, Modula-2 considers the two arrays to belong to the same data type. But, when the second form is used, they are regarded as being different types (Fig. 7.15). Therefore in case 2 the 'Speed:=Delta;' statement fails on type compatibility grounds. Nevertheless, statement set (i) *is* valid because all *elements* of the two arrays are the same type, that is, INTEGER. Remember that the assignment action relates individual elements; thus type compatibility rules are still obeyed.

DECLARATION	STATEMENT
Delta, Speed : ARRAY [1 .. MaxNumber] OF INTEGER ;	Delta [1] : = Speed [1] — VALID Delta : = Speed ——— VALID
Delta : ARRAY [1 .. MaxNumber] OF INTEGER ; Speed : ARRAY [1 .. MaxNumber] OF INTEGER ;	Delta [1] : = Speed [1] — VALID Delta : = Speed ——— INVALID

Fig. 7.15 Problems of type incompatibility

Arrays as types

Modula-2 enables us to declare an array structure as a data type. Subsequently variables can be declared as belonging to that type, as follows:

TYPE Vector = ARRAY[1..100] OF INTEGER;
VAR
  Speed, Delta :Vector;

i.e. the type declaration form is

TYPE Name = ARRAY IndexType OF ComponentType;

This layout is easy to follow and understand. By using this the programmer, when working with arrays, is much less likely to make mistakes. Such mistakes occur most often when using procedures or when mixing arrays from different modules. In fact this declaration form forces the compiler to check for name equivalence rather than structural equivalence.

7.2.5 Multidimensional arrays

What we've dealt with so far are so-called 'one-dimensional' arrays. These are directly analogous to vectors in matrix algebra. For instance the linear equation

$$a_1 X_1 + a_2 X_2 + a_3 X_3 = Y$$

can be written in matrix form as

$$[a_1 \; a_2 \; a_3] \begin{bmatrix} X_1 \\ X_2 \\ X_3 \end{bmatrix} = Y$$

Listing 7.5 will perform the necessary mathematical calculations.

That's fine so far, but how do we go about calculating matrix operations, typified by the need to solve equations of the form:

$$a_{11} X_1 + a_{12} X_2 + a_{13} X_3 = Y_1$$
$$a_{21} X_1 + a_{22} X_2 + a_{23} X_3 = Y_2$$

In matrix notation this is

```
MODULE VectorMultiplication;
(************************************************************)
(*        This is a part program showing the use of arrays  *)
(*        in multiplying two vectors - Listing 7.5          *)
(************************************************************)
TYPE
   Elements = [1..3];
   Vector = ARRAY Elements OF REAL;
VAR
   Alpha, X:Vector;
   Y:REAL;
   J:Elements;

BEGIN
   Y:=0.0;
   FOR J:= 1 TO 3 DO
      Y:= Y + (Alpha[J]*X[J]);
   END; (* end of forloop *)
END VectorMultiplication.
```

Listing 7.5

$$\begin{bmatrix} a_{11} & a_{12} & a_{13} \\ a_{21} & a_{22} & a_{23} \end{bmatrix} \begin{bmatrix} X_1 \\ X_2 \\ X_3 \end{bmatrix} = \begin{bmatrix} Y_1 \\ Y_2 \end{bmatrix}$$

Here there are two 'A' vectors, each one being a one-dimensional array. To handle the whole problem we use an 'array of arrays' structure, alternatively known as 'multidimensional arrays'. In this particular case the declaration would be

TYPE Matrix = ARRAY [1..2] OF ARRAY [1..3] OF REAL;
VAR
   Alpha:Matrix;

Nowhere in Modula-2 are array structures defined in mathematical form as 'rows' and 'columns'. However these are very widely used in engineering calculations. Therefore it is useful to think in such terms when handling arrays (Fig. 7.16). Alternatively, for three-dimensional operations, it is useful to consider them as expressing coordinate information (e.g. Cartesian or

TYPE
   Matrix = ARRAY [1..2] OF ARRAY [1..3] OF REAL;
                    ↑ Double Subscript ↑

VAR
   Alpha : Matrix ;

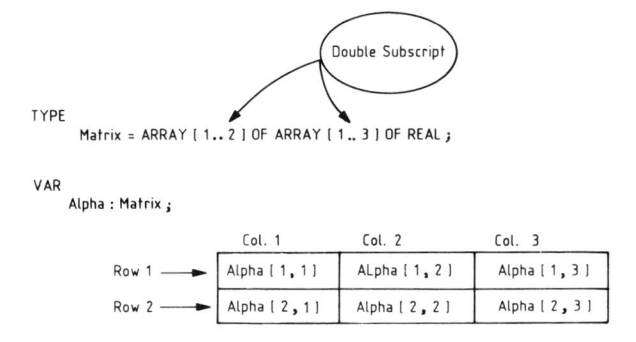

	Col. 1	Col. 2	Col. 3
Row 1	Alpha [1,1]	Alpha [1,2]	Alpha [1,3]
Row 2	Alpha [2,1]	Alpha [2,2]	Alpha [2,3]

Fig. 7.16 Two-dimensional array – row-column interpretation

146 Structured data types – arrays and sets

Spherical). Note that the matrix subscripting used above defines the row and column structure.

For the situation described here the elements of the 'A' matrix are accessed as follows;

a_{11} Alpha [1,1] (interpreted as row1/column1 intersection)
a_{13} Alpha [1,3] (interpreted as row1/column3 intersection)
a_{21} Alpha [2,1]

In cases like this the use of typed indices makes the program much clearer and understandable.

TYPE AlphaRow = [1..2];
TYPE AlphaColumn = [1..3];
TYPE Matrix = ARRAY AlphaRow OF ARRAY AlphaColumn
                                                OF REAL;

VAR
  Alpha:Matrix;

Hence, when we write

Alpha[SubscriptX,SubscriptY]

the X subscript refers to the row identifier, Y pointing to the column position (i.e. the subscript order must correspond to the declaration order). Listing 7.6 illustrates these points.

```
MODULE MatrixMultVector;
(***************************************************************)
(*       This part program shows the use of arrays for         *)
(*       multiplying a matrix by a vector - Listing 7.6        *)
(***************************************************************)
TYPE
   AlphaRow = [1..3];
   AlphaColumn = [1..2];
   Matrix = ARRAY AlphaRow OF ARRAY AlphaColumn OF REAL;

   Elements = [1..3];
   Vector = ARRAY Elements OF REAL;
VAR
   Alpha:Matrix;
   X,Y:Vector;
   I,J:Elements;

BEGIN
   (*initialise Y vector *)
   FOR I:= 1 TO 2 DO
      Y[I]:=0.0;
   END; (* end of initialisation *)

   FOR I:= 1 TO 2 DO
      FOR J:=1 TO 3 DO
         Y[I]:= Y[I] + (Alpha[I,J]*X[J]);
      END; (* end of J forloop *)
   END; (* end of I forloop *)
END MatrixMultVector.
```

Listing 7.6

7.2.6 Array declarations – final comments

Let's collect together the various points we've met concerning array declarations (and add a little bit more, Fig. 7.17). The basic form of array declaration is

```
VAR
    Accel : ARRAY [ 1 .. 10 ] OF INTEGER ;
```

```
CONST
    Low = 1;
    High = 10 ;
VAR
    Accel : ARRAY [ Low .. High ] OF INTEGER ;
```

```
TYPE
    SpeedValues = ARRAY [ 1 .. 10] OF INTEGER
VAR
    Accel : SpeedValues;
```

```
CONST
    FirstMeasurement = 1 ;
    LastMeasurement = 10 ;
TYPE
    Measurements = [ FirstMeasurement .. LastMeasurement] ;
    SpeedValues = ARRAY Measurement OF INTEGER ;
VAR
    Accel : SpeedValues;
```

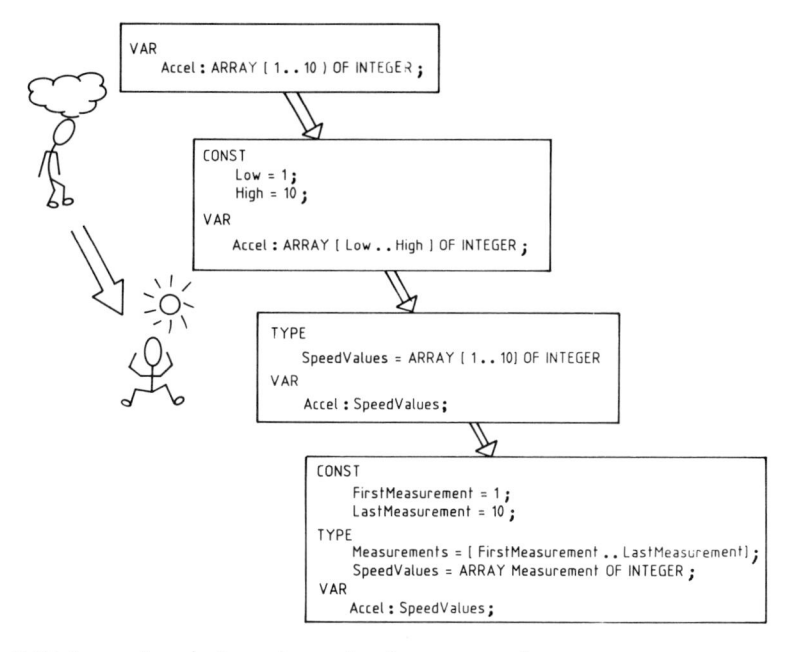

Fig. 7.17 Improving clarity and security of array operations

Example:
```
VAR
    Name: ARRAY [X..Y] OF TYPE;
VAR
    Accel: ARRAY [1..10] OF INTEGER;
```

This may also be written as

Accel: ARRAY [Low..High] OF INTEGER;

provided that Low and High have already been declared.

The program can be made clearer and less error-prone by declaring the array as a type and assigning variables to this type, as follows:

```
TYPE
    SpeedValues = ARRAY[1..10] OF INTEGER;
VAR
    Accel:SpeedValues;
```

Even greater clarity results from declaring the array range as a type and then using its name in the array declaration.

```
TYPE
  Measurements = [1..10];
  SpeedValues = ARRAY Measurements OF INTEGER;
VAR
  Accel:SpeedValues;
```

This can be taken one stage further, as in

```
CONST
  FirstMeasurement = 1;
  LastMeasurement = 10;
TYPE
  Measurements = [FirstMeasurement..LastMeasurement];
  SpeedValues = ARRAY Measurement OF INTEGER;
VAR
  Accel:SpeedValues;
```

For two-dimensional arrays the basic form of declaration is:

```
VAR
  Coefficients: ARRAY[1..10] OF ARRAY[2..6] OF INTEGER;
```

This can also be written as

```
VAR
  Coefficients: ARRAY[1..10], [2..6] OF INTEGER;
```

Clarity can be added (as shown earlier) by declaring the range bounds as constants, as follows:

```
CONST
  Low1 = 1;
  High1 = 10;
  Low2 = 2;
  High2 = 6;
VAR
  Coefficients: ARRAY[Low1..High1], [Low2..High2] OF INTEGER;
```

For greatest program reliability the following form is useful:

```
CONST
  Low1 = 1;
  High1 = 10;
  Low2 = 2;
  High2 = 6;
TYPE
  RowElements = [Low1..High1];
  ColumnElements = [Low2..High2];
  Matrix1 = ARRAY RowElements, ColumnElements OF INTEGER;
VAR
  Coefficients :Matrix1;
```

With a three-dimensional array the declaration form is:

VAR
    Coordinates ARRAY [1..5], [3..6], [0..10] OF INTEGER;

Note: For a three-dimensional array (say 'Coefficients') individual elements are accessed using three subscripts. The form shown earlier corresponds to

    y:= Coefficients[3,7,2];

An alternative form is

    y:= Coefficients[3][7][2];

The first is most suitable for use with vector and matrix operations. The second, however, is better for non-mathematical functions, as follows:

TYPE
    Book = ARRAY Pages, Lines, Words OF INTEGER;
VAR
    Catch22:Book;

Then an individual word can be accessed by writing:

    y:= Catch22[68][5][1];

i.e. page 68, line 5, word 1.

Listing 7.7 illustrates many of the points discussed here relating to array operations.

7.2.7 Using arrays in procedures

It should be no surprise that arrays can be used in procedures, this being straightforward when the array is confined within the procedure. However, when the array is a formal parameter then the situation is slightly more complicated. Remember that the declaration format for a procedure using a value parameter is

    PROCEDURE ProcedureName(ParameterName:TYPE);

typified by

    PROCEDURE Check(x1:INTEGER);

From this it should be clear that, when using array parameters, the array type must be also be declared. The following format must be used in Modula-2:

    PROCEDURE Vector(Alpha: RowVector);

where RowVector is a previously declared array type. We cannot write

    PROCEDURE Vector(Alpha: ARRAY[1..N] OF TYPE)

Listing 7.8 gives an example which uses arrays as procedure parameters.

150 Structured data types – arrays and sets

```
MODULE MatrixMultMatrix;
(*************************************************************)
(* This is a part program showing the use of arrays in multiplying a  *)
(* matrix by a matrix.  Inbuilt are declarations to ensure that matrix *)
(* rules are automatically obeyed.  The calculation is                 *)
(*                Y = A*X                                              *)
(* where A, X and Y are all matrices.  A has dimensions 3 x 2 (row by  *)
(* column), X has dimensions 2 x 2.  Therefore Y dimensions are 3 x 2  *)
(*              LISTING 7.7                                            *)
(*************************************************************)
CONST
   MaxArow = 3;      (* the number of A row-elements *)
   MaxAcolumn = 2;   (* the number of A column-elements *)
   MaxXcolumn = 2;   (* the number of X column-elements *)
   MaxXrow = MaxAcolumn;    (* matrix rules *)
   MaxYrow = MaxArow;       (* matrix rules *)
   MaxYcolumn = MaxXcolumn; (* matrix rules *)
  TYPE
   Arow = [1..MaxArow];
   Acolumn = [1..MaxAcolumn];
   MatrixA= ARRAY Arow,Acolumn OF REAL;

   Xrow = Acolumn;    (* matrix algebra rules *)
   Xcolumn = [1..MaxXcolumn];
   MatrixX = ARRAY Xrow,Xcolumn OF REAL;

   Yrow = Arow;        (* matrix rules *)
   Ycolumn = Xcolumn;  (* matrix rules *)
   MatrixY = ARRAY Yrow,Ycolumn OF REAL;

 VAR
    A: MatrixA;
    X: MatrixX;
    Y: MatrixY;
    I,J,K: INTEGER;

 BEGIN
    (*initialise the Y matrix *)
    FOR I:= 1 TO MaxYrow DO
       FOR J:= 1 TO MaxYcolumn DO
          Y[I,J]:=0.0;
       END; (* end For J *)
    END; (* end For I *)
    FOR I:= 1 TO MaxArow DO
       FOR J:= 1 TO MaxXcolumn DO
          FOR K:= 1 TO MaxXrow DO
             Y[I,J]:= Y[I,J] + (A[I,K]*X[K,J]);
          END; (* end For K *)
       END; (* end For J *)
    END; (* end For I *)
 END MatrixMultMatrix.
```

Listing 7.7

7.2.8 Open array parameters

That's all right as far as it goes, but let's stand back and have another look at this example. Although the procedure carries out array multiplication perfectly well it is quite limited in use. Why? Well, when using procedures, formal and actual parameters must be the same type; therefore formal and

```
MODULE VectorMultiplication;
(*****************************************************************)
(*        This is a part program showing the use of arrays       *)
(*        as procedure parameters.  The procedure calculates     *)
(*        the multiplication of two vectors, returning a scalar. *)
(*                          Listing 7.8                          *)
(*****************************************************************)

TYPE
   RowVector = ARRAY [1..10] OF REAL;
VAR
   WorkDone :REAL;
   Force, Distance :RowVector;

PROCEDURE VectorMultVector (Alpha,X:RowVector):REAL;
VAR
   Y:REAL;
   J:INTEGER;

BEGIN
   Y:=0.0;
   FOR J:= 1 TO 10 DO
      Y:= Y + (Alpha[J]*X[J]);
   END; (* end of forloop *)
   RETURN Y;
END VectorMultVector; (* end of procedure *)

BEGIN
   .
   .
   WorkDone:=VectorMultVector(Force,Distance);
   .
   .
END VectorMultiplication.
```

Listing 7.8

actual array bounds must also be the same (Fig. 7.18). Thus the procedure 'VectorMultVector' can only be used for a specific fixed-size array. In other words, every time we change the size of the vector (or matrix) we need to develop a different procedure. Clearly this is unacceptable in a modern language, especially one that places so much stress on the use of library

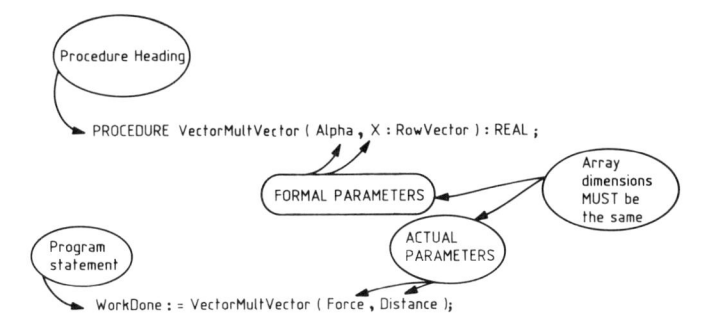

Fig. 7.18 Basic use of array parameters

152 Structured data types – arrays and sets

functions. Professor Wirth was well aware of such a limitation; he has included the 'open array' parameter structure to cope with this problem.

For the previous example the procedure declaration, when using open arrays, is written

    PROCEDURE VectorMultVector (Alpha, X:ARRAY OF REAL):REAL;

or, in general terms

    PROCEDURE ProcedureName(ArrayName:ARRAY OF ArrayType);

By using this form we can pass an array of any size into the procedure. In other words the size of the array is 'open' (Fig. 7.19).

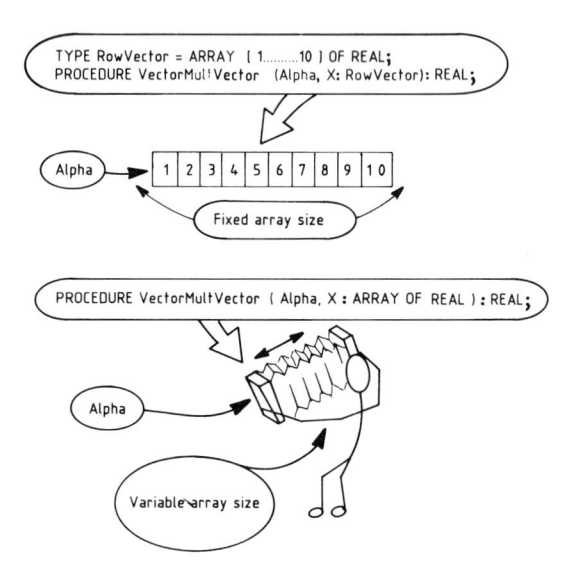

Fig. 7.19 Comparing fixed with variable (open) array parameters

Listing 7.9 shows how open array parameters are used. You can see that an extra variable (MaxSize) was used to control the forloop. This is an unnecessary complication as Modula-2 gives us a very simple way of avoiding this construct. Before detailing it let's first look more deeply at how formal array parameters are handled. Without this we may well run into trouble when using array parameters.

Modula-2 considers all open array formal parameters as arrays having the lower bound set to zero. The upper bound is set by the size of the *actual* array. For instance, consider two array declarations:

    ForceVector = ARRAY [1..10] OF INTEGER;
    WorkVector = ARRAY [11..30] OF INTEGER;

Now write a procedure using formal array parameters, say

```
MODULE Vector2Multiplication;
(*****************************************************************)
(*        This is a part program showing the use of open          *)
(*        array parameters. The procedure calculates the          *)
(*        multiplication of two vectors, returning a scalar.      *)
(*                        Listing 7.9                             *)
(*****************************************************************)
TYPE
   MechVector = ARRAY [0..10] OF REAL;
   ElecVector = ARRAY [0..20] OF REAL;
VAR
   WorkDone, Power :REAL;
   Force, Distance :MechVector;
   Voltage, Current :ElecVector;
CONST
   MechSize = 10;
   ElecSize = 20;

PROCEDURE VectorMultVector (Alpha,X:ARRAY OF REAL; MaxSize:INTEGER):REAL;
VAR
   Y:REAL;
   J:INTEGER;
BEGIN
   Y:=0.0;
   FOR J:= 0 TO MaxSize DO
      Y:= Y + (Alpha[J]*X[J]);
   END; (* end of forloop *)
   RETURN Y;
END VectorMultVector; (*end of procedure *)

BEGIN
   WorkDone:=VectorMultVector(Force,Distance,MechSize);
   Power:=VectorMultVector(Voltage,Current,ElecSize);
END Vector2Multiplication.
```

Listing 7.9

PROCEDURE Test(Alpha: ARRAY OF INTEGER);

Then, when we write

Test(ForceVector)

the element Alpha[0] is interpreted as being the first element of the actual array (ForceVector[1]), Alpha[9] being regarded as ForceVector[10]. likewise, for the statement

Test(WorkVector)

Alpha[0] denotes WorkVector[11], Alpha[19] denoting WorkVector[30]. In general then

Actual array range   [y..z]   e.g. [11..30]
Corresponding formal array range [0..(z-y)]   [0..19]

Compile and run the program of Listing 7.10. Examine the results obtained and make sure that you understand why these came about.

154 Structured data types — arrays and sets

```
MODULE FormalArrayBounds;
(***************************************************************)
(*        This program should be incorrect at run time.  It     *)
(*        is designed to show how the lower bound of an open    *)
(*        array parameter is numbered  -  Listing 7.10          *)
(***************************************************************)
FROM InOut IMPORT WriteInt, WriteString, WriteLn;
FROM RealInOut IMPORT WriteReal;
FROM MathLib0 IMPORT real;
CONST
   MechSize = 10;
TYPE
   MechVector = ARRAY [1..MechSize] OF REAL;
VAR
   Force :MechVector;
   K :INTEGER;

PROCEDURE PrintValue(Alpha :ARRAY OF REAL; MaxSize:INTEGER);
VAR
   Y:REAL;
   J:INTEGER;
BEGIN
   Y:=0.0;
   FOR J:= 1 TO MaxSize DO
      WriteString('Element no. '); WriteInt(J,2); WriteString(' = ');
      WriteReal(Alpha[J],6); WriteLn;
   END; (* end of forloop *)
END PrintValue; (*end of procedure *)

BEGIN
   FOR K:=1 TO MechSize DO
      Force[K]:=real(K);
   END;
   PrintValue(Force, MechSize);
END FormalArrayBounds.
```

Listing 7.10

Now we can introduce the use of the standard Modula-2 function 'HIGH'. This is used with arrays to define the value of the top bound as defined in the formal array range. Thus

HIGH(ForceVector) returns the value 9
HIGH(WorkVector) returns the value 19

or, generally, for actual array bounds [y..z], 'HIGH ArrayName' gives the value (z−y) (Fig. 7.20).

We can use this to significantly simplify working with arrays, as illustrated in Listing 7.11.

Unfortunately, at the present time, the open array feature is only defined for one-dimensional arrays. However, the basic definition of Modula-2 can be simply extended to include open array parameters for multidimensional arrays. It is expected that newer compilers will support this construct. For the moment programmers have to devise their own methods for implementing such constructs; one solution is given by Ford and Wiener (1985).

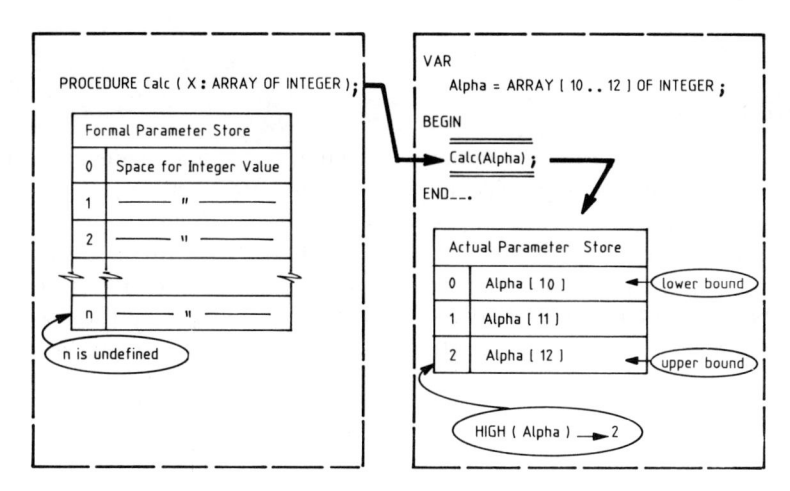

Fig. 7.20 Open array bounds

```
MODULE Vector3Multiplication;
(******************************************************************)
(*      This is a part program showing the use of the HIGH        *)
(*      function in conjunction with array manipulation.          *)
(*                       Listing 7.11                              *)
(******************************************************************)
TYPE
    MechVector = ARRAY [1..10] OF REAL;
    ElecVector = ARRAY [1..20] OF REAL;
VAR
    WorkDone, Power :REAL;
    Force, Distance :MechVector;
    Voltage, Current :ElecVector;

PROCEDURE VectorMultVector (Alpha,X:ARRAY OF REAL):REAL;
VAR
    Y:REAL;
    J:INTEGER;

BEGIN
    Y:=0.0;
    FOR J:= 0 TO HIGH(Alpha) DO        (* note the use of HIGH *)
        Y:= Y + (Alpha[J]*X[J]);
    END; (* end of forloop *)
    RETURN Y;
END VectorMultVector; (* end of procedure *)

BEGIN
    WorkDone:=VectorMultVector(Force,Distance);
    Power:=VectorMultVector(Voltage,Current);
END Vector3Multiplication.
```

Listing 7.11

7.3 Sets

7.3.1 Introduction

Sets are similar to arrays in many ways. First, individual elements of a set belong to some base type. Second, all elements are of the same base type ('homogeneous'), either subranges or enumerations. Third, elements can be accessed directly, i.e. it is a direct access method. Now for the differences. The set elements must be constants; further, the size of the set (i.e. the number of elements contained within it) can be changed by the program. Note that if an element is a constant then it is impossible to alter its value. This gives us a clue to the use of sets. If values are fixed then we can't use them in the same way as arrays. All we can do is to check whether a set element is there, add elements to the set, or delete elements as required. Set use is best shown by example, but first let's look at set declaration and the interpretation of set expressions.

7.3.2 Set structuring and declaration

In Modula-2 the base type of sets must be a scalar, being limited to BOOLEAN, CHAR, INTEGER and CARDINAL. From a practical point of view set sizes are limited, usually being machine dependent. In general we can only deal with relatively small sets. So it is not surprising that base types are enumerated or subrange ones.

Let's build ourselves a set which has three elements: alpha, beta and delta. First we declare an enumerated type (Fig. 7.21) to hold these elements, *viz*:

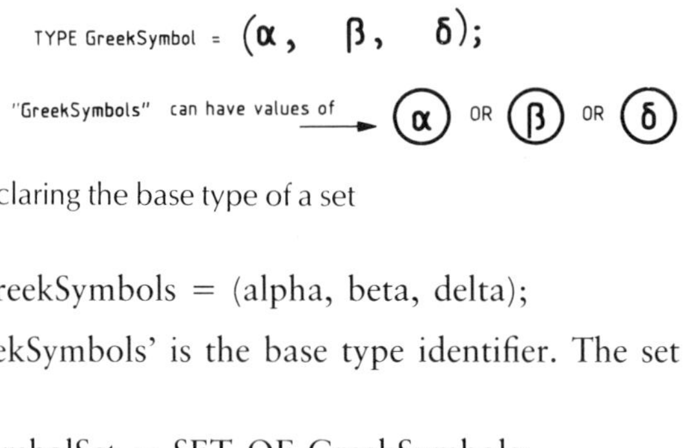

TYPE GreekSymbol = (α, β, δ);

"GreekSymbols" can have values of → (α) OR (β) OR (δ)

Fig. 7.21 Declaring the base type of a set

    TYPE GreekSymbols = (alpha, beta, delta);

where 'GreekSymbols' is the base type identifier. The set type is declared next:

    TYPE SymbolSet = SET OF GreekSymbols;

'SymbolSet' being the set type identifier (Fig. 7.22). After this, variables and constants can be declared as belonging to the type 'SymbolSet':

    VAR Letters :SymbolSet;

This variable 'Letters' is used to hold a set of elements defined by 'SymbolSet'. As stated earlier, the number actually held at any time can be varied. Here, for instance, it may range from nothing (the empty set) to all

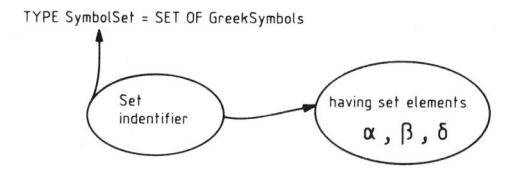

Fig. 7.22 Set declarations

three values (Fig. 7.23). But, in such instances, how do we show which elements are present?

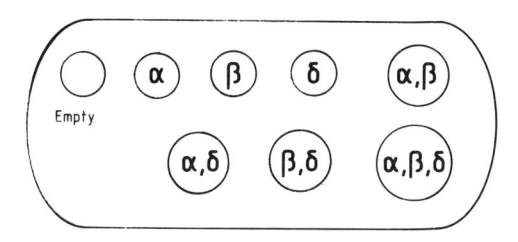

Fig. 7.23 Possible set values

The technique adopted in Modula-2 is to list them within curly brackets, as follows:

{ }, {alpha}, {beta}, {delta},
{alpha, beta}, {alpha, delta}, {beta, delta},
{alpha, beta, delta}

Note again that set elements are constants which are either present or absent. Thus it is very easy to calculate the maximum number of set values. Using binary arithmetic, for N elements there are 2^N possible combinations.

When set information is written using the curly bracket enclosure we have no indication which set these elements belong to. Suppose, for instance, we come across an expression 'ControlReg:=Beta;' in a program. Unless it's a short program, or we've got a very good memory, we won't have a clue as to which set Beta belongs to. To help with this problem it is normal practice to precede the brackets with the set identifier. (One exception, 'bitset', will be covered later.) Therefore, in the example given here we have

SymbolSet{alpha} or SymbolSet{beta, delta}, etc.

Thus we identify the set type and the actual elements being operated on within the set. What about the listing order of the elements? For instance, is there any difference between

SymbolSet{beta, delta} and SymbolSet{delta, beta}?

The answer is no; all we're looking for is the presence (or otherwise) of set members, not their order.

158 Structured data types – arrays and sets

Pulling together the information given above (Fig. 7.24), we get Listing 7.12).

VAR
    LettersX, LettersY, LettersZ, NewLetters: SymbolSet;

LettersX := SymbolSet { α, β, δ };
LettersY := SymbolSet { α, δ };
LettersZ := SymbolSet { δ, β };

RESULTS IN → LettersX, LettersY, LettersZ

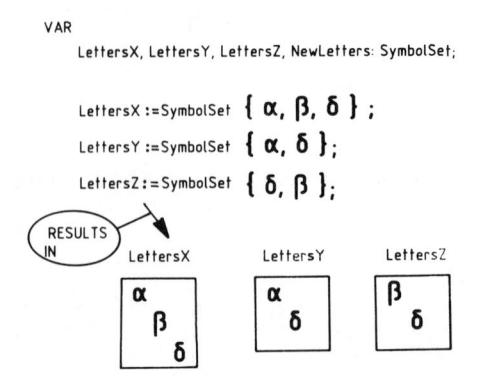

LettersX: α, β, δ
LettersY: α, δ
LettersZ: β, δ

Fig. 7.24 Assignment of set members

```
MODULE SetDemo;
(****************************************************************)
(*      This is a simple illustration of SET                    *)
(*      declaration and use.  The program                       *)
(*      performs no useful function. Listing 7.12               *)
(****************************************************************)
TYPE
   GreekSymbols = (alpha, beta, delta);
   SymbolSet = SET OF GreekSymbols;
VAR
   Letters :SymbolSet;
CONST
   UniqueSymbol = SymbolSet{alpha};
   OtherSymbols = SymbolSet{delta, beta};

BEGIN
   Letters:=SymbolSet{ };        (* forming an empty set *)
   Letters:=SymbolSet{alpha};    (* 'Letters' now holds alpha only *)
   Letters:=UniqueSymbol;
   Letters:=OtherSymbols;
END SetDemo.
```

Listing 7.12

It is valid to use a range specification to simplify and clarify the text. For instance, both of the following are equivalent:

    SymbolSet{alpha, beta, delta} and SymbolSet{alpha..delta}

Furthermore, suppose we had made the following declaration:

    TYPE GreekSymbols = (alpha, beta, delta, gamma, phi, rho);

Then SymbolSet{alpha, beta, delta, rho} and SymbolSet{alpha..delta, rho} are directly equivalent.

7.3.3 Set operations

Before we look at the use of sets in a real situation we need to understand:

(a) what operations we can carry out on sets (Fig. 7.25); and
(b) how we can evaluate the results of such operations (Fig. 7.26).

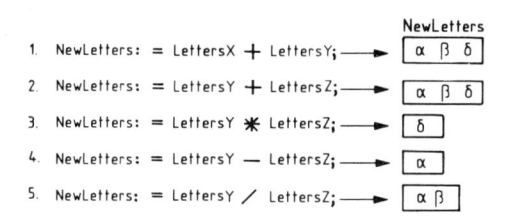

```
                                              NewLetters
1.  NewLetters: = LettersX + LettersY;  ───►  │ α β δ │
2.  NewLetters: = LettersY + LettersZ;  ───►  │ α β δ │
3.  NewLetters: = LettersY * LettersZ;  ───►  │   δ   │
4.  NewLetters: = LettersY − LettersZ;  ───►  │ α     │
5.  NewLetters: = LettersY / LettersZ;  ───►  │ α β   │
```

Fig. 7.25 Set operations

TEST	RESULT
LettersY = LettersZ	FALSE
LettersY <> LettersZ	TRUE
LettersZ <= LettersX	TRUE
LettersX >= LettersZ	TRUE
LettersY >= LettersZ	FALSE
LettersZ IN LettersX	TRUE

Fig. 7.26 Using the relational operators

In Modula-2, the operators which can be used on set variables are listed in Table 7.1; the relational operators applicable to sets are given in Table 7.2.

Modula-2 provides two standard functions for use with sets: INCL and

Table 7.1 Operators used with set variables

Operator	Name	Logical	Example	Result
+	Union	OR	X + Y	The resulting set has elements which belong to X, Y or both.
*	Intersection	AND	X.Y	The resulting set elements belong to both X and Y.
~	Difference		X.(NOT Y)	The resulting set has elements which belong to X but are not in Y.
/	Symmetric difference	EX-OR	X O Y	The resulting set has elements which belong either to X or to Y, but not to both.

Table 7.2 Set relational operators

=	Equality	X = Y	Boolean result, true if X = Y.
<>	Inequality	X<>Y	Boolean, true if X and Y are not equal.
<=	Inclusion (set is contained in)	X<=Y	Boolean, true if set X is contained in set Y.
>=	Inclusion (set contains)	X>=Y	Boolean, true if set X contains set Y.
IN	Membership	x IN Y	Boolean, true if ELEMENT x is contained in SET Y.

EXCL (Fig. 7.27). INCL ('include') adds a member to the set whilst EXCL (yes, you've guessed it, 'exclude') removes a member.

In Listing 7.13 a number of these operations are given. Read through this and satisfy yourself that you understand it. Modify it to exercise the various other set operators.

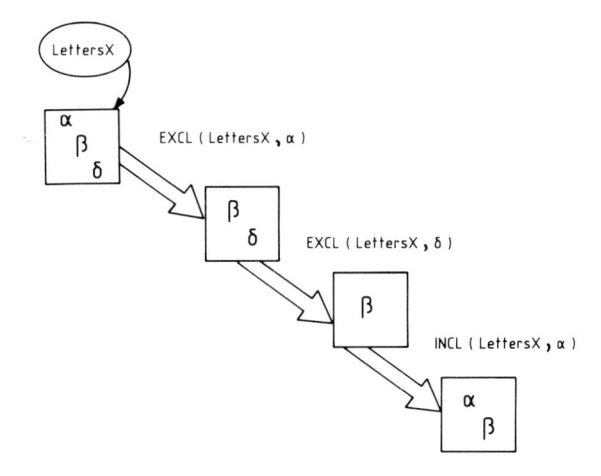

Fig. 7.27 Deleting and adding set members

7.3.4 Using sets

There are three main reasons for using sets:

- Mathematical operations
- Validity testing
- Control of individual bits within computer words.

The first item applies to fairly specialised areas of mathematics; therefore no more will be said here concerning this.

The second function can be best explained by using an example. Listing

```
MODULE SetOperationsDemo;
(*******************************************************************)
(*      This illustrates various set operations.  The         *)
(*      program itself is trivial. - Listing 7.13.            *)
(*******************************************************************)
FROM InOut IMPORT WriteInt, WriteLn, WriteString, Read, ReadInt;
TYPE
   GreekSymbols = (alpha, beta, delta, gamma);
   SymbolSet = SET OF GreekSymbols;
VAR
   Letters, NewSet :SymbolSet;
   i: GreekSymbols;
CONST
   UniqueSymbol = SymbolSet{alpha};
   OtherSymbols = SymbolSet{gamma, beta};

BEGIN
      Letters:=SymbolSet{alpha};                (* simple assignment *)
      IF alpha IN Letters THEN
         WriteString('alpha present'); WriteLn;
      END; (*end if *)
      IF beta IN Letters THEN
         WriteString('beta present'); WriteLn;
      END; (* end if*)

      INCL(Letters, beta);                      (* add set member *)
      IF beta IN Letters THEN
         WriteString('beta now included'); WriteLn;
      END; (* end if*)

      EXCL(Letters, alpha);                     (* delete set member *)
      IF alpha IN Letters THEN
         WriteString('program gone wrong');
      ELSE
         WriteString('alpha excluded'); WriteLn;
      END; (* end if-then-else *)

      IF Letters<=OtherSymbols THEN      (* check for set inclusion *)
         WriteString('Letters contained in set OtherSymbols'); WriteLn;
      END; (* end if *)

      IF OtherSymbols>=Letters THEN      (* check for set inclusion *)
         WriteString('OtherSymbols set contains Letters'); WriteLn;
      END; (* end if *)

      NewSet:= (UniqueSymbol+OtherSymbols);       (* union of sets *)
      FOR i:= alpha TO gamma DO
         IF i IN NewSet THEN
            WriteString('ordinal value ');
            WriteInt(ORD(i),1); WriteString(' present'); WriteLn;
         END; (* end if *)
      END; (* end forloop *)

END SetOperationsDemo.
```

When this program is run the following sequence will appear on the screen;

    alpha present
    beta now included
    alpha excluded
    Letters contained in set OtherSymbols

```
OtherSymbols set contains letters
ordinal value 0 present
ordinal value 1 present
Ordinal value 3 present
When this program is run the following sequence will appear on the
screen;

alpha present
beta now included
alpha excluded
Letters contained in set OtherSymbols
OtherSymbols set contains letters
ordinal value 0 present
ordinal value 1 present
Ordinal value 3 present
```

Listing 7.13

7.14 shows a simplified version of the program 'LoopExit' which was used in Chapter 3 to demonstrate the CASE operation. The program puts up a menu on the screen, requiring a response from the operator. In the original program an invalid reply was trapped by the CASE 'else' statement. Here the SET construct is used to prevent the program even accepting such invalid answers.

The final item, that of bit management, is probably the most important application for the embedded systems programmer. Here we use the only standard set in Modula-2, BITSET. Using the BITSET construct we can handle single bits of a processor word quickly and easily. Yet this can be written in Modula-2, providing visibility, clarity and security. BITSET examples applied to processor specific functions will be given in Chapter 9; for the moment we'll outline its general features.

First, this is a standard type, hence it doesn't need declaring. However, if a declaration *was* required then the following form would be used:

TYPE BITSET = SET OF [O..K]

where the subrange is of type CARDINAL, having values 0, 1, 2, . . . K. For an N-bit processor we normally have K = (N−1).

If a set listing (i.e. the curly bracket construct) is not accompanied by a set identifier the compiler assumes it to be a BITSET.

Assume that the processor word length is 16 bits; then K is 15. Writing

```
VAR
    UART :BITSET
```

	MSB	LSB
then UART:={ } produces the bit pattern	0000 0000	0000 0000
UART:={0,1,2,3}	0000 0000	0000 1111
UART:={15, 14}	1100 0000	0000 0000

Sets   163

```
MODULE TestValidity;
(*************************************************************)
(*      This is a simple illustration of the use of          *)
(*      the set operation to check the validity of data      *)
(*      entered at a computer keyboard - Listing 7.14        *)
(*************************************************************)
FROM InOut IMPORT WriteInt, WriteLn, WriteString, Read, ReadInt;
TYPE
    Numbers = [0..15];
    SetOfNumbers = SET OF Numbers;
VAR
    Answer:Numbers;
    Reply:CHAR;
    Input:INTEGER;
CONST
    ValidNumber = SetOfNumbers{1,2};

BEGIN
    LOOP
        WriteString('System Alarms - Set-up procedure'); WriteLn;
        WriteString('Select Alarm group by number'); WriteLn;
        WriteString('1. Main Propulsion'); WriteLn;
        WriteString('2. Generators'); WriteLn;

        (* this is the start of the new section.  Only valid numbers, i.e.,
           1 and 2, will be accepted by the system.  Anything else
           generates the 'invalid entry' response.  *)

        REPEAT (*Reading the keyboard input until a valid number is sent *)
            ReadInt(Input); WriteLn;
            Answer:=Numbers(Input);   (* note the type transfer action *)
            IF Answer IN ValidNumber THEN
                WriteLn;
            ELSE
                WriteString('Invalid entry, retry'); WriteLn;
            END; (* end if-then-else *)
        UNTIL Answer IN ValidNumber;
        (* this is the end of the new section *)

        CASE Input OF
            1: WriteString('Main Propulsion Selected')|
            2: WriteString('Generators Selected')
        END; (*this is the end of the CASE statement*)

        WriteLn;WriteString('OK to proceed?'); WriteLn;
        Read(Reply); WriteLn;
        IF Reply = 'y' THEN EXIT END;
    END;     (* end of loop *)

    WriteString('Program finished - goodbye');
END TestValidity.
```

Listing 7.14

One last point concerning sets is their size, that is, the number of elements within the set. First, practical systems considerably limit set sizes (16 elements is not unusual). Second, sizes vary between different computers or compilers. Therefore set operations tend to be highly unportable features of programs.

Size limits can be overcome by combining the array and the set construct. This is illustrated in part in Listing 7.15.

```
MODULE LargeBitset;
(******************************************************************)
(*  This illustrates the basic mechanism by which large sets     *)
(*  can be constructed  -  Listing 7.15                          *)
(******************************************************************)
FROM InOut IMPORT WriteInt, WriteLn, WriteString, Read, ReadInt;
TYPE
    ASCIICharacters = ARRAY [0..7] OF BITSET;
VAR
    CodeValue :ASCIICharacters;
    k :INTEGER;

BEGIN
   (* create a null or empty set *)
   FOR k:=0 to 7 DO
      CodeValue[k]:={ };
   END; (* of for *)

   (* insert letter 'b' into its correct position *)
   Row:= ORD(b) DIV 16;
   Col:= ORD(b) MOD 16;
   INCL{CodeValue[Row], Col};

   WriteString('Program finished - goodbye');
END LargeBitset.
```

Listing 7.15

Review

Are you sure you now:

- Understand the use of structured data types.
- Appreciate the need for a variety of structures.
- Understand the use of array and set types.

Chapter 8

Structured data types – records and dynamic structures

As shown previously, all individual data elements within array and set data structures are the same type. This, generally, has been good enough to satisfy engineering and scientific computing needs. In fact, most early languages (e.g. Fortran 2, Coral66) only support limited constructs for structured variables. Unfortunately these constructs are unsuited for handling large amounts of data, especially data involving different types. We find that data structures are needed which allow different types to be mixed together. We also need to be able to manipulate the contents of such data structures both collectively and individually. Moreover, it must also be possible to work with large quantities of data. As a result, component parts may themselves be structured.

We also saw that arrays and sets have a fixed size. Even the open array type, when brought into being by a procedure call, is fixed. If such structures are used for handling large amounts of data then computer storage space will soon be exhausted. Data like this is usually dynamic, i.e. in a constant state of change. Consequently the amount of storage space needed during a program run can change considerably. What is the best way to deal with this? The solution is to employ data structures which expand and contract as our requirements change, being disposed of when no longer required.

In this chapter you'll meet data structures which have been devised to match the needs outlined above. After having studied it you will:

- Understand the concept the use of the record data structure.
- Be able to work with record contents either as complete entities or as individual elements.
- Understand and use variant records.
- Understand the concepts of dynamic data structures.
- Understand the concept and use of pointers.
- Understand how to construct a simple last-in first-out file.
- Appreciate that dynamic data structures are potential sources of software unreliability.

166 Structured data types – records and dynamic structures

8.1 Records

8.1.1 The whats and whys of records

In the real world we often work with items which are related to each other, yet are of different types. For instance, the specification of a ship's propulsion control system states (in part):
  'Group warnings will be given on the Visual Display Unit for the following units;

Port Gas Turbine
Stbd. Gas Turbine
Port Cruise Diesel
Stbd. Cruise Diesel
. . .

For the Gas Turbines the following alarms will be provided:

Power Turbine fire
Gas generator overspeed
GG vibration
. . .

It is far more logical for the marine engineer to relate individual alarms to a specific propulsion unit rather than to consider a grouping of, say, fire alarms. Moreover, it is much more useful to use names instead of cryptic identifiers. After all, 'Port Gas Turbine, Fire' is slightly more attention getting than 'Alarm 27'.

Consider now how we deal with such information. We may talk, for instance, about the 'Port Gas Turbine alarms' as if they are a single object or entity. In other cases we are concerned with an individual item within the group, as with the fire alarm.

Now let's look at this in the context of developing a program for such a system. If we have a data structure which matches our view of the real world then we are likely to produce programs which are:

- Meaningful
- Readable
- Understandable
- Maintainable.

Obviously for this job both the array and set structures are unsuitable (why?). What we use instead is a new construct, the record. Actually, there is nothing new about the record concept. Consider how we'd keep data relating to an engine fitted to a ship (Fig. 8.1). Here we've made up a form which defines all information to be recorded. To identify it, it is given a reference number. When it is used, appropriate data are entered into the boxes concerned. So, in informal terms, we could describe it as in Fig. 8.2. And

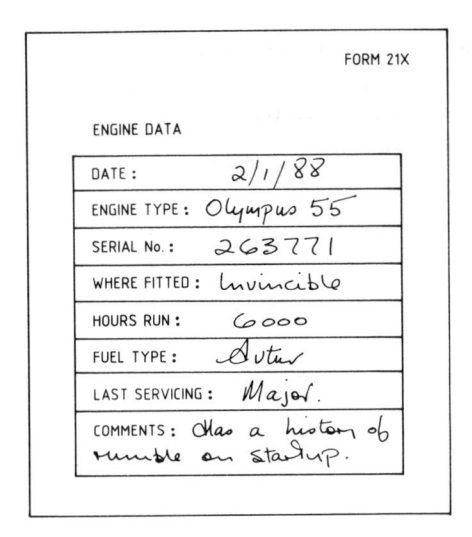

```
                    FORM 21X

    ENGINE DATA

    DATE:          2/1/88
    ENGINE TYPE:   Olympus 55
    SERIAL No.:    263771
    WHERE FITTED:  Invincible
    HOURS RUN:     6000
    FUEL TYPE:     Avtur
    LAST SERVICING: Major.
    COMMENTS:      Has a history of
                   rumble on startup.
```

Fig. 8.1 A conventional manual record

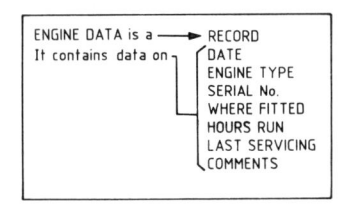

```
    ENGINE DATA is a ——▶ RECORD
    It contains data on ─┬─ DATE
                         │  ENGINE TYPE
                         │  SERIAL No.
                         │  WHERE FITTED
                         │  HOURS RUN
                         │  LAST SERVICING
                         └─ COMMENTS
```

Fig. 8.2 Informal description of the record form

really that's all there is to the record. Now for the software equivalent of our pencil and paper system.

In programming terms a record is defined as a direct access, heterogeneous, fixed-size data structure. It has the following features:

- It allows a mix of data types.
- The complete data structure can be handled as if it is a single object.
- Each component (element) within the structure can be accessed and manipulated individually.
- Names are used to identify the complete structure *and* its elements.

Let's illustrate these points, and the formal construct of records, using a few examples.

8.1.2 Declaring and using records – an introduction

Let us build up a record for the port gas turbine, at this stage including only three alarms. Four items have to be declared to the compiler:

168 Structured data types – records and dynamic structures

- The name of the record structure ('PropulsionEngine').
- The fact that it is a record.
- The individual components of the record.
- The type of each component.

Consider the requirements to form a record for the propulsion engine (Fig. 8.3). In this case the declaration format is:

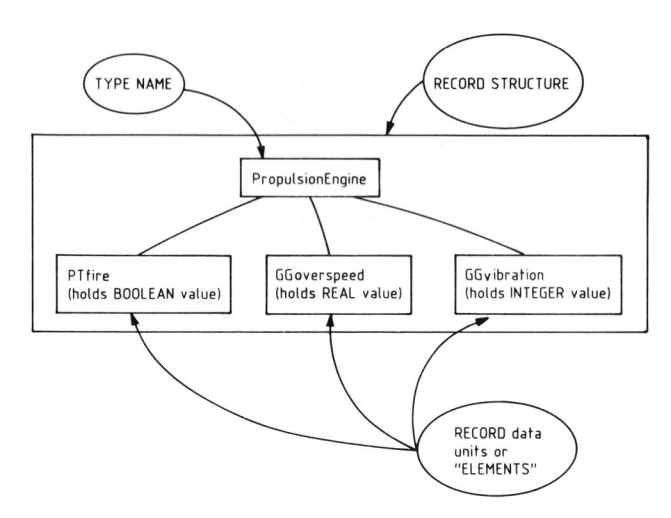

Fig. 8.3 Structure of record type 'PropulsionEngine'

```
TYPE
   PropulsionEngine =  RECORD
                         PTfire :BOOLEAN;
                         GGoverspeed :REAL;
                         GGvibration :INTEGER;
                       END;
```

Variables belonging to this record type are declared in the usual way, as follows:

```
VAR
   PortGasTurbine, StbdGasTurbine :PropulsionEngine;
```

Thus we have two variables: PortGasTurbine and StbdGasTurbine (Fig. 8.4). It should be realised that record type declarations (as with all other type declarations) do not reserve computer storage. This takes place only when variables are declared to belong to that type. Each variable has a set of individual components, these being PTfire, GGoverspeed and GGvibration. When used in the program they are accessed by name, as follows:

   PortGasTurbine.PTfire

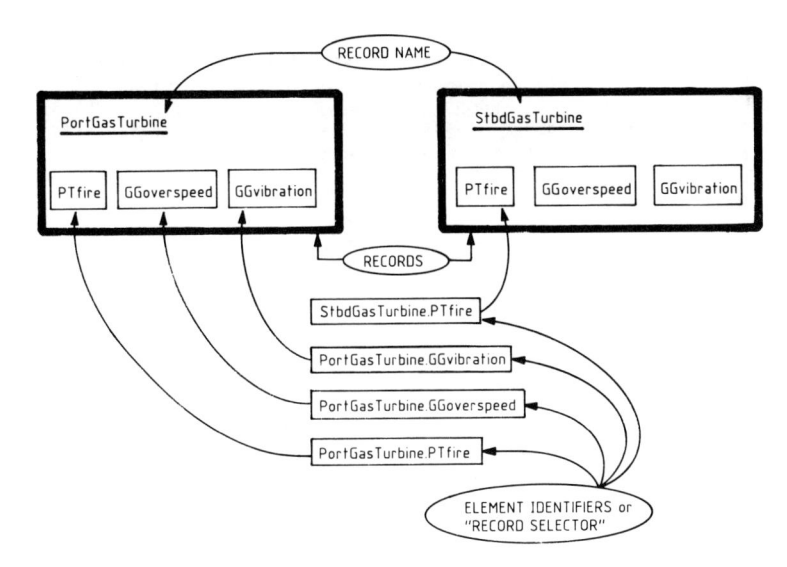

Fig. 8.4 Identifying variables of type record

  StbdGasTurbine.PTfire
  PortGasTurbine.GGvibration

Let's use this in a simple example (Listing 8.1).
  Now for a few definitions. In the above example the grouping

  PTfire :BOOLEAN;
  GGoverspeed :REAL;
  GGvibration :INTEGER;

is called the 'record field list' or the 'record field list sequence' (Fig. 8.5). We can regard 'PTfire :BOOLEAN;' as being 'field number 1' or 'field list number 1', 'GGoverspeed :REAL' as field 2, etc.
  The name 'PTfire' is called the 'field identifier' whilst the type designator 'BOOLEAN' is called the 'field type'. It can be seen that individual components within a record are accessed using their field identifiers attached to the variable name, as, for instance,

  PortGasTurbine.GGvibration

This individual element identifier is called the 'record variable designator'.
  The order in which field lists are written is not important. Note well that the variables are those declared in the variable listing, e.g. 'StbdGasTurbine', having individual components such as 'StbdGasTurbine.PTfire', etc. The record field names by themselves (e.g. PTfire, etc.) are *not* variables.
  The syntax diagram for the record type is shown in Figs. 8.6 and 8.7
  Just to recap, when using records the normal format is:

170 Structured data types – records and dynamic structures

```
MODULE RecordTest;
(*********************************************************************)
(*          This is a simple demonstration of the declaration        *)
(*          and use of the RECORD construct - Listing 8.1            *)
(*********************************************************************)
FROM InOut IMPORT WriteInt, WriteLn, WriteString, ReadInt;
TYPE
    PropulsionEngine = RECORD
                           PTfire :BOOLEAN;
                           GGoverspeed :REAL;
                           GGvibration :INTEGER;
                       END;
VAR
    PortGasTurbine, StbdGasTurbine :PropulsionEngine;
    Input :INTEGER;

BEGIN
    WriteString('Enter the Port Turbine vibration trip level - mm ');
    ReadInt(Input); WriteLn;
    PortGasTurbine.GGvibration:= Input; (* setting the trip level *)

    WriteString('Enter the Stbd Turbine vibration trip level - mm ');
    ReadInt(Input); WriteLn;
    StbdGasTurbine.GGvibration:= Input; (* setting the other trip level *)

    (* This shows that the trip levels have been set *)
    WriteString('The Port Turbine vibration alarm trip level is ');
    WriteInt(PortGasTurbine.GGvibration, 3); WriteLn;

    WriteString('The Stbd Turbine vibration alarm trip level is ');
    WriteInt(StbdGasTurbine.GGvibration, 3); WriteLn;
END RecordTest.
```

Listing 8.1

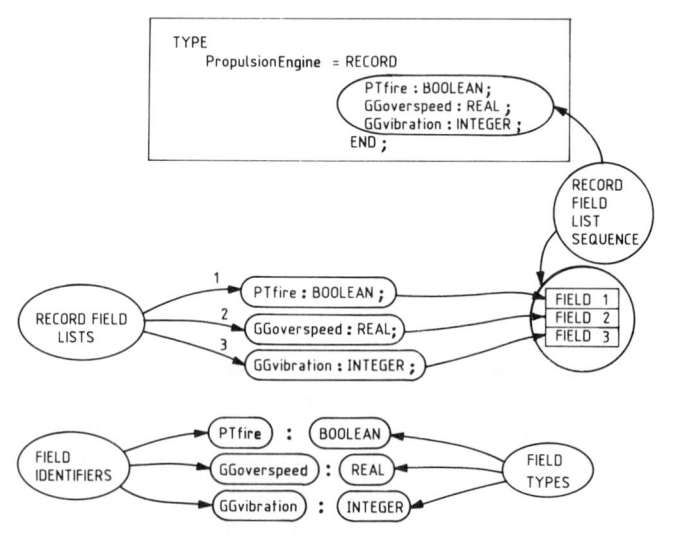

Fig. 8.5 Defining the parts of a record

Records   **171**

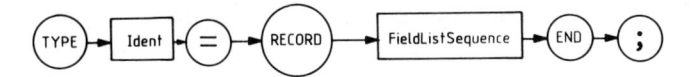

Fig. 8.6 Record type syntax

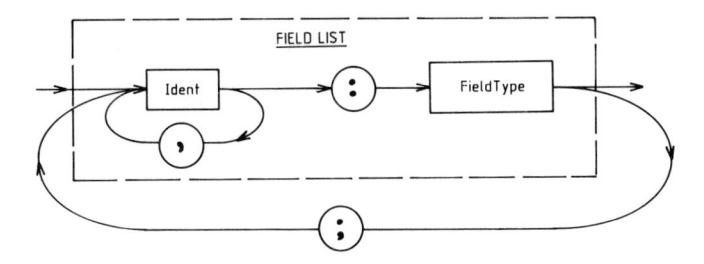

Fig. 8.7 Syntax of the field list sequence

```
TYPE Structure = RECORD  (Structure is the name of the type)
                Alarm:INTEGER;  (*This is the *)
                Filter :REAL;    (*field list  *)
                END;
```

Both 'Alarm' and 'Filter' are field names; 'INTEGER' and 'REAL' are field types.

8.1.3 Working with records

Handling individual components

The example above shows how to work with individual record components (Fig. 8.8). Very little more needs to be said as the process is straightforward. Record elements are declared in exactly the same way as program variables

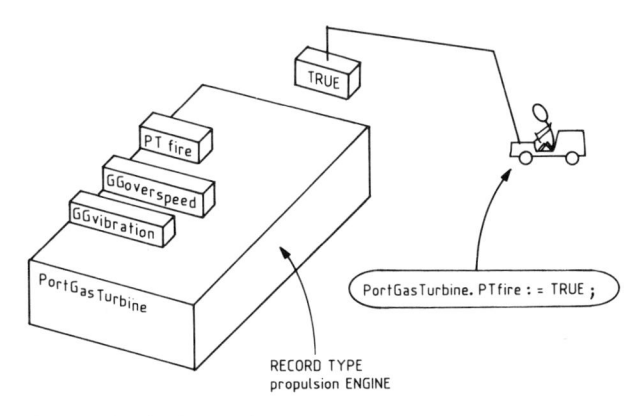

Fig. 8.8 Handling individual record components

172 Structured data types – records and dynamic structures

(go back and look). The only difference is that they are located in the RECORD section.

Handling the complete data structure as a single unit
Suppose in our propulsion system all gas turbines are set up for the same conditions. By using the approach shown above every individual item would have to be set up separately, a fairly tedious process. Furthermore, there is always the chance of making mistakes. What can be done about this? Well, this is where the ability to handle complete records as a single unit is useful. Let's start by doing a new record declaration as follows:

```
TYPE
    PropulsionEngine = RECORD
                GGoverspeed :REAL;
                GGvibration, BearingTemp :INTEGER;
            END;
VAR
    PortGasTurbine, StbdGasTurbine, GasTurbines :PropulsionEngine;
```

Within the program, we can set up all values in the record variable 'Gas-Turbines', a once-only activity. Then we can proceed to copy them (assign them) *en bloc* to the other records (Fig. 8.9); this eliminates the need to enter

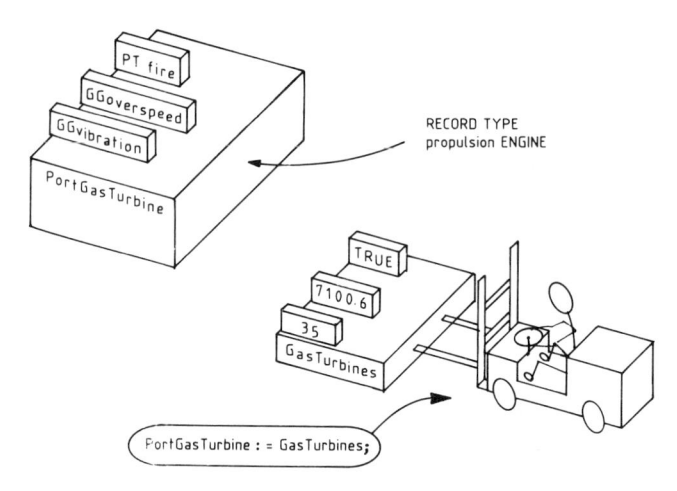

Fig. 8.9 Handling complete records

up the component values for these other records. Listing 8.2 illustrates this point.

Simplifying record processing – the WITH statement
Consider that we wish to set up all the individual elements in the record. We would be faced with writing out something like:

Records

```
MODULE Record1Test;
(*************************************************************)
(*          This is a demonstration showing how to manipulate  *)
(*          RECORDs as single units (or entities) - Listing 8.2 *)
(*************************************************************)
FROM InOut IMPORT WriteInt, WriteLn, WriteString, ReadInt;
TYPE
   PropulsionEngine = RECORD
                        GGoverspeed :REAL;
                        GGvibration, BearingTemp :INTEGER;
                      END;
VAR
   PortGasTurbine, StbdGasTurbine, GasTurbines :PropulsionEngine;
   Input :INTEGER;

BEGIN
   WriteString('Enter the Gas Turbine vibration trip level - mm ');
   ReadInt(Input); WriteLn;
   GasTurbines.GGvibration:= Input;
   WriteString('Enter the Gas Turbine bearing temp. trip level - Deg C');
   ReadInt(Input); WriteLn; WriteLn;
   GasTurbines.BearingTemp:= Input;

   PortGasTurbine:=GasTurbines; (* copying complete record *)
   StbdGasTurbine:=GasTurbines; (* copying again *)


   (* proving that the construct works *)
   WriteString('The Port Turbine vibration alarm trip level is ');
   WriteInt(PortGasTurbine.GGvibration, 3); WriteLn;
   WriteString('The Stbd Turbine vibration alarm trip level is ');
   WriteInt(StbdGasTurbine.GGvibration, 3); WriteLn; WriteLn;
   WriteString('The Port Turbine bearing temp. trip level is ');
   WriteInt(PortGasTurbine.BearingTemp, 4); WriteLn;
   WriteString('The Stbd Turbine bearing temp. trip level is ');
   WriteInt(StbdGasTurbine.BearingTemp, 4); WriteLn;
END Record1Test.
```

Listing 8.2

```
GasTurbines.GGoverspeed: = 7000.0;
GasTurbines.GGvibration := 100;
GasTurbines.BearingTemp:= 150;
```

Now this is a tedious process, especially when the records become complex. Help is at hand though, through the use of the 'WITH' statement of Modula-2. This allows us to write such statements in a shortened form. Those above, for instance, can be rewritten using a 'WITH clause', as follows:

```
WITH GasTurbines DO
   GGoverspeed:= 7000;
   GGvibration := 100;
   BearingTemp:= 150;
END;
```

Building complex records
Any record can itself be made up of other structured data types such as arrays and records, and also enumerated types. Further, we can form arrays

174 Structured data types – records and dynamic structures

of records (or, if you're feeling really masochistic, arrays of records which are themselves made up of structured types...). Let's look at a few examples, starting with a subrange type (Listing 8.3). Extending this to the use of arrays we get Listing 8.4.

A more complex structure still is given in Listing 8.5. Here two records are

```
////////////////////////////////////////////////////////////////////
TYPE
   RunningHours = [0..10000]; (* this is a subrange type *)
   EngineData = RECORD
                   Hours :RunningHours; (* constrained to the subrange *)
                END;
VAR
   Olympus :EngineData;

BEGIN
   Olympus.Hours:=2075;
   WriteString(' The Olympus running hours are ');
   WriteInt(Olympus.Hours, 5); WriteLn;
END Test.
////////////////////////////////////////////////////////////////////
```

Listing 8.3


```
MODULE Record2Test;
(*************************************************************)
(*           Using arrays in RECORDs - Listing 8.4            *)
(*************************************************************)
FROM InOut IMPORT WriteInt, WriteLn, WriteString, ReadInt;
TYPE
   RunningHours = [0..10000];
   ShipName = ARRAY [0..20] OF CHAR; (* here is the array declaration *)
   EngineData = RECORD
                   Hours :RunningHours;
                   Ship :ShipName;(* Ship now is an array type *)
                END;
VAR
   Olympus :EngineData;

BEGIN
   Olympus.Hours:=2075;
   Olympus.Ship:= 'Andromeda';
   WriteString(' The Olympus running hours are ');
   WriteInt(Olympus.Hours, 5); WriteLn;
   WriteString(' The engine is fitted to ');
   WriteString(Olympus.Ship); WriteLn;
END Record2Test.
```

When this is run the following is printed on the terminal screen;

The Olympus running hours are 2075
The engine is fitted to Andromeda

//

Listing 8.4

Records

```
MODULE TwoRecords;
(**************************************************************)
(*           A more complex RECORD example - Listing 8.5      *)
(**************************************************************)
FROM InOut IMPORT WriteInt, WriteLn, WriteString, ReadInt;
TYPE
   RunningHours = [0..10000];
   ShipName = ARRAY [0..20] OF CHAR;
   FuelName = ARRAY [0..10] OF CHAR;
   EngineData = RECORD  (* the first record *)
                   Fuel :FuelName;
                   Hours :RunningHours;
                END;
   PropulsionUnit = RECORD (* the second record *)
                   Ship :ShipName;
                   Engines :EngineData; (* a record type variable *)
                END;
VAR
   Olympus55 :PropulsionUnit;

BEGIN
   Olympus55.Engines.Hours:=2075; (* note the variable designator form *)
   Olympus55.Engines.Fuel:='Avtur';
   Olympus55.Ship:= 'Andromeda';
   WriteString(' The engine is fitted to ');
   WriteString(Olympus55.Ship); WriteLn;
   WriteString(' The running hours are ');
   WriteInt(Olympus55.Engines.Hours, 5); WriteLn;
   WriteString(' The fuel type is ');
   WriteString(Olympus55.Engines.Fuel); WriteLn;
END TwoRecords.

           When this program is executed, the following printout results;

The engine is fitted to Andromeda
The running hours are  2075
The fuel type is Avtur
```

Listing 8.5

declared. The first one, 'EngineData', contains two elements. The second 'Propulsion Unit', includes 'Engines' as one of its elements. This has the structure of the record 'Engine Data'. A variable, 'Olympus-55', is declared to be of type 'PropulsionUnit'. This results in the record structure of Fig. 8.10 for the variable 'Olympus55'. The method of element selection is shown in Fig. 8.11.

The next example here (Listing 8.6) includes an array of records; structurally it appears as in Fig. 8.12.

By nesting WITH statements, more compact code can be written, as shown in Listing 8.7.

To show the use of the array of records a modified version of the previous example is given in Listing 8.8. Two sets of engine records are set up, designated 55 and 56. A single statement set prints out the information contained within these records.

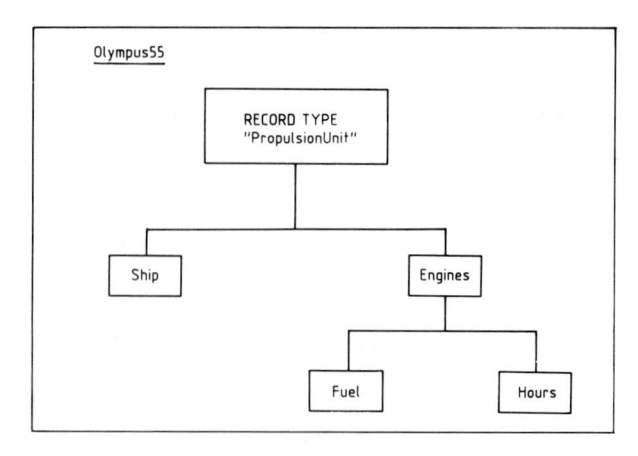

Fig. 8.10 Structure of the record variable 'Olympus55' (Listing 8.5)

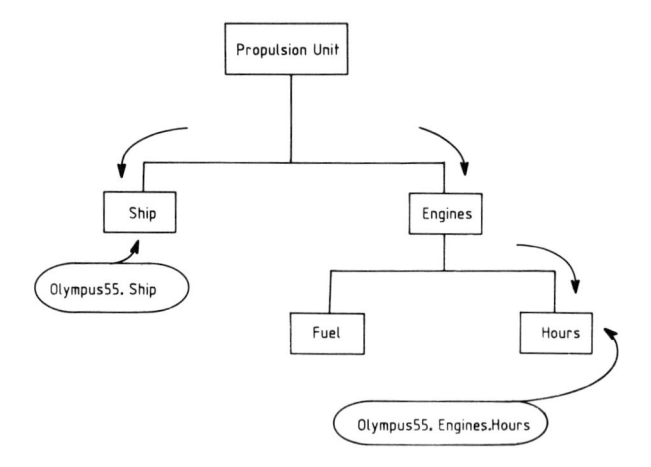

Fig. 8.11 Element selection in a complex record structure

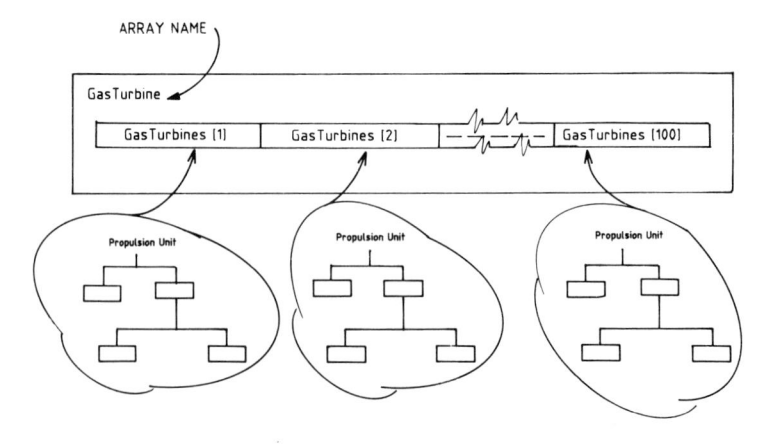

Fig. 8.12 Example – array or records (Listing 8.6)

```
MODULE Test;
(*********************************************************************)
(*           Using an array of RECORDs - Listing 8.6              *)
(*********************************************************************)
FROM InOut IMPORT WriteInt, WriteLn, WriteString, ReadInt;
TYPE
   RunningHours = [0..10000];
   Name = ARRAY [0..20] OF CHAR;
   EngineData = RECORD
                   SerialNo:Name;
                   Fuel :Name;
                   Hours :RunningHours;
               END;
   PropulsionUnit = RECORD
                       Ship :Name;
                       Engines :EngineData;
                    END;
VAR
   Olympus55 :PropulsionUnit;
   GasTurbine: ARRAY [1..100] OF PropulsionUnit; (* here is the Array of
                                                    of records           *)
BEGIN
   WITH Olympus55 DO
      Engines.SerialNo:= '55';
      Engines.Hours:=2075;
      Engines.Fuel:='Avtur';
      Ship:= 'Andromeda';
      GasTurbine[1]:=Olympus55;
      WriteString(' Maintenance Record ');
      WriteString('- Olympus Serial No.');
      WriteString(Engines.SerialNo); WriteLn; WriteLn;
      WriteString(' The engine is fitted to ');
      WriteString(Ship); WriteLn;
      WriteString(' The running hours are ');
      WriteInt(Engines.Hours, 5); WriteLn;
      WriteString(' The fuel type is   ');
      WriteString(Engines.Fuel); WriteLn;
   END; (* end of with *)
END Test.
```

                   LISTING 8.6

Running this program gives the following writeout on the terminal;

Maintainance Record - Olympus Serial No. 55

The engine is fitted to Andromeda
The running hours are 2075
The fuel type is Avtur

Listing 8.6

8.1.4 Variant records

Up to now we've considered records to have a fixed size, i.e. a fixed number of fields. In fact, Modula allows the structure to vary, giving rise to the 'variant record' construct. Suppose that we have set up a record to define the operational state of missile systems on a number of warships, as follows:

178 Structured data types – records and dynamic structures

```
MODULE Record3Test;
(*********************************************************************)
(*           Using the WITH construct in RECORDs                     *)
(*                      Listing 8.7                                  *)
(*********************************************************************)
FROM InOut IMPORT WriteInt, WriteLn, WriteString, ReadInt;
TYPE
    RunningHours = [0..10000];
    Name = ARRAY [0..20] OF CHAR;
    EngineData = RECORD
                    SerialNo:Name;
                    Fuel :Name;
                    Hours :RunningHours;
                 END;
    PropulsionUnit = RECORD
                        Ship :Name;
                        Engines :EngineData;
                     END;
VAR
    Olympus55, Olympus56 :PropulsionUnit;
    GasTurbine: ARRAY [1..100] OF PropulsionUnit;
    n :INTEGER;

BEGIN
    WITH Olympus55 DO
        WITH Engines DO
            SerialNo:= '55';
            Hours:=2075;
            Fuel:='Avtur';
            Ship:= 'Andromeda';
            GasTurbine[1]:=Olympus55;

            WriteString(' Maintenance Record ');
            WriteString('- Olympus Serial No.');
            WriteString(SerialNo); WriteLn; WriteLn;
            WriteString(' The engine is fitted to ');
            WriteString(Ship); WriteLn;
            WriteString(' The running hours are ');
            WriteInt(Hours, 5); WriteLn;
            WriteString(' The fuel type is   ');
            WriteString(Fuel); WriteLn;
        END; (* end of Engines with *)
    END; (* End of Olympus55 with *)
END Record3Test.
```

Listing 8.7

```
TYPE MissileSystem = RECORD
                Seadart :BOOLEAN;
                Seawolf :BOOLEAN;
                Ikara   :BOOLEAN;
                Seaslug :BOOLEAN;
             END;
```

We could go ahead and include these fields in every record, filling in the record as appropriate to the ships, Nottingham, Broadsword and Andromeda (Listing 8.9). What we have done is to create three records which are identical. However, we are only using certain fields within each record. The un-

```
MODULE Record4Test;
(*************************************************************)
(*          Using an array of RECORDs - another example      *)
(*                        Listing 8.8                        *)
(*************************************************************)
FROM InOut IMPORT WriteInt, WriteLn, WriteString, ReadInt;
TYPE
   RunningHours = [0..10000];
   Name = ARRAY [0..20] OF CHAR;
   EngineData = RECORD
                   SerialNo:Name;
                   Fuel :Name;
                   Hours :RunningHours;
                END;
   PropulsionUnit = RECORD
                       Ship :Name;
                       Engines :EngineData;
                    END;
VAR
   Olympus55, Olympus56 :PropulsionUnit;
   GasTurbine: ARRAY [1..100] OF PropulsionUnit;
   n :INTEGER;

BEGIN (* the first set of engine information *)
   WITH Olympus55 DO
      WITH Engines DO
         SerialNo:= '55';
         Hours:=2075;
         Fuel:='Avtur';
         Ship:= 'Andromeda';
      END; (* end of Engines with *)
   END; (* End of Olympus55 with *)
   GasTurbine[55]:=Olympus55;

   WITH Olympus56 DO (* the second set of engine information *)
      WITH Engines DO
         SerialNo:= '56';
         Hours:=1509;
         Fuel:='Avtur';
         Ship:= 'Nottingham';
      END; (* end of Engines with *)
   END; (* End of Olympus56 with *)
   GasTurbine[56]:=Olympus56;

   FOR n:=55 TO 56 DO (* this causes both records to be written out *)
      WITH GasTurbine[n] DO
         WITH Engines DO
            WriteString(' Maintenance Record ');
            WriteString('- Olympus Serial No.');
            WriteString(SerialNo); WriteLn; WriteLn;
            WriteString(' The engine is fitted to ');
            WriteString(Ship); WriteLn;
            WriteString(' The running hours are ');
            WriteInt(Hours, 5); WriteLn;
            WriteString(' The fuel type is   ');
            WriteString(Fuel); WriteLn; WriteLn; WriteLn;
         END; (* end of Engines with *)
      END; (* end of GasTurbine with *)
   END; (* end of Forloop *)
END Record4Test.
```

The following screen printout results when the program is run;

```
Maintainance Record - Olympus Serial No. 55

The engine is fitted to Andromeda
The running hours are 2075
The fuel type is Avtur



Maintainance Record - Olympus Serial No. 56

The engine is fitted to Nottingham
The running hours are 1509
The fuel type is Avtur
```

Listing 8.8

```
MODULE Record5Test;
(***********************************************************************)
(*          This demonstrates inefficency in the fixed            *)
(*          RECORD construct - Listing 8.9                        *)
(***********************************************************************)
FROM InOut IMPORT WriteInt, WriteLn, WriteString, ReadInt;
TYPE
   MissileSystem = RECORD
                      Seadart :BOOLEAN;
                      Seawolf :BOOLEAN;
                      Ikara   :BOOLEAN;
                      Seaslug :BOOLEAN;
                   END;
VAR
   Nottingham, Andromeda, Broadsword :MissileSystem;
CONST
   Operational = TRUE;
   NotOperational = FALSE;

BEGIN
   WITH Nottingham DO
      Seadart:=Operational;
   END;
   WITH Andromeda DO
      Seaslug:=Operational;
   END;
   WITH Broadsword DO
      Seawolf:=Operational;
      Ikara:=NotOperational;
   END;
END Record5Test.
```

Listing 8.9

used fields constistute wasted computer storage space. What we really want is a record structure that varies depending on its use (after all, it is highly unlikely that an individual ship will have all missile types fitted). In Modula this is provided by a record which has alternative parts, the 'variant record' structure. Using this we can vary the number of fields, and their type, for a record variable. We do not, note, declare a new record type.

In the record declaration we define the fields that are conditional by using the CASE statement. Taking the above example we write the record as follows:

```
TYPE
   ShipClass = (F21, F22, D42);
   MissileSystem = RECORD
                    CASE Class :ShipClass OF
                      D42 :Seadart :BOOLEAN;|
                      F22 :Seawolf, Ikara :BOOLEAN;|
                      F21 :Seaslug :BOOLEAN;
                    END;
                  END;
VAR
   Nottingham, Andromeda, Broadsword :MissileSystem;
```

Figure 8.13 shows the conceptual use of the selection process; Fig. 8.14

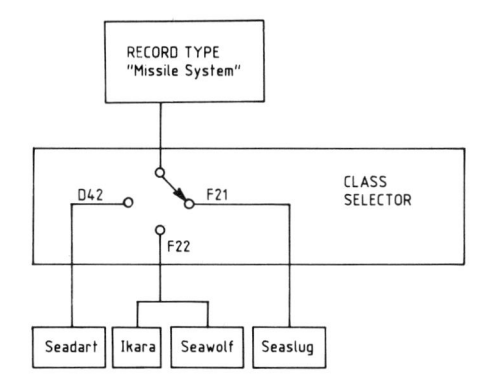

Fig. 8.13 Record with alternative parts

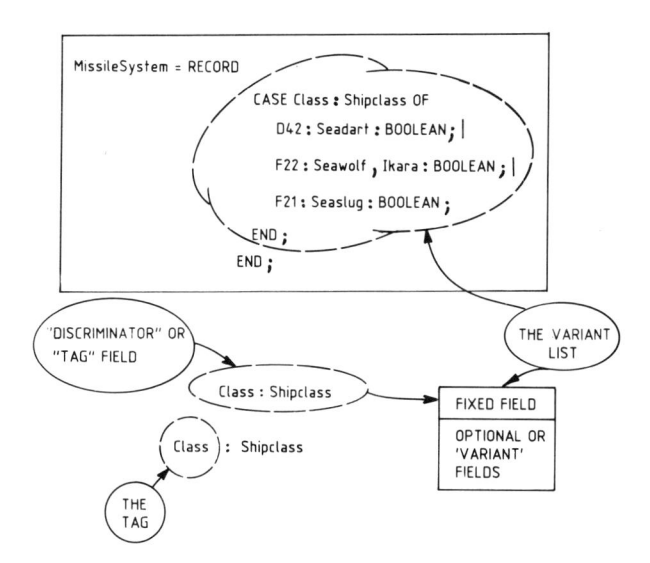

Fig. 8.14 Variant record structure

formally describes the variant record structure in more detail. The field 'Class :ShipClass' is called the 'discriminator' or 'tag' field; 'Class' is defined as the 'discriminator identifier' or 'tag'. This is a non-variant field. Following the CASE clause is the variant field list sequence, being composed of three fields. Note the use of the vertical bar separator. Each field is associated with a specific value of the tag. For instance, when the value D42 is assigned to 'Class' only the field labelled with D42 (Seadart) is selected.

Well, how does this work in practice? Suppose we set up a record for the variable 'Nottingham'. In doing this we must assign a value to the tag identifier; here we'll use D42, as follows:

Nottingham.Class:=D42;

Once we've done this only the field named 'Seadart' is associated with the record for Nottingham.

As an example of the use of variant records, lets modify the previous program to that of Listing 8.10.

```
MODULE Record6Test;
(*********************************************************************)
(*          This is a demonstration of the use of                    *)
(*          Variant Records - Listing 8.10                           *)
(*********************************************************************)
FROM InOut IMPORT WriteInt, WriteLn, WriteString, ReadInt;
TYPE
    ShipClass = (F21, F22, D42);
    MissileSystem = RECORD
                    CASE Class :ShipClass OF
                        D42 :Seadart :BOOLEAN;
                        F22 :Seawolf, Ikara :BOOLEAN;
                        F21 :Seaslug :BOOLEAN;
                        END;
                    END;
VAR
    Nottingham, Andromeda, Broadsword :MissileSystem;
CONST
    Operational = TRUE;
    NotOperational = FALSE;

BEGIN
    Nottingham.Class:=D42; (* setting the Nottingham record tag to D42 *)
    Andromeda.Class:=F21;  (* setting the Andromeda record tag to D42 *)
    Broadsword.Class:=F22; (* setting the Broadsword record tag to F22 *)
    WITH Nottingham DO
        Seadart:=Operational;
    END; (* end of with *)
    WITH Andromeda DO
        Seaslug:=Operational;
    END; (* end of with *)
    WITH Broadsword DO
        Seawolf:=Operational;
        Ikara:=NotOperational;
    END; (* end of with *)
END Record6Test.
```

Listing 8.10

Q8.1 What is the fundamental difference between types such as INTEGER, REAL, etc. and arrays, records and sets?

Variables declared to be a record type having variant parts may cause us trouble. After all, the compiler will treat them as being type compatible; yet they actually may differ in their structure because the variant parts are used differently. Such a situation may easily lead to programming errors; Wirth himself states that it should be used with great caution.

8.2 Dynamic data structures

8.2.1 Introduction

Let's just have another look at how we store and access data in our system. In simple terms we can visualise data storage locations as being much the same as a set of 'pigeon holes' for letters (Fig. 8.15). Each hole has a unique identifier number or 'address'. By using this address we can obtain the information contained within the hole. Only one item of information is held within each location. Therefore, for one of our earlier specimen programs ('CalcAcceleration') we might well have the situation shown in Fig. 8.16. Here the first data item is Xnew, the next Xold, and so on. To get the value contained within the first 'box' we only need to refer to the item by its name, actual addressing being handled by the compiler.

What we have here is a 'static' data storage structure, i.e. the data store size is fixed. By defining our system data we also define the amount of memory space needed to support it. Implicit is the assumption that we'll always know how much storage is needed when the program runs. Do we, though? Consider the requirement to monitor production line machinery, maintaining a log of equipment status. We would like to know which systems are running, those defective, those shut down, etc. This is going to be a dynamic log; after all, in the real world, equipment states continually change. Therefore we cannot say exactly how much data storage is needed

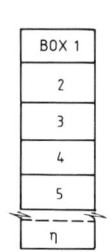

BOX No.	CONTENTS	
BOX 20	X new (INTEGER)	← VARIABLE
BOX 21	X old (I)	← VARIABLE
BOX 22	Y new (I)	← VARIABLE
BOX 23	Y old (I)	← VARIABLE
BOX 24	ACCEL [1]	⎫
BOX 25	ACCEL [2]	⎬ ARRAY "ACCEL"
BOX 26	ACCEL [3]	⎭

Fig. 8.15 Data storage – concept

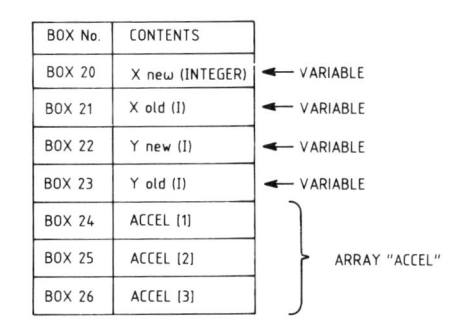

Fig. 8.16 Static data storage

184 Structured data types – records and dynamic structures

at any one instant. This presents us with a problem if our data structures are fixed. The data store must be large enough to cope with the worst case situation, i.e. a maximum amount of data needing to be stored. And yet most of the time we won't actually have a full set of data; hence we end up wasting memory space.

Looking at a totally different aspect of the problem, suppose we are asked to generate a maintenance log for the machinery. This should show when maintenance is required, and its nature. Now, not only will this be dynamic (we can't predict when equipment will fail) but the order of items within the log will change. Certain items must be given high priority, even if they've just arrived in the log (the managing director's PC being No.1 on the list). So here we have to store data which not only changes its size but is also subject to constant reorganisation.

It is in response to such needs that 'dynamic data structures' have been devised. Their main use is for handling large quantities of information; sensibly then, we have to be talking about structured as opposed to simple data types.

8.2.2 Dynamic variables and pointers

From a practical point of view our store size cannot be infinite. After all, there's only a certain amount of memory available in our computers. But, within this constraint, we can use it to its maximum if each and every memory location is available for use. Hence the first 'must' for a dynamic data structure is that it can use storage locations wherever they happen to be available. Such a case is shown in Fig. 8.17. Here the items belonging to the maintenance log are located as shown, using memory storage as and when available. From this it can be seen that its size can be changed to meet differing situations.

Fine. But it does raise some interesting questions. As the amount of data changes how do we add and delete information? Further, how do we find individual elements (called 'nodes') within the structure? These are funda-

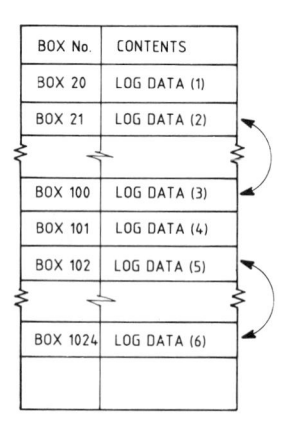

BOX No.	CONTENTS
BOX 20	LOG DATA (1)
BOX 21	LOG DATA (2)
BOX 100	LOG DATA (3)
BOX 101	LOG DATA (4)
BOX 102	LOG DATA (5)
BOX 1024	LOG DATA (6)

Fig. 8.17 Dynamic data structure – basic concept

mental points, requiring an efficient solution to minimise store requirements. The answers define the nature of dynamic data structures. In practice this has led to the use of sequential data storage techniques for dealing with dynamic variables. Note, however, that this doesn't restrict the data types which can be used as dynamic variables.

Figure 8.18 is a redrawn version of Fig. 8.17, defined as a linked list. Each element or node now holds two pieces of information. The first is the data itself, the second being the address of the next node in the list. This address is called a 'pointer'. We access data through the use of the pointer, not by name. Two final pieces of information are still needed, the start and the finish of the list. The first item added to a list automatically defines the start; the last needs to be identified as such. This is done by pointing to nothing, the so-called 'nil' pointer.

Dynamic variables are not generated by the compiler. They come into being as a result of program execution. In such a situation it is natural that the number of variables produced will vary from time to time, including the case where none are present. This underlines the fact that we only have as many variables as are actually needed at that time.

When the program runs there are really only three actions which we want to carry out on the data structure:

- Add variables
- Delete variables
- Manipulate variables

Specific statements are used to add and delete variables, as shown later. However, the technique for accessing variables is conceptually quite different to those described earlier; we do it through the use of pointers, and not names. Remember, variables stored within a dynamic structure do not have individual names, only data values and locations.

8.2.3 Working with dynamic variables

The starting point here is to look at the declarations which must be made before working with dynamic variables. In the first case we need to define

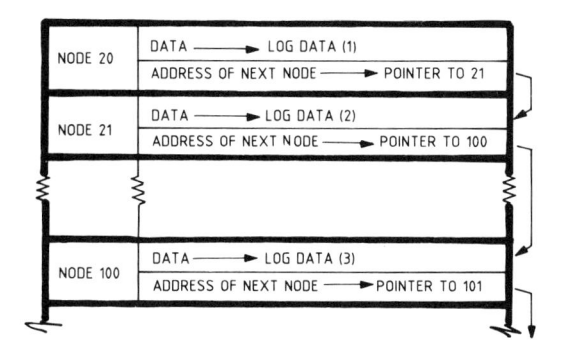

Fig. 8.18 Linked list construct

various pointer types; then for each one we must specify which variable type a pointer points to. It is then 'bound' to that particular data type and cannot point to any other. Generally,

   TYPE NodePointer = POINTER TO Node;

Example:

   TYPE LogPointer = POINTER TO RunningHours;

In the example, the pointer type 'LogPointer' is bound to data objects of the type RunningHours. Extending this we have:

TYPE
   RunningHours = [0..9000];
   LogPointer = POINTER TO RunningHours;
VAR
   Log :LogPointer;

Thus, 'log' is of type 'LogPointer', this being bound to 'RunningHours'. To create a new node of type RunningHours we write

   NEW(Log)

This statement causes memory space to be reserved for RunningHours. The value of Log is the address of this storage area. Now this node has no name and can only be accessed using its address. This is done by 'dereferencing' the pointer, written as

   Log^

which is interpreted as 'the item whose address is held in Log'. We can use it in the following way;

   Log^:=Hours;

This will allocate the value held in 'Hours' to 'RunningHours', the latter being defined as an 'anonymous' variable (anonymous because you cannot access RunningHours by using its name).

To delete a node from the structure the following statement is used:

   DISPOSE(Log)

Both NEW and DISPOSE are standard functions supplied with Modula. However, to use these, procedures ALLOCATE and DEALLOCATE must be imported into the client module.

Listing 8.11 is a very simple example of the use of pointers.

Figure 8.19 shows what happens as we progress through the program. It also demonstrates clearly the difference between static and dynamic variables. It should also be clear that Log is a POINTER TO a dynamic variable (of type 'RunningHours'); it is not itself the variable.

The above example has been produced to show the basics of pointer operations and dynamic variables. Normally the data structures involved

Dynamic data structures   **187**

```
MODULE DynamicVar;
(*********************************************************************)
(*          This is an ultra-simple demonstration of the use of      *)
(*          Dynamic Variables and Pointers - Listing 8.11            *)
(*********************************************************************)
FROM InOut IMPORT WriteInt, WriteLn, WriteString, ReadInt;
FROM Storage IMPORT ALLOCATE, DEALLOCATE;
TYPE
    RunningHours = [0..9000];
    LogPointer = POINTER TO RunningHours;
VAR
    Log :LogPointer;
    Y, Hours :INTEGER;

BEGIN
(*A*)    Hours:=0;
        Y:=0;
(*B*)    NEW(Log);
        WriteString('enter running hours'); WriteLn;
(*C*)    ReadInt(Hours); WriteLn;
(*D*)    Log^:=Hours;
(*E*)    Y:=Log^;
        WriteString('you entered ');
        WriteInt(Y,5);
(*F*)    DISPOSE(Log);
END DynamicVar.
```

Listing 8.11

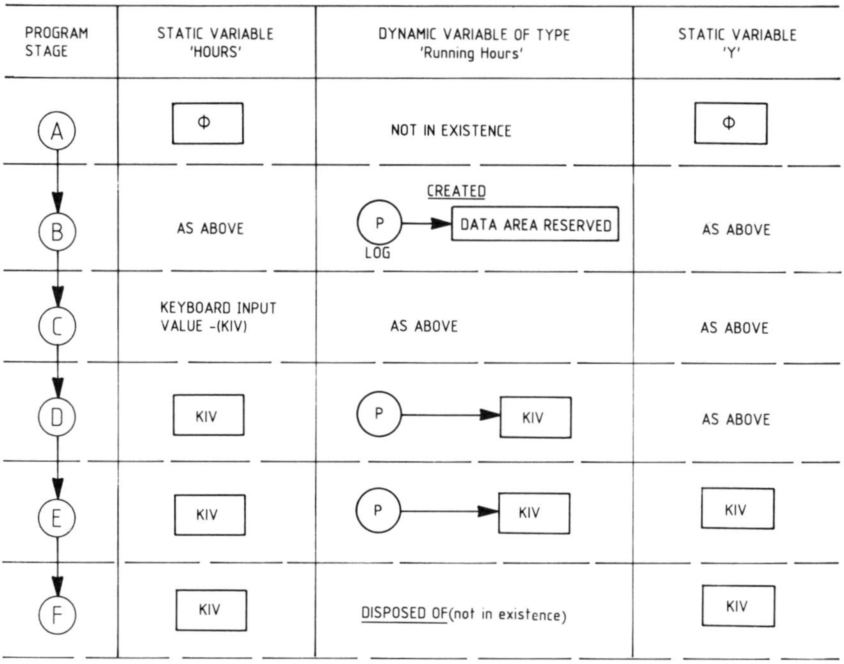

PROGRAM STAGE	STATIC VARIABLE 'HOURS'	DYNAMIC VARIABLE OF TYPE 'Running Hours'	STATIC VARIABLE 'Y'
A	ϕ	NOT IN EXISTENCE	ϕ
B	AS ABOVE	CREATED P(LOG) → DATA AREA RESERVED	AS ABOVE
C	KEYBOARD INPUT VALUE -(KIV)	AS ABOVE	AS ABOVE
D	KIV	P → KIV	AS ABOVE
E	KIV	P → KIV	KIV
F	KIV	DISPOSED OF (not in existence)	KIV

Fig. 8.19 Operating with static and dynamic variables

188 Structured data types – records and dynamic structures

```
MODULE Dynamic2Var;
(***********************************************************************)
(* This is a further demonstration of the use of Dynamic                *)
(* Variables, involving the record structure - Listing 8.12             *)
(***********************************************************************)
FROM InOut IMPORT WriteInt, WriteLn, WriteString, ReadInt;
FROM Storage IMPORT ALLOCATE, DEALLOCATE;
TYPE
   Text = ARRAY[0..20] OF CHAR;
   LogPointer = POINTER TO LogList;
   LogList = RECORD
               RunningHours :INTEGER;
               LastService: Text;
               FuelConsumption: REAL;
            END;
VAR
   Log :LogPointer;
   Y, Hours :INTEGER;

BEGIN
   NEW(Log);
   WriteString('enter running hours'); WriteLn;
   ReadInt(Hours); WriteLn;
   Log^.RunningHours:=Hours;
   Y:=Log^.RunningHours;
   WriteString('you entered ');
   WriteInt(Y,5);
END Dynamic2Var.
```

Listing 8.12

are much larger, typically being records. The program of Listing 8.12 shows the use of the record structure in such an application.

Q8.2 When the above example was compiled it required 197 bytes of code and 8 bytes of data. After an additional pointer, 'Log2', was introduced the code size remained the same but the data size increased to 12 bytes. Now an extra variable, 'SerialNo:INTEGER', was added to the record structure. It was found that both the code and data sizes were unchanged. Explain this.

At this stage let's review the basic operations involved when using pointers. First, pointers need to be brought into existence (Fig. 8.20); then data storage space can be established (Fig. 8.21). Only now can data be

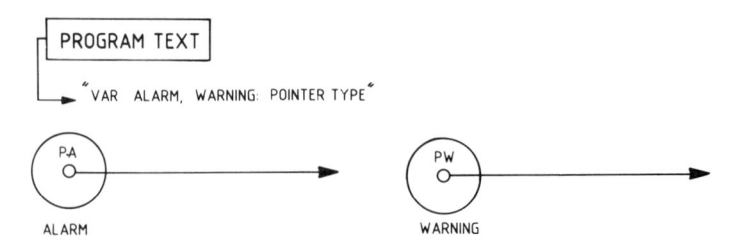

Fig. 8.20 Defining the existence of pointers

Dynamic data structures **189**

loaded into this space (Fig. 8.22). We can manipulate data and pointers as shown in Figs. 8.23 and 8.24, finally disposing of the data space when it is no longer required (Fig. 8.25). We can also define that a pointer does *not* point to an object (Fig. 8.26). This feature is used to establish the end of a linked set of data stores.

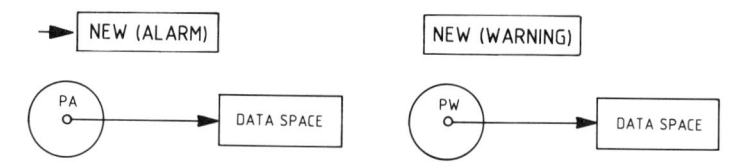

Fig. 8.21 Creating data storage space

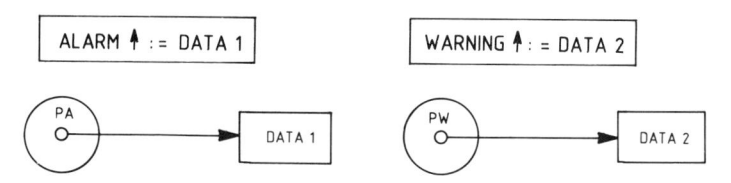

Fig. 8.22 Putting data into the data stores

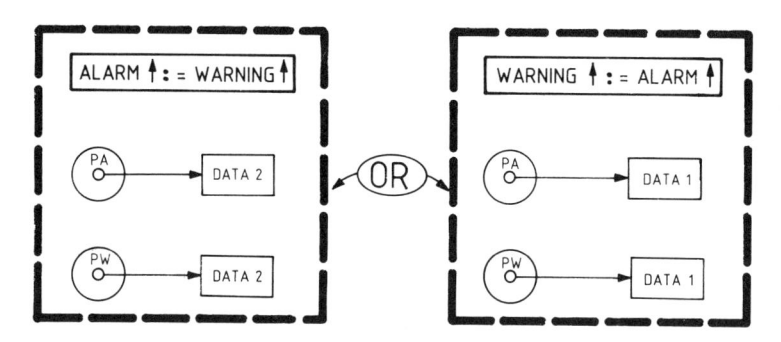

Fig. 8.23 Moving data around

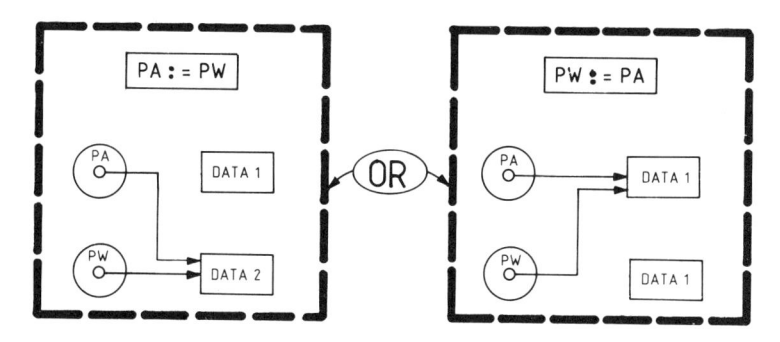

Fig. 8.24 Changing pointer values

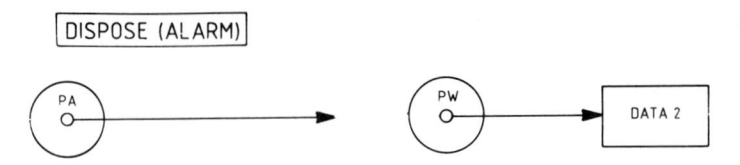

Fig. 8.25 Disposing of storage space

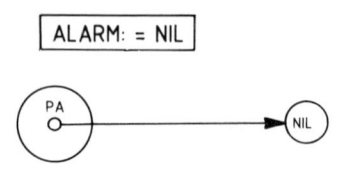

Fig. 8.26 Pointing the pointer to no object

8.2.4 Linking data items

So far we've successfully managed to create a store space for a data item, put data into the store, and finally dispose of the space. Good. But that is only the first step. What we want to do is to form a dynamically varying data space which consists of a whole grouping of store locations, as illustrated in Fig. 8.17. What is missing in the present arrangement is the pointer carried with each data item, used for pointing to the next item in the list. This is demonstrated in the following example, 'Dynamic3Var'. Before going through this, one important point needs to be looked at. We establish a pointer within the data item by using the following type declaration.

```
TYPE
   LogPointer = POINTER TO LogList;
   LogList = RECORD
            LastDataStore: LogPointer;
         END;
```

We've already said that a pointer type is bound to one specific node data type and cannot point to any other. Now the pointer carried within the data structure points to the next store location. But the next data item is exactly the same type as the current one; therefore all pointer types must be the same. This explains the reason for the declaration form used above. Unfortunately, no matter whether we first declare LogPointer followed by LogList or else reverse the declaration order, we always end up with a forward reference. For instance, as shown, LogPointer refers to LogList before LogList is declared. This is the only case in Modula where forward referencing can be made.

Listing 8.13 shows the creation and use of two data stores. It is straight-

```
MODULE Dynamic3Var;
(*******************************************************************)
(*           This is a demonstration of linking                     *)
(*           Dynamic Variables together - Listing 8.13              *)
(*******************************************************************)
FROM InOut IMPORT WriteInt, WriteLn, WriteString, ReadInt, ReadString;
FROM Storage IMPORT ALLOCATE, DEALLOCATE;
TYPE
   Message = ARRAY [1..30] OF CHAR;
   LogPointer = POINTER TO LogList;
   LogList = RECORD
                ServicePriority:INTEGER;
                Machine :Message;
                LastDataStore : LogPointer;
             END;

VAR
   HeadOfList, Log :LogPointer;
BEGIN
   HeadOfList:=NIL;
   NEW(Log);
   WriteString('Enter Machine Description'); WriteLn;
   ReadString(Log^.Machine); WriteLn;
   WriteString('enter service priority'); WriteLn;
   ReadInt(Log^.ServicePriority); WriteLn; WriteLn;
   Log^.LastDataStore:= HeadOfList;
   HeadOfList:=Log;

   NEW(Log);
   WriteString('Enter Machine Description'); WriteLn;
   ReadString(Log^.Machine); WriteLn;
   WriteString('enter service priority'); WriteLn;
   ReadInt(Log^.ServicePriority); WriteLn; WriteLn;
   Log^.LastDataStore:= HeadOfList;
   HeadOfList:=Log;

   WriteString('The last machine was ');
   WriteString(HeadOfList^.Machine); WriteLn;
   WriteString('Its priority is ');
   WriteInt(HeadOfList^.ServicePriority, 2); WriteLn;

   Log:=Log^.LastDataStore;
   WriteString('The first entry was ');
   WriteString(Log^.Machine); WriteLn;
   WriteString('Its priority is ');
   WriteInt(Log^.ServicePriority, 2); WriteLn;

END Dynamic3Var.
```

Listing 8.13

forward but has been written out explicitly so that the reader can follow the sequence of events. These are further depicted graphically in Fig. 8.27.

8.2.5 Last-in first-out list

The example given in Listing 8.14:

- takes in data from the keyboard;
- dynamically allocates storage for each entry;

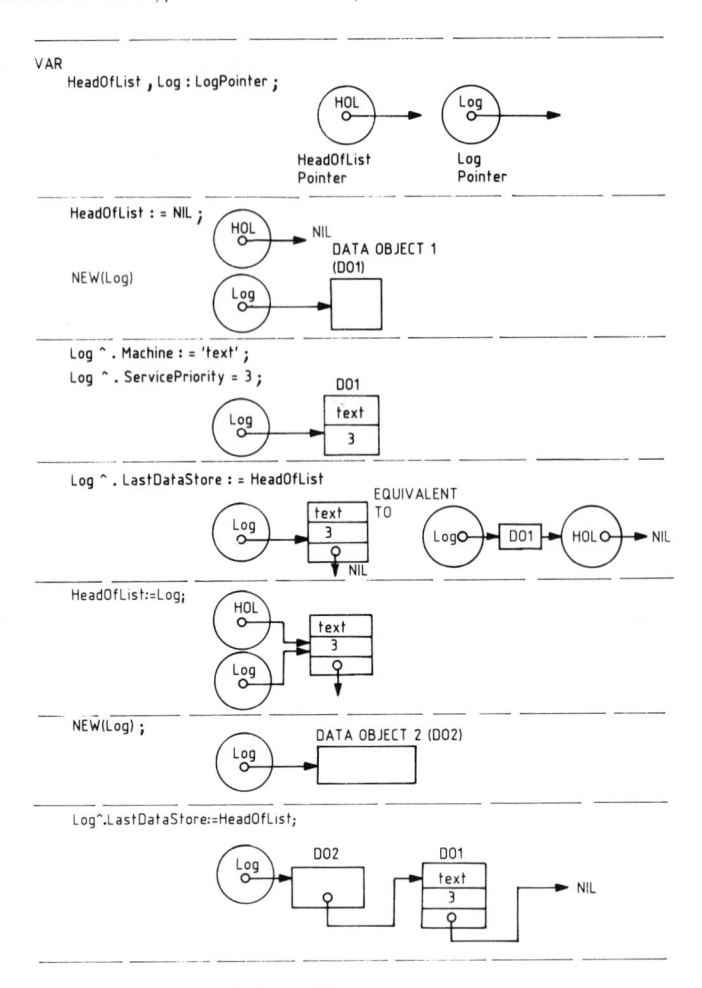

192 Structured data types – records and dynamic structures

Fig. 8.27 Linking data items (Listing 8.13)

- appends each new entry to the data list;
- links this to the previous data store location;
- terminates data entry when 0 is entered as the service priority;
- writes out the stored information, with the last entry shown first; and
- deletes each data node when the information has been retrieved.

This is the action of a 'last-in first-out' (LIFO) data store (also known as a first-in last-out (FILO) store).

8.2.6 Implications for engineering design

By now it should be clear that dynamic data structures are really useful (or necessary) for handling large amounts of data. Engineering tasks of this size

Dynamic data structures

```
MODULE Dynamic4Var;
(****************************************************************)
(*                                                              *)
(*         This is a further demonstration of the use of        *)
(*              Dynamic Variables - listing 8.14                *)
(****************************************************************)
FROM InOut IMPORT WriteInt, WriteLn, WriteString, ReadInt, ReadString;
FROM Storage IMPORT ALLOCATE, DEALLOCATE;
TYPE
   Message = ARRAY [1..30] OF CHAR;
   LogPointer = POINTER TO LogList;
   LogList = RECORD
                EntryNumber :INTEGER;
                ServicePriority:INTEGER;
                Machine :Message;
                LastDataStore : LogPointer;
             END;
VAR
   HeadOfList, Log, Temp :LogPointer;
   N, Priority :INTEGER;

BEGIN
   HeadOfList:=NIL;
   WriteString('enter service priority'); WriteLn;
   ReadInt(Priority); WriteLn;
   N:=0;

   WHILE Priority <> 0 DO
      INC (N);
      NEW(Log);
      WriteString('Enter Machine Description'); WriteLn;
      ReadString(Log^.Machine); WriteLn; WriteLn;
      Log^.ServicePriority:= Priority;
      Log^.LastDataStore:= HeadOfList;
      Log^.EntryNumber:=N;
      HeadOfList:=Log;
      WriteString('enter service priority'); WriteLn;
      ReadInt(Priority); WriteLn;
   END; (* end of while *)

   REPEAT
      WriteString('entry No.');
      WriteInt(Log^.EntryNumber,3); WriteString(' - ');
      WriteString(Log^.Machine); WriteLn;
      WriteString('Its priority is ');
      WriteInt(Log^.ServicePriority, 2); WriteLn; WriteLn;
      Temp:=Log^.LastDataStore;
      DISPOSE(Log);
      Log:=Temp;
      DEC(N);
   UNTIL N = 0;
END Dynamic4Var.
```

Listing 8.14

are likely to be programmed by software engineers or the like. In contrast, most problems tackled by individual engineers are on a much smaller scale. For that reason the description of dynamic data structures will stop right here. Further information can be found in Knepley and Platt (1985) (a good, well-written introduction to the topic), Beidler and Jackowitz (1986) (for a more detailed treatment) and Sincovec and Wiener (1986) (for an advanced view of the subject).

More importantly, the use of dynamic data structures raises questions concerning program reliability. Three particular points need to be considered:

- The use of pointers.
- Confusion between pointers and objects which are referred to by pointers.
- The need to dispose of dynamic data objects.

These are discussed in detail by Young (1982).

In general purpose computing, program failures aren't usually catastrophic. The same is not true for real-time engineering applications. Software errors may well produce dangerous situations, sometimes leading to injury or death. For such applications dynamic data structures should be used with great care (if at all).

8.3 Opaque types

This is yet another item which appears to be out of place. Types, after all, have been considered in Chapter 5. But this subject involves definition module export declarations; perhaps it should have come in Chapter 6? However, the real reason for waiting until now is that opaque exports are restricted to pointers; moreover they only concern data types which are made up of component parts. In general this appears to be used only with the record structure.

Suppose that we have the following declaration in a definition module:

TYPE
   PropulsionEngine = RECORD
                        PTfire :BOOLEAN;
                        GGoverspeed :REAL;
                        GGvibration :INTEGER;
                      END;

then the importing module has access and control of all elements within the record structure (nothing new here). This is called a 'transparent export'. There are situations where this may be undesirable. In such cases the following type export declaration can be made:

TYPE
   PropulsionEngine;

This is followed up by a full declaration of the type within the implementation module.

This is defined to be an 'opaque export', the corresponding type being referred to as an 'opaque' type. When this type is imported into a client module the record can be handled only as a complete entity. No access can be made to the component parts. Consequently, in the client module, all we can do is to declare variables as belonging to this type and carry out assignment statements.

Review

At this point you should:

- Understand the concept and use of the record data structure.
- Be able to work with record contents either as complete entities or as individual elements.
- Understand and use variant records.
- Understand the concepts of dynamic data structures.
- Understand the concept and use of pointers.
- Understand how to construct a simple last-in first-out file.
- Appreciate that dynamic data structures are potential sources of software unreliability.

Chapter 9

Accessing processor hardware

Everything that has been covered so far is standard to Modula-2. Different compilers may have different library features but, once this is allowed for, any program should run on any computer system. Now, just stop for a moment and consider this point. Why should this be the case? The answer is that our computer comes with an operating system which provides an interface between the Modula-2 software and system features. So when we insert a program statement such as 'WriteString...', the operating system is responsible for printing out screen information at program run time. To us, the user, the operation is automatic and unseen, i.e. 'transparent'. But what do we do when we need to use a feature which is non-standard as far as the operating system is concerned? Or what if we are working with a bare board in a target (embedded) system environment? In both cases the only way to achieve our goals is to interact with the system at the chip level. Can this be done in Modula-2? Generally, yes, although we may not write all the source code in the Modula-2 language itself.

This chapter sets out to show:

- Why we need to access device (chip) hardware.
- What access features are needed.
- How Modula-2 supports operations of this type.
- How these are used in a specific target system.

9.1 Introduction – the need for device access

Do we need to manipulate hardware at the chip level? Well, if our software is destined to run on a standard operating system, and the system is already installed on our machine, then we don't. In such cases control of the computer devices is done by 'systems software', our own programs being defined as 'applications software' (Fig. 9.1).

Unfortunately for the engineer, many computer-based real-time engineering functions don't use standard operating systems. Software tends to be tailor-made for the task in hand, with little or no distinction between sys-

Introduction – the need for device access 197

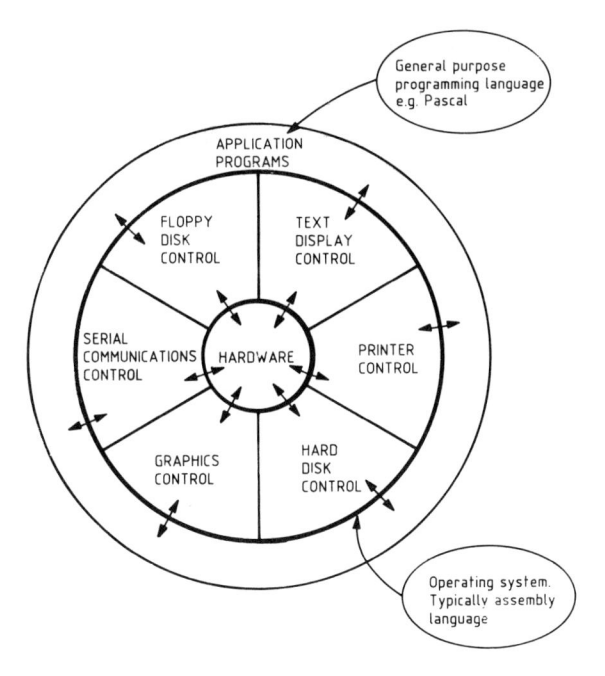

Fig. 9.1 General purpose machine – hardward/software structure

tems and applications software. In fact, software in smaller embedded systems is considered to be 'applications' only, interacting directly with the computer hardware (Fig. 9.2). Systems like these are many and diverse, ranging from aircraft flight controllers to microwave ovens; hence the need for unique, as opposed to general purpose, software.

Adapting hardware behaviour to meet varying requirements is not restricted just to embedded schemes. The systems programmer, for instance, faces similar problems when installing operating systems on new or modified hardware.

A second set of problems arises when dealing with designs which use different processors. A brief comparison is given in Table 9.1 of the Intel

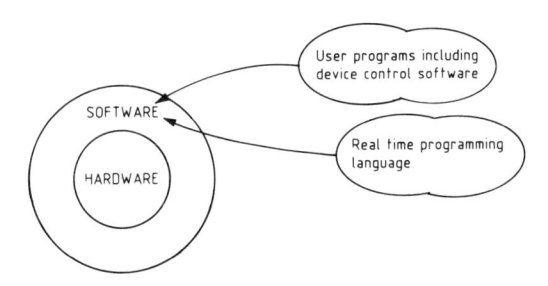

Fig. 9.2 Embedded real-time computer – hardware/software structure

Table 9.1 Outline comparison – Intel 8085 vs. 8086

	8085	8086
Address range	64 kbyte	1 Mbyte
Data word size	8 bits	16 bits
Serial I/O	Yes	No
Vectored hardware interrupts	4	1
Software interrupts	No	Yes

8085 and 8086 microprocessor; this shows just how much variation can be found, even in devices from the same manufacturer. From this it is clear that operating systems have to be adaptable if they're ever going to work on different processors. Even when the processor is fixed, designs will still differ concerning:

- Use of memory space for code, data and stack
- Amount of code in read-only store
- Amount of read/write store
- Special store provisions, such as non-volatile devices
- Address locations of these devices
- Location, size and activating methods for interrupt driven programs

So, software engineers who wish to venture beyond the comfortable confines of applications programming have to get involved in hardware manipulation.

9.2 Facilities needed to access devices

9.2.1 General comments

Before looking at what Modula-2 offers, let's define what we *do* need for the access and control of computer hardware. Our requirements can be grouped roughly into five areas:

- Memory accesses, for the control of code, data and stack operations.
- Interrupt handling.
- Peripheral device interfacing and control.
- Support of special machine operations, as in I/O mapping methods in Intel processors.
- Software aspects relating to these and other requirements.

9.2.2 Memory operations

This is of particular interest to the embedded (usually microprocessor-based) systems designer (Fig. 9.3). In such applications non-volatile storage

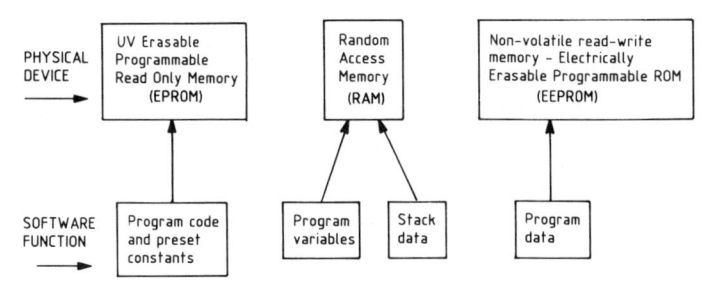

Fig. 9.3 Memory devices – use in microprocessor systems

is used for the program code. Almost always this is programmed into UV Erasable Programmable Read Only Memory (EPROM) integrated circuit devices. Data (i.e. program variables) are held in read/write store, normally Random Access Memory (RAM). Some applications call for the use of non-volatile read/write data stores, this function being performed by battery-backed RAM or Electrically Erasable Programmable ROM (EEPROM). The stack, being a read/write data store, must be located in RAM.

These physical devices are mapped into the processor address space, their locations being determined mainly by processor characteristics. For instance, EPROM must be mapped at the bottom of memory in the Z80 (Fig. 9.4). This comes about because, on power-up, program execution begins at location 0000H. The 8086, however, restarts with its instruction pointer pointing to location FFFF0H; hence EPROM must be located at the top of memory in this instance. Thus the software engineer must take into account the mapping scheme in use when compiling the program (as it's rather difficult to write information into EPROM).

In other cases it may be that we want to handle information which resides in specific memory locations (absolute addresses). This is, for instance, one way of communicating between devices, the so-called 'shared memory' method (Fig. 9.5). Here we need to be able to specify precisely the addresses of the memory locations we're reading to or writing from.

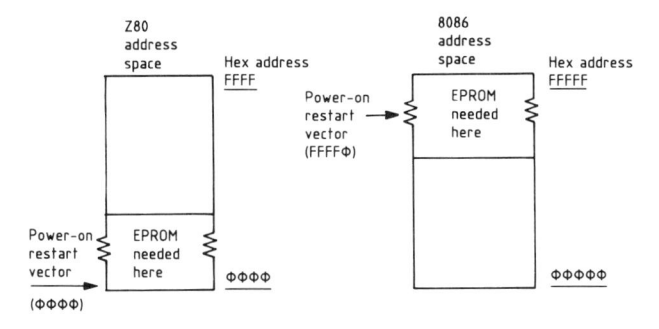

Fig. 9.4 Mapping of memory devices

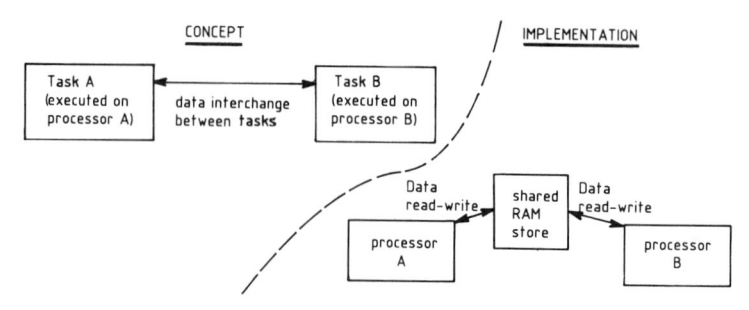

Fig. 9.5 Use of shared memory

9.2.3 Management of peripheral devices

Virtually everything except processor and memory devices come into this category. Included are items such as programmable timers, interrupt controllers, serial I/O controllers, maths chips, analogue-to-digital converters, etc.; the list is immense. Generally, though, they have three factors in common:

- They are mapped at specific absolute addresses.
- Both read and write operations are performed on them.
- Individual bits within a data word have specific meanings.

Where peripherals are mapped into memory then, to the processor, they look like RAM. Thus the first two points need no further discussion. However, bit management is a different matter. We need this facility for two main reasons, both associated with programmable devices or processor subsystems. In the first case we may want to establish the status of the device being accessed; in the second we may wish to change its operational mode. Both status and control information is handled using word (in smaller systems, byte) data transfers. For such applications the information carried by the word is set by individual bits within the word. As an example, Fig. 9.6 shows the make-up of two registers from a Signetics serial communications controller. From this it is obvious that, when interacting with peripherals, we must be able to examine and modify data words bit by bit. And, for the sake of clarity and reliability, it is better to do this using high-level language statements.

9.2.4 Interrupt handling

Interrupts have three main roles. First, they enable us to guarantee to meet stringent timing requirements of programs. This is a common aspect of closed-loop control systems. Second, they simplify the implementation of multi-tasking or handling processor – I/O interaction as asynchronous operations. Finally, they can get us out of dangerous situations, such as loss of program control, dividing by zero, etc. Different processors use different

STATUS REGISTER							
BIT7	BIT6	BIT5	BIT4	BIT3	BIT2	BIT1	BIT0
RECEIVED BREAK	FRAMING ERROR	PARITY ERROR	OVERRUN ERROR	TxEMT	TxRDY	FFULL	RxRDY
0 = no 1 = yes	0 = no 1 = yes	0 = no 1 = yes	0 = no 1 = yes	0 = no 1 = yes	0 = no 1 = yes	0 = no 1 = yes	0 = no 1 = yes

CONTROL REGISTER						
BIT7	BIT6	BIT5	BIT4 BIT3	BIT2	BIT1 BIT0
RX RTS CONTROL	RX INT SELECT	ERROR MODE	PARITY MODE	PARITY TYPE	BITS PER CHAR
0 = no 1 = yes	0 = RXRDY 1 = FFULL	0 = char 1 = block	00 = with parity 01 = force parity 10 = no parity 11 = multi-drop mode	0 = no 1 = yes	00 = 5 01 = 6 10 = 7 11 = 8

Fig. 9.6 Interacting with peripherals – status and control features

hardware/software interrupt control methods. But no matter how these are actually implemented, we always end up using absolute addressing methods. Typically, we locate the interrupt program at a defined absolute address in memory; the processor is then 'vectored' to this address when the interrupt is activated (Fig. 9.7). Alternatively, the compiler fixes the program location; we then 'plant' the necessary reference to this at an absolutely defined address in the interrupt vector area. When an interrupt occurs, program control is initially transferred to the appropriate location in the vector area (Fig. 9.8). The program residing here is usually quite short; normally it performs limited housekeeping functions and then transfers program execution to its interrupt program.

Variations of these exist, of course.

9.2.5 Special machine operations

Occasionally processors provide facilities which are unique to their design. For instance, on Intel processors, data can be transferred quickly and effi-

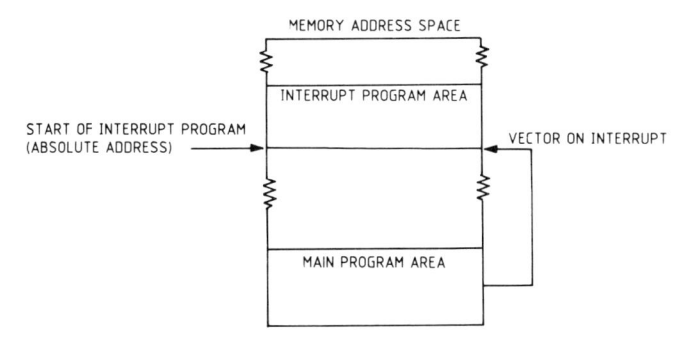

Fig. 9.7 Interrupt operation – 1

202 Accessing processor hardware

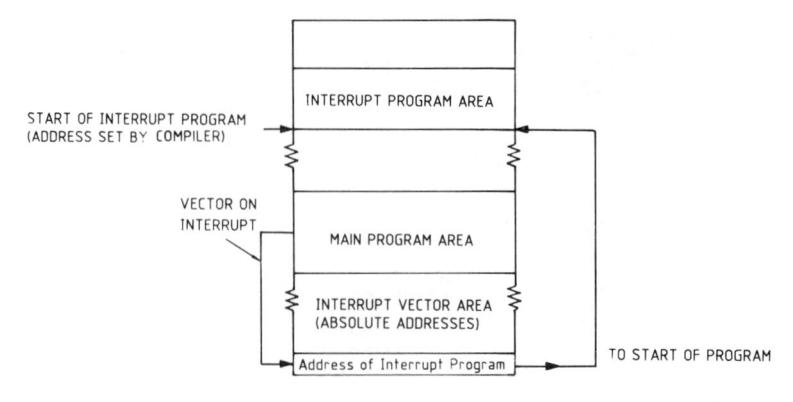

Fig. 9.8 Interrupt operation – 2

ciently using their 'IN' and 'OUT' instructions. Peripheral devices which respond to these instructions are mapped into the so-called 'I/O' space. Address decoding is performed in conjunction with a signal generated by the processor on one of its output pins. There is no overlap with the memory space. It would be contradictory to include such instructions as standard in a general purpose high-level language; this would make it much less portable (or else dangerous) in use. Yet we still need to be able to invoke all facilities provided by the processor.

9.2.6 Software issues

The primary requirement is that we should be able to do as much as possible using high-level statements. These are easy to understand, straightforward to maintain, and are much less likely to hold unwitting mistakes. Nevertheless, there will be some occasion when the high-level approach fails. Therefore we must be able to insert low-level statements, either in assembly language or machine (hex) form, into the high-level code.

Where strong typing is a feature (as in Modula-2), type transfer facilities must be available.

Finally, it is highly desirable that program modules developed in different languages can be bound (linked) together. At the very least, assembler modules must be handled by the linker.

9.3 Low-level facilities in Modula-2

9.3.1 Overview

Device access and control is carried out using the so-called 'low-level' or 'machine dependent' facilities. Let's first see what low-level features Modula-2 provides as standard.

Once we've decided to use a particular microprocessor we have to live with its functions. Software designers can tailor a compiler for a specific processor, enabling us to access its functions from the high-level code. Even so, the functions and operation of *complete* computers vary from design to design. It is just not feasible for the language writer to take such individual designs into account. Hence standard implementations of Modula-2 will fail to meet all our needs; extensions are needed to cope with these design variations. Modula-2 compilers are designed so that low-level facilities are supplied by the 'pseudo' library module 'SYSTEM'. Although this is a library module it is closely related to the compiler, being specific to the target processor. As such, it is not provided as a separate module but may be regarded as part of the total compiler package.

In this section we'll look briefly at facilities which should generally be provided by the SYSTEM module. The next section shows how these are used in a specific target design. Great care must be taken when using low-level facilities. These are machine, and sometimes device, dependent. The resulting software is usually not portable; moreover the compiler error checking power is seriously reduced when handling such facilities. It is recommended that *any* code so produced is kept in clearly identified modules.

9.3.2 Type WORD

All data types we've met so far are uniquely defined. The compiler interprets the meaning of the bit pattern of variables according to the type rules. Yet there are cases when we, and not the compiler, want to decide on the meaning and attributes of stored information. This is where the type WORD comes in.

WORD is defined to be a data storage unit (Fig. 9.9); its size depends on the computer being used. No meaning is attached to the binary pattern held within the word location; we interpret it as we see fit. Each data store location can be individually addressed.

In the Logitech 8086 compiler, WORD is two bytes long; other implementations may use one byte (8-bit machines) or 4 bytes (32-bit machines). Thus, in the Logitech system, an INTEGER value uses one word of storage, while a REAL number occupies four words.

The *only* way the data held by a variable of type WORD can be changed is through the use of the assignment statement. This, though, would appear

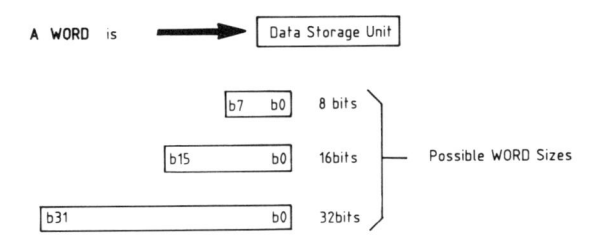

Fig. 9.9 Data storage unit WORD

to make it a pretty useless item. After all, if all we can do is to assign a WORD variable to another WORD variable we're not going to get very far. Now this is where we really need to get around the strong typing of Modula-2. By using type transfer facilities we can interact with other types and so manipulate WORD variables in the usual way.

Listing 9.1 illustrates this point in a very simple way.

```
MODULE TestWord;
(*****************************************************************)
(*      This is an example of working with WORD variables.      *)
(*      Assignment only is carried out but type transfer has    *)
(*      to be used to mix types - Listing 9.1                   *)
(*****************************************************************)
FROM SYSTEM IMPORT WORD;
FROM InOut IMPORT WriteCard, WriteInt, WriteLn;
VAR
   TestCode :WORD;
   Input, Output1 :INTEGER;
   Output :CARDINAL;

BEGIN
   TestCode:=WORD(8FFFH);      (* Planting a hexadecimal value at a
                                  specific location.              *)
   Output:=CARDINAL(TestCode); (* Interpreting the value as CARDINAL.
                                  Note it involves assignment with type
                                  transfer *)
   WriteCard(Output, 5); WriteLn;

   Output1:=INTEGER(TestCode); (* Interpreting the stored value as an
                                  INTEGER *)
   WriteInt(Output, 5);
END TestWord.
```

Listing 9.1

Where would we find the features of WORD an advantage? Suppose we have a serial communications link to another computer which transfers data to us as a series of words. Assume that the first word gives the destination address, the second the number of message words, and the next 100 are, say, INTEGER values of numerical data. By defining these to be words we can treat the first two words as being of type CARDINAL, the others as being INTEGER.

Note well that to use WORD variables the programmer has to take responsibility for their use. For that reason he needs to fully understand how data is stored within his computer.

9.3.3 Type ADDRESS

Earlier we've seen the need to be able to get at specific, absolute, machine addresses. This feature is provided in Modula-2 through the use of type ADDRESS.

ADDRESS is a pointer, being implicitly defined as:

TYPE ADDRESS = POINTER TO WORD

Thus, items of type ADDRESS designate specific locations in memory. Following the normal rules for pointers, any ADDRESS variable can be de-referenced.

Note that a variable of type ADDRESS can be assigned a value held by any other ADDRESS variable. An example using an ADDRESS type is given in Listing 9.2.

```
MODULE TestAddress;
(*****************************************************************)
(*      This is an example of working with variables of type     *)
(*      ADDRESS - listing 9.2.                                   *)
(*****************************************************************)

FROM SYSTEM IMPORT WORD, ADDRESS;
FROM InOut IMPORT ReadInt, WriteCard, WriteInt, WriteString, WriteLn;

VAR
   TestCode, NewTestCode :WORD;
   Input :INTEGER;
   Output :CARDINAL;
   CodeIs, CopiedPointer :ADDRESS;  (* memory address designators *)

BEGIN
   WriteString('Enter value'); WriteLn;
   ReadInt(Input); WriteLn;
   TestCode:=WORD(Input);
   CodeIs^:=TestCode;              (* The value of TestCode is placed in
                                      the location designated by CodeIs *)
   NewTestCode:=CodeIs^;           (* The value in the memory location
                                      denoted by CodeIs is assigned to
                                      NewTestCode *)
   Output:=CARDINAL(NewTestCode);
   WriteString('The value pointed to by CodeIs is ');
   WriteCard(Output, 4); WriteLn;

   CopiedPointer:=CodeIs;
   WriteString('The value pointed to by CopiedPointer is ');
   WriteCard(CARDINAL(CopiedPointer^),4); WriteLn;
END TestAddress.
```

Listing 9.2

What happens when a value is assigned to a variable of type ADDRESS? Suppose, for instance, that an address variable 'CodeIs' is assigned a value 2000. Then the result is that CodeIs points to the data word held at location 2000.

Some arithmetic operations can be used on operands of type ADDRESS. What can be done in practice depends entirely on the particular compiler being used. More will be said on this in Section 9.4.

9.3.4 Obtaining system information (SIZE, TSIZE and ADR)

Modula-2 provides us (Fig. 9.10) with facilities to:

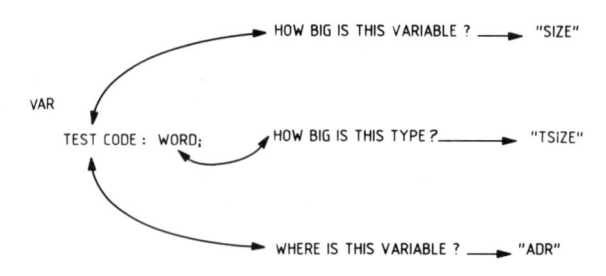

Fig. 9.10 System dependent attributes of program items

- Determine how much storage space a variable uses (its SIZE).
- Determine how much storage space is used for specific types (the type size, TSIZE).
- Find the memory address of a variable (its address, ADR).

Finding the size of a variable
We can find out how much space any variable occupies by using the standard function procedure 'SIZE'. When applied to a variable its answer gives the number of memory storage locations used by that variable. The returned value is of type CARDINAL. SIZE can be defined as:

> PROCEDURE SIZE (VariableName : VariableType):CARDINAL;

Listing 9.3 gives an example for the use of SIZE.

```
MODULE TestSize;
(*******************************************************************)
(*      This is an example of the use of the function          *)
(*      procedure SIZE - Listing 9.3                            *)
(*******************************************************************)
FROM SYSTEM IMPORT SIZE;
FROM InOut IMPORT WriteCard, WriteString, WriteLn;
VAR
   Input :INTEGER;
   VariableSize :CARDINAL;

BEGIN
   Input:=35;
   VariableSize:=SIZE(Input);
   WriteString('The storage space of variable Input (an integer) is ');
   WriteCard(VariableSize, 4); WriteLn;
END TestSize.
```
Listing 9.3

Finding the size of a type
To find out the amount of storage space used by any individual type we use the procedure 'TSIZE', also a standard Modula-2 function procedure. When applied to a type its answer gives the number of memory storage locations required by that type (Listing 9.4). It can be defined as:

```
MODULE TestTypeSize;
(*****************************************************************)
(*      This is an example using the function procedure TSIZE to  *)
(*      obtain the memory space used by type REAL -Listing 9.4    *)
(*****************************************************************)
FROM SYSTEM IMPORT TSIZE;
FROM InOut IMPORT WriteCard, WriteString, WriteLn;
VAR
   TypeSize :CARDINAL;

BEGIN
   TypeSize:=TSIZE(REAL);
   WriteString('The storage space for type REAL is ');
   WriteCard(TypeSize, 4); WriteLn;
END TestTypeSize.
```

Listing 9.4

    PROCEDURE TSIZE (TypeName):CARDINAL;

Finding memory addresses
To find the address of a variable in memory we use 'ADR', another standard function procedure. When this operates on a variable it gives us the memory location (the pointer value) of that variable. ADR is defined as:

    PROCEDURE ADR (VariableName : VariableType):ADDRESS;

An example using ADR will be given later.

9.3.5 Managing individual bits – type BITSET

Normally we handle individual bits of a word only when dealing with peripheral devices. Typically the status of a device is obtained by reading its status register; its mode is set by writing command words to its control registers. In each case specific meanings are attached to the values of individual bits within the data word. The BITSET construct allows us to:

- Examine individual bits
- Set/reset bits
- Mask off bits
- Shift bits

These operations can be more clearly understood when used for real applications (see Section 9.4).

9.4 Using Modula-2 in a target system

9.4.1 A general comment

When writing about low-level facilities one is presented with an insoluble problem: describing these in general terms is both unsatisfying and incomplete. After all, they are meant to be used in specific applications. Yet applying them to a particular computer system is difficult for the reader; it requires a level of knowledge which he may not have. Catch 22 again!

I have decided to opt for the latter approach. After all, it really does show the whys and hows of such features in practical systems. The reader will have to take some aspects on trust. Suspicious types can always read the data books.

Some points have been considered in a fair amount of detail. This might seem to be out of place in a text like this. But, if your intention is to program embedded systems, you *must* appreciate compiler limitations. Those which implement only standard versions of the language assume support from a standard operating system. For embedded applications, language extensions are always required. After going through this section you'll understand why this is true, even if your processor is different from the one described here.

9.4.2 The target system

The system described here is part of a single-board computer (Fig. 9.11) based on the Intel iAPX188 microprocessor component range. Only a limited part of the circuit is shown (Fig. 9.12). At the heart of the process-

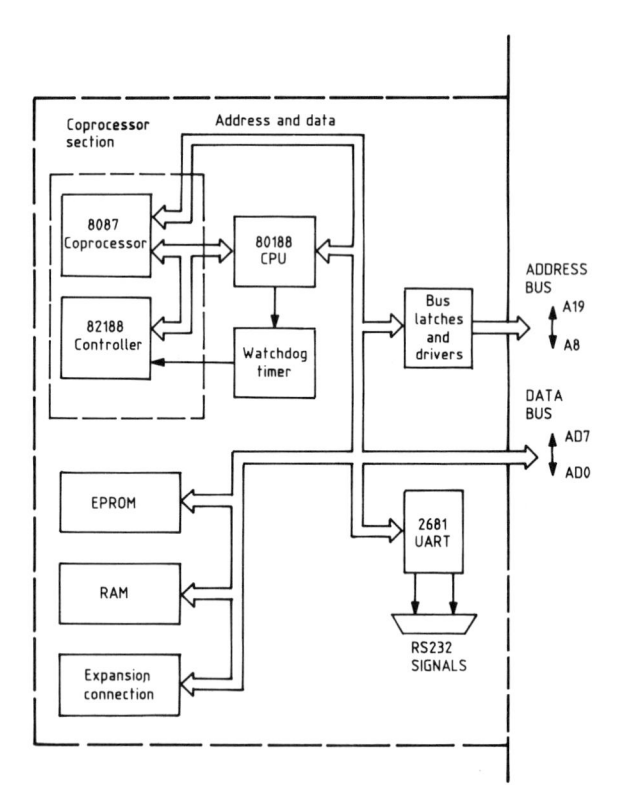

Fig. 9.11 Target system – block diagram

ing section is a highly integrated microprocessor, the 80188 device. It can address a maximum memory address space of 1 Mbyte and an I/O space of 64 kbyte.

Supporting this is an Intel 8087 Numeric Data Coprocessor, used for fast maths operations. This is interfaced to the 80188 by an Intel 82188 bus controller. Three sockets are provided for on-board memory devices, designed to accept standard 'byte-wide' memory chips. As shown, socket 1 is used for EPROM, socket 2 for RAM, and socket 3 can be set for either type. Notice how the chip-select lines (CS, pin 20 of the sockets) are connected; this will become important later on.

ICs 7, 8 and 11 are used merely to increase the electrical drive capability of the signals which originate from the microprocessor (i.e. a 'buffer' function). IC9 performs two functions. First, it acts as a buffer. Second, it latches address information A0–A7 generated by the microprocessor on lines AD0–AD7. This point needs explanation for those unfamiliar with Intel processors.

Lines AD0–AD7 are used to output both address and data information. This corresponds to the lower eight address signals and the eight data bits. Clearly these cannot be present simultaneously. What is done is to time-share the AD lines, address information being presented in the first time slot, this being followed by the data handling phase. IC9 'grabs' and latches the address information when it appears on the AD lines, ignoring subsequent signals. Control of the latch is done through the use of the 188's ALE (address latch enable) signal.

9.4.3 The 80188 microprocessor

The 80188 processor contains not only a microprocessor, but also a number of commonly used peripheral devices. These are based on those used with the 8088 microprocessor (as used in the IBM PC). The major internal blocks are (Fig. 9.13):

- Microprocessor section
- Chip select unit (programmable)
- Interrupt controller (programmable)
- Timers (programmable)
- Direct memory access controller (programmable)
- Clock generator

Control of the programmable devices is achieved by using a set of registers inside the microprocessor: the 'peripheral control block'. These are grouped as one block of 256 bytes, and may be mapped into memory or I/O space (Fig. 9.14). The addresses of the various registers within the control block are shown in Fig. 9.14, these being relative to a base value. This base address is user programmable. Thus changing the base preset value moves the location of the control block within the memory or I/O address space.

210 Accessing processor hardware

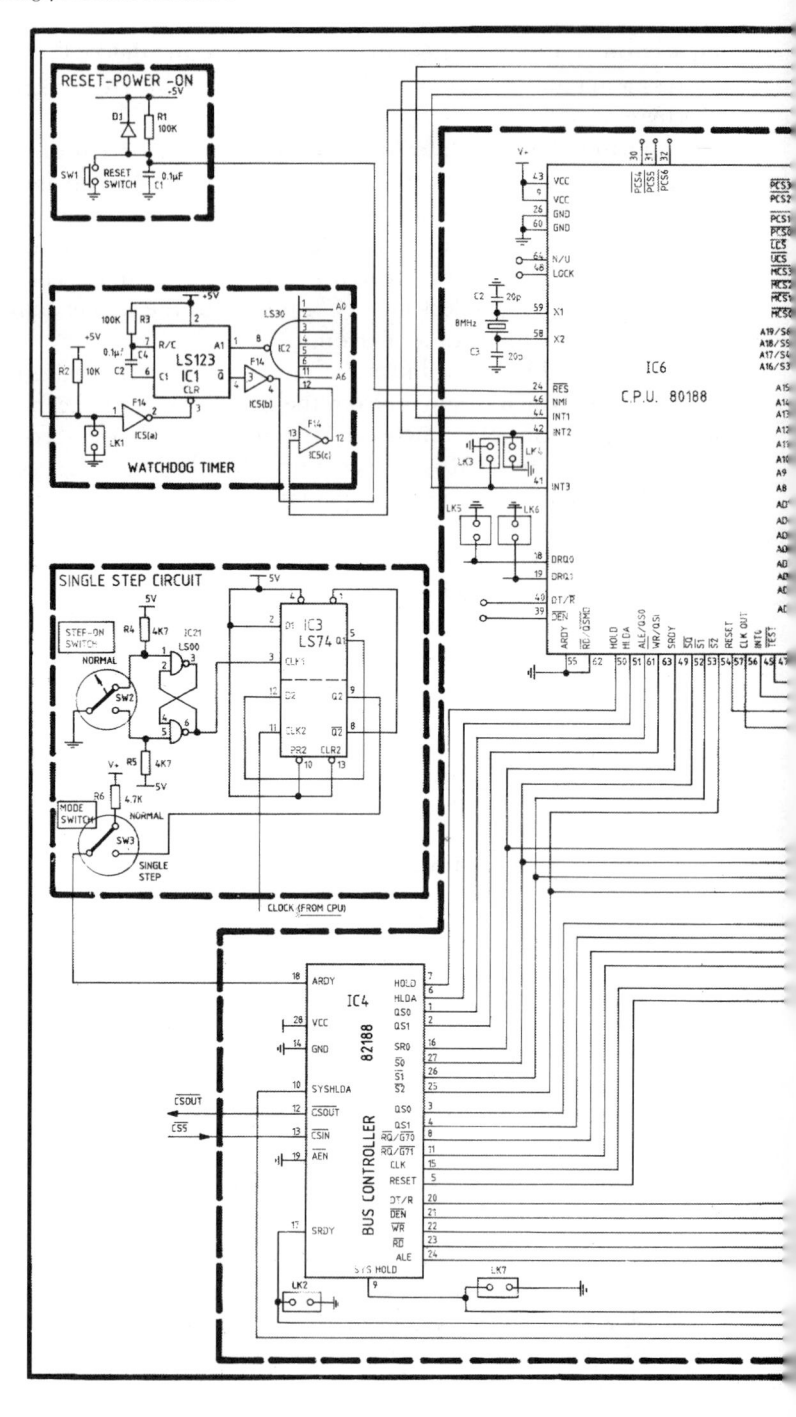

Fig. 9.12 Target system circuit diagram

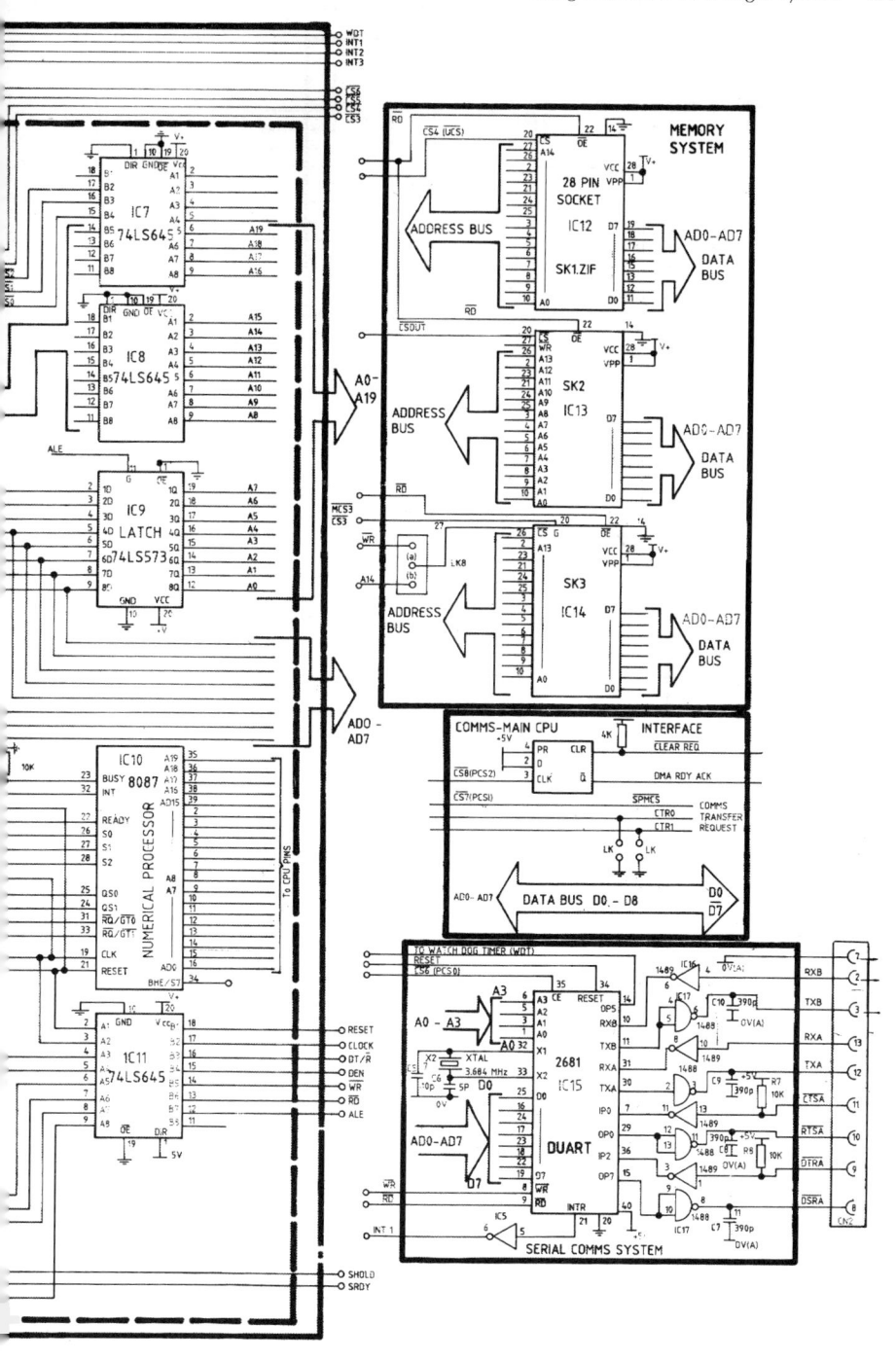

Using Modula-2 in a target system **211**

212 Accessing processor hardware

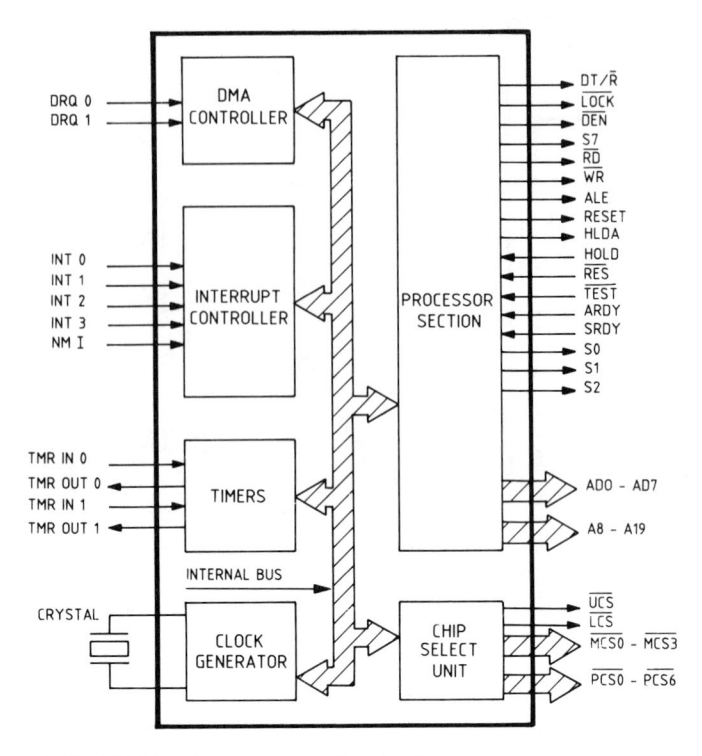

Fig. 9.13 INTEL 80188 microprocessor block diagram

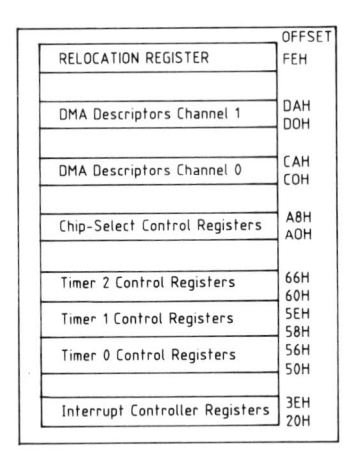

Fig. 9.14 80188 peripheral control block – address map

In the following sections low-level features of Modula are demonstrated for the manipulation of the control block. Specifically, these are features provided within the Logitech compiler.

9.4.4 Memory operations and absolute addressing

Assume that the peripheral control block is mapped into memory at this stage. We are now going to re-program one of the chip select registers to alter the memory area controlled by the upper chip select line. To be precise, the upper chip select (UCS) line is to be active for all addresses between F8000(H) and FFFFF(H), i.e. a 32 kbyte range. To do this we need to load the value FE38(H) into the UCS register. This register is located at address A0(H) in the control block. Assume that the control block base address is F0000(H). Thus the absolute address of the UCS register is F00A0(H). Here we have a case where it is essential to invoke absolute addressing; this brings in the use of constants of type ADDRESS. However, before doing this we have to understand the addressing technique used in the Intel 16-bit processors.

The 80188 can address a maximum memory space of 1 Mbyte, this being organised in sets of segments. Each segment is a linear contiguous sequence of bytes; the maximum segment size is 64 kbytes. A 20-bit number is needed to handle the full 1 Mbyte range. In the 80188, the actual address value is formed by adding two values together: the 'base segment' and the 'offset' (Fig. 9.15). Each of these is a 16-bit number. The offset is straightforward, its value being that as written down. The segment value must be multiplied by 16 to get its actual value. So, if we have

Offset = 1234(H), Segment = F000(H) then actual address = F1234(H)

i.e. the segment value is implicitly assumed to be F0000(H). For quick calculations of actual addresses, remember that multiplying by 16 is equivalent to a leftward shift of one nibble.

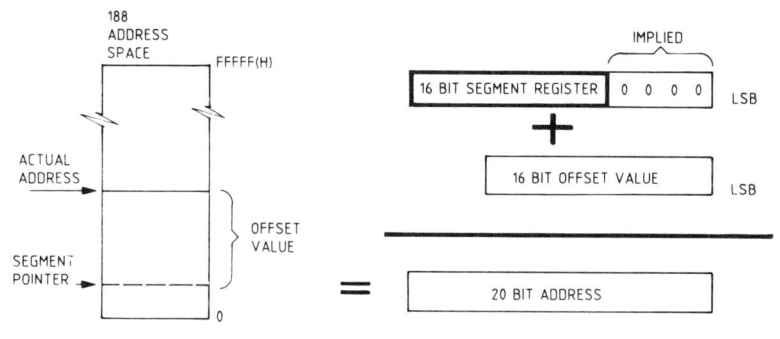

Fig. 9.15 Forming addresses in the 188 processor system

Now, as previously stated, objects of type ADDRESS designate specific locations in memory. Its standard (implicit) definition is

TYPE ADDRESS = POINTER TO WORD

Unfortunately, this is not sufficient to meet our needs. Therefore a language extension is provided by the Logitech compiler; it gives a second definition to ADDRESS, as follows:

TYPE ADDRESS = RECORD
                    OFFSET:CARDINAL;
                    SEGMENT:CARDINAL;
             END;

As a result, ADDRESS constants may be declared as ‹segment:offset›, as shown in Listing 9.5. One small point must be mentioned to avoid confusion. Hexadecimal values must be written having a leading decimal digit. For instance, F00A0(H) is written as 0F00A0; otherwise it would be considered by the compiler to be an identifier.

The example in Listing 9.5 is rather cumbersome in places. Also, it's easy to get things wrong because we've loosened the compiler type checking capability through the use of WORD. The Logitech compiler simplifies

```
MODULE TestChipSelect1;
(*****************************************************************)
(*       This is an example of the use of type ADDRESS           *)
(*       for accessing absolutely defined memory locations.      *)
(*                       Listing 9.5                             *)
(*****************************************************************)
FROM SYSTEM IMPORT WORD, ADDRESS;

VAR
   UpperMemoryRange:ADDRESS;
CONST
   UpperChipSelectRegister = 0F000H:00A0H;
   (* This defines the address of the upper memory chip select
      register to be F00A0(H), i.e., (F000 x 16) + (00A0). By its
      declaration format the constant is of type ADDRESS.        *)

   (* We now set up the register value which will select an
      address range of 32 kByte.                                 *)
   UpperMemory8kByte = 0FE38H;

BEGIN

   UpperMemoryRange:=UpperChipSelectRegister;
   (* the variable, which is of type ADDRESS, has been loaded with
      the address 0F000H:00A0H.                                  *)

   UpperMemoryRange^:=WORD(UpperMemory8kByte);
   (* the location pointed to by UpperMemoryRange is loaded with
      the value 0FE38H.  Note the need to use a type transfer
      operation to overcome type incompatibilites.               *)

END TestChipSelect1.
```

Listing 9.5

memory mapped operations by using absolutely located variables. It provides a simpler form of declaration for such variables, the construct being

VAR IdentifierName[AbsoluteAddress] : IdentifierType;

An example of this is given in Listing 9.6.

```
MODULE TestChipSelect2;
(*****************************************************************)
(*      This example uses absolutely defined variables            *)
(*         for accessing memory locations - listing 9.6           *)
(*****************************************************************)
VAR
   (* Here we declare the variable 'UpperChipSelectRegister' to
      be of type CARDINAL, having an absolute address of F00A0(H).
      The segment value is F000(H), the offset being 00A0(H).     *)
   UpperChipSelectRegister[0F000H:00A0H] :CARDINAL;
 CONST
   UpperMemory8kByte = 0FE38H;

BEGIN
   UpperChipSelectRegister:=UpperMemory8kByte;
END TestChipSelect2.
```

Listing 9.6

It is *very* important that low-level operations are always considered to be non-portable. They are totally bound up with the architecture of the target system. As such they are very unlikely to run properly, if at all, on other installations.

9.4.5 Code inserts

If we actually programmed an EPROM with the object code produced by the 'TestChipSelect' program we'd find a major problem. The processor would first execute the instructions to set up the upper chip select register, but it would then carry on reading information from the EPROM, running into an unprogrammed area. As a result we lose control of the system. There are a number of ways to get over this, one solution being to stop program execution. This is done using the 'HALT' instruction in assembly code, its equivalent hexadecimal value being F4(H). The question is, how do we incorporate this with the Modula source code? It isn't possible to use assembly language statements in the high-level source code (as this is never subjected to an assembly process) However, it *is* possible to use object (hexadecimal) code values, these being defined as CODE inserts. Listing 9.7 shows the use of this feature to halt the processor at the end of program execution.

9.4.6 Bit handling

When dealing with the control and monitoring of peripheral devices, bit handling is all important. The programmer must have the ability to set/reset

```
MODULE TestChipSelect3;
(*******************************************************************)
(*         This is an example of the use of CODE inserts          *)
(*         within the modula souce file - listing 9.7             *)
(*******************************************************************)
FROM SYSTEM IMPORT CODE;
VAR
   UpperChipSelectRegister[0F000H:00A0H] :CARDINAL;
 CONST
   UpperMemory8kByte = 0FE38H;

BEGIN
   UpperChipSelectRegister:=UpperMemory8kByte;
   CODE(0F4H);
END TestChipSelect3.
```

Listing 9.7

individual bits in a control word. He must also be able to interrogate status word information, bit by bit. Languages designed for embedded systems provide these facilities. For instance, Coral66 has the 'BITS' feature, enabling the programmer to handle individual or groups of bits within a data word. Modula goes much further in terms of abstraction; further, such operations are implemented fairly easily using the 'BITSET' type. It is assumed that the reader is familiar with the use of sets and BITSET from Chapter 7.

Example 1 – individual bit manipulation

To show this in action we're going to program timer 1 of the 80188 to act as a timing generator. Its internal clock is to be used as the clocking source for the timer; the output is to be taken from pin T1 OUT to an external device. It is required to generate a timing signal which has a period of 200 μs (i.e. a frequency of 5 kHz.). The 80188 internal clock frequency is 2 MHz.

Two registers in the control block are important to us: 'count' and 'control word'. The first, the count register, is loaded with the count value. This is counted down by one at each clock interval once the timer is enabled. During this time the T1 OUT line is high, going low for one clock cycle at the end of count. Provided the timer resets to the count value and the cycle continues, a repetitive waveform will be produced on the timer output line. Thus the timing signal period is determined by both the internal clock frequency and the number loaded into the count register.

This brings in the use of the control word register. The operational mode of the timer is determined by specific bits within this register. Details of the bit functions are given below. This information is included *not* to help you program the 80188 (an unlikely requirement for the average reader) but to appreciate the example 'Timer1Test'.

Individual bits of the mode/control word are programmed as follows:

Bit 0 – CONT
   1 – Continuous running of timer

    0 – Stop (halt) at next maxcount
Bit 1 – ALT
    1 – Use both maxcount registers
    0 – Use maxcount register A only
Bit 2 – EXT
    1 – External clock used, this being on the 'T IN' pin
    0 – Internal source used for clock
Bit 3 – P
    This is only applicable if internal clocking (EXT = 0) is used; otherwise it is ignored.
    1 – Timer 2 output used as the clock source
    0 – CPU derived clock used as the timer clock source
Bit 4 – RTG
    This bit is only active for internal clocking (EXT=0).
    1 – The timer acts as a digital one-shot, being triggered by a rising edge of the T IN signal.
    0 – T IN signal controls the timer count. A logic high allows counting; a low stops the counter.
Bit 5 – MC
    This is a status bit, indicating the maxcount register state. The bit is set whenever the register reaches the present maxcount value.
Bit 12 – RIU
    This is a status bit, indicating which maxcount register is in use (logic 1 = B). This bit cannot be written to. Further, it is always cleared (logic 0) when the A register only is being used.
Bit 13 – INT
    1 – Allows the timer to generate an interrupt on every terminal count
    0 – Inhibits interrupt generation
Bit 14 – INH
    This bit controls the updating of bit 15, EN, when a new control word is written to the timer.
    1 – The state of EN is modified by the control word
    0 – A control word write has no effect on EN
Bit 15 – EN
    This is applicable to internal clocking functions of the timer.
    1 – Timer clocking is enabled
    0 – Timer clocking disabled

Identifiers used for the bits are taken from the Intel iAPX188 User's Manual (1985).

The addresses of the register are absolutely defined, being given in the program example. Note that to produce a 5 kHz signal using a 2 MHz clock, the count register must be loaded with the value 400 (Listing 9.8). When the program in Listing 9.8 is run in the target system, timer control word will be set to

    1100   0000   0000   0001

218 Accessing processor hardware

```
MODULE Timer1Test;
(*****************************************************************)
(* This is an example illustrating bit manipulation using the    *)
(* BITSET construct.  Timer 1 of the 188 is loaded with a        *)
(* count value of 400; it is then counted out using a 2 MHz.     *)
(* clock.  The timer is set into the continuous mode, thus       *)
(* generating a 5 kHz. signal - listing 9.8                      *)
(*****************************************************************)
FROM SYSTEM IMPORT CODE;
VAR
    Timer1ControlWord[0F00H:005EH] :BITSET;
    Timer1CountRegisterA[0F00H:005AH] :CARDINAL;
CONST
    Halt = 0F4H;

    (* These constants set up the 188 timer mode control word bits *)
    ContinuousMode = 0;
    BothMaxcountRegisters = 1;
    ExternalClocking = 2;
    Timer2asClock = 3;
    RetriggerMode = 4;
    GenerateInterrupt = 13;
    AllowENupdating = 14;
    EnableInternalClocking = 15;

    (* This is the timer maxcount value *)
    CountTime = 400;
    (* end of setting 188 timer control data *)

BEGIN
    Timer1CountRegisterA:=CountTime; (* setting up the count value *)
    Timer1ControlWord:={ContinuousMode, AllowENupdating,
                    EnableInternalClocking}; (* setting up the timer *)
    CODE(Halt);
END Timer1Test.
```

Listing 9.8

This could have equally well been achieved by writing

   Timer1ControlWord:=0C001H;

or

   Timer1ControlWord:={0, 14, 15}

I'll leave it to you to judge which is the more meaningful method.

In this example new names have been made up for the control word bits. This should make it easier to understand the timer setting. Control of the timer is now quite straightforward. For instance, to cause it to generate interrupts we write:

   INCL(Timer1ControlWord, GenerateInterrupt);

and to stop the timer

   EXCL(Timer1ControlWord, ContinuousMode);

Example 2 – bit masking

We typically use 12-bit analogue-to-digital converters (ADCs) in data acquisition systems. As most microprocessors are byte oriented the result obtained by reading the digitised output of the ADC is a 16-bit one. Clearly the top four bits are meaningless; therefore we must ensure that these are set to a safe value. For our case we wish to set these to zero; all other bits must be unaffected.

This can be done through the use of the set intersection function together with the correct mask word (Fig. 9.16, Listing 9.9).

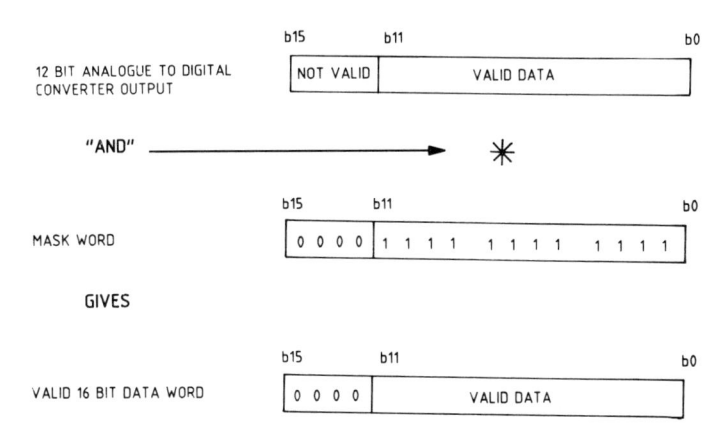

Fig. 9.16 Masking of bits

```
MODULE BitMaskTest;
(*******************************************************************)
(*      This is an example illustrating bit manipulation      *)
(*      using the SET intersection operation. The objective   *)
(*      is to ensure that the four most significant bits of   *)
(*      of the value 'ADCvalue' are set to zero -listing 9.9  *)
(*******************************************************************)
FROM InOut IMPORT WriteString, WriteLn, WriteHex;
FROM CardinalIO IMPORT ReadHex;
VAR
   ADCvalue :CARDINAL;
   ADCbits :BITSET;
CONST
   ADCmask = {0..11};

BEGIN
   WriteString('enter ADC test value, four hex digits'); WriteLn;
   ReadHex(ADCvalue); WriteLn;
   ADCbits:=BITSET(ADCvalue);
   ADCbits:= ((ADCbits) * (ADCmask)); (* here is the masking operation *)
   WriteHex(CARDINAL(ADCbits),4); WriteLn;
END BitMaskTest.
```

Listing 9.9

220 Accessing processor hardware

```
MODULE BitShiftTest;
(*******************************************************************)
(*      This is an example illustrating bit manipulation        *)
(*      using intersection and shifting operations. We wish     *)
(*      to extract three nibbles from a 16 bit word and output  *)
(*      these to the console - listing 9.10                     *)
(*******************************************************************)
FROM InOut IMPORT WriteString, WriteLn, WriteHex;
FROM CardinalIO IMPORT ReadHex;
VAR
   Testvalue, DACvalue :CARDINAL;
   Testbits, DACbits :BITSET;
CONST
   Testmask = {0..11};
   DACmask = {0..3};
   NibbleShift = 16;
   ByteShift = 256;

BEGIN
   WriteString('enter Test test value, four hex digits'); WriteLn;
   ReadHex(Testvalue); WriteLn;
   Testbits:=BITSET(Testvalue);
   Testbits:= (Testbits)*(Testmask);
   WriteHex(CARDINAL(Testbits),4); WriteLn; WriteLn;
   WriteString('Here come the DAC nibble values, low one first');
   WriteLn;
   DACbits:= (Testbits)*(DACmask);
   WriteHex(CARDINAL(DACbits),4); WriteLn;
   DACbits:=BITSET(CARDINAL(Testbits) DIV NibbleShift);
   DACbits:= (DACbits)*(DACmask);
   WriteHex(CARDINAL(DACbits),4); WriteLn;
   DACbits:=BITSET(CARDINAL(Testbits) DIV ByteShift);
   WriteHex(CARDINAL(DACbits),4); WriteLn;
END BitShiftTest.
```

Listing 9.10

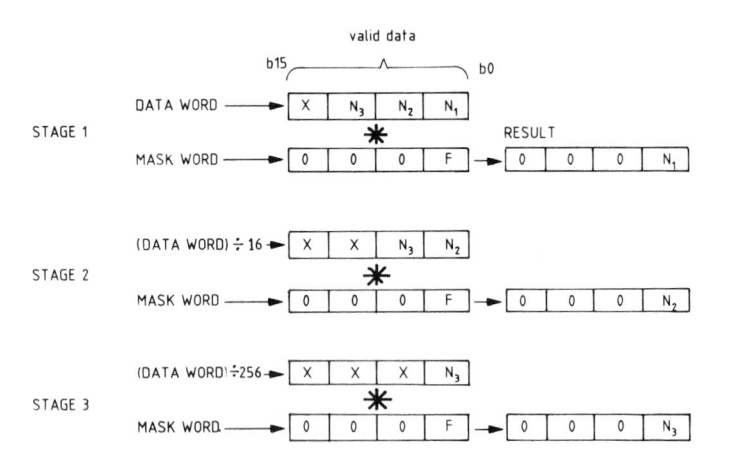

Fig. 9.17 Use of mask and shift features for bit extraction

Example 3 – bit extraction
There are cases where we want to extract a specific set of bits from a data word. For instance, the analogue device AD7542 digital-to-analogue converter (DAC) must be loaded up one nibble at a time. As it is a 12-bit converter, three loads must be carried out. Further, we must extract the individual nibbles from the complete 16-bit data word before loading up the DAC. Listing 9.10 shows how this is done through the use of shift and mask operations. Our objective is to first extract one nibble at a time. This is then inserted into the least significant nibble position in a 16-bit word with the leading 12 bits set to zero. The procedure adopted is shown in Fig. 9.17. This could have been written in a more elegant way. However, the objective is to show clearly what happens as the code executes, not to be clever.

9.4.7 Interrupts

General operation
The 80188 can service either hardware- or software-generated interrupts. An internal interrupt controller is used to handle those originating in hardware.

In general, interrupt operation is much the same whether the request is hardware- or software-generated. First we'll describe a hardware-initiated sequence (Fig. 9.18).

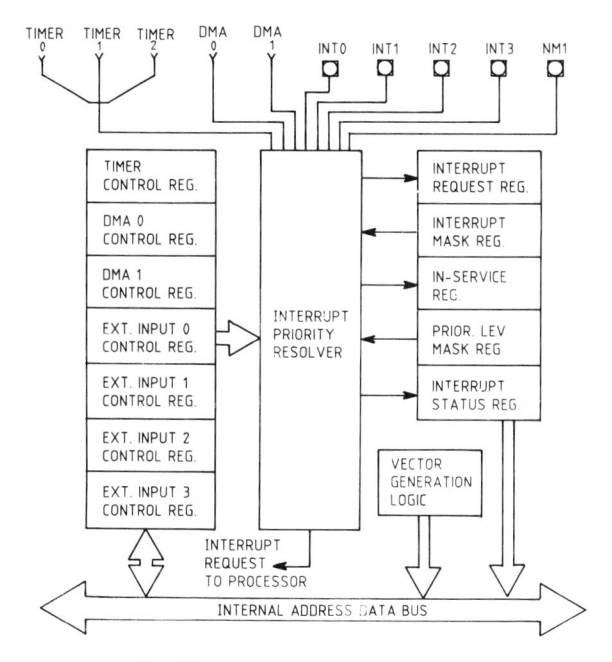

Fig. 9.18 Interrupt controller block diagram

- An interrupt occurs. Hardware sources signal the interrupt controller; this generates a single interrupt signal to the CPU.
- The CPU issues an 'interrupt acknowledge' signal.
- The interrupt controller responds by outputting the vector address of the interrupt being serviced.
- The CPU reads this code and uses it to call the corresponding interrupt procedure. However, prior to actually doing this, it saves essential but limited processor register information (see next section).

Two particular points must be clearly understood. First, what is the value of the vector address? Second, what information is contained at this address?

Interrupt vectors and the interrupt sequence

The 80188 uses the first 1 kbyte of address space to hold the addresses of ('pointers to') the interrupt service routines. This is organised as 256 four-byte pointers (Fig. 9.19). Each pointer consists of a two-byte code segment (CS) and a two-byte instruction pointer (IP) value. Together these form the ⟨segment⟩⟨offset⟩ combination needed to define a specific location in memory.

Each interrupt is given a vector type number. The position of the corresponding pointer in the interrupt vector table is calculated by multiplying the vector type by four. A number of interrupt vectors are preset in the 188 (Fig. 9.20). Thus the pointer for timer 0 interrupt is located at (4×8 = 32 decimal), i.e. 20H.

Should timer 0 obtain interrupt service, the interrupt controller outputs '8' in response to the 'interrupt acknowledge' signal from the CPU. This is

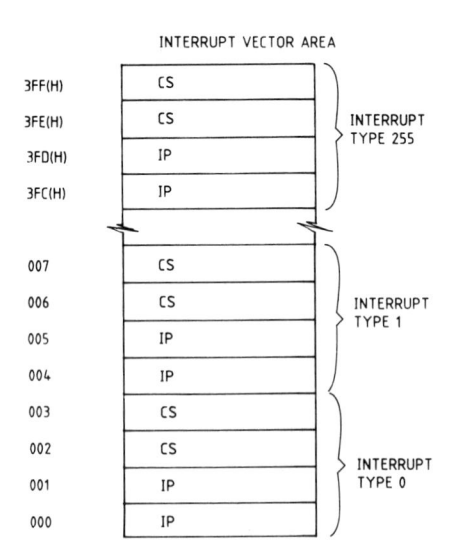

Fig. 9.19 Interrupt routines – address vectors

Fig. 9.20 80188 interrupt vectors

INTERRUPT NAME	VECTOR TYPE	DEFAULT PRIORITY
Divide Error Exception	0	1
Single Step Interrupt	1	12
NMI	2	1
Breakpoint Interrupt	3	1
INTO Detected Overflow Exception	4	1
Array Bounds Exception	5	1
Unused-Opcode Exception	6	1
ESC Opcode Exception	7	1
Timer 0 Interrupt	8	2A
Timer 1 Interrupt	18	2B
Timer 2 Interrupt	19	2C
Reserved	9	3
DMA 0 Interrupt	10	4
DMA 1 Interrupt	11	5
INTO Interrupt	12	6
INT1 Interrupt	13	7
INT2 Interrupt	14	8
INT3 Interrupt	15	9

picked up by the CPU and manipulated so that CS and IP are loaded up with the pointer values set into location 20H. Program execution is then transferred to the address set by the pointer.

Hence the overall sequence of events for a timer 0 interrupt is:

- Interrupt controller generates INT REQ to CPU.
- CPU responds with INT ACK.
- Controller places vector address 08H on the 188 internal bus.
- The 188 uses this value (multiplied by four) to index into the vector table. This location carries the CS and IP values of the interrupt service routine (the pointer to the routine).
- The 188 pushes the current CS, IP and flags onto the stack.
- It now loads CS and IP with the values from the vector table and proceeds with the interrupt service routine.

Software-generated interrupts

Interrupts may be generated by software in two different ways. First, certain specific errors resulting from instruction execution automatically invoke interrupt action. For instance, a divide error is generated if the quotient resulting from a division is too big to be handled by the computer number system.

Alternatively, the programmer himself may insert an interrupt instruction into the source code using the INT function. Thus the instruction

INT 20

generates an interrupt of type 20. The pointer for this service routine is located at 80 decimal (50H) in the vector table.

Here we have another example of a machine operation which cannot be executed by a standard Modula instruction. But interrupt calls are extremely important and must always be made as visible as possible. We don't really want to bury them as inline code. For this reason the Logitech compiler provides an extension in the SYSTEM module to set software interrupts, the SWI procedure. It is defined as

SWI (InterruptVectorNumber; CARDINAL);

Hence the instruction SWI(20) performs the same operation as INT20.

Locating the interrupt service routine
The actual mechanics of handling interrupts are discussed in Section 10.6

9.4.8 Special machine operations

Occasionally one meets processors which have unique features. In order to handle such facilities, extensions must be made to the language standard. The example here is the use of an I/O area as well as a memory access area in Intel processors. The purpose of this is to provide an address space for peripheral devices without overlapping the processor memory space.

Further, the code produced for such operations is usually fast and compact.

One can usually eliminate the need to use I/O instructions by memory mapping all peripherals. So, monitoring and control of these devices can be done using standard high-level language operations. In the 80188, however, it is impossible to avoid the use of I/O commands. On power-up or reset, the processor peripheral control block is mapped into the I/O space. It can be remapped into the memory area, but the remapping must be done via an I/O operation.

Only four commands are needed for 80188 I/O data transfer: IN (either byte or word) and OUT (again, byte or word). To eliminate the use of inline code, language extensions:

INBYTE, INWORD, OUTBYTE, OUTWORD

are provided by the Logitech compiler. These are actually procedures supplied in the SYSTEM module. Each has the same general export definition form, *viz*:

INBYTE (port:CARDINAL; VAR value BYTEorWORD);
INWORD (port: CARDINAL; VAR value WORD);

Listing 9.11 uses these features. It should be noted that the base address for the control block is FF00H; all register addresses are relative to this. The code performs the same function as the example TestChipSelect1 of Section 9.4.4. However, for this case, it is assumed that the peripheral control block is mapped into the I/O space.

9.4.9 Finding addresses – the use of the ADR function

We've met this briefly already. Now let's apply it to an actual system involving 188 addressing techniques. In Listing 9.12 an array variable is used

```
MODULE TestChipSelect2;
(*****************************************************************)
(*      This example uses I/O instructions to access devices    *)
(*      in the input/output space - listing 9.11                *)
(*****************************************************************)
FROM SYSTEM IMPORT OUTWORD, CODE;
CONST
   UpperChipSelectRegister = 0FFA0H;
   (* This will allow us to access the upper memory chip select
      register at address FFA0H in the peripheral control block *)

   (* We now set up the register value which will select an
      address range of 32 kByte. *)
   UpperMemory8kByte = 0FE38H;
   Halt = 0F4H;

BEGIN
   OUTWORD(UpperChipSelectRegister, UpperMemory8kByte);
   CODE(Halt);
END TestChipSelect2.
```

Listing 9.11

```
MODULE TestAddress;
(****************************************************************)
(*  Here the function procedure ADR is used to obtain the       *)
(*  the absolute memory address of a variable - listing 9.12    *)
(****************************************************************)

FROM SYSTEM IMPORT WORD, ADDRESS, ADR, SIZE;
FROM InOut IMPORT WriteCard, WriteString, WriteLn, WriteHex;
TYPE
   AbsoluteAddress = ARRAY [0..1] OF CARDINAL;
VAR
   UpperChipSelectRegister[0F000H:00A0H]:CARDINAL;
   AddressSize :CARDINAL;
   TestCodeIs :ADDRESS;
   AddressIs : AbsoluteAddress;

BEGIN
   TestCodeIs:=ADR(UpperChipSelectRegister);(*TestCodeIs gets the address
                                                     of TestCode *)
   AddressIs:=AbsoluteAddress(TestCodeIs); (* Type transfer *)
   WriteString('The address is (OFFSET) ');
   WriteHex(AddressIs[0], 4); WriteLn;
   WriteString('The address is (SEGMENT) ');
   WriteHex(AddressIs[1], 4); WriteLn;
END TestAddress.

When this is run it will output the following to the console;

The address is (OFFSET) 00A0
The address is (SEGMENT) F000
```

Listing 9.12

to handle the absolute address returned by ADR. Normally standard types (e.g. CARDINAL) would be used for this; unfortunately for computers with large memory addressing capabilities (as with the Intel 80188) the address pointer is not compatible with any of the standard types.

Review

Do you realise:

- Why we need to access device (chip) hardware?
- What access features are needed?
- How Modula-2 supports operations fo this type?
- How these are used in a specific target system?

Chapter 10
Concurrent processing

Up to this time we have, with a single exception, assumed that the computer processes one task, and one task only. The exception in question involves the use of interrupts. Interrupts were shown to be a way by which the computer can switch jobs at unpredictable times, so responding to so-called 'asynchronous' events. This may have given the impression that running multiple tasks on one machine is not a normal or routine event. And yet, apart from very trivial tasks, most applications do consist of a multiplicity of jobs. For instance, we may wish to use a word processing package and a compiler simultaneously under the control of a standard commercial operating system. In an embedded application we may have to consider simultaneous running of a control loop, a data communications channel and a display system. Operations such as these are described as being 'concurrent', the related software topic being that of 'concurrent programming'.

To handle interrupts directly means that we must have a detailed knowledge of the computer hardware. Moreover, great care must be taken in their use; simple mistakes can be disasterous. So, it would be very convenient to be able to generate software for concurrent tasks without getting involved in such detail. This is where Modula-2 scores again. It has actually been designed so that the programmer can develop concurrent programs using Modula-2; there is no need to resort to assembly language operations.

After having studied this chapter you will:

- Understand the difference between sequential and parallel activities.
- Appreciate the use of multiprocessing and multitasking.
- Understand and implement multitasking of independent tasks.
- Understand and implement multitasking of interacting tasks.
- Be able to operate with the co-routine feature (processes) of Modula-2.
- Realise the need for safe synchronisation controls when tasks interact.

10.1 Concurrency – an introduction

Let's consider the situation portrayed in Fig. 10.1. Here we have two different tasks running under the control of a single computer system. At this stage nothing has been said about how many separate processors are contained within this system. Further, nothing has been said about task interaction.

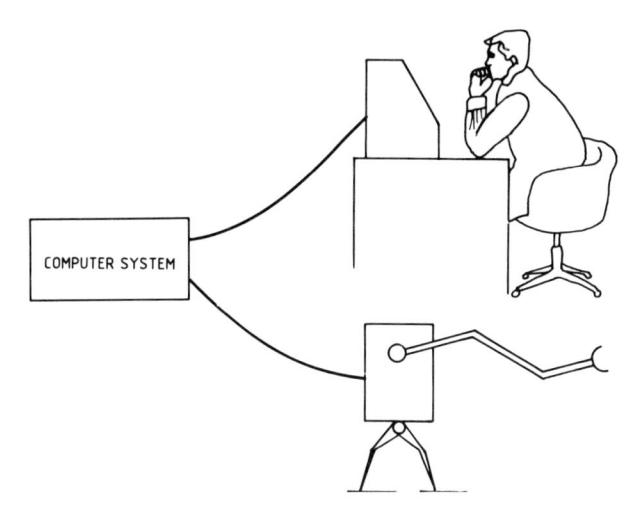

Fig. 10.1 Computer based tasks

Assume that both operations are to run simultaneously. This can be shown diagrammatically as in Fig. 10.2. Here we have true parallel task execution, that is, each task actually runs at the same time. To be able to do this we *must* have a separate processor dedicated to each function (Fig. 10.3). This is a proper multiprocessor system, being the only way to implement true 'multiprocessing'.

Now consider the situation where only one processor is available, yet the two tasks have to be carried out. One solution might be to use the method shown in Fig. 10.4. Here each task is performed in sequence, the program being a continuous loop. Control merely passes from the robot task to the

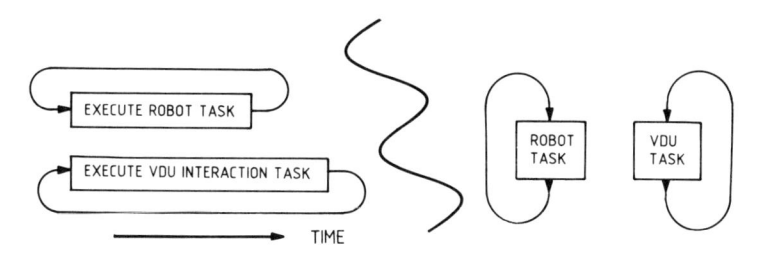

Fig. 10.2 Simultaneous task or process operation (parallel execution)

228 Concurrent processing

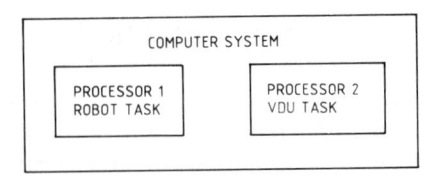

```
                COMPUTER SYSTEM
        ┌─────────────┐  ┌─────────────┐
        │ PROCESSOR 1 │  │ PROCESSOR 2 │
        │ ROBOT TASK  │  │ VDU TASK    │
        └─────────────┘  └─────────────┘
```

Fig. 10.3 Hardware support for parallel processing

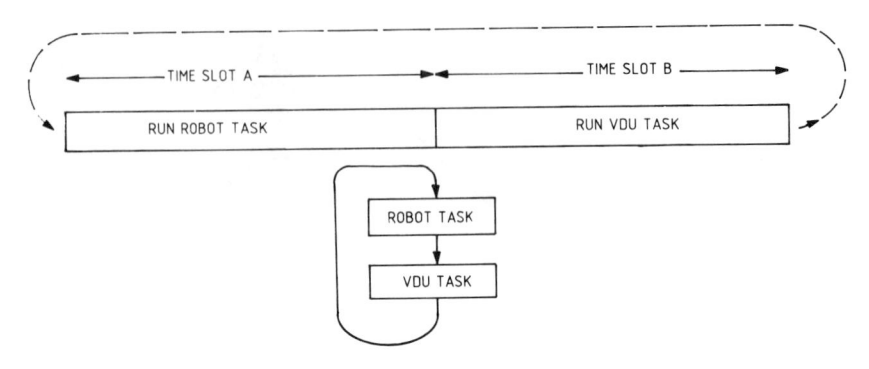

Fig. 10.4 Simple sequential task operation

VDU task to the robot task...and so on. This technique has a lot going for it. It is simple to implement, it is well controlled and predictable, and it should be relatively straightforward to de-bug. In fact, such methods have been widely used in slow systems such as process control. Any time critical functions within such systems have normally been managed using interrupts. Unfortunately, there are situations where we can't (or may not want to) use such an approach. While one task is being serviced by the computer the other is idle (or out of control). In fast embedded systems, tasks may be left uncontrolled only for very short periods. For keyboard interaction the waiting for computer responses can be totally frustrating. Accepting that we are stuck with only one processor, what can we do in these circumstances?

The key here is to realise that, for many tasks, the job can be carried out in short bursts, pausing between activities. For such applications, say producing flight navigation information on a cockpit display, the job would then appear to be carried out as one continuous activity. The operator is unaware of the start–stop nature of the job (assuming, of course, the pauses are quite short). So, where more than one task has to be carried out on a single processor, we may be able to time-share the resources between tasks (Fig. 10.5). As shown here each individual task is either running or suspended; they take it in turns to use the computing facilities. This produces the illusion of running two tasks simultaneously in the system; the reality is different. Such an approach is called 'multitasking'.

For either multiprocessing or multitasking, each task may be in one of four possible states (Fig. 10.6).

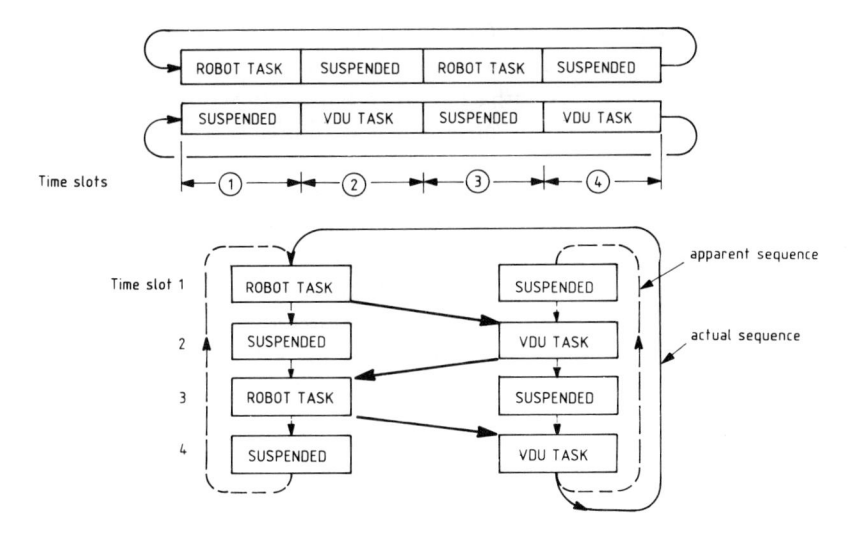

Fig. 10.5 Time-sharing of tasks (multitasking)

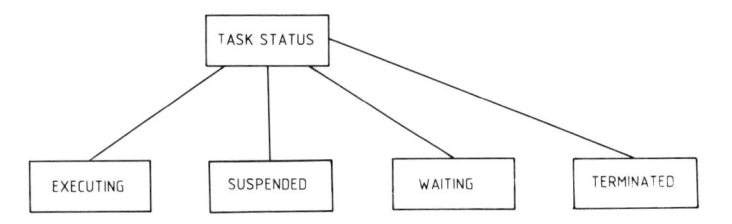

Fig. 10.6 Possible task states

The underlying ideas are much the same for multiprocessing and multitasking. In reality, though, multiprocessor software is generally much more complex than that of a uniprocessor system. Hence most of the Modula-2 features described here are placed in the context of multitasking.

It is possible to introduce some element of concurrency by using special hardware. A processor system, for instance, might include a graphics chip to control a colour display function. In this case, picture information is drawn up by the graphics device asynchronous to, and separate from, the main processor. Such features are specific to design and so are not considered here.

10.2 Interacting and non-interacting tasks – their coordination

In the discussion so far we haven't stated whether the robot and VDU tasks actually interact. Clearly, if the VDU operator sends commands to the robot we have an interacting system. If, on the other hand, the VDU is being used for word processing only, no task interaction takes place. Even so, what they must do is to *cooperate* with each other in using the computer resources. In its simplest form this cooperation involves shutting down one task and starting up the other.

Let's first assume that the tasks are non-interacting, i.e. the functions performed are independent of each other. The way in which the tasks run and communicate with each other can be shown as in Fig. 10.7. Here, the non-running task sits waiting for a 'start' command whilst the other is using system resources. The running task carries out part of its total function, suspends itself, and starts up the other task. It, in turn, waits for the start-up command. On receiving it, it resumes task execution from where it previously left off.

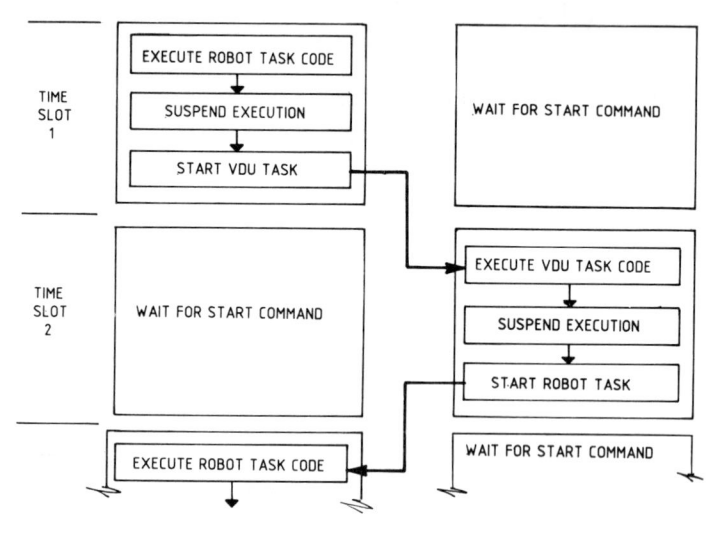

Fig. 10.7 Cooperation between independent tasks

This represents the simplest form of concurrency, often found in time-shared computer installations. A good example of this is the typical college computer system used by students for programming work. In such instances each task is essentially an individual, private one. Normally, users do not need, or wish, to interact with each other. As a result the problem (as far as the computer operating system is concerned) is reduced to handling task information and allocating computer time to users.

Let's now assume that the VDU operator can control and monitor the robot from his console. Here the tasks must cooperate in a number of ways (Fig. 10.8). Task transfer still has to be implemented; nothing has changed there. However, the tasks now have to communicate with each other. For instance, the operator may set the maximum velocity of movement of the

Fig. 10.8 Cooperation between interacting tasks

robot via the keyboard input. This then has to be picked up by the servo controllers of the robot drive mechanism. In the same way, status information acquired by the robot sensors may need to be displayed on the VDU screen. Such communication functions can be carried out using data sharing methods.

Finally, the tasks must be coordinated or synchronised. The following is a simple example of the need for such coordination. Suppose, for instance, the robot is carrying out a delicate operation, based on information already supplied by the operator. Also suppose that changing this information part way through the operation would produce a dangerous situation. Now, although we're quite happy to time-share both tasks, it is essential to block off up-dating of the control data until this critical operation in completed. In other words, the update and use of such information must be synchronised.

It is easy to forget that, in a single-processor system, only one task runs at any one instant. This fundamental fact ensures that there cannot be a clash for the use of computing resources. It is also unlikely that tasks will clash over the use of other, peripheral, resources. Suspended tasks should normally give up the use of all facilities. It *is* possible through the use of sloppy programming to have a 'deadlock' situation. Deadlocks occur, for instance, when two (or more) tasks come to a complete standstill because of missing information. Consider the case where

Task A needs the result of a computation from task B before it can proceed; and
Task B is waiting for the result from A before *it* can complete

and there you have a deadlock.

Deadlocks are much more likely to be met in multiprocessor systems where tasks actually do run simultaneously (and usually asynchronously); further, there is often extensive sharing of hardware resources.

10.3 Subroutines, co-routines and processes

The present discussion limits itself to concurrency within a single-processor system, the so-called 'quasi-concurrent' mode of operation. In other words, we have a multitasking system. Our objective is to run a number of tasks or processes on this machine, writing all software in Modula-2.

First, what is a process? This *may* be defined as a 'program in execution' though it is said that there is no universally agreed definition (Deitel, 1984).

232 Concurrent processing

For our purposes we take a process as being equivalent to a task (Fig. 10.9). Each individual process has specific identifying features, these being its code, data and operational status.

The concurrent software is structured using 'co-routines'; consider these to be a set of programs which execute in a multitasking environment (Fig. 10.10). Each specific co-routine is implemented as a process. In Modula-2 a process has a very precise specification (Fig. 10.11), and is actually written as a procedure. From its structure it can be seen to be completely self-contained. Thus each process is essentially an independent program. *But*, because they are contained (compiled) within one overall program, information can be transferred between them using signals and data values.

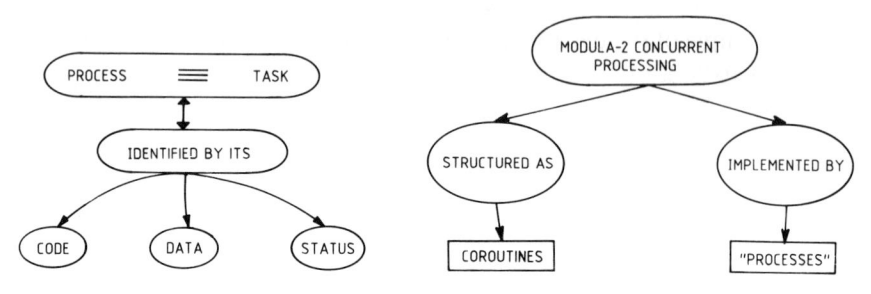

Fig. 10.9 Process – general definition

Fig. 10.10 Concurrency in Modula-2

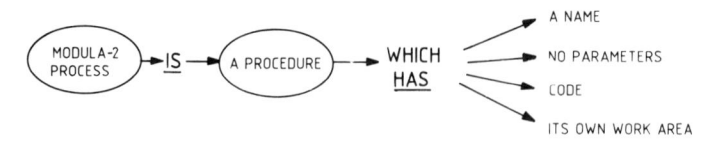

Fig. 10.11 Processes in Modula-2

Previously we've regarded procedures as being high-level language equivalents of subroutines. This is not strictly correct; it depends whether or not the procedure is used as a process. When a procedure is used in the normal sense it acts as a subroutine (Fig. 10.12). At each call of the subroutine by the foreground program (say) the current state of the processor is saved and program control branches to the subroutine. On completion of the subroutine a return is made to the point of call. Processor status is restored, and execution of the foreground program recommences. On any subsequent call of the procedure this action is repeated. From this description it is clear that the *called* program is subordinate to the *calling* (foreground) one.

Now let's look at co-routines. Suppose that we've implemented the foreground program (Fig. 10.12) as a process; we've also included a second process 'Beta'. First it is important to realise that there is no boss/slave relationship here; all processes have equal standing. Second, only one process may have use of the processor. Third, transfer of control between processes can take place at any point in their programs. Fourth, transfer has to be

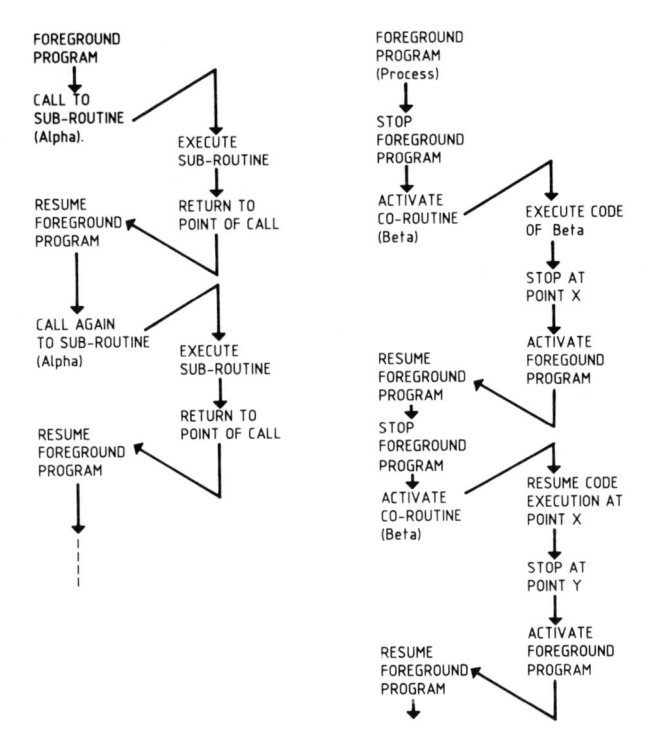

Fig. 10.12 Subroutines vs. co-routines – conceptual differences

actively implemented by the running process. Assume initially that the foreground program process is running. At some point it suspends itself and activates process Beta. The current state of the processor is saved before the transfer to Beta takes place. Beta now begins to run until it decides to return control to the foreground program. All processor information related to the current state of Beta is saved, the process suspended, and control transferred to the foreground program. At some later stage control is once more transferred back to Beta. Beta now picks up at the point at which it previously left off, executes a certain amount of code, transfers control back to... and so on in an alternating fashion. In other words, we have two cooperating sequential processes.

10.4 Using co-routines (processes) in Modula-2

10.4.1 Introductory aspects

There are a number of distinct stages in the life of a Modula-2 co-routine or process (Fig. 10.13). (From now on we'll use the word 'process' to refer to a specific task.) Initially it has to be created and then activated before it enters its normal state. Once in this state it will either be running or else it will be

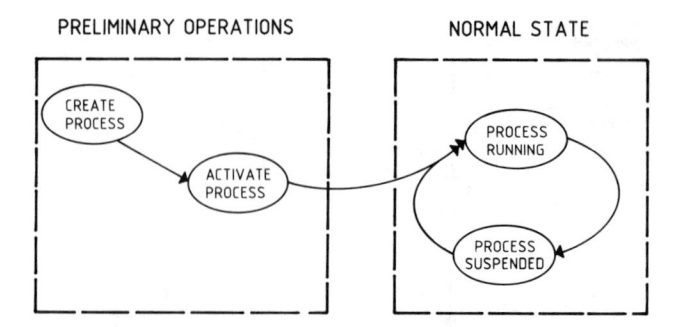

Fig. 10.13 The stages of a Modula-2 process

suspended; there is no in-between condition. Fine. So how do we go through these stages?

First let's consider the preliminary operations (Fig. 10.14). In order to create the task we have to write the code needed to carry out its function. This code is written within a procedure; note that it cannot have parameters. We then 'allocate' this procedure to a process, reserve a working area of memory for the process, and finally give the process a name. Now we are in a position to activate the process.

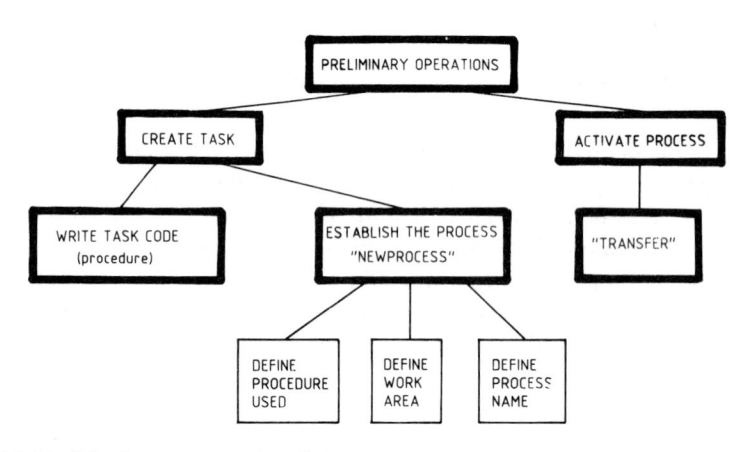

Fig. 10.14 Bringing a process into being (Listing 10.1)

The process is established by use of the standard procedure NEWPROCESS. Its format is:

NEWPROCESS(ProcedureName, AddressOfWorkSpace,
           SizeOfWorkSpace, NameOfProcess);

and is defined as:

PROCEDURE NEWPROCESS(P:PROC, A:ADDRESS, n:CARDINAL,
                                        VAR new:ADDRESS);

Activation is carried out using the procedure TRANSFER, its format being:

TRANSFER(FromProcessName, ToProcessName);

It is defined as:

PROCEDURE TRANSFER(VAR source, destination :ADDRESS);

These actions are shown in Listing 10.1. The code of the process is contained in the procedure 'DemoProcess', the actual process being named 'FirstProcessExample'. Processes and procedures are considered to be syntactically different; hence the need for the two different names in the parameter list of the NEWPROCESS procedure.

Processes are deemed to be variables of type PROCESS; here two are declared: 'FirstProcessExample' (already described) and 'OpeningProcess'.

```
MODULE ProcessTest1;
(*********************************************************)
(*      This is the first stab at using the process      *)
(*      construct - listing 10.1.                        *)
(*********************************************************)
FROM SYSTEM IMPORT ADDRESS, NEWPROCESS, PROCESS, TRANSFER,
                  WORD, ADR, SIZE;
FROM InOut IMPORT WriteString, WriteLn;
VAR
    FirstProcessExample, OpeningProcess :PROCESS;
    ProgramArea :ARRAY [0..255] OF WORD;

(* Here is the code of the process *)
PROCEDURE DemoProcess;
BEGIN
    (* we arrive into the process at this point *)
    WriteString('Now in the Demo Process'); WriteLn;

    TRANSFER (FirstProcessExample, OpeningProcess);
    (* we leave the process now, returning to OpeningProcess *)

END DemoProcess;


BEGIN (* ProcessTest1 *)
    NEWPROCESS(DemoProcess, ADR(ProgramArea), SIZE(ProgramArea),
               FirstProcessExample);
    TRANSFER (OpeningProcess, FirstProcessExample);
    (* we leave the main program at this point.  On return the next
       statement is executed *)

    WriteString('Back in the opening process now'); WriteLn;
END ProcessTest1.
```

LISTING 10.1

This is a demonstration of the creation and activation of a single process. Note that to avoid hiccups in the operating system the base address of the data area is not defined in absolute terms. Instead it is left to the compiler to sort it out; it does it using the ADR function.

Listing 10.1

The use of 'OpeningProcess' may at first seem mysterious (in line with much software work). To appreciate its use we have to understand that the main program is itself regarded as a process. Therefore to activate any other process we have to make an explicit transfer to that process. But the TRANSFER procedure has, as one of its parameters, the name of the process which is currently active. And nowhere have we named the 'main program' process. It appears to be a no-go situation. The TRANSFER procedure requires a name, yet we haven't given the process a name. All is not lost, however. What happens (in this particular case) is that the name given to the active process in the TRANSFER procedure is automatically associated with the main program one. So, as a result of writing

TRANSFER(OpeningProcess, FirstProcessExample);

the main program is treated as the process named 'OpeningProcess'. Any suitable name may be used to identify the main program.

At this stage we have seen how to create a process, transfer into it from the main program process, and return back to this process. Now let's extend this work further.

10.4.2 Independent processes

Review the two functions shown in Fig. 10.7: the robot task and the VDU task. These are, as shown, independent of each other. Thus we can implement a task operation as shown in Fig. 10.15. Two processes are used, one for each function. While one runs the other is suspended; activation and suspension are carried out using the TRANSFER procedure. Each process runs in a continuous loop, with control alternating between the two. The program for this is given in Listing 10.2. Note that each process has been written as a separate procedure. The main program code has been used

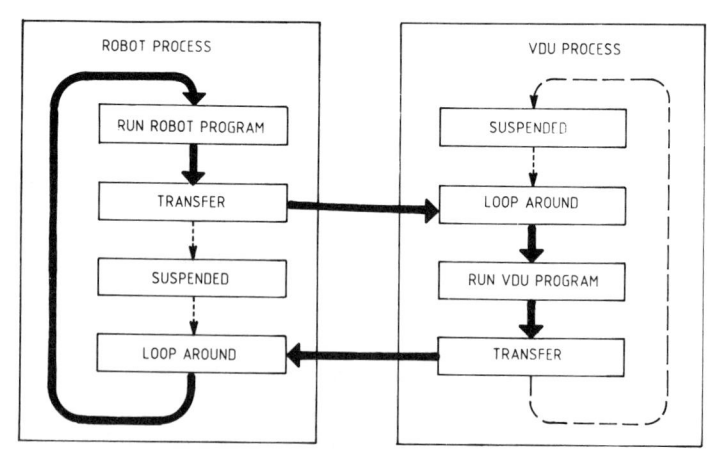

Fig. 10.15 Two independent processes – steady-state cooperation (Listing 10.2)

```
MODULE ProcessTest2;
(*****************************************************************)
(*        This is a simple example of two independent           *)
(*        processes in action - listing 10.2                    *)
(*****************************************************************)
FROM SYSTEM IMPORT ADDRESS, NEWPROCESS, PROCESS, TRANSFER,
                  WORD, ADR, SIZE;
FROM InOut IMPORT WriteString, WriteLn, Read;
VAR
   RobotProcess, OpeningProcess, VDUprocess :PROCESS;
   RobotProgramArea :ARRAY [0..255] OF WORD;
   VDUprogramArea :ARRAY [0..255] OF WORD;
   KBinput :CHAR;
   N :CARDINAL;

PROCEDURE DemoRobot;
BEGIN
   LOOP
      WriteString('Robot Demo running'); WriteLn;
      WriteString('Ready to transfer control, Y or N?'); WriteLn;
      REPEAT
         Read(KBinput);
      UNTIL KBinput = 'Y'; (*end repeat*)
      TRANSFER (RobotProcess, VDUprocess);
   END; (*end loop *)
END DemoRobot;

PROCEDURE DemoVDU;
BEGIN
   N:=0;
   LOOP
      INC(N);
      IF N>5 THEN EXIT END;
      WriteString('VDU Demo running'); WriteLn;
      WriteString('Ready to transfer control, Y or N?'); WriteLn;
      REPEAT
         Read(KBinput);
      UNTIL KBinput = 'Y'; (*end repeat*)
      TRANSFER (VDUprocess, RobotProcess);
   END; (*end loop *)
   TRANSFER(VDUprocess, OpeningProcess);
END DemoVDU;

BEGIN (* ProcessTest2 *)
   NEWPROCESS(DemoRobot, ADR(RobotProgramArea), SIZE(RobotProgramArea),
              RobotProcess);
   NEWPROCESS(DemoVDU, ADR(VDUprogramArea), SIZE(VDUprogramArea),
              VDUprocess);
   TRANSFER (OpeningProcess, RobotProcess);
   WriteString('Finish of demo'); WriteLn;
END ProcessTest2.
```

This is a demonstration of the creation and activation of two processes.
Note that in order to transfer control between processes the transfer
instruction must be carried within the appropriate procedure. The robot
process is the one first activated.

Listing 10.2

merely to bring the processes into being and to start the system up. It plays no part in subsequent operations.

This example illustrates one of the dangers of using processes. Within each process the system waits for a correct keyboard response. Until this arrives the tasks effectively stop. Other processes cannot regain control and resume operation. Therefore, where processes are used to provide concurrency, any individual process can bring the whole system to a grinding halt. This is both irritating and frustrating when running analysis/simulation/etc. programs on your own machine; it is intolerable in an embedded system. Defensive programming techniques, together with hardware fallback (the watchdog timer) is essential in such circumstances.

This is the simplest form of concurrency that we're likely to meet. As shown, each task takes it in turn to run. This makes it almost identical to that of the simple sequential operation depicted in Fig. 10.4. However, Fig. 10.16 shows how much more powerful this method is. Moreover, task transfer can be a conditional function, allowing us to carry out as much or as little as we desire at any particular time. The program for Fig. 10.16 is given in Listing 10.3.

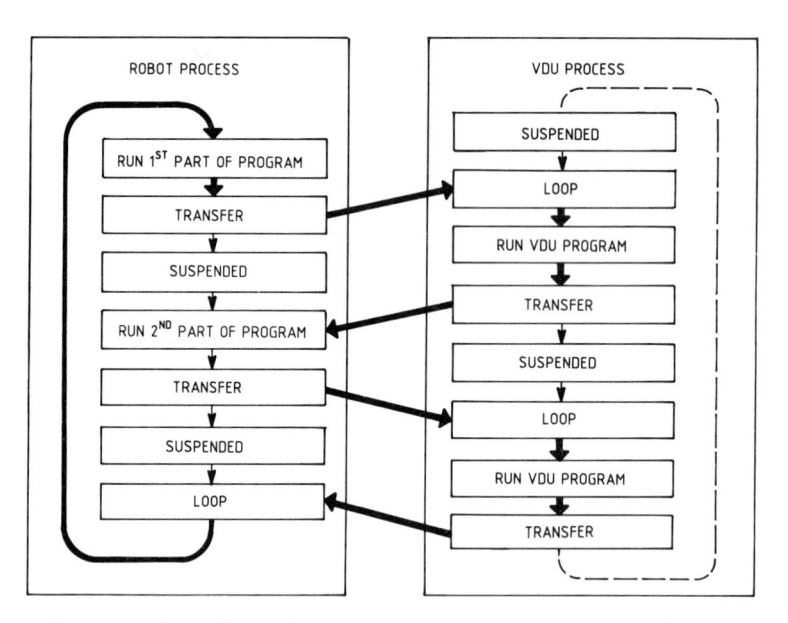

Fig. 10.16 Two independent tasks – unequal time-sharing (Listing 10.3)

10.4.3 Interacting processes – using flags for coordination

Let's now look at the problem of tasks which are interdependent or 'interacting'. Staying with the ideas of robotic tasks, consider the situation shown in Fig. 10.17. Here robot 1 makes components while robot 2 builds (assem-

Using co-routines (processes) in Modula-2 **239**

```
MODULE ProcessTest3;
(*****************************************************************)
(*      This is a further example of two independent        *)
(*      processes in action. - listing 10.3.                *)
(*****************************************************************)
FROM SYSTEM IMPORT ADDRESS, NEWPROCESS, PROCESS, TRANSFER,
                  WORD, ADR, SIZE;
FROM InOut IMPORT WriteString, WriteLn, Read;
VAR
   RobotProcess, OpeningProcess, VDUprocess :PROCESS;
   RobotProgramArea, VDUprogramArea :ARRAY [0..255] OF WORD;
   KBinput :CHAR;

PROCEDURE DemoRobot;
BEGIN
   LOOP
      WriteString('Robot Demo now at start'); WriteLn;
      WriteString('Ready to transfer control, Y or N?'); WriteLn;
      REPEAT
         Read(KBinput);
      UNTIL KBinput = 'Y'; (*end repeat*)
      TRANSFER (RobotProcess, VDUprocess);
      WriteString('Robot Demo on second run'); WriteLn;
      WriteString('Ready to transfer control, Y or N?'); WriteLn;
      REPEAT
         Read(KBinput);
      UNTIL KBinput = 'Y'; (*end repeat*)
      TRANSFER (RobotProcess, VDUprocess);
   END; (*end loop *)
END DemoRobot;

PROCEDURE DemoVDU;
BEGIN
   LOOP
      WriteString('VDU Demo running'); WriteLn;
      WriteString('Ready to transfer control, Y or N?'); WriteLn;
      REPEAT
         Read(KBinput);
      UNTIL KBinput = 'Y'; (*end repeat*)
      TRANSFER (VDUprocess, RobotProcess);
   END; (*end loop *)
END DemoVDU;


BEGIN (* ProcessTest3 *)
   NEWPROCESS(DemoRobot, ADR(RobotProgramArea), SIZE(RobotProgramArea),
              RobotProcess);
   NEWPROCESS(DemoVDU, ADR(VDUprogramArea), SIZE(VDUprogramArea),
              VDUprocess);
   LOOP
      TRANSFER (OpeningProcess, RobotProcess);
   END; (*end loop *)
END ProcessTest3.
```

This is a demonstration of control transfer between two processes.
Note that RobotProcess runs in two steps for each single complete run of
the VDUprocess.

Listing 10.3

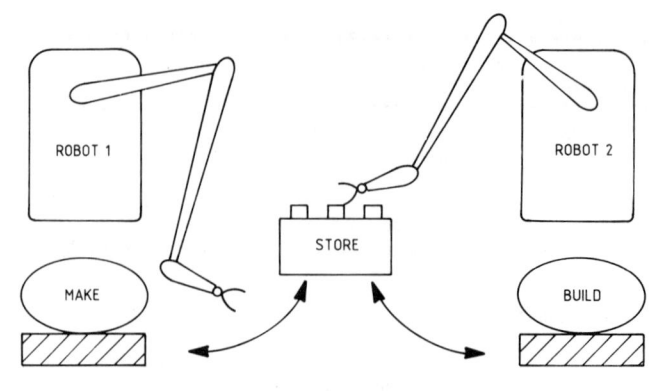

Fig. 10.17 Interacting tasks

bles) units using these component parts. The meeting point between the two is the store. Robot 1 spends most of its time making components. When the 'make' pile is large enough, and the store has gone empty, it loads the lot into the store as one action. Robot 2 comes along and fetches completed components from the same store. Where it differs from Robot 1 is that it removes only one item at a time. During these operations it is essential that both robots do not try to get at the store simultaneously.

The system can be in one of three possible states, as shown in Fig. 10.18.

STORE STATE	ACTION	FLAG STATUS
NORMAL -1	ROBOT 1 MAKING ROBOT 2 BUILDING	NOT LOADING NOT EMPTY
LOW -2	ROBOT 1 MAKING ROBOT 2 WAITING	NOT LOADING EMPTY
REPLENISH -3	ROBOT 1 LOADING ROBOT 2 WAITING	LOADING NOT EMPTY

Fig. 10.18 Cooperation between interacting tasks – use of flags

Its status is defined by the condition of two signals or 'flags': 'LoadingStore/not-loading' and 'StoreEmpty/not-empty'. Each robot pursues its own job while the store is in the normal state. If it goes empty the 'StoreEmpty' flag is set; robot 1 then tops it up. To prevent robot 2 entering the store during the loading period the 'LoadingStore' flag is set before the operation commences. So, robot 1 can only enter the store after the empty flag has been set; robot 2 is barred from this area when the loading flag is in the set state. This means that both tasks need to share information, i.e. the condition of the flags. In this case the common information is stored in a data area which can be accessed by both tasks (Fig. 10.19).

To put some flesh on this problem let's show the required operations as a

Using co-routines (processes) in Modula-2   241

Fig. 10.19 Data-sharing technique for task communication

flow chart (Fig. 10.20). Read through this to see how the two tasks proceed quite differently. Process transfer has been omitted from the diagram for clarity at this stage.

The program to simulate these functions is shown in Listing 10.4. As in the previous example, the main program is used only for establishing pro-

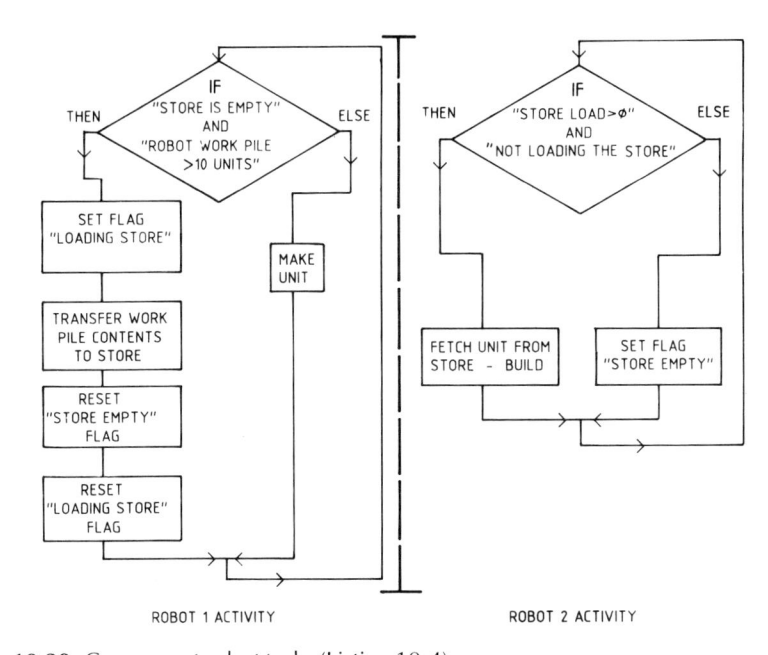

Fig. 10.20 Concurrent robot tasks (Listing 10.4)

```
MODULE ProcessTest4;
(*******************************************************************)
(*      This is a simple example of two interacting            *)
(*      processes in action - listing 10.4.                    *)
(*******************************************************************)
FROM SYSTEM IMPORT ADDRESS, NEWPROCESS, PROCESS, TRANSFER,
                WORD, ADR, SIZE;
FROM InOut IMPORT WriteString, WriteLn, WriteCard, Write, Read;
VAR
    Robot1Process, OpeningProcess, Robot2process :PROCESS;
    Robot1ProgramArea :ARRAY [0..255] OF WORD;
    Robot2programArea :ARRAY [0..255] OF WORD;
    Robot1WorkPile, StoreLoad, I :CARDINAL;
    StoreEmpty, LoadingStore :BOOLEAN;

PROCEDURE Delay;
VAR
```

242 Concurrent processing

```
      Escape : CHAR;
   CONST
      CursorLeft = 'D';
      CursorRight = 'C';
   BEGIN
      Escape:=CHR(27);
      FOR I:=1 TO 100 DO
         Write(Escape);Write(CursorRight);  Write(Escape);Write(CursorLeft)
      END;(*of for*)
   END Delay;

   PROCEDURE DemoRobot1;
   BEGIN
      Robot1WorkPile:=0;
      LOOP
         TRANSFER (Robot1Process, Robot2process);
         IF StoreEmpty AND (Robot1WorkPile>10) THEN
            LoadingStore:=TRUE;
            WriteString('Robot1 loading - Loading - Loading '); WriteLn;
            StoreLoad:=Robot1WorkPile;
            Robot1WorkPile:=0;
            Delay;
            WriteString('Robot1 loading finished');
            WriteLn; WriteLn; WriteLn;
            LoadingStore:=FALSE;
            StoreEmpty:=FALSE;
         ELSE
            WriteString('Robot1 making'); WriteLn;
            INC(Robot1WorkPile);
            Delay;
         END; (*end of if *)
      END; (*end loop *)
   END DemoRobot1;

   PROCEDURE DemoRobot2;
   BEGIN
      StoreLoad:=0;
      LOOP
         IF (StoreLoad > 0) AND (NOT LoadingStore) THEN
            DEC(StoreLoad);
            WriteString('Robot2 building - StoreLoad is ');
            WriteCard(StoreLoad, 2); WriteLn;
            Delay;
         ELSE
            StoreEmpty:=TRUE;
         END; (*end of if *)
         TRANSFER (Robot2process, Robot1Process);
      END; (*end loop *)
   END DemoRobot2;


   BEGIN (* ProcessTest4 *)
      NEWPROCESS(DemoRobot1, ADR(Robot1ProgramArea),
                 SIZE(Robot1ProgramArea), Robot1Process);
      NEWPROCESS(DemoRobot2, ADR(Robot2programArea),
                 SIZE(Robot2programArea), Robot2process);

      LOOP
         TRANSFER (OpeningProcess, Robot1Process);
      END; (*end loop *)
   END ProcessTest4.
```

Listing 10.4

cesses and starting operations. It plays no further part in operations. An additional procedure, 'Delay', is used merely to give the program writer time to observe the action of the program as it runs. While it is active the screen cursor just moves rapidly backwards and forwards one step at a time (this procedure may not be portable to all systems).

The problems raised by using shared variables to communicate between processes is beyond this text. For further information on this and related topics (such as the use of monitors) see Deitel (1985).

10.5 Multiple task synchronisation

10.5.1 Introduction

We are beginning to get into advanced waters here. However, no text on Modula would be complete without a description of facilities provided specially for task synchronisation.

To appreciate the need for these observe the requirements shown in Fig. 10.21. These are typical of many embedded real-time systems. It could represent, for instance, a flight control system. Process 1 is the closed-loop control function of the autopilot, 2 supports man–machine interfacing, 3 enables the flight controller to 'talk' to other avionic systems, 4 looks after the safety of the aircraft, and 5 provides flight air data to the crew. Clearly these are going to interact considerably. We could use the combination of flags and the process transfer mechanism to write the software for such an application. Even in a single-processor installation task coordination then becomes difficult to manage. Not only do we have to consider the 'when', but also the 'who to'. In cases such as these a different approach is needed. This problem was first faced for real by developers of the early operating systems. A number of techniques were developed; the one described here has proved to be sound, effective and fairly straightforward to apply in concurrent applications. Basically each process explicitly indicates its status by using a set of signals; synchronisation is achieved through the use of these signals.

The following description applies to a single-processor structure. It does, however, also form the basis for synchronisation within multiprocessor systems.

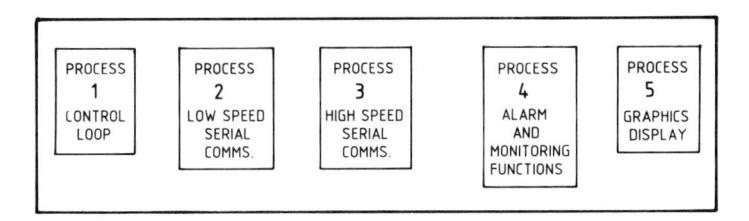

Fig. 10.21 Embedded system – typical multiple task requirement

10.5.2 Synchronising operations

Modula provides us with a data type 'SIGNAL' for use in the synchronising of processes. Fundamentally, signals denote the state of a process. A number of operations can be carried out through the use of signals (Fig. 10.22). Before looking into these in detail let's first see why we need them and how they function.

Fig. 10.22 The synchronising signals of Modula-2

Assume that a system has three processes. Only one (say X) can possibly be running at any one time in our uniprocessor installation. Process X reaches a point when it needs to activate one (or both) of the others. To do this it SENDs the appropriate signal and suspends itself.

Process Y has been sitting there, waiting for the 'wake-up' signal. It gets into the wait state initially through the use of a WAIT operation. This operation not only suspends execution of the process; it also defines the name of the 'wake-up' signal.

What if the third process (Z) is also waiting for the same wake-up signal? Do Y and Z fight it out for use of system resources? Common sense says no; in fact some form of priority has to be used to avoid contention. The simplest is based on a first-come first-served idea, discussed later under queues in Section 10.5.5.

Suppose we have the situation just described, that is, process Y being active, Z and X suspended. We've decided that process Z should run next if it is waiting for the signal from X; otherwise X should be reactivated. How can we handle such a requirement? Here the next operation to be described, 'Awaited', comes into use. Using this we check to see if any processes are waiting for a particular signal. As a result decisions can be made concerning future program actions, i.e. if Z is waiting then we'll send the wake-up signal to that process.

So far, so good. One small (but important) detail remains to be sorted out. The signals define specific status conditions. How do we ensure that, on program start-up (initialisation), everything functions in a controlled and secure manner? Here the fourth signal operation is needed, that of 'Init'. This initialises the signal variable associated with the operation; it must be carried out before the variable is used.

One final operation has to considered. It really has nothing to do directly with the handling of signals but must be used where signals are involved. It is concerned with bringing a process into being and then activating it. Previously this has been done using the NEWPROCESS and TRANSFER procedures. Now they are combined in the one procedure, 'StartProcess'. The other reason for mentioning 'StartProcess' is that it is held in the same library module ('Processes') as the others. The procedure is defined as

PROCEDURE StartProcess(P:PROC; n:CARDINAL);

Here P is the procedure which is actually executed when the process is active; n is the number of words of workspace allocated to it.

The other procedures are:

PROCEDURE SEND(VAR s:SIGNAL);   This causes signal s to be sent. Any one process waiting for s is given control.

PROCEDURE WAIT(VAR s:SIGNAL);   The current process suspends execution and waits for the signal s.

PROCEDURE Awaited(s:SIGNAL):BOOLEAN;
   This is a function procedure which tests to see if any process is waiting for s. If so, the result is TRUE.

PROCEDURE Init(VAR s:SIGNAL);   The signal s is initialised. Directly after invoking this, Awaited(s) returns the result FALSE.

The definition module 'Processes' also exports the type SIGNAL.

One final general point needs to be made. The actual behaviour of processes when using these techniques may depend on your compiler. Be aware of this. Always check out operations, especially for target system software.

10.5.3 Starting up a process which uses signals

Before we can activate a process we have to write its code. There is nothing new here; once again we use procedures (Fig. 10.23). As before, no para-

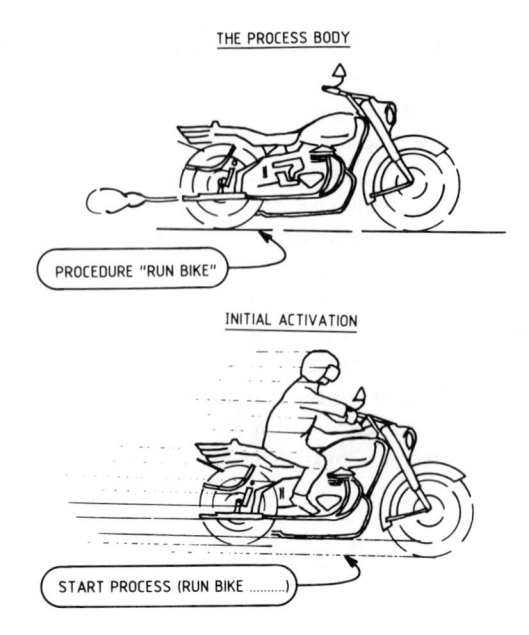

Fig. 10.23 Starting a process

meters can be attached to such procedures. What *is* different though is that no name is given to the process. This may seem odd; but remember that now there are no explicit transfers between processes, only signalling. Names play no part in these operations; hence they just aren't needed.

We'll demonstrate these activities through the use of a simple example (Listing 10.5). Here we have written two procedures: 'RunBikeX' and 'RunBikeY'; neither have parameters. These are going to be our processes. In the body of the main program 'StartUpProcess' we activate 'RunBikeY', allocating appropriate workspace to it. At this stage signals have been omitted to keep the description clear.

When this program is run, process 'RunBikeY' is activated, and the system enters the infinite loop within this process.

As a self-test:

- Start up 'RunBikeX' only
- Put in both 'StartProcess' statements
- Repeat this, changing the order of the 'StartProcess' statements.

From the results obtained deduce the rules used by your compiler for process activation.

10.5.4 Using SEND, WAIT and Awaited operations

We'll start with sending a signal as this results in one of two possible outcomes. If a signal is sent, and another process is waiting for that signal, then

Multiple task synchronisation

```
MODULE StartUpProcess;
(***************************************************************)
(*      This is a simple example showing how to create and     *)
(*      then activate a process - activation is by use of      *)
(*      the 'StartProcess' procedure - listing 10.5.           *)
(***************************************************************)
FROM InOut IMPORT WriteString, WriteLn;
FROM Processes IMPORT StartProcess;

PROCEDURE RunBikeX;
BEGIN
    WriteString('Bike X now running'); WriteLn;
    LOOP
    END; (*end of loop *)
END RunBikeX;

PROCEDURE RunBikeY;
BEGIN
    WriteString('Bike Y now running'); WriteLn;
    LOOP
    END; (*end of loop *)
END RunBikeY;

BEGIN (* StartUpProcess *)
    WriteString('Foreground process running'); WriteLn;
    StartProcess(RunBikeY,500);
END StartUpProcess.
```

Listing 10.5

clearly the running process should suspend itself. But if nobody is waiting for the signal if would be pretty pointless to stop the current process. And that's the way it works in Modula. This is demonstrated in Listing 10.6. When this program is run, the following text appears on your screen:

Foreground process running
Bike X now running
X running again
X running again
etc.
etc.
. . .

In this example the variable of type SIGNAL is 'Stop'; note its initialisation before being used.

Now let's look at the wait operation just by itself. Whenever a process executes a WAIT procedure it enters a suspended state. Only when it sees the appropriate signal does it wake-up. This is shown in Listing 10.7, using only one signal, 'Stop'. When this program runs the following appears on your screen:

Foreground process running
Bike X now running
FG process on run 2

```
MODULE SendSignal;
(*******************************************************************)
(*     This example shows that generating a SEND signal has no     *)
(*     effect unless a process is waiting for it - listing 10.6.   *)
(*******************************************************************)
FROM InOut IMPORT WriteString, WriteLn;
FROM Processes IMPORT SIGNAL, SEND, WAIT, Init, StartProcess;
VAR
    Xdone, Ydone :SIGNAL;

PROCEDURE RunBikeX;
BEGIN
    WriteString('Bike X now running'); WriteLn;
    SEND(Xdone);
    LOOP
        WriteString('X running again'); WriteLn;
    END; (*end of loop *)
END RunBikeX;

PROCEDURE RunBikeY;
BEGIN
    WriteString('Bike Y now running'); WriteLn;
    LOOP
    END; (*end of loop *)
END RunBikeY;

BEGIN (* SendSignal*)
    WriteString('Foreground process running'); WriteLn;
    Init(Xdone);
    StartProcess(RunBikeX,500);
    StartProcess(RunBikeY,500);
END SendSignal.
```

Listing 10.6

X on re-run 1
FG process on run 3
X on re-run 2

By now you should be able to follow this through by reading the source code itself. Observe that the main program is itself treated as a process.

10.5.5 Process queueing

Two interesting points to be considered are:

- How is fairness of use given to the different processes?
- If a process is suspended as a result of sending a signal, *but* it hasn't generated a WAIT signal, how does it restart?

Both problems are solved, in fact, by the same solution. We merely make the processes queue-up for service. When a process is suspended it joins the back of the queue. The process at the front of the queue can now take its place. Whether it actually does so depends on the current state of signals in

```
MODULE WaitSignal;
(***************************************************************)
(*         This shows how processes interact through            *)
(*         the use of the WAIT signal - listing 10.7.           *)
(***************************************************************)
FROM InOut IMPORT WriteString, WriteLn;
FROM Processes IMPORT SIGNAL, SEND, WAIT, Init, StartProcess;
VAR
    Stop :SIGNAL;

PROCEDURE RunBikeX;
BEGIN
    WriteString('Bike X now running'); WriteLn;
    WAIT(Stop);
    WriteString('X on re-run 1'); WriteLn;
    WAIT(Stop);
    WriteString('X on re-run 2'); WriteLn;
    WAIT(Stop);
END RunBikeX;


BEGIN (* WaitSignal *)
    WriteString('Foreground process running'); WriteLn;
    Init(Stop);
    StartProcess(RunBikeX,500);
    WriteString('FG process on run 2'); WriteLn;
    SEND(Stop);
    WriteString('FG process on run 3'); WriteLn;
    SEND(Stop);
END WaitSignal.
```

Listing 10.7

the system. If for any reason it can't run, it goes to the back of the queue; the next process along may now take command of the system.

This is demonstrated by the examples given in Listings 10.8 and 10.9. First consider Listing 10.8. Notice that the main program (now called the foreground process) uses a SEND operation. The other processes use WAIT. The program module sets up the situation shown in Fig. 10.24, giving both the start-up condition and that of the steady-state. Note that the foreground process suspends because of the SEND operation. It is automatically revived when its turn comes round in the queue even though it isn't waiting for a particular signal.

The second point raised above, that of fairness of use, is demonstrated by using two identical WAIT signals. When the foreground process sends the GO signal both processes are waiting for it. However, only the first one in the queue is allowed to respond. Thus, when this module is run and enters the steady-state condition, the screen text goes as follows:

FG running again
X now running again
FG running again
Y now running again
FG running again

250 Concurrent processing

```
MODULE ProcessQueue;
(*****************************************************************)
(*      This example illustrates the cyclic nature of            *)
(*      process queues - listing 10.8.                           *)
(*****************************************************************)
FROM InOut IMPORT WriteString, WriteLn, Write;
FROM Processes IMPORT SIGNAL, SEND, WAIT, Init, StartProcess;
VAR
   GO :SIGNAL;
   I :CARDINAL;

PROCEDURE Delay;
VAR
   Escape : CHAR;
CONST
   CursorLeft = 'D';
   CursorRight = 'C';
BEGIN
   Escape:=CHR(27);
   FOR I:=1 TO 100 DO
      Write(Escape);Write(CursorRight);  Write(Escape);Write(CursorLeft);
   END;(*of for*)
END Delay;

PROCEDURE RunBikeX;
BEGIN
   WriteString('Bike X now running'); WriteLn;
   WAIT(GO);
   LOOP
      Delay;
      WriteString('X now running again'); WriteLn;
      WAIT(GO);
   END; (*end of loop *)
END RunBikeX;

PROCEDURE RunBikeY;
BEGIN
   WriteString('Bike Y now running'); WriteLn;
   WAIT(GO);
   LOOP
      Delay;
      WriteString('Y now running again'); WriteLn;
      WAIT(GO);
   END; (*end of loop *)
END RunBikeY;

BEGIN (*ProcessQueue*)
   WriteString('Foreground process running'); WriteLn;
   Init(GO);
   StartProcess(RunBikeX,500);
   WriteString('FG on run 2'); WriteLn;
   StartProcess(RunBikeY,500);
   LOOP
      Delay;
      WriteString('FG running again'); WriteLn;
      SEND(GO);
   END; (*end of loop*)
END ProcessQueue.
```

Listing 10.8

Multiple task synchronisation

```
MODULE ProcessRunning;
(***************************************************************)
(*     This shows the running of three processes and  their    *)
(*     interaction via SEND and WAIT signals - listing 10.9.   *)
(***************************************************************)
FROM InOut IMPORT WriteString, WriteLn;
FROM Processes IMPORT SIGNAL, SEND, WAIT, Init, StartProcess;
VAR
   GO, Finish, Xdone, Ydone :SIGNAL;

PROCEDURE RunBikeX;
BEGIN
   WriteString('Bike X now running'); WriteLn;
   WAIT(GO);
   WriteString('X on run 2'); WriteLn;
   SEND(Xdone);
   WAIT(Ydone);
   WriteString('X on run 3'); WriteLn;
   SEND(Xdone);
   WAIT(Ydone);
   WriteString('Error if this comes up'); WriteLn;
END RunBikeX;

PROCEDURE RunBikeY;
BEGIN
   WriteString('Bike Y now running'); WriteLn;
   WAIT(Xdone);
   WriteString('Y on run 2'); WriteLn;
   SEND(Ydone);
   WAIT(Xdone);
   WriteString('Y on run 3'); WriteLn;
   WAIT(Finish);
   END RunBikeY;


BEGIN
   WriteString('Foreground process running'); WriteLn;
   Init(Xdone);
   Init(Ydone);
   Init(GO);
   WriteString('FG process starting up X'); WriteLn;
   StartProcess(RunBikeX,500);
   WriteString('FG process starting up Y'); WriteLn;
   StartProcess(RunBikeY,500);
   WriteString('Back to the FG process'); WriteLn;
   SEND(GO);
   WriteString('FG process - 4'); WriteLn;
END ProcessRunning.


        When this is run the following occurs;
        Foreground process running
        FG process starting up X
        Bike X now running
        FG process starting up Y
        Bike Y now running
        Back to the FG process
        X on run 2
        Y on run 2
        FG process - 4
```

Listing 10.9

252 Concurrent processing

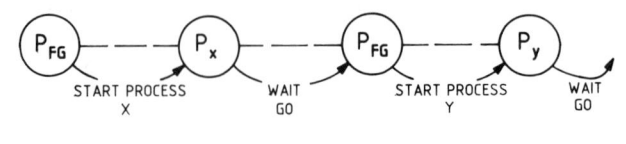

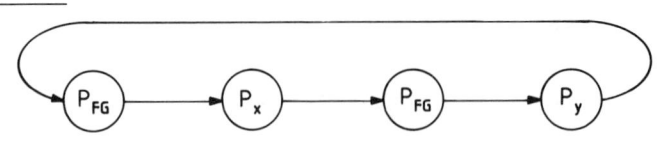

P_{FG} - Foreground Process
P_X - Process X
P_Y - Process Y

Fig. 10.24 Process queuing

X now running again
FG running again
Y now running again
...and so on.

As an exercise, examine the code of example Listing 10.9, predict what should happen, and run the program. Don't be surprised at the difference between prodictions and reality; it just points out the need to clearly think through your program.

Listing 10.10 incorporates the 'Awaited' signal.

```
MODULE Process2Running;
(*****************************************************************)
(*  This shows the of three  processes and their interaction    *)
(*   via the SEND, WAIT and Awaited signals - listing 10.10.    *)
(*****************************************************************)
FROM InOut IMPORT WriteString, WriteLn;
FROM Processes IMPORT SIGNAL, SEND, WAIT, Init, Awaited, StartProcess;
VAR
    GO, Finish, Xdone, Ydone :SIGNAL;

PROCEDURE RunBikeX;
BEGIN
    WriteString('Bike X now running'); WriteLn;
    WAIT(GO);
    WriteString('X on run 2'); WriteLn;
    SEND(Xdone);
    WAIT(Ydone);
    WriteString('X on run 3'); WriteLn;
    SEND(Xdone);
    WAIT(Ydone);
    WriteString('Error if this comes up'); WriteLn;
END RunBikeX;
```

```
PROCEDURE RunBikeY;
BEGIN
   WriteString('Bike Y now running'); WriteLn;
   WAIT(Xdone);
   WriteString('Y on run 2'); WriteLn;
   SEND(Ydone);
   WAIT(Xdone);
   WriteString('Y on run 3'); WriteLn;
   WAIT(Finish);
   END RunBikeY;


BEGIN
   WriteString('Foreground process running'); WriteLn;
   Init(Xdone);
   Init(Ydone);
   Init(GO);
   WriteString('FG process starting up X'); WriteLn;
   StartProcess(RunBikeX,500);
   WriteString('FG process starting up Y'); WriteLn;
   StartProcess(RunBikeY,500);
   WriteString('Back to the FG process'); WriteLn;
   SEND(GO);
   WriteString('FG process - 4'); WriteLn;
   IF Awaited(Ydone) THEN
       WriteString('Process X stopped correctly'); WriteLn;
   END;(*end if*)
END Process2Running.


          When this is run the following occurs;
          Foreground process running
          FG process starting up X
          Bike X now running
          FG process starting up Y
          Bike Y now running
          Back to the FG process
          X on run 2
          Y on run 2
          FG process - 4
          Process X stopped correctly
```

Listing 10.10

10.6 Interrupt handling

In Chapter 9 we saw the need for, and the use of, interrupts. This is a useful point to return to the subject, and view interrupt activities as processes. Only a short, general discussion will be given here. In order to use interrupts in target systems you need to have a good knowledge of both the hardware design and the compiler being used. Specifically, how does it support runtime activities?

Consider now the various stages in installing and activating an interrupt handler into the source code. First we have the writing of the body of the interrupt handling routine. Once again this is encapsulated inside a procedure, e.g.

PROCEDURE Receiver;
...
...
END Receiver;

At some stage the process must be established and, as before, the NEWPROCESS procedure is used, as, for instance,

NEWPROCESS(Receiver, ADR(workspace), SIZE(workspace), receiverP);

Here a process 'receiverP' has been defined, having the code of procedure 'Receiver'.

We activate it using the TRANSFER procedure:

TRANSFER(mainP, receiverP);

where 'mainP' is the foreground process.

So far, so good. However, this process should normally run only when a specific interrupt signal occurs. What we now need to do is to establish the relationship between this process and a particular interrupt vector. Once this is done we can then return control to the foreground process. We do this through a new procedure, IOTRANSFER:

IOTRANSFER(receiverP, mainP, AsyncInterrupt);

This statement is located in the process 'receiverP'. When the program reaches this for the *first* time control is transferred back to 'mainP'. However, what is also does is to say that when the interrupt 'AsyncInterrupt' occurs then process 'receiverP' is to be activated. Once control of the system is transferred to the interrupt routine program execution begins with the statement following the IOTRANSFER statement.

IOTRANSFER is formally defined as:

PROCEDURE IOTRANSFER(VAR source,
                          destination:PROCESS;
                    InterruptVectorNumber:CARDINAL)

where 'source' is the interrupt service routine and 'destination' is the routine which was interrupted.

An alternative view of IOTRANSFER is that it is equivalent to a WAIT operation, only now the activating signal must come from an interrupting source.

One final point concerns systems which have a number of interrupt sources (the normal state of affairs). We must be able to cope with simultaneous multiple interrupt requests in these designs. Clearly only one can be serviced at a time. We can set the system up on a first-come first-served basis; alternatively, important items can be given precedence. This is done by allocating priorities to the individual interrupting sources and responding (typically) as follows:

- No interrupts being serviced: Any interrupt signal will be seen to immediately.
- A low priority interrupt being serviced: Any higher priority interrupt signal will be serviced immediately.
- The highest priority interrupt is being serviced: This cannot be interrupted.

Using Modula-2, priorities can be specified in the header of a module, as for instance:

IMPLEMENTATION MODULE HighSpeedComms[7];

where '7' is the priority number. Priorities can be set in program, implementation and local modules.

In practice, this feature is highly system dependent. If it is used reference should be made to the appropriate compiler manual.

Review

Do you:

- Understand the difference between sequential and parallel activities?
- Appreciate the use of multiprocessing and multitasking?
- Understand multitasking of independent tasks?
- Understand multitasking of interacting tasks?
- Appreciate the co-routine feature (processes) of Modula-2?
- Realise the need for safe synchronisation controls when tasks interact?

Appendix A

EBNF and syntax diagrams

A.1 EBNF as a metalanguage

EBNF stands for 'Extended Backus–Naur Form' (of notation), and is one widely used method to define the formal rules, the 'syntax', of programming languages. As such it is called a 'metalanguage', that is, a language used to describe another language. It is based on BNF which was invented by John Backus and used in the defining report on Algol 60, 'Report on the Algorithmic Language ALGOL60', the editor being Peter Naur. Hence the name.

Why should it be necessary to invent a language to describe programming languages? After all we seem to get by in most situations with ordinary English. True, but everyday language tends to be imprecise, ambiguous or ambivalent. The objective in using a metalanguage is to remove these factors so that programming languages can be precisely defined and interpreted. Some computer scientists argue that so far this has never been achieved; however, we'll content ourselves with the tools at hand and use EBNF, together with syntax diagrams, to describe the rules of Modula-2.

We can build up our full set of language rules through the use of four basic operations:

- Concatenation
- Choice
- Option (this here has a different meaning to choice)
- Repetition

Let's describe what we mean by using the words BIRTHDAYPRESENT, TOOL and BOX. If we mean that the present is to consist of both a tool and a box then we write

   BIRTHDAYPRESENT = TOOL BOX

which is the concatenation of the two words TOOL and BOX. If, on the other hand, we mean either a tool or a box then we write

BIRTHDAYPRESENT = TOOL | BOX

where | means OR. Where the present may be a tool, but alternatively we may send nothing (the option), then we have

BIRTHDAYPRESENT = TOOL or NOTHING

written as [TOOL]. In the final situation we may decide to send one tool, two, or maybe three, and so on, or even nothing, giving

BIRTHDAYPRESENT = NOTHING, One TOOL, Two TOOLs, etc.

written as BIRTHDAYPRESENT = {TOOL}.

More concisely, if we represent four objects as A, B, C and D, then we can define a whole variety of relationships between them using EBNF notation. For instance,

```
A = B|C|D. means   A = B or C or D
A = [B].           A = Nothing (empty) or B
A = B[C].          A = B or BC
A = {B}.           A = Empty or B or BB or BBB, etc.
A = B{D}.          A = B or BD or BDD or BDDD etc.
```

Through the use of parentheses (round brackets to you) the objects can be grouped together as, for instance,

A = (B|C)D. meaning A = BD or CD

QA.1 Explain the meaning of the following relationships which are defined using EBNF:

(a) B[C]D
(b) B[CD]
(c) B{C}D
(d) B{CD}
(e) {B}CD
(f) B(C|D)
(g) [B|C]D
(h) {B|C}D

Answers:

(a) BD BCD   (b) B BCD
(c) BD BCD BCCD ...   (d) B BCD BCDCD ...
(e) CD BCD BBCD ...   (f) BC BD   (g) D BD CD
(h) D BD CD BBD CCD BCD CBD BBCD ...

There is a good reason for you to gain an understanding of EBNF. Modula-2 was designed by Professor Nicklaus Wirth; he describes the working definition of the language using EBNF. This has been reproduced in Appendix B.

A.2 Syntax diagrams

Syntax diagrams are a way of expressing the rules of a language in pictorial form. For many people, information is conveyed much more easily when it's presented as a picture instead of using words. Assimilation and understanding is readily achieved; moreover, these are more likely to be correct. If this is true then we should be able to explain their use with few words. Given below are the EBNF concepts outlined earlier, now explained using diagrams. Appendix B states the language rules in this form.

EBNF NOTATION   SYNTAX DIAGRAM

BIRTHDAYPRESENT
= TOOL BOX

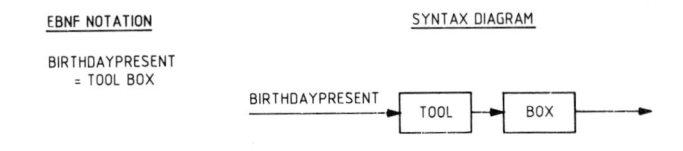

Fig. A.1

EBNF NOTATION   SYNTAX DIAGRAM

BIRTHDAYPRESENT
= [TOOL]

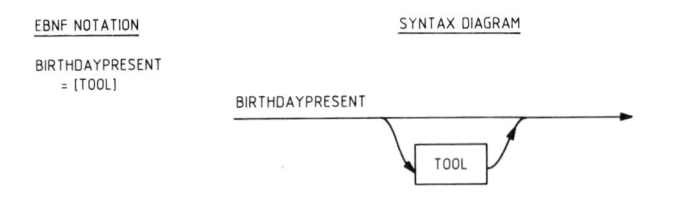

Fig. A.2

EBNF NOTATION   SYNTAX DIAGRAM

BIRTHDAYPRESENT
= TOOL/BOX

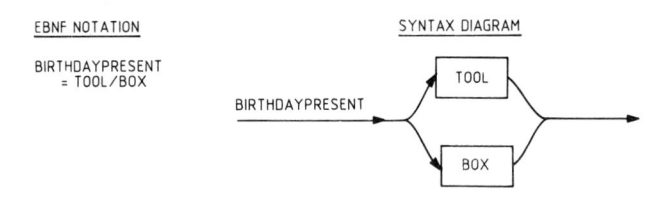

Fig. A.3

EBNF NOTATION   SYNTAX DIAGRAM

BIRTHDAYPRESENT
= {TOOL}

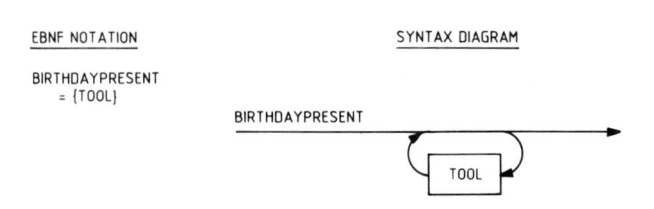

Fig. A.4

Syntax diagrams 259

EBNF NOTATION

A = B|C|D

SYNTAX DIAGRAM

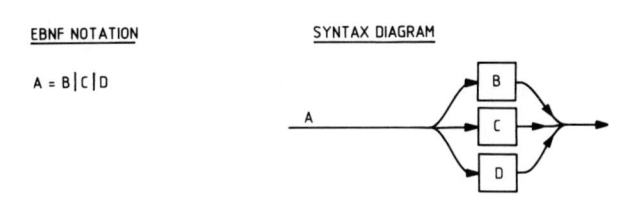

Fig. A.5

EBNF NOTATION

A = B[C]

SYNTAX DIAGRAM

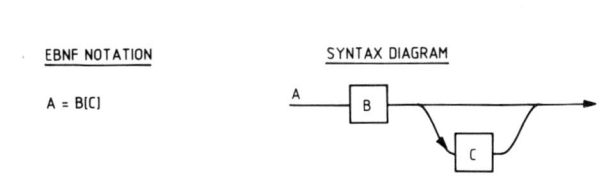

Fig. A.6

EBNF NOTATION

A = B{D}

SYNTAX DIAGRAM

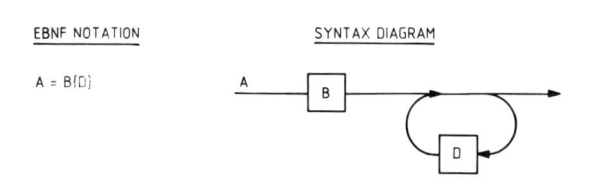

Fig. A.7

EBNF NOTATION

A = B[C]D

SYNTAX DIAGRAM

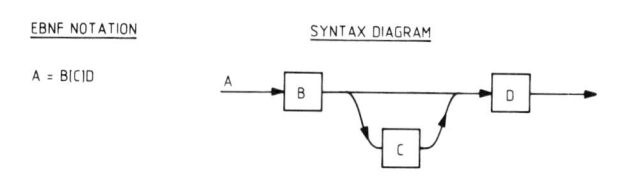

Fig. A.8

EBNF NOTATION

A = {B/C}D

SYNTAX DIAGRAM

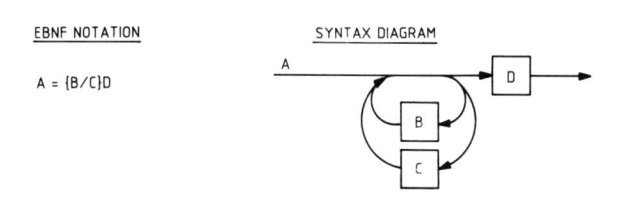

Fig. A.9

Appendix B
Modula-2 language definition

The formal definition of Modula-2 is given in this appendix. It is based on that produced by Professor Nicklaus Wirth in his book, *Programming in Modula-2*, Springer-Verlag, 1985, and is reproduced with permission.

B.1 The syntax of Modula-2

1 ident = letter{letter | digit}.
2 number = integer | real.
3 integer = digit{digit} | octalDigit{octalDigit} ("B"|"C") |
4   digit{hexDigit} "H".
5 real = digit{digit} "." {digit} [ScaleFactor].
6 ScaleFactor = "E" ["+"|"−"] digit{digit}.
7 hexDigit = digit|"A"|"B"|"C"|"D"|"E"|"F".
8 digit = octalDigit|"8"|"9".
9 octalDigit = "0"|"1"|"2"|"3"|"4"|"5"|"6"|"7".
10 string = "'" {character} "'" | '"' {character} '"'.
11 qualident = ident{"." ident}.
12 ConstantDeclaration = ident "=" ConstExpression.
13† ConstExpression = expression.
14 TypeDeclaration = ident "=" type.
15 type = SimpleType | ArrayType | RecordType | SetType |
16   PointerType | ProcedureType.
17 SimpleType = qualident | enumeration | Subrange Type.
18 enumeration = "(" IdentList ")".
19 IdentList = ident{"," ident}.
20† SubrangeType = [qualident] "[" ConstExpression ".." ConstExpression "]".
21 ArrayType = ARRAY SimpleType {"," SimpleType} OF type.
22 RecordType = RECORD FieldListSequence END.
23 FieldListSequence = FieldList{";" FieldList}.

24 FieldList = [IdentList ":" type |
25†   CASE[ident] ":" qualident OF variant{"|" variant}
26   [ELSE FieldListSequence] END].
27† variant = [CaseLabelList ":" FieldListSequence].
28 CaseLabelList = CaseLabels{"," CaseLabels}.
29 CaseLabels = ConstExpression[".." ConstExpression].
30 SetType = SET OF SimpleType.
31 PointerType = POINTER TO type.
32 ProcedureType = PROCEDURE[FormalTypeList].
33 FormalTypeList = "("[[VAR] FormalType
34   {"," [VAR] FormalType}]")" [":" qualident].
35 VariableDeclaration = IdentList ":" type.
36 designator = qualident{"." ident | "["ExpList"]" | " ↑ "}.
37 ExpList = expression{"," expression}.
38 expression = SimpleExpression[relation SimpleExpression].
39 relation = "=" | "#" | "<" | "<=" | ">" | ">=" | IN.
40 SimpleExpression = ["+"|"−"] term {AddOperator term}.
41 AddOperator = "+" | "−" | OR.
42 term = factor{MulOperator factor}.
43 MulOperator = "*" | "/" | DIV | MOD | AND.
44 factor = number | string | set | designator[ActualParameters] |
45   "("expression")" | NOT factor.
46 set = [qualident] "{"[element{"," element}]"}".
47† element = expression[".." expression].
48 ActualParameters = "("[ExpList]")".
49 statement = [assignment | ProcedureCall |
50   IfStatement | CaseStatement | WhileStatement |
51   RepeatStatement | LoopStatement | ForStatement |
52   WithStatement | EXIT | RETURN [expression]].
53 assignment = designator ":=" expression.
54 ProcedureCall = designator[ActualParameters].
55 StatementSequence = statement{":" statement}.
56 IfStatement = IF expression THEN StatementSequence
57   {ELSIF expression THEN StatementSequence}
58   [ELSE StatementSequence] END.
59 CaseStatement = CASE expression OF case {"|" case}
60   [ELSE StatementSequence] END.
61† case = [CaseLabelList ":" StatementSequence].
62 WhileStatement = WHILE expression DO StatementSequence END.
63 RepeatStatement = REPEAT StatementSequence UNTIL expression.
64 ForStatement = FOR ident ":=" expression TO expression
65   [BY ConstExpression] DO StatementSequence END.
66 LoopStatement = LOOP StatementSequence END.
67 WithStatement = WITH designator DO StatementSequence END.
68 ProcedureDeclaration = ProcedureHeading ";" block ident.

69 ProcedureHeading = PROCEDURE ident [FormalParameters].
70 block = {declaration} [BEGIN StatementSequence] END.
71 declaration = CONST{ConstantDeclaration ";"} |
72   TYPE{TypeDeclaration ";"} |
73   VAR{VariableDeclaration ";"} |
74   ProcedureDeclaration ";" | ModuleDeclaration ";".
75 FormalParameters =
76   "("[FPSection{";" FPSection}]")" [":" qualident].
77 FPSection = [VAR] IdentList ":" FormalType.
78 FormalType = [ARRAY OF] qualident.
79 ModuleDeclaration =
80   MODULE ident [priority] ";" {import} [export] block ident.
81 priority = "["ConstExpression"]".
82 export = EXPORT [QUALIFIED] IdentList ";".
83 import = [FROM ident] IMPORT IdentList ";".
84 DefinitionModule = DEFINITION MODULE ident ";"
85†   {import} {definition} END ident ".".
86 definition = CONST {ConstantDeclaration ";"} |
87   TYPE{ident["=" type] ";"} |
88   VAR{VariableDeclaration ";"} |
89   ProcedureHeading ";".
90 ProgramModule = MODULE ident [priority] ";" {import} block ident ".".
91 CompilationUnit = DefinitionModule | [IMPLEMENTATION] ProgramModule.

B.2 Modula-2 syntax diagrams

This section contains a description of the rules of Modula-2 using syntax diagrams. These conform to those given in *Programming in Modula-2* (Third Edition), by Professor N. Wirth. Generally their order ties in with the presentation of material within the text.

Diagram Name	Fig. No.
ActualParameters	B38
AddOperator	B15
ArrayType	B54
assignment	B19
block	B33
CaseLabels	B26
CaseLabelList	B25
CaseStatement	B24
CompilationUnit	B53
ConstantDeclaration	B13

ConstExpression	B14
declaration	B34
definition	B51
DefinitionModule	B50
designator	B62
digit	B3
element	B68
enumeration	B42
ExpList	B63
export	B48
expression	B20
factor	B66
FieldList	B59
FieldListSequence	B58
FormalParameters	B35
FormalType	B55
FormalTypeList	B45
ForStatement	B29
FPSection	B36
hexDigit	B6
ident	B1
IdentList	B12
IfStatement	B23
import	B49
integer	B9
letter	B2
LoopStatement	B30
ModuleDeclaration	B46
MulOperator	B16
number	B8
octalDigit	B5
PointerType	B64
priority	B47
ProcedureCall	B37
ProcedureDeclaration	B31
ProcedureHeading	B32
ProcedureType	B44
ProgramModule	B52
qualident	B4
real	B10
RecordType	B57
relation	B17
RepeatStatement	B27
set	B67
SetType	B56

SimpleExpression	B21
SimpleType	B41
statement	B65
StatementSequence	B18
string	B7
SubrangeType	B43
term	B22
type	B40
TypeDeclaration	B39
VariableDeclaration	B11
variant	B60
WhileStatement	B28
WithStatement	B61

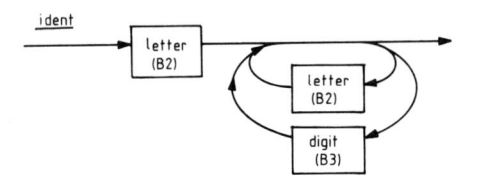

Fig. B.1

Fig. B.2

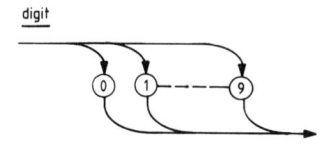

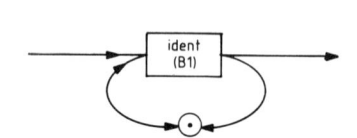

Fig. B.3

Fig. B.4

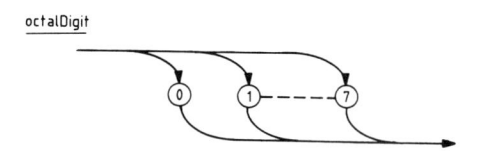

Fig. B.5

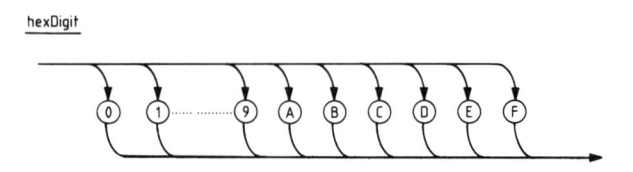

Fig. B.6

Modula-2 syntax diagrams **265**

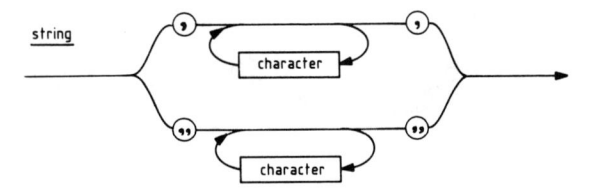

Fig. B.7

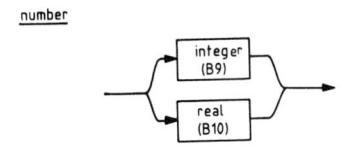

Fig. B.8

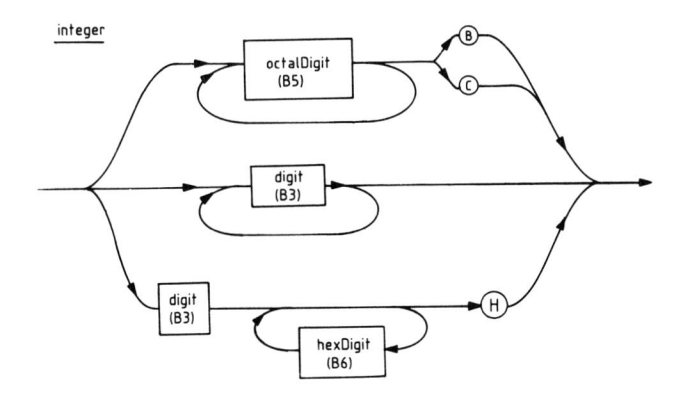

Fig. B.9

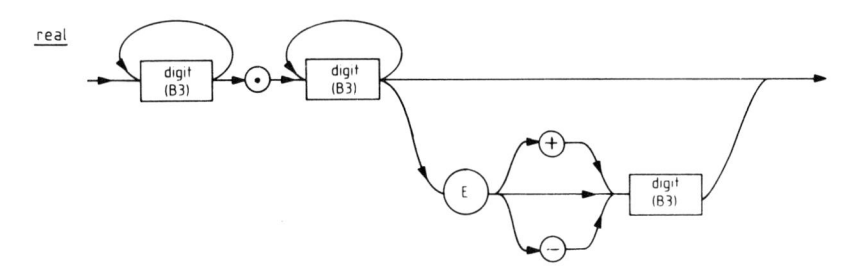

Fig. B.10

266 Appendix B Modula-2 language definition

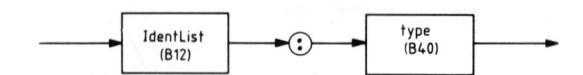

Fig. B.11

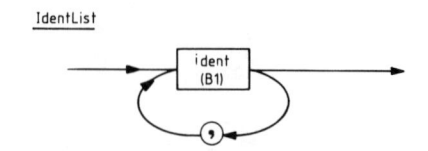

Fig. B.12

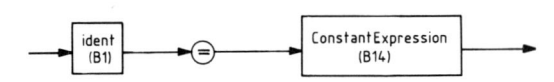

Fig. B.13

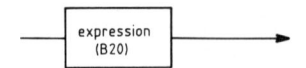

Fig. B.14

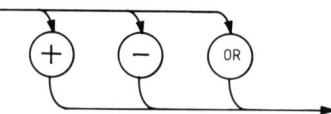

Fig. B.15

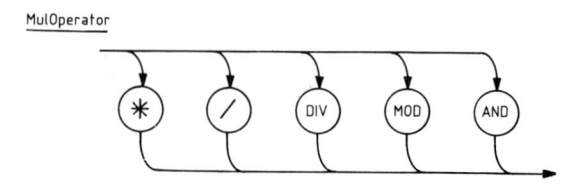

Fig. B.16

Modula-2 syntax diagrams **267**

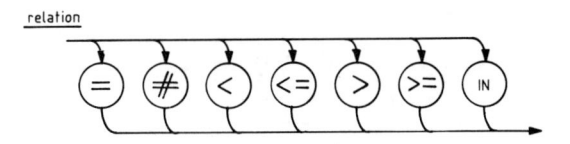

Fig. B.17

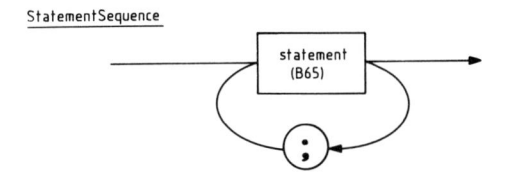

Fig. B.18

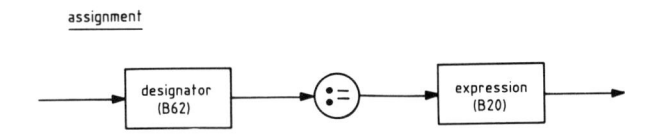

Fig. B.19 •

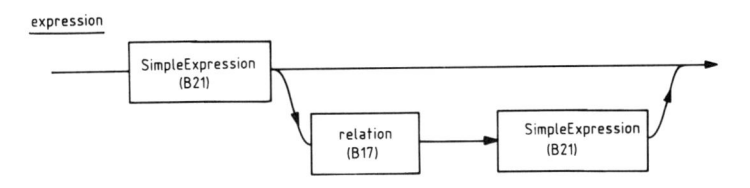

Fig. B.20

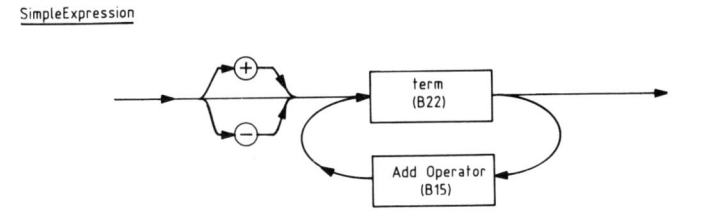

Fig. B.21

268 Appendix B Modula-2 language definition

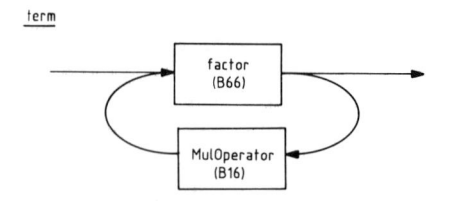

Fig. B.22

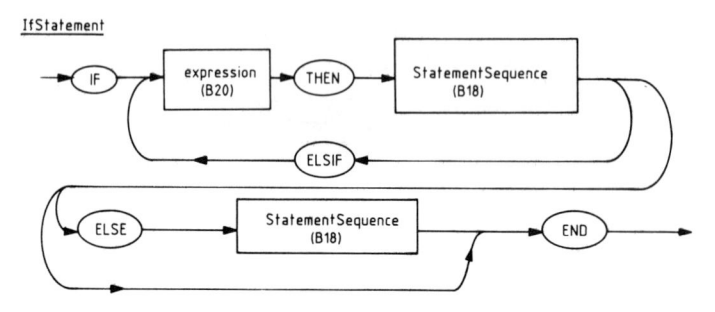

Fig. B.23

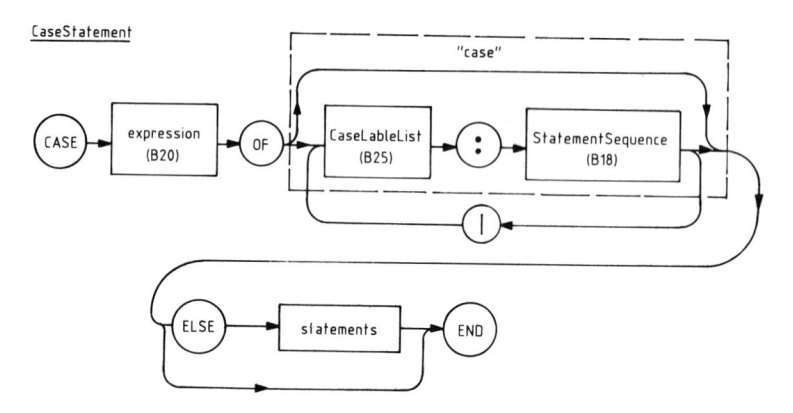

Fig. B.24

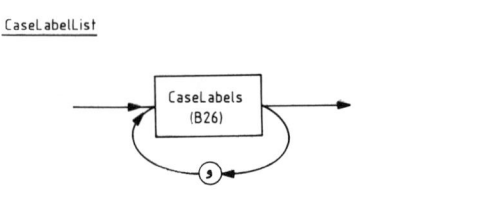

Fig. B.25

Modula-2 syntax diagrams **269**

CaseLabels

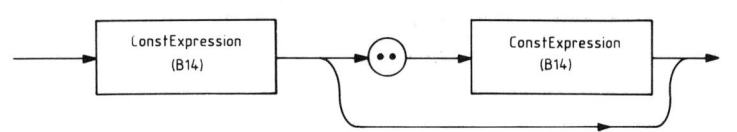

Fig. B.26

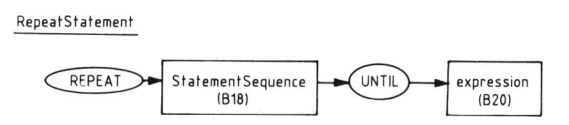

RepeatStatement

Fig. B.27

WhileStatement

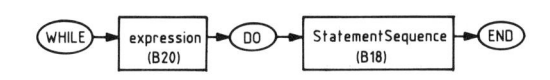

Fig. B.28

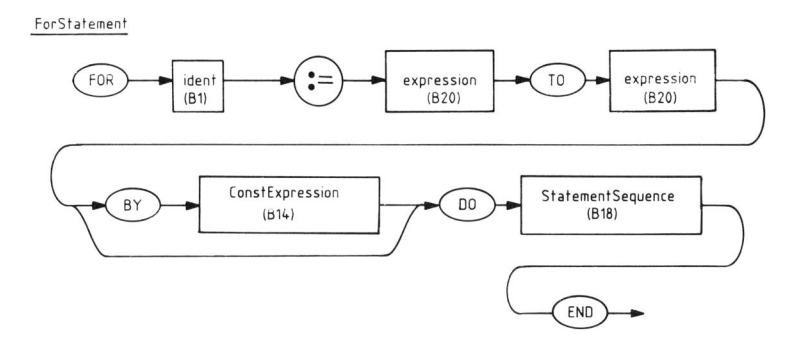

ForStatement

Fig. B.29

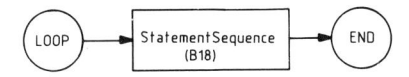

LoopStatement

Fig. B.30

270 Appendix B Modula-2 language definition

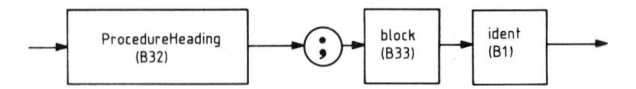

Fig. B.31

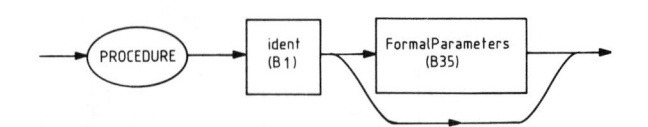

Fig. B.32

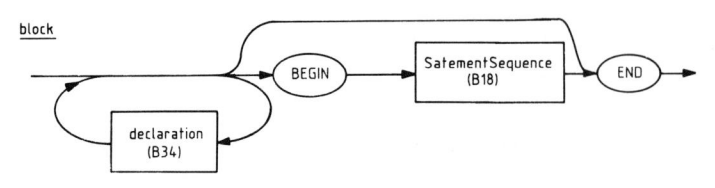

Fig. B.33

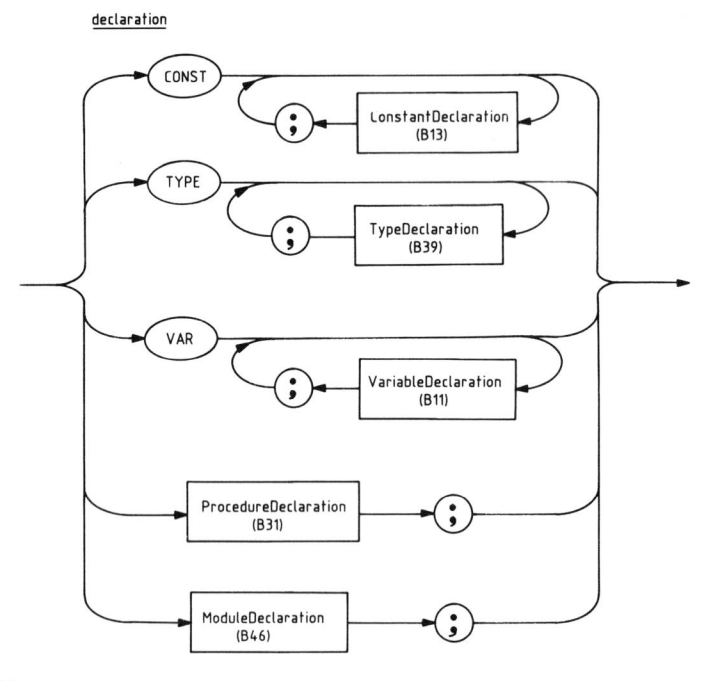

Fig. B.34

Modula-2 syntax diagrams **271**

FormalParameters

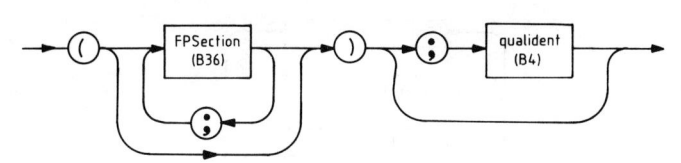

Fig. B.35

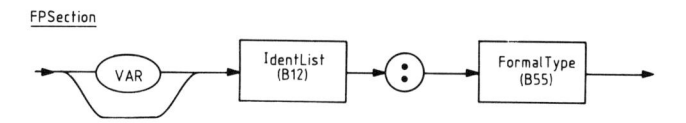

FPSection

Fig. B.36

ProcedureCall

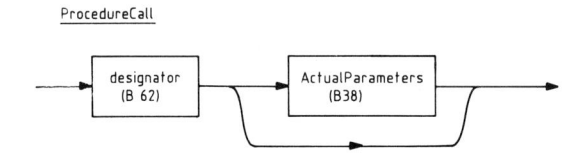

Fig. B.37

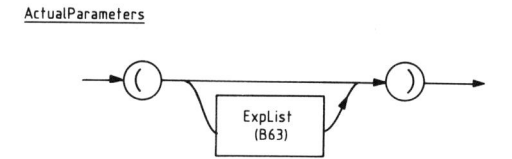

ActualParameters

Fig. B.38

TypeDeclaration

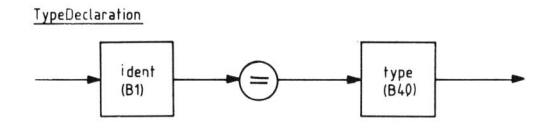

Fig. B.39

272 Appendix B Modula-2 language definition

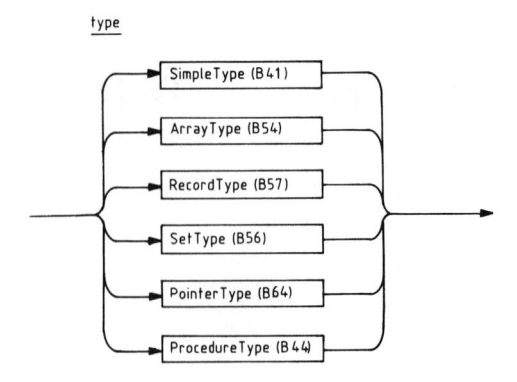

Fig. B.40

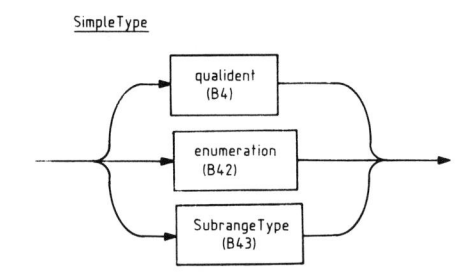

Fig. B.41

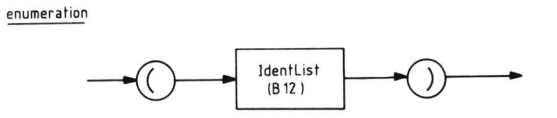

Fig. B.42

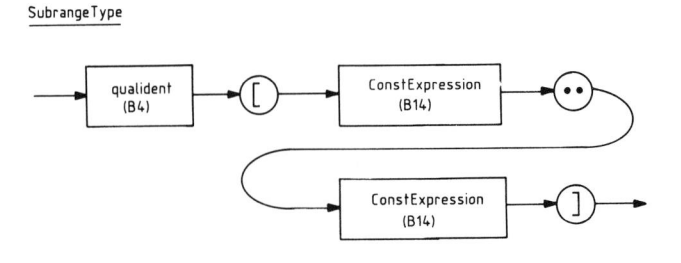

Fig. B.43

Modula-2 syntax diagrams 273

ProcedureType

→─(PROCEDURE)──→[FormalTypeList (B45)]──→

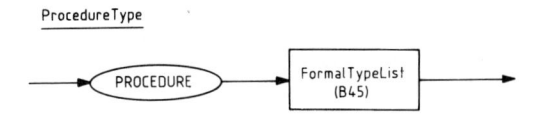

Fig. B.44

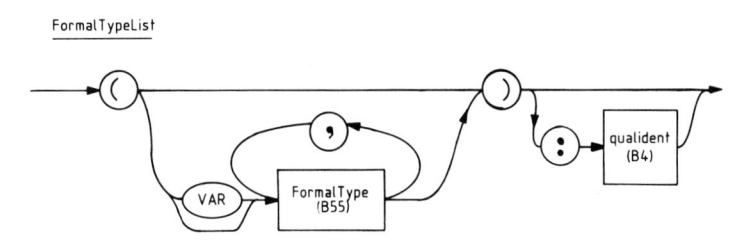

FormalTypeList

→─(( )─┬─────────────────────┬─( ))─┬──────────────────────────────→
        │ ┌──────(,)──────┐ │   │
        └─┬─(VAR)─┬─[FormalType (B55)]─┘   └─(:)─[qualident (B4)]─┘
          └───────┘

Fig. B.45

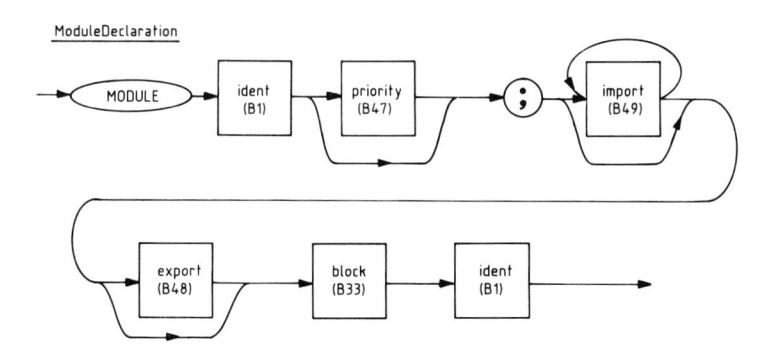

ModuleDeclaration

→─(MODULE)──→[ident (B1)]──→[priority (B47)]──→(;)──┬─[import (B49)]─┐
                                                          └──────────────────┘
    ┌─[export (B48)]─┐
    └──────────────────┴──→[block (B33)]──→[ident (B1)]──→

Fig. B.46

priority

→─([ )──→[ConstExpression (B14)]──→( ])──→

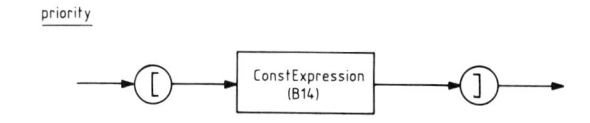

Fig. B.47

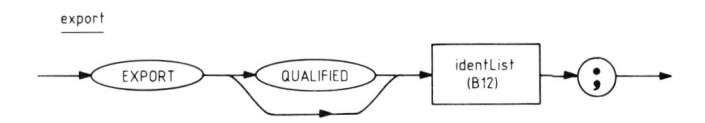

export

→─(EXPORT)──┬─(QUALIFIED)─┬──→[identList (B12)]──→(;)──→
              └───────────────┘

Fig. B.48

274 Appendix B Modula-2 language definition

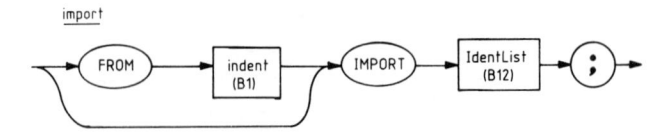

Fig. B.49

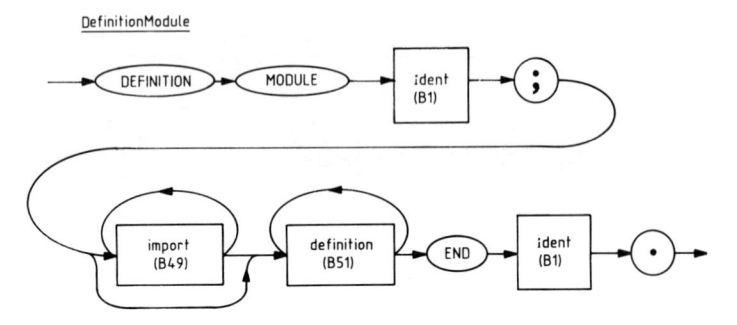

Fig. B.50

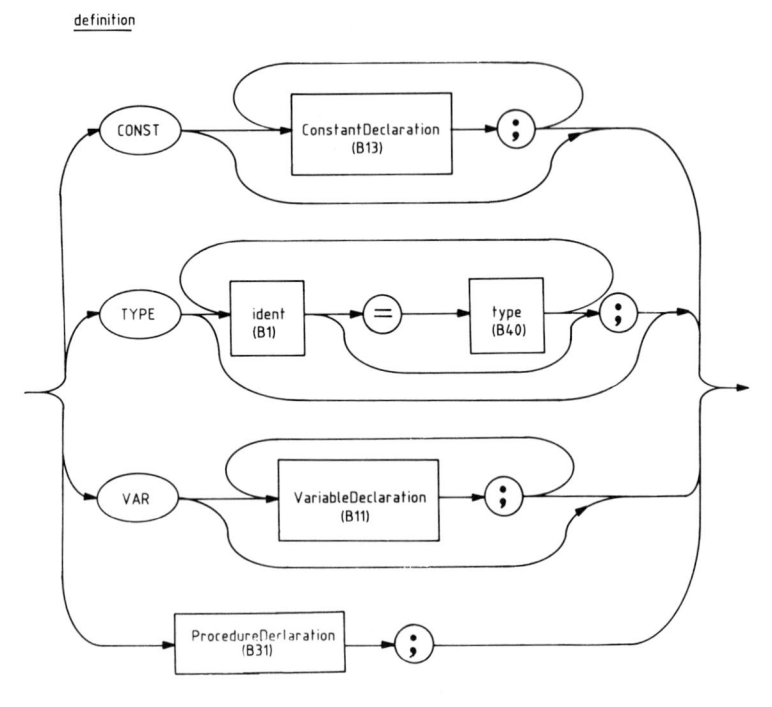

Fig. B.51

Modula-2 syntax diagrams **275**

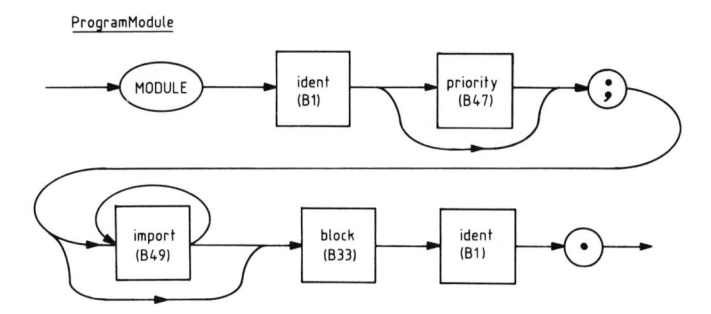

Fig. B.52

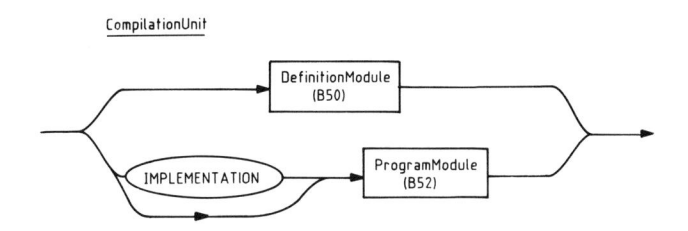

Fig. B.53

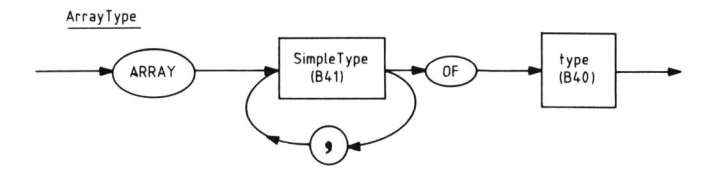

Fig. B.54

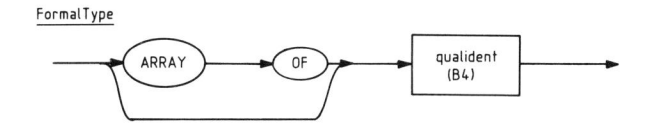

Fig. B.55

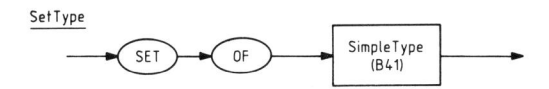

Fig. B.56

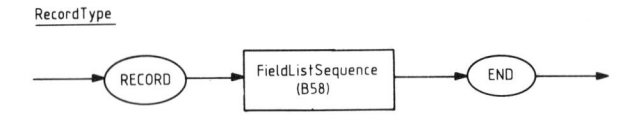

Fig. B.57

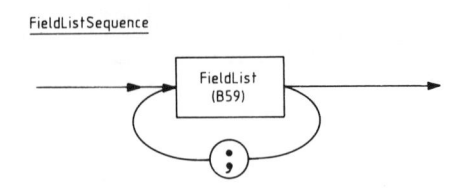

Fig. B.58

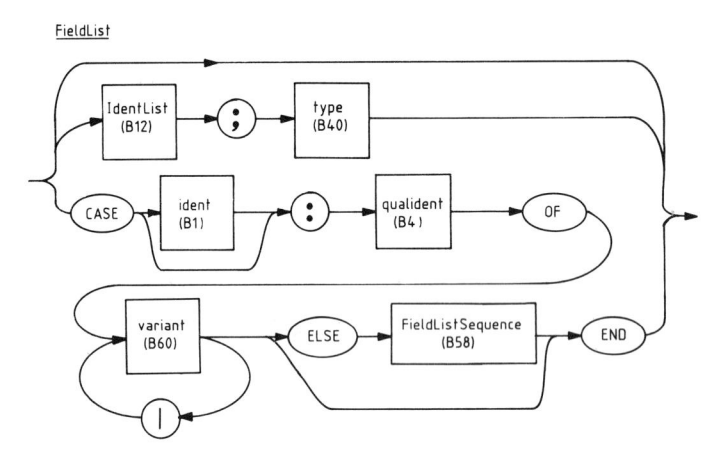

Fig. B.59

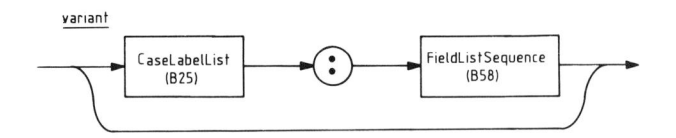

Fig. B.60

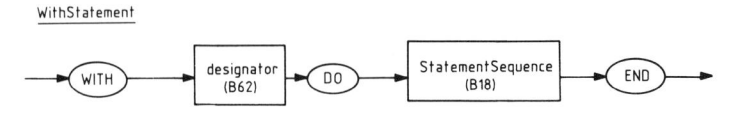

Fig. B.61

Modula-2 syntax diagrams **277**

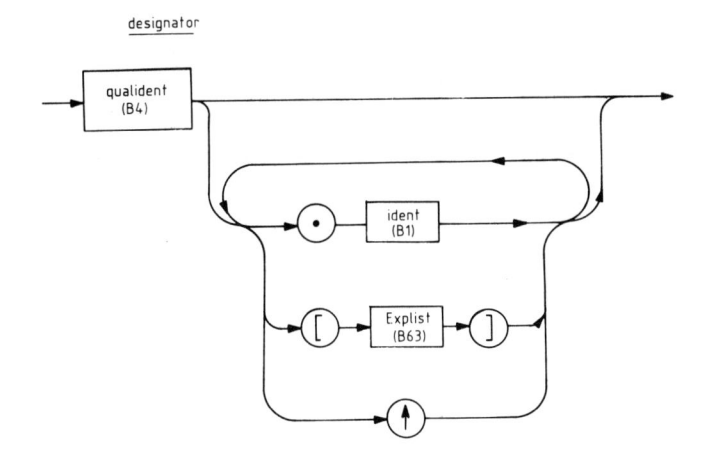

Fig. B.62

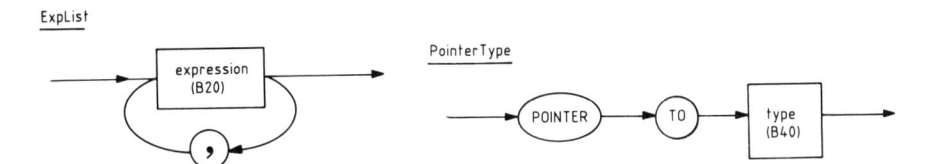

Fig. B.63

Fig. B.64

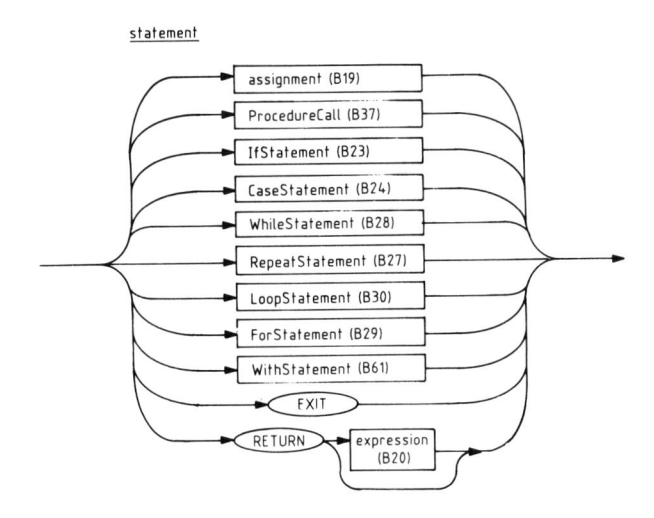

Fig. B.65

278   Appendix B Modula-2 language definition

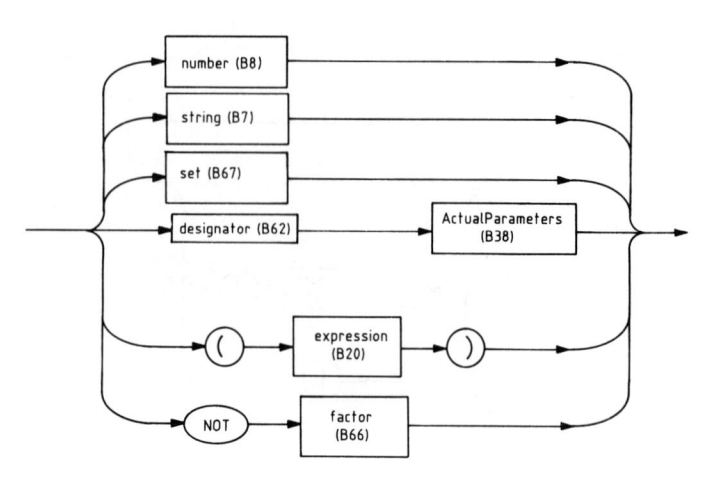

Fig. B.66

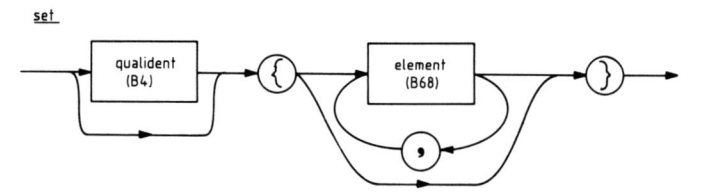

Fig. B.67

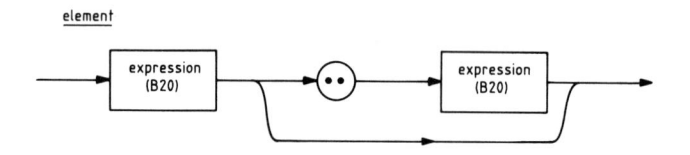

Fig. B.68

Appendix C
Modula-2 language features

C.1 Reserved words

AND	ELSIF	LOOP	REPEAT
ARRAY	END	MOD	RETURN
BEGIN	EXIT	MODULE	SET
BY	EXPORT	NOT	THEN
CASE	FOR	OF	TO
CONST	FROM	OR	TYPE
DEFINITION	IF	POINTER	UNTIL
DIV	IMPLEMENTATION	PROCEDURE	VAR
DO	IMPORT	QUALIFIED	WHILE
ELSE	IN	RECORD	WITH

C.2 Operators and delimiters

+	addition, set union, unary plus
–	subtraction, set difference, unary minus
*	Multiplication, set intersection
/	real division, symmetric set difference
:=	assignment
&	logical (Boolean) AND
~	logical (Boolean) NOT
=	equal
<>	not equal
<	less than
>	greater than
<=	less than or equal to, subset
>=	greater than or equal to, superset
( )	parentheses
[ ]	array index brackets, index brackets

{ }   set brackets
(* *)   comment delimiters
;   statement delimiter
..   subrange delimiter
| alternative delimiter
.   end of module delimiter
,
:

C.3 Operator precedence

Highest (first)   NOT,~
second   *, /, DIV, MOD, AND
third   +, −, OR
fourth (lowest)   =, <>, <, >, <=, >=, IN

C.4 Standard predefined identifiers

(i) **Constants:** FALSE TRUE NIL

(ii) **Types:** BITSET BOOLEAN CARDINAL CHAR INTEGER PROC REAL
(note that LONGINT and LONGREAL are defined by Wirth but may not be implemented).

(iii) **Procedures and function procedures:**

ABS(x)   Used to find the absolute value of a number. Returns the absolute value of x. This matches the argument type.

CAP(x)   Used to convert characters to uppercase form. Returns the uppercase version of the character x. This is of type CHAR. If x is lower case no action is taken.

CHR(x)   Given an ordinal number, it is used to find its corresponding character. Returns the character whose ordinal number is x. The Logitech compiler expects a cardinal value for x.

DEC(x)   Decrements x by 1. x may be CARDINAL, INTEGER, CHAR, or any enumerated or subrange types. For CHAR or enumerated types, decrementing a variable gives its predecessor in the enumeration list (x:=x−1).

DEC(X,n)   Decrements x by n.

DISPOSE(x) Releases the storage space occupied by the data referenced by pointer x. This is bound up with the use of system module procedures ALLOCATE and DEALLOCATE.

EXCL(a,x)   Deletes the element x from the set a (a:=a−{x}).

FLOAT(x)   Used to convert a cardinal number to its real equivalent. Returns a REAL value for a cardinal.

HALT	Stops the program.
HIGH(x)	Used to find the numerical value of the high index bound of an array. x is an array variable.
INC(x)	Reverse operation to DEC(x).
INC(x,n)	Reverse to DEC(x,n).
INCL(a,x)	Reverse to EXCL(a,x). a:=a+{x}.
MAX(T)	Used to find the maximum value of a type T.
MIN(T)	Used to find the minimum value of a type T.
NEW(x)	Creates a data storage space referenced by pointer x (see comments relating to DISPOSE).
ODD(x)	This checks if x (INTEGER or CARDINAL) is an odd or even value. Returns a Boolean result TRUE if x is odd, otherwise returns FALSE.
ORD(x)	Used to find the ordinal value of an item in an enumerated list. The return value is CARDINAL.
SIZE(x)	Use to find the amount of memory storage required by a variable x. Implemented in the Logitech compiler as SIZE, imported from SYSTEM module.
SIZE(T)	Used to find the amount of memory storage required by a type T. Implemented in module SYSTEM as TSIZE.
TRUNC(x)	This truncates a real value x to its integral part in CARDINAL form.
VAL(T,x)	Used to find the value of an element in any enumerated list. T is the type, x is the ordinal value in the list.

(iv) Facilities provided by the module SYSTEM.
   Note that the following items may be implementation dependent.
   (a) **Types:** BYTE, WORD, PROCESS, ADDRESS

   (b) **Procedures and function procedures:**

ADR(x)	This gives the storage address of the variable x. The answer, returned is of type ADDRESS.
IOTRANSFER(P1,P2,n)	Transfers program execution from process P2 to process P when interrupt n occurs. P1 is defined to be the "interrupt handler" P2 is the "interrupted process"
NEWPROCESS(PB,WA,WS,x)	This creates a new process. PB is the procedure which is executed. WA is the address of the workspace of this procedure. WS is the memory size (workspace size) allocated to this PROCESS. x is the name given to the PROCESS.

SIZE(x)	Used to find the amount of memory storage required by a variable. The answer is of type cardinal.
TRANSFER(P1,P2)	Transfers program execution from process P1 to process P2.
TSIZE(T)	Used to find the amount of memory storage required by a type T.

C.5 Control statements

CASE expression OF
  ConstantExpression: StatementSequence; |
  ConstantExpression: StatementSequence; |
  .
  .
  ConstantExpression: StatementSequence;
ELSE
  StatementSequence;
END;

IF BooleanExpression THEN
  StatementSequence;
END;

IF BooleanExpression THEN
  StatementSequence;
ELSE
  StatementSequence;
END;

IF BooleanExpression THEN
  StatementSequence;
ELSIF BooleanExpression THEN
  StatementSequence;
ELSIF BooleanExpression THEN
  StatementSequence;
  .
  .
ELSE
  StatementSequence;
END;

FOR variable:=expression TO expression DO
  StatementSequence;
END;

FOR variable:=expression TO expression BY constant DO
  StatementSequence;
END;

WHILE BooleanExpression DO
  StatementSequence;
END;

REPEAT
  StatementSequence;
UNTIL BooleanExpression;

LOOP
  StatementSequence;
END;

LOOP
  StatementSequence;
  EXIT;
  StatementSequence;
END;

WITH RecordVariable DO
  StatementSequence;
END;

Appendix D

Program development for micros

D.1 Introduction

Many students are familiar with software development on mini or mainframe systems, but when programs are produced for microcomputers the development process is different, especially for target system software. This appendix sets out to introduce the reader to the broader aspects of program development techniques for microprocessors. Most electronic engineers will be familiar with these. However, computer scientists and software engineers should find it a useful guide.

To understand the various stages of program development let's start in the computer system itself. Figure D.1 shows the basic or core structure of any microcomputer. This applies to all such systems, including personal computers and embedded (target) applications.

In PCs the EPROM usually only carries a small program designed to get the machine up and running. This is the so-called 'bootstrap' loader. Main programs run from RAM, these being down-loaded from disk. In embedded systems all program code is carried in EPROM. RAM is used for variables,

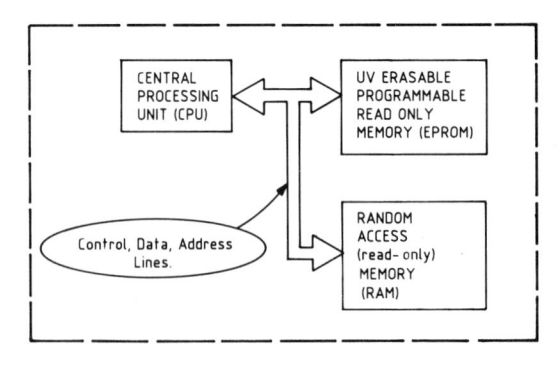

Fig. D.1 Basic microcomputer structure

Introduction **285**

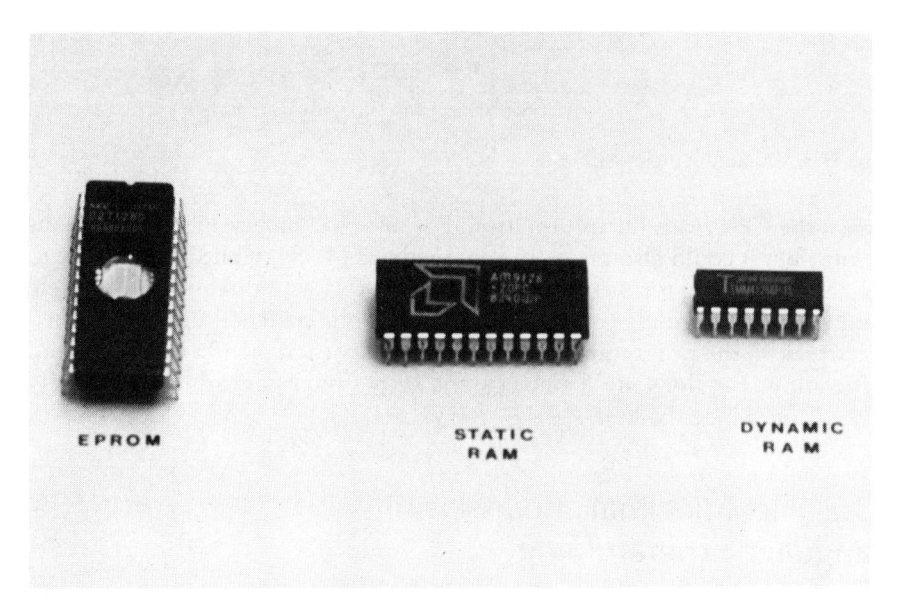

Fig. D.2 EPROM and RAM integrated circuits

including stack data. In any case, whether RAM or EPROM (Fig. D.2) is used to hold the code, system functioning is the same. The bit pattern stored in these memories acts as the instructions and data for the CPU. Examples of instructions applicable to the Intel 188 processor are given in Fig. D.3. These are the simplest ones, involving only one byte (8 bits). More complex ones exist within the instruction set, some being as much as five bytes long.

In most systems data is stored in byte or word (16-bit) form. It is accessed by placing the appropriate address on the system address bus (Fig. D.4), activating access control signals, and reading the resulting output on the data lines. This, by the way, is a very simple explanation; CPU operation is made more complex because the interpretation of the code word depends on

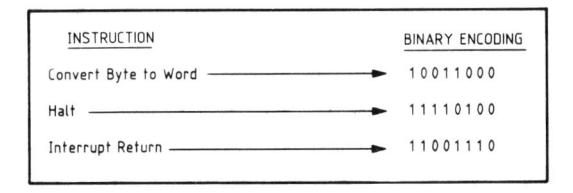

INSTRUCTION	BINARY ENCODING
Convert Byte to Word	1 0 0 1 1 0 0 0
Halt	1 1 1 1 0 1 0 0
Interrupt Return	1 1 0 0 1 1 1 0

Fig. D.3 Computer instructions – example

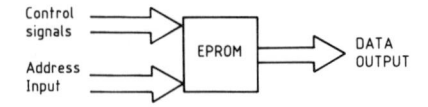

Fig. D.4 Obtaining processor data

when the CPU reads the information. For instance, binary 11110100 means 'Halt'; but it could also mean 'the data value 244'. So, while it is possible to use binary coding for program development, this would require a complete and full understanding of CPU operation, infinite patience and a masochistic streak in the programmer. Nevertheless, always remember that any and all computer actions are defined by the stored binary information (usually called the 'object code').

D.2 Hexadecimal and assembly language programming

In some cases it actually is convenient to prepare code and data for direct loading into the memory devices. An instance is the execution of tests whilst developing the computer hardware. For our convenience we could do with a shorthand form of binary coding. A very widely used method is that of hexadecimal coding (Fig. D.5). In this format the 'Halt' instruction becomes 'F4'. What are the advantages of using such coding? First, the amount of typing is cut down, by a factor of four. Second, and more importantly, the code is more recognisable. Therefore, mistakes are reduced. But such information cannot be directly applied to the memories as these have to be programmed in binary format. Translation from hex to binary is needed. Two commonly used methods are shown in Fig. D.6. Where the program is to run from RAM the translation is carried out using a monitor or utility program. These are often found on low-cost kits designed for elementry teach-

BINARY	HEXADECIMAL
0000	0
0001	1
0010	2
⋮	⋮
1001	9
1010	A
1011	B
1100	C
1101	D
1110	E
1111	F

Fig. D.5 Binary-hexadecimal conversion

Hexadecimal and assembly language programming **287**

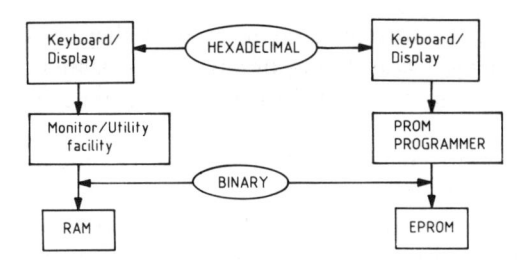

Fig. D.6 Hexadecimal programming

ing of microprocessor programming. Conversely, when code is to be loaded into EPROM, a PROM programmer (Fig. D.7) is used to perform hex to binary conversion.

Hexadecimal coding is useful only in specialised circumstances, and then only for very short programs. The next (higher) stage in the abstraction process is to use plain language statements to define CPU actions. For brevity, mnemonics are used, as for instance,

```
Convert byte to word ——> CBW
Halt                 ——> HLT
Interrupt return     ——> IRET
```

Fig. D.7 PROM programmer

When CPU instructions are expressed in this form they are said to be written in 'assembly language'. Translation of source text statements into executable binary instructions is carried out using a program called an 'assembler' (Fig. D.8).

Various outputs are available from assemblers; much depends on the specific product. For EPROM-based software the output file must be compatible with PROM programmers. One very widely used file structure which meets this requirement is that of 'Intel Hex format'.

Clearly the assembler programs must be run on a processor-based system

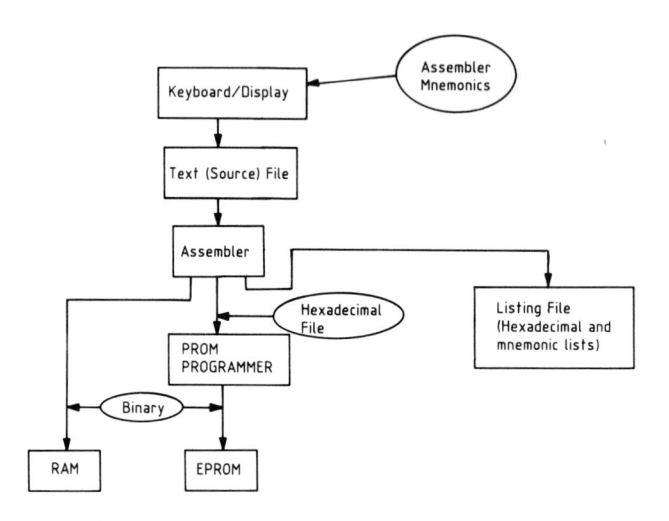

Fig. D.8 Assembly language programming

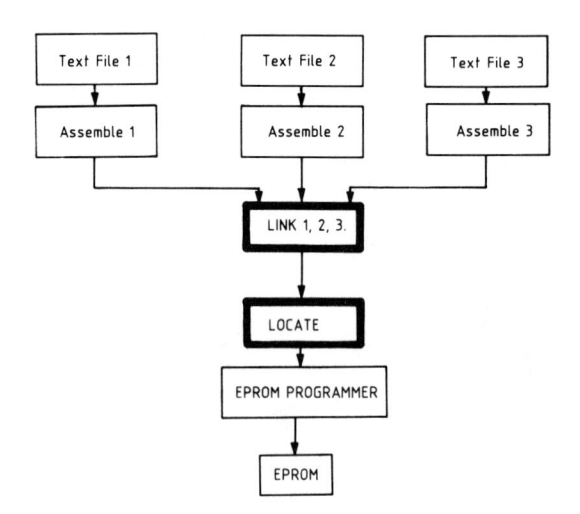

Fig. D.9 The linker and locator

(the host). When the host processor is the same type as that for which the code is intended, the package is called a 'resident assembler', or merely 'assembler'. When they are different then it is known as a 'cross-assembler'.

Assembly languages not only use mnemonics for instructions, they also support symbolic representation of data and addresses. In the latest ones provision is made for the use of IF-THEN and REPEAT-WHILE type statements. It has been estimated that productivity using assemblers is ten times greater than that using hex coding.

Assemblers usually provide us with the facility to develop programs in modular or segmented fashion (Fig. D.9). Joining these together and sorting out all cross-references is carried out by a software package called the 'linker'. If the resulting program is to be loaded down into a target system further information is needed. This concerns the address locations of the Code, Data and Stack. Such information is fed into the 'locator' software package, which then sorts out all the actual or 'absolute' addresses.

D.3 High-level language programming

High-level languages have been around for quite some time now. Well-known names include Fortran, Algol, Cobol and Pascal. Until recently,

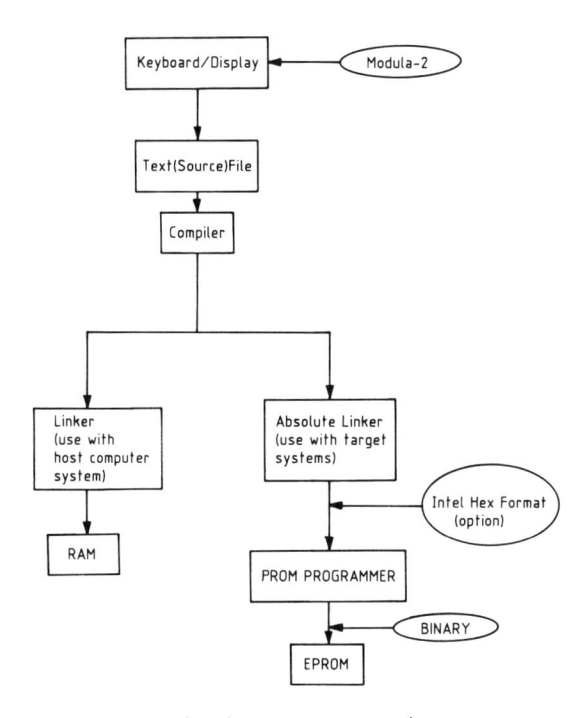

Fig. D.10 Modula-2 program development – Logitech system

though, few were available for real-time embedded systems, exceptions being Coral66 (UK defence language), RTL-2 (designed by ICI), PL/M from Intel and MPL from Motorola. This situation is changing, but it is still true that relatively few packages are around which generate PROM programming information, the so-called 'ROMable code' output. The Modula-2 Logitech package outlined here is designed to produce such code.

Figure D.10 shows the various steps involved in going from a Modula-2 text input file to executable code. The source text file (say 'Filter2.mod') is first processed by a compiler which produces a number of output files. The one which concerns us most is that holding the object code in linkable format, given the file extension '.lnk' (i.e. Filter2.lnk). All individually compiled modules are now linked together into a single file using the linking command.

If the program is to be run on the host computer then the 'normal' linker is used. This produces a single load and executable module, the object file having the extension '.lod'. Where the code is destined for a target system then the absolute linker package is used; its output can be sent directly to a PROM programmer. The absolute linker, in this implementation, also carries out the task of the locator.

The following extremely simple example (Listing D.1) is included to show how obscure assembler coding is when compared with Modula.

```
MODULE CodeExample;
(*****************************************************************)
(*  This example shows a Modula program and its corresponding    *)
(*  assembler code list  -  Listing D.1                          *)
(*****************************************************************)
VAR
   x1,x2,y1,y2 : INTEGER;

BEGIN
   x1:= OFH; (* decimal 15 *)
   x2:= 7H;
   y1:= x1 DIV x2;
   y2:= x1 MOD x2;
END CodeExample.
```

The Intel 8086 code produced by the compiler relating directly to the maths operations above is given below.

```
CS:     MOV DS,[0000]
MOV     WORD[0000],000F
MOV     WORD[0002],0007
MOV     AX,[0000]
CWD
IDIV    WORD[0002]
MOV     [0004],AX
MOV     AX,CX
CWD
IDIV    WORD[0002]
MOV     [0006],DX
```

Listing D.1

References

Beidler, J. and Jackowitz, P. (1986). *Modula-2*. PWS Engineering and Computer Science, Boston. ISBN 0-87150-912-1.

Ford, G.A. and Wiener, R.S. (1985). *Modula-2, A Software Development Approach*. John Wiley & Sons, New York, ISBN 0-471-87834-0.

Intel Corporation (1985). *Microsystem Components Handbook*, Vol. I, pp. 3–106 to 3–160. Intel Corp., Santa Clara, CA 95051, USA. ISBN 0-917017-22-6.

Knepley, E. and Platt, R. (1985). *Modula-2 Programming*. Reston Publishing Company Inc., Virginia. ISBN 0-8359-4602-9.

Logitech Modula-2/86, *Compiler Manual LU–GU101–2*, Logitech, Inc., 805 Veterans Blvd., Redwood City, CA 94063, USA.

Sincovec, R.F. and Wiener, R.S. (1986). *Data Structures Using Modula-2*. John Wiley & Sons, New York. ISBN 0-471-81489-X.

Wirth, N. (1985). *Programming in Modula-2* (3rd Edn). Springer-Verlag, Berlin. ISBN 3-540-15078-1.

Young, S.J. (1982). *Real Time Languages – Design and Development*. Ellis Horwood Ltd, Chichester, UK. ISBN 0-85312-251-2.

Answers to selected questions

Q1.1 Read Appendix C.

Q1.3 Look this out in your syntax diagrams.

Q1.4 When looking for errors in the program code. It provides a simple method of 'removing' compilable code by bracketing it with the comment delimiters. This avoids the need to actually delete text and then having to later type it back into the program.

Q1.5 The compilation will fail. Strings must be limited to a single line at a time.

Q2.1 'Three' must be declared before it can be used.

Q2.2 This will depend on your compiler. It will probably pass the compilation stage but should throw up a run-time error. Check this out. TRUNC returns a CARDINAL result; but CARDINALs represent positive numbers only.

Q2.3 The same, because Modulus(35) = Modulus(−35).

Q2.4 It is caused by the truncation effects of DIV.

Q2.5 Normal Boolean rules apply here. That is, the evaluation is
(a AND b AND c) OR (d).

Q2.6 It is obvious that these must be Boolean types, i.e. having only the value of true or false.

Q3.3 For the example given it is likely to be equal to its terminating value, *but*, according to the rules of Modula-2, it is considered to be undefined. So do not rely on it having any particular value.

Q3.4 The step value is defined to be a constant expression. That is, it must appear in the constant declarations section, and conform to the syntax of an expression. However, the start and finish range values may be specified by expressions.

Q4.1 If we use value parameters an extra 10 000 store locations have to be provided for the copied items. There may be insufficient data storage available.

Q4.2 With this format there is no confusion between a function procedure call and a variable assignment.

Q4.3 (a) When a procedure is invoked the current status of the processor has to be saved before the procedure runs. If parameters are involved, these have to be placed in specific store locations. On completion of the procedure system status must be restored. This all takes time. And with recursive procedures this may happen many times on a single call of the procedure in the program statement sequence.

(b) A small system may not have enough RAM storage space to hold all temporary information during the recursive operation.

Q5.1 Cardinality – 2; ordinality – false, true.

Q5.2 Truth table for short circuited Boolean AND function

AND (basic logic) X Y (Z=X AND Y)	AND (positive logic form) X Y Z	
F F F	0 0 0	
F T F	0 1 0	
F X F	0 X 0	X means 'Undefined'
T F F	1 0 0	
T T T	1 1 1	

Evaluation of the remaining logical operations is left to the reader as an exercise.

Q5.3 The compiler will flag up an error of 'identifier declared twice'.

Q5.4 At code generation time a listing error 'out of range' would be produced.

Q5.6 The compiler will give a 'type incompatibility' message.

Q7.1 At the end of each forloop identical values would be held in locations Speed[1], Speed[2] and Speed[3].

Q7.2 The first 100 locations will be set to zero and the value printed out. Then the operating system will abort the program, signalling a 'range error'.

For embedded operations such operating system support is unlikely to be available. In any case, all such exception conditions *must* be allowed for. Loss of program control is not acceptable.

Q7.3 They must be if the original and the copy are to be identical. But that is the only reason for this format.

Q7.4 The data structure consists of 100 store locations, each one capable of storing a single REAL variable. The first location is identified as Vector[1], the last one being Vector[100].

Q7.5 The array bound 'MaxNumber' is not allowed to be of type REAL.

Q7.6 (i) This is a case of a forward reference to an item, 'MaxNumber'. That is, we are trying to use MaxNumber before it is declared. Forward references are not allowed in Modula except in the case of pointer structures.

(ii) Variables are not allowed as array bounds.

Q8.1 INTEGER and REAL are base types whilst arrays, etc. are 'type constructors', i.e. they are constructed from base types.

Q8.2 Code is produced for executable statements. Data space is allocated for all variables. Thus when Log2 was introduced an extra 4 bytes were provided to hold the variable value, but the statements were not changed. As a result the code allocation remained the same.

The field identifier affects the type declaration. No code is generated, neither is any data area reserved as a result of such declarations.

Index

ABS 24, 280
absolute addresses 199, 289
absolute addressing 213
absolute linker 290
absolute machine addresses 204
actual addresses 289
actual parameters 67
addition 20, 22
ADR 205, 206, 225
ADDRESS 204, 214
    language extension 214
ALLOCATE 187
AND 29, 89, 279, 280
anonymous variable 186
applications software 196
arithmetic expressions 20
ARRAY 136, 279
array (see also open arrays)
    bounds 137
    declarations 136, 142
    elements 137
    index 137
    multidimensional 144, 145
    one-dimensional 144
    size 136, 139
    subscript 137
    three-dimensional 149
    two-dimensional 148
    type 149
array structure
    concept 135
arrays 134
    as formal parameters 149, 152
    as types 144
    compact assignment operation 143
    in procedures 149
    presetting 138
    transferring data between variables 140
    transferring values 138
    type compatibility 143
    typed indices 146
    with open parameters 150
arrays of arrays 145
ASCII 84
assembler 288
assembly language 202, 288
assembly language programming 286
assignment of procedures 103
assignment symbol 6
automatic change module 129
Awaited 244, 246

BEGIN 4, 279
bit
    extraction 221
    handling 215
    management 200
    masking 219
BITSET 162, 207, 216, 280
block structure 7
BOOLEAN 17, 20, 29, 89, 280
boolean expressions 29
bootstrap loader 284
bounds and indexing
    of arrays 141
BY 47, 279
BYTE 14
byte-wide memory chips 209

CAP 280
CARDINAL 15, 280
cardinality 83

case list 41
CASE – reserved word, 279, 281
case sensitive 4, 9
CASE statement 35, 39
   in variant records 180
CHAR 17, 83, 280
   enumeration 84
character constants 17
character operations 17
CHR 84, 100, 280
clients 116
code inserts 215
columns 145
command words 207
comments 9
communication between modules 115
compact array assignment operation 143
compilation 5
   methods 113
compiling
   library modules 128
complex records 173
complex structure
   element selection 175
concurrency 227
conditional fields
   in variant records 180
conjunction (logical AND) 89
CONST 14, 279
constant expression 14, 20
constants 12
control information 200
control registers 207
control statements 281
control transfer (between processes) 232
cooperating sequential processes 233
co-routines 232
CPU 284
cross-assembler 289

data storage unit 203
data structure 132
data types 80, 190
   hetrogeneous 133
   homogeneous 133
deadlocks 231
DEALLOCATE 187
DEC 280
declarations 4, 68
declarations section 6
DEFINITION 119, 279
definition modules 117, 119, 128
   procedure declarations 119
   structure 119

delimiters 6, 279
dereferencing
   of ADDRESS variables 205
   of pointers 187
device access 196
device status 200, 207
discriminator 181
discriminator field 181
disjunction (logical OR) 89
DISPOSE 186, 190, 280
DIV 20, 279, 280
division 20, 22
DO
   in FOR statement 46
   in WHILE statement 44
   in WITH clause 173
   reserved word 279
dynamic 63
   range 25
   variable declaration 185
   variables 123, 184
dynamic data structures 183
   linked list 185
   nodes 184
   sequential data storage techniques 184

EBCDIC 84
EBNF 7, 256
EEPROM 199
ELSE 34, 279, 281
ELSIF 35, 279, 282
ELSIF statement 35
END 4, 279
entier 21
enumerated type 83
   user defined 93
enumeration 83
EPROM 199
equivalence
   name 144
   structural 144
EXCL 160, 218, 280
executable code 290
executable statements 5
EXIT
   reserved word, 279, 282
   statement 49
EXPORT 119, 279
export
   list 120
   opaque 195
   statements 116, 125, 128
   transparent 194

EXPORT QUALIFIED 119
expressions 19, 28
Extended Backaus-Naur Form (EBNF) 7

field
   identifier 169
   list number 169
   number 169
   type 169
fieldwidth 10
finding
   memory addresses 207
   the size of a type 206
   the size of a variable 206
fixed-point 15
Flags 241
Flags for process coordination 238
FLOAT 21, 101, 281
floating-point 15
FOR 46, 279, 282
formal array parameters 152
formal parameters 67
   order 71
FOR-TO statement 45
forward referencing 191
FROM 11, 279
function designators 76
function procedures 73
   empty parameter list 75
   type 74
functional decomposition 115

global 60, 61, 109
GOTO 33

HALT, 281
hetrogeneous data types 133
hexadecimal coding 286
hexadecimal programming, 286
hierarchical decomposition 115
HIGH 154, 281
homogeneous data types 133
host 289

identifiers 7
IF 33, 279, 281
IF-THEN-ELSE statement 33
IF-THEN statement 33
IMPLEMENTATION 120, 279
implementation modules 117, 120, 128
   revision of 129
   structure 120
IMPORT 11, 279

import
   listings 116
   statements 11, 125, 128
IN 160, 279
INC, 281
INCL 159, 218, 281
independent
   compilation 113
   design 109
   operation 111
   processes 236
indexing
   of arrays 141
INBYTE 224
individual bit manipulation 216
Init 245
Initialisation
   modules 130
   of signal 247
INTEGER 4, 15, 281
Intel
   iAPX188 208
   80188 microprocessor 209
   8087 Numeric Data Coprocessor 209
   82188 bus controller 209
Intel Hex format 288
Interacting tasks 238
Interdependent tasks 238
interrupt
   controller 221
   handling 200, 253
   sequence 222
   service routine 254
   vector 254
   vector area 201
   vectors 222, 254
interrupts 221
   software-generated 223
INWORD 224
I/O space 202
IOTRANSFER 254

language definition 260
language features 279
last-in-first-out list 192
library 11
library modules 114, 117
   revision of 129
library module processes 245
library module SYSTEM 203, 224
lifetime of variables 122
linkable format 290
linked list 185
   finish 185

298 Index

start 185
linker 289
linking of modules 117
list 185
literal constants 12
local
  constants 62
  modules 115, 122, 124
  variables 62
locality 59
local module
  calls 126
  compilation 128
  export statements 125
  import statements 125
  program code 127
location parameters 71
locator 289
logical operations 29
Logitech compiler 16
LONGINT 280
LONG REAL 280
LOOP 48, 279, 282
LOOP statement 49
low-level facilities 202, 207
low-level statements 202

machine dependent facilities 202
machine (hex) form 202
management of peripheral devices 200
mask word 219
MathLibO 28
matrix algebra 144
MAX, 281
memory operations 198, 213
MIN, 281
mnemonics for instructions 289
MOD 24, 279, 280
mode setting 207
modular
  compilation 113
  design 109, 289
  operation 111
MODULE 4, 6, 107
modules (see also definition modules,
    implementation modules, library
    modules, local modules, program
    modules) 114
  initialisation 130
monitor program 286
monolithic
  compilation 113
  design 108
  operation 110

multidimensional arrays 144, 145
Multiple tasks – synchronisation 243
multiplication 20, 22
multiprocessing 227
multiprocessor system 227
multitasking 228

named constants 13
name equivalence 94, 144
negation (logical NOT) 89
nested
  procedures 63, 77
  WITH statements 175
nested-IF statement 35
NEW 186, 189, 281
new data types 91
NEWPROCESS 234, 254
NIL 190
nil pointer 185
nodes 184
non-interacting tasks 229
NOT 29, 89, 279, 280
numeric 20

object code 286
ODD, 281
OF 137, 279
one-dimensional arrays 144
opaque
  exports 195
  types 194
open array parameters 150
  in procedure declaration 150
open arrays 152
  as formal parameters 152
  for multi-dimensional arrays 154
  for one-dimensional arrays 154
  in procedure declarations 152
operands 7
operational mode 200
operator 7, 279
operator class 25
operator precedence 24, 280
OR 29, 89, 279, 280
ORD 84, 100, 281
order 67
ordinality 83
OUTBYTE 224
OUTWORD 224
overflow 25

parameter 68
parentheses 27
peripheral control block 209

POINTER 186, 279
pointer 184, 185
  dereferencing 186
  nil pointer 185
  type 190
POINTER TO 186
predefined types 82
presetting
  array variables 138
priorities 255
PROC 106, 280
PROCEDURE 59, 279
procedure 58
  as a parameter 105
  as processes 234
  assignment of 103
procedure type declaration 103
procedure types 103
Process – definition 231
Process startup 245
  activation 246
  queueing 248
PROCESS – type 235
program
  design 57
  module 114
program code
  inside a local module 127
PROM programmer 287
proper procedure 58

QUALIFIED 119, 279
qualified identifier 9
Quasi-current operations 231
quotient 23

RAM 199
Read 18
ReadInt 12
ReadReal 16
REAL 15, 280
real
  library procedure 21
  numbers 81
RealInOut 16
RECORD 168, 279
record
  concept 166
  field identifier 169
  field list 169
  field list number 169
  field list sequence 169
  field number 169
  field type 169
  storage allocation 168
  variable designator 169
records 166
  complex 173
  declaration 167
  handling individual components 171
  handling the complete data structure 172
  the WITH statement 172
  variant 175
  when to use them 167
recursive procedures 77
relational operators 29
remainder 24
REPEAT 44, 279, 282
REPEAT-UNTIL statement 44
repetition 43
reserved words 4, 279
resident assembler 289
RETURN 76, 279
RETURN statements 74
revising
  definition modules 129
  implementation modules 129
  library modules 129
ROMable code 290
rows 145

scalar types 14
scope 59, 63
  of identifiers 123, 127
selection 33
semantics 20
SEND 244, 246, 249
sequential data storage techniques 184
SET 156, 279
set
  base type identifier 156
  evaluation 159
  identifier 162
  listing 162
  operation 156
  size 163
  standard functions 159
    EXCL 160
    INCL 159
  type 156
set intersection function 219
sets 156
  declaration 156
  structuring 156
  when to use them 160
setting modes 206
short circuit operations 89

side-effects 111
SIGNAL 245
simple variables 132
SIZE 205, 206, 281
software-generated interrupts 223
special machine operations 201, 223
stack data 285
standard predefined identifiers 280
StartProcess 245
statements 5, 19
static
   data storage structure 183
   variables 123, 124
status of a device 200, 207
status register 207
string 17
strong typing 82, 98, 202
structural
   compatibility 93
   equivalence 144
structured
   data 132
   programming 33
   variables 132
subrange
   bounds 97, 98
   syntax 96
subrange types 95
   user defined 95
subscript (of an array) 137
subtraction 20, 22
suspended process 247
SWI 223
synchronising of tasks 244
syntax diagrams 7, 256, 262–278
syntax rules 20
SYSTEM (library module) 203, 224
systems programmer 197
systems software 196

tag 181
tag field 181
task cooperation 230
task coordination 229
task synchronisation 231
target system 207, 208
text string 10
THEN 33, 279
three-dimensional arrays 149
TO 46, 279
TRANSFER 235, 254
transferring
   array values 138
   data between array variables 140

transparent export 194
TRUNC 21, 101, 280
TSIZE 205, 206
two-dimensional arrays 148
TYPE 94, 279
type
   attributes 81
   coercion 103
   conversion 21, 98
   conversion functions 100
   declaration 190
   mixing 21
   transfer 102, 202
   transfer facilities 204
type –
   in a function procedure 74
   in an array declaration 137
   of formal parameters 67
   of procedure 103
type compatibility
   of arrays 142
   of records 182
typed 4
typed indices 146
types 4, 14, 79
   hetrogeneous 133
   homogeneous 133
   opaque 194
   predefined 82

UNTIL 44, 279
user defined
   enumeration types 95
   subrange types 95
using
   records 167
   sets 160
utility program 286

VAL 101, 281
value parameters 68
VAR
   in declaration section 6
   in parameter list 71
   reserved word, 279
variable list 6
variable parameters 71
variables 6, 284
   anonymous 186
   dynamic 123
   simple 132
   static 123
   variant records 175
   type compatibility 182

variant record structure 178
  CASE statement 180
  conditional fields 180
  discriminator 181
  discriminator identifier 181
  tag 181
  tag field 181
vectored 201
vectors 144
visibility 124

WAIT 244, 246, 249, 254
WHILE 44, 279, 282
WHILE-DO statement 44
WITH 172, 279
WITH
  clause 173
  nested statement 175
  statement 172
WORD 203
Write 18
WriteInt 10
WriteLn 10
WriteReal 16
WriteString 10